NOTABLE MOMENTS OF WOMEN IN MUSIC

by Jay Warner

HAL LEONARD BOOKS
NEW YORK

Published in 2008 by Hal Leonard Books
An Imprint of Hal Leonard Corporation
7777 West Bluemound Road
Milwaukee, WI 53213

Trade Book Division Editorial Offices
19 West 21st Street, New York, NY 10010

Photo credits: Etta James, pg. 70, copyright Gilles Petard Collection/Redferns; Brenda Lee, pg. 73, copyright Rob Verhorst/Referns; Connie Francis, pg. 79, by GAB Archives/Redferns; Mary J. Blige, pg. 427, copyright Gilles Petard Collection/Redferns. Roxy Saint, pg. 437, appears courtesy of Dan Scott. Cover photos and all other interior photos appear courtesy of Photofest.

Printed in the United States of America

Book design by Clare Cerullo

Library of Congress Cataloging-in-Publication Data is available upon request.

ISBN 978-1-4234-2951-7

www.halleonard.com

Additional Praise for Jay Warner's
NOTABLE MOMENTS OF
WOMEN IN MUSIC

"I am proud to be mentioned in a book of such quality with women of such talent and prestige."

—*Dolly Parton*

"Notable Moments of Women in Music *is a tribute by a truly first-rate entertainment archivist, Jay Warner. His behind-the-scenes look into the world of female musicians and vocalists of the last hundred years is more than a fascinating timeline—it's heartfelt recognition of the struggles for females in all entertainment media and the passion it takes to find success."*

—*Marie Osmond*

To the women who helped me form my admiration of,
passion for, angst about, frustration from, delight with,
and love for the opposite sex, just some of whom are
Jackie, Ellen, Laura, Susan, Sue, Tammy, Patricia,
Jane, Eileen, and Maxine

CONTENTS

ACKNOWLEDGMENTS

To my biggest believers: my mother, Ray, and my father, Bob, my uncle Archie "Willie" Friedberg, my aunt Sydelle and uncle Hymie Sherman, Dean Griffith, Sam Shatzman, my cousins Deanna Griffith Presley, Roger Griffith, Michael Wechsler, and Jerry Pato, and especially my loving and loyal wife, Jackie. May your spirit, faith, and love forever guide me and may God always bless you.

I'd also like to thank a few long-standing friends and supporters and business associates who have given of themselves truly out of friendship: Dennis Wolfe, Sam Atchley, John Wilson, Barry and Chris Peterman, Phil Kozma, Chas Peate, Ellis Rich, Lars Wiggman, David and Ismay Gresham, Ichiro Asatsuma, Peter Schoonhoven, Pieter van Bodegraven, Mark Altman, Jochem Gerrits, Adelfa Lanfranchi, Alfredo Gramitto Ricci, Philip Mortlock, Paul Menes, Barry Menes, Igor, Ralph Murphy, Peter Benson Malick, Ron Nadel, Steve Pina, Jon Stroll, Mary Wilson, Evie Sands, Jerry Wagner, Debbie Crawford, Mindi Abair, Ellis Hall, Max and Michele Langstaff, Linda Mensch, Mary Jo Menella, Alex Barkaloff, Eric Wolfson, Steve Bedell, Floyd Lieberman, Fred Frank, Stanley Kahan, Stu Silfen, Joe Smith, Peter Foldy, Stu Nadel, Dick and Nancy Hieronymous, Perry Santos, Dee Erwin, David Chackler, and Joe Isgro. I feel rich indeed to know you and wish you everything I wish for those I hold most dear.

Special thanks to my loyal assistant, Rex Sampaga, and to Diane Gershuny for her invaluable contribution to this work.

A special thought of appreciation to David Rish, James Economou, Michael Duffy, Sol Perez, and especially Mary Maish. And in memoriam:

Acknowledgments

Sid Seidenberg, Wes Farrell, Rick James, Johnny Bragg, Joel Dorn, and Bert De Coteaux.

Lastly, I want to thank the entire Hal Leonard organization, whom I have been privileged to know and work with for over twenty years, especially Keith Mardak, Jeff Schroedl, John Cerullo, Larry Morton, Brad Smith, Belinda Yong, Bernadette Malavarca, and Jenna Young. I appreciate your belief in my work.

FOREWORD

Moments.

They pile upon each other and gradually create our life stories and journeys. We keep moving right along, in a fast-paced world, time moving fast along with it. And in all we do, most of us have some point of reflection, where we pause and ask—How did I get here? Where am I going?

Yes, I've really learned the value of moments—from the simple to the pivotal. Some are especially crystallized. Opening the box that encased my first guitar at eight years old. Learning my first note. The notes turning into chords. Discovering the outlet of writing and performing—how music felt safe and free. Heading to bed, sneaking the AM radio on, keeping it low as *Sgt. Pepper* seeped into my subconscious. I remember the fiery, hopeful energy the songs I loved sent through me. Restless legs under my sheets. Wanting to sing along to the choruses, but it was night and I couldn't. So I mouthed the words with my eyes closed. The Kansas breezes swept across my face and I dreamed into the night of someday stages.

You see, Leavenworth wasn't necessarily the hot music center, and I wasn't surrounded by a lot of people longing for music like I was. But I had access to the art through films and through the radio. I had the Supremes. I had Janis Joplin, and so many others. And my fire was lit. Because I learned of them, I learned of myself and discovered where my soul really belonged. I discovered my own dream and my own way to contribute. And that dream would be the great door opener in my mind and my life and the fodder for so many more moments and experiences on all levels. Making my first album. The surreal seconds of recognizing my own song on the radio while racing to catch a train in London. It would lead me to my major loves and my major accomplishments. From adolescent eagerness to real-world success, to love, to loss, to babies, to illness, to survival, and to resurgence—it's been awesome.

So, I find a true value in reflection, whether it's listening to early songs or looking at old photos from the road. That pause allows me to experience what's behind me in a whole new way, and in turn I recharge and create again.

Reading this book is much like that kind of reflective experience. It's as if we're looking at a photo album, picture after picture. We can turn to any year, any month, and see events, one by one, that tell the story of women in music. How their efforts shaped culture. And no moment is too small. Many brave women have been standing up, singing big and bold, inspiring the next wave. It's important to recognize that and pay some homage.

Thanks to Jay Warner for doing that—compiling the stories of females in music in a way that gives us a glimpse into their many contributions. I believe in the importance of that effort and feel glad to be a part of this homage.

You know, you have to wonder: We're nearly at the end of the first decade of the new millennium. We're in an election year. What music is being created now? What moments are we living? What impact is music, music of women, playing in all of it?

We may be too close to see at this time, but no doubt it *is* making an impact. I hope for many more moments. More and more doors swinging open. I believe walking through will be more and more women. I am excited for new larks. Rocking. Spreading the dream to countless spirits, maybe even small-town Kansas kids.

—Melissa Etheridge

Introduction

The Beginning

Notable Moments of Women in Music History breaks apart the myth that it's a man world, though it certainly was in the dawning days of pop music. From 1890 to 1950, of the Top 100 recording artists, only nineteen were solo women vocalists, not including one vocal group (the Andrews Sisters) and half of the duo of Ada Jones and Billy Murray. This despite the fact that popular artists—and future legends—abounded, from Marian Anderson, Bessie Smith, and Pearl Bailey to Helen Morgan, Ethel Merman, and Kate Smith, among many others. It's still a struggle today, but as recently as November 2007, 27 percent of the pop charts were represented by women.

More than a hundred years since British-born Ada Jones and her superlative contralto, mastery of ethnic dialects, and infectious humor caught the ears of the American public with the 1905 No. 3 hit "My Carolina Lady" (on Thomas Edison's label, Edison Records), the contributions of women in all genres of music are undeniable. While early suffragettes were blazing a path of recognition and equal rights, women devoted to music careers were in their own way paving a similar road as wide as any superhighway. Against a backdrop ranging from post–Civil War Reconstruction, the Spanish–American War, and the beginning of the recording era through the invention of radio and TV, the baby-boom generation, and the digital mass-media age, American society has served as a breeding ground for the development of music where women have contributed in a way men never could.

Each era, and each decade, presented immense challenges, hardships, and struggles, as well as opportunities for women. Until the 1960s, "respectable" women were thought of mainly as men's homebound mates, frowned upon if they were anything other than homemakers and child raisers. When women were accepted as entertainers in the late 1800s and early 1900s, it was in the environments of dance halls, bars, nightclubs, and vaudeville theaters. Though men often fell in love and/or lust with the sexy chanteuses' and bawdy bar girls' vocal and physical charms, these were not the type of women they would dare bring home, let alone marry. Early female singers (with the exception of opera stars, who had a cultural acceptability carried over from Europe) faced a double standard in society and were often harshly treated by the so-called reputable women of the time.

The early women's rights movement had as much to do with the acceptance and diversity of women in the music industry as the Emancipation Proclamation had to do with the freedom of blacks in America. In fact, that "separate but equal" establishment added many great black female vocalists and musicians to the swelling ranks of their sisterhood in song.

Whether they were songwriters, musicians, vocalists, or any combination of the three, women in music often had to shock the then-current establishment in order to gain recognition and popularity, when all men had to do for the most part was open their mouths and sing. From nineteenth-century stage queen Jenny Lind to early-twentieth-century bawdy star Mae West to 1990s provocative rocker Sinead O'Connor, women always seem to have to do a little more than men to get their due, and for the most part they've rarely disappointed. Women in music have always been among the most adventurous in society.

Running throughout history is the theme of the woman with the gift to captivate men and relate to other women with her ability to express shared feelings and ideas through music. As more and more women began standing up for themselves, lyrics evolved and a new era began, with the likes of Lesley Gore declaring "You Don't Own Me," Helen Reddy proclaiming "I Am Woman," and Donna Summer venting "She Works Hard for the Money." In turbulent times, there were as many women as men marching for peace, and the movement's themes were often framed by women like Joan Baez, Mimi Farina, Judy Collins, and Peter, Paul and Mary's Mary Travers. But the heart and soul of women's appeal in music has always been the love song, and no man can compare with the heart-wrenching effects of a woman like Ruth Etting singing a 1920s torch song, a scorching blues ballad from the lips of Billie Holiday, or the numerous song sirens of the twentieth and twenty-first centuries, including Barbra Streisand, Tina Turner, Ella Fitzgerald, Aretha Franklin, Mariah Carey, Celine Dion, and so many others.

"It isn't where you come from, it's where you're going that counts."—Ella Fitzgerald

THE FIRST GUTSY GIRLS

1900–1939

A mid Reconstruction in America after the Civil War, the country was expanding west, and opportunistic, adventurous female singers saw the new frontier as an opportunity for a better life, just as hundreds of thousands of families did. These women, however, were not of the "settle down and raise a family" variety. They liked the freedom of being free-spirited and being able to say yes or no at will. For every star such as the famed Grace Spencer (the first female to record on Victor, which became RCA), there were countless other obscure singers in the bars and emporiums of the nation hoping to get their chance. The industrialized East Coast, meanwhile, was developing more of a European sophistication musically, and concert halls became the venues for such stalwarts as the legendary Jenny Lind, known as the Swedish Nightingale and who was also the love of Hans Christian Andersen's life. Brought to America by showman P. T. Barnum, Lind earned a thousand dollars a night starring in ninety-three concerts in 1850 while giving most of the proceeds to American charities.

In the pre-1900s era, before recordings, radio, newspapers, or dime-store novels, word of mouth was the wind on which popularity traveled. And so it was for vocalists plying their trade in cabarets and clubs, featuring musical styles such as pop, opera, early jazz, blues, vaudeville, and folk.

Many vocalists came out of churches, both white and black, cutting their teeth on spirituals before adventuring into various popular forms the church considered "the devil's music." Right through the 1950s, when spiritual and gospel artists sang pop or R&B, they often changed their name so as not to be ostracized by family and the church.

With the dawning of the recording age, after Emil Berliner and Thomas Edison had invented and developed the early phonograph and player discs (1870s), recordings of the various early stars proliferated as the average American family could, by the turn of the twentieth century, afford a $40 phonograph and its 35-cent to 50-cent single-sided discs. Stars of the day like Geraldine Farrar, who began recording in 1900, Louise Homer (1905), Nellie Melba (1905), and Ernestine Shumann-Heink (1908) brought opera to the masses. Lucy Marsh (1908) and Alice Nielsen (1905), who started in opera, crossed over to popular music and Broadway musicals to the delight of fans.

Broadway and vaudeville were well represented by the Florodora Girls (these girls were the first Broadway musical cast members to record a song from their show) (1901), Estelle Manne (1898) (who also sang with the Lyric Quartet), Blanche Ring (1902), Grace Spencer (1900), and Helen Trix (1907). Among fan favorites, and the first superstar, Ada Jones started her pop recording career in 1904, going on to eventually have an incredible 108 chart hits, forty-four of those in duets with turn-of-the-century icon Billy Murray (take that, Madonna!). In 1900, the first black vocal group, the Dinwiddie Colored Quartet, recorded, opening the vinyl frontier for everyone from Billie Holiday to Alicia Keys.

The years 1910–1919 featured the First World War and women who gave the nation a respite from the conflict with their musical offerings. Opera stars included Francis Alda, Sophie Braslau, Elida Morris, and Maggie Tate. Broadway lights never darkened as Elsie Baker, Inez Barbour, Helen Clark, Elizabeth Brice, and the incomparable Mae West brought their talents to the stage as well as recordings. These and other artists merged their Broadway belting with pop, vaudeville, and even minstrel-show styles to entertain the public. Pop stars like Nora Bayes, Alma Gluck, Elizabeth Wheeler, the That Girl Quartet (probably the first successful all-female singing group), and the legendary Sophie Tucker dazzled live audiences and record listeners alike with their charms and styles. Classical violinist Kathleen Parlow was a star of great magnitude, and trumpet-playing Edna White and her quartet were as popular then as Kenny G is today. Ragtime rebel Dolly Connolly set toes a-tapping, and of course numerous female vaudeville stars like Belle Baker, Ann Chandler, Elsie Janis, and Margaret Farrell kept the fun-filled style popular in the teens. Even the White House got in on the act as patriotic music was represented on the early hit charts by Margaret Woodrow Wilson (daughter of President Woodrow Wilson) with her stirring rendition of "The Star-Spangled Banner."

The Roaring Twenties of Prohibition, bootlegging, and the nation's dynamic growth was a "let's have fun" era until the Great Depression, beginning in 1929, sobered the nation. Radio exploded in the early 1920s; there were over 500 stations by 1922, and more than 1,000 by 1924. Many stars emerged through radio programs while the antics of unconventional women known as "flappers" became the rage, along with the era's femme fatale singers. Torch-song balladeers like Ruth Etting, Libby Holman, and the quintessential "torcher," Helen Morgan, rung every heartfelt note from every song they interpreted.

Jazz spilled out of New Orleans to flood the country with the sounds of Adelaide Hall, Marion Harris, and Edith Wilson. Mamie Smith's hit "Crazy Blues," the first authentic blues recording, set the stage for the likes of Ma Rainey, Clara Smith, Dolly Kay, Ethel Waters, Alberta Hunter, and Bessie Smith (later recognized as the world's greatest blues singer), whose 1923 "Down Hearted Blues" became the first blues million seller.

Pop and Broadway styles were well represented by stars like Gertrude Lawrence, Annette Hanshaw, the enormous talent (and size) of Kate Smith, and the irreverent legend Fanny Brice (whom Barbra Streisand portrayed in *Funny Girl*).

With the advent of film, movies would become the predominant source of pop hits in the thirties while radio would help expand and sustain artists' careers.

> *"I opened as a unknown and I left two years later as a star."*
> *—Billie Holiday on her performance at Café Society*

Actors/singers like the Andrews Sisters, Dorothy Lamour, Joan Crawford, Irene Dunn, Jane Froman, Alice Faye, Betty Hutton, Ruby Keeler, Jeanette McDonald, and the glorious Judy Garland graced the screen in full voice. The Golden Age of jazz vocals began with the huge success of Billie Holiday, Mildred Bailey, the Boswell Sisters (the first superstar girl group and forerunner of the Andrews Sisters), Maxine Sullivan, and the incomparable Ella Fitzgerald.

The repeal of Prohibition in 1933 stimulated the opening of thousands of cocktail lounges and bars where performers could ply their trade. The swing and big-band era began in the 1930s, and many bands featured female vocalists who often went on to achieve solo success after their apprenticeship. Such stalwarts included Helen O'Connell, Ginny Simms, Dolly Dawn, Helen Forrest, and Harriet Hillard (who married her band-leading boyfriend, Ozzie Nelson, to become the most popular mom on 1950s TV).

Broadway also had its bellwethers as the likes of Ella Logan, Gertrude Niesen, Hildegarde, Mary Martin, and the "big as a barn" sound of Ethel Merman lit up the stages of New York. Country music began to be recognized in the late twenties and early thirties with the success of the Carter family, featuring Sarah and Maybelle. Maybelle's daughter, June, carried on the family tradition and later sang with her husband, Johnny Cash, as June Carter Cash.

The feminine contribution to music over the first four decades of the twentieth century—from vaudeville and minstrel stars to the best and most interesting artists in pop, jazz, blues, opera, big band, Broadway, country, radio, and film—made for a pioneering time, creating a pleasurable period for both music lovers and women watchers.

1873

June
Notable birthdays: (June 1) Ada Jones

1883

May
Notable birthdays: (May 26) Mamie Smith

1884

January
Notable birthdays: (January 13) Sophie Tucker

1886

April

Notable birthdays: (April 26) Gertrude "Ma" Rainey

1887

September

Notable birthdays: (September 19) Cora "Lovie" Austin

1890

May

Notable birthdays: (May 1) Ada Brown

1891

October

Notable birthdays: (October 29) Fanny Brice

1892

August

Notable birthdays: (August 17) Mae West

1895

April

Notable birthdays: (April 1) Alberta Hunter, (April 15) Bessie Smith

October

Notable birthdays: (October 31) Ethel Waters

November

Notable birthdays: (November 17) Katie Crippen

1897

June
Notable birthdays: (June 3) Memphis Minnie

1898

February
Notable birthdays: (February 3) Lil Harding Armstrong

July
Notable birthdays: (July 21) Sarah Dougherty (Carter Family)

1900

February
Notable birthdays: (February 3) Mabel Mercer

1901

November
Notable birthdays: (November 5) Etta Moten Barnett

1902

October
Notable birthdays: (October 31) Julia Lee

1903

November
Notable birthdays: (November 9) Margaret Fay Shaw

1905

March

Notable birthdays: (March 15) Bertha "Chippie" Hill

May 20

Ada Jones made her chart debut with "My Carolina Lady," reaching No. 3. One of the first women to record regularly in this era, Ada's often regarded as the "First Lady of the American Phonograph"! She would have sixty-four solo hits through 1919, and forty-four more in duets with Billy Murray from 1907 until 1922.

1906

October 15

Singer/pianist Victoria Spivey, one of the great blues interpreters from the 1920s, was born. Best known for her "Black Snake Blues" in 1926, Victoria performed up until her passing in 1976.

June

Notable birthdays: (June 3) Josephine Baker

1907

June

Notable birthdays: (June 18) Jeanette McDonald

November

Notable birthdays: (November 23) Ruth Etting

December

Notable birthdays: (December 3) Connee Boswell (Boswell Sisters)

1908

January

Notable birthdays: (January 16) Ethel Merman

1909

February
Notable birthdays: (February 9) Carmen Miranda

May
Notable birthdays: (May 10) Maybelle Addington (Carter Family)

1910

April
Notable birthdays: (April 10) Brigitte Mira

July 30
One of vaudeville's greatest entertainers, brassy and flamboyant Sophie Tucker made her pop-chart debut with "That Lovin' Rag," reaching No. 3. The "Last of the Red Hot Mamas," as she was known, had twenty-one pop hits through 1937.

1911

May
Notable birthdays: (May 13) Maxine Sullivan

October
Notable birthdays: (October 26) Mahalia Jackson

1912

October
Notable birthdays: (October 25) Minnie Pearl

1913

January 4
Ada Jones, the most popular female vocalist of the pre-1920s, hit the top of

the pop charts with "Row! Row! Row!," reaching No. 1 for three weeks. It was Ada's forty-seventh of an amazing sixty-four solo hits through 1919, not including another forty-four hits with singing partner Billy Murray from 1907 through 1922.

March 29

The most famous of the early twentieth-century opera singers, Geraldine Farrar actually hit the popularity charts ten times from 1907 through 1916. She reached the hit list today with "Rigoletto: Deh! Non Parlare al Misero" (Recall Not the Past"), rising to No. 6.

June 14

New York Metropolitan Opera star Alma Gluck reached the pop charts with "Abide with Me," rising to No. 10.

Notable birthdays: (June 23) Helen Humes

1915

March

Notable birthdays: (March 20) Sister Rosetta Thorpe

"Once, when we were playing at the Apollo, [Billie] Holiday was working a block away at the Harlem Opera House. Some of us went over between shows to catch her, and afterwards we went backstage. I did something then, and I still don't know if it was the right thing to do—I asked her for her autograph."
—*Ella Fitzgerald*

April 7

One of the all-time great blues singers, Eleanora "Billie" Holiday was born today in Baltimore. She took her name from her favorite actress, silent-screen star Billie Dove, but her fans dubbed her "Lady Day." A line from her a biography noted: "Mom and Pop were just a couple of kids when they got married. He was eighteen, she was sixteen and I was three."

Notable birthdays: (April 7) Billie Holiday (Eleanora Fagan), (April 30) Mabel Scott

July

Notable birthdays: (July 6) LaVerne Andrews (Andrews Sisters)

December

Notable birthdays: (December 19) Edith Piaf

1916

October

Notable birthdays: (October 29) Hadda Brooks

December 2

A superb singer of the 1920s, Marion Harris made her chart debut with "I'm Gonna Make Hay While the Sun Shines in Virginia," reaching No. 8. It was the first of forty-three hits through 1930.

1917

March 17

Ada Jones and Billy Murray, one of the most successful duos of all time, hit the charts with "What Do You Want to Make Those Eyes at Me For," reaching No. 3. It was the twosome's forty-second of a career forty-four hits.

Notable birthdays: (March 1) Dinah Shore, (March 20) Vera Lynn

June

Notable birthdays: (June 30) Lena Horne

November 3

Popular teens and twenties vocalist Nora Bayes charted with George M. Cohen's "Over There," the song most synonymous with World War I. It stayed at No. 1 for three weeks, becoming her biggest recording of thirty-nine hits from 1910 through 1923. Nora (born Dora Goldberg) began her career on the Broadway stage in 1901 at age twenty-one.

Notable birthdays: (November 12) Jo Stafford (Pied Pipers)

1918

January

Notable birthdays: (January 3) Maxine Andrews (Andrews Sisters)

March

Notable birthdays: (March 29) Pearl Bailey

April

Notable birthdays: (April 25) Ella Fitzgerald, (April 12) Helen Forrest

1919

March 15

Romanian-born Alma Gluck rose to stardom with the New York Metropolitan Opera. On this day, she charted with the last of her nineteen pop hits, "Bring Back My Bonnie to Me," with vocal support from the famous Orpheus Quartet. Alma was married to concert violinist Efrem Zimbalist. Their son, Efrem Zimbalist Jr., starred in TV's *The F.B.I.,* and their granddaughter, Stephanie, starred in TV's *Remington Steele.*

August

Notable birthdays: (August 30) Kitty Wells

October

Notable birthdays: (October 18) Anita O'Day

1920

February
Notable birthdays: (February 16) Patty Andrews (Andrews Sisters)

May
Notable birthdays: (May 11) Beryl Bryden, (May 26) Peggy Lee

August 10
Mamie Smith's "Crazy Blues" was issued and became the first successful authentic blues recording.

August 21
A terrific singer who began her career out of necessity, not desire, Savannah Churchill was born today. When her husband died in a car accident in 1941, she began performing to support her two children. Recording mostly with the vocal group the Four Tunes, she scored her biggest hits with "I Want to Be Loved," which was No. 1 on the R&B charts for eight weeks, and "Daddy Daddy" (No. 3 R&B). She also played a mean violin.

Notable birthdays: (August 17) Georgia Gibbs, (August 21) Savannah Churchill

November
Notable birthdays: (November 11) Annisteen Allen

1921

January
Notable birthdays: (January 31) Carol Channing

February
Notable birthdays: (February 7) Wilma Lee Cooper, (February 26) Betty Hutton

September 17
From vaudeville to Broadway musicals to recordings, Ethel Waters was a pioneering blues singer who debuted on the pop chart today with "Down Home Blues" (No. 5). Ethel introduced the original version of "Stormy Weather" in 1933, taking it to No. 1, and it became her trademark song. Lena Horne would have a hit with it in 1943.

1922

February 11

The legendary Fanny Brice (Fannie Borach) debuted on the pop chart with "My Man," reaching No. 1. Fanny was a fixture in the Ziegfeld Follies from 1910 to 1923 and became famous as Baby Snooks on 1940s radio. The Barbra Streisand film *Funny Girl* was based on her life.

April

Notable birthdays: (April 3) Doris Day, (April 5) Gale Storm

May

Notable birthdays: (May 25) Kitty Kallen

July

Notable birthdays: (July 21) Kay Starr

1923

February 16

Bessie Smith made her recording-studio debut, cutting "Gulf Coast Blues" and "Down Hearted Blues," which eventually became her first single that June. Bessie went on to be known as the "Empress of the Blues."

March

Notable birthdays: (March 25) Bonnie Guitar

June 9

Legendary blues vocalist Bessie Smith made her chart debut with "Down Hearted Blues," reaching No. 1 for four weeks on the pop hit list. The record would go on to sell over a million copies, almost exclusively to the black community, an almost unheard of accomplishment for the times. Bessie began her career touring with another blues great, Ma Rainey. Bessie's recordings were so popular that they were greatly responsible for saving the fragile Columbia label from bankruptcy.

Notable birthdays: (June 22) Ella Johnson

Bessie Smith.

1924

March
Notable birthdays: (March 27) Sarah Vaughan

April
Notable birthdays: (April 21) Clara Ward

May
Notable birthdays: (May 1) Big Maybelle

June
Notable birthdays: (June 7) Dolores Gray, (June 27) Rosalie Allen

July

Notable birthdays: (July 7) Mary Ford (Les Paul and Mary Ford), (July 22) Margaret Whiting

August 23

Vaudevillian Blossom Seeley danced onto the pop list with "Don't Mind the Rain," reaching No. 8. Blossom was first married to Hall of Fame pitcher Rube Marquard and later performer Lew Fields. The 1952 film *Somebody Loves Me* was based on Blossom's and Lew's lives.

Notable birthdays: (August 29) Dinah Washington

September

Notable birthdays: (September 12) Ella Mae Morse, (September 20) Gogi Grant

November

Notable birthdays: (November 27) Bonnie Lou

December 27

Vaudeville star Belle Baker, known as "The Ragtime Singer," charted with "Hard Hearted Hannah," reaching No. 13. She was also the first artist to record "All of Me," one of the most recorded songs of the era.

1925

January 31

Pioneering blues singer Ma Rainey (Gertrude Pridgett) hit the pop charts with "See See Rider Blues," rising to No. 14. The "Mother of the Blues," Rainey was highly influential among many women blues artists, including Bessie Smith. In fact, music historian Chris Albertson wrote of Rainey, "If there was another woman who sang the blues before Rainey, nobody remembered hearing her." The 1985 Broadway musical *Ma Rainey's Black Bottom* was based on her life.

June

Notable birthdays: (June 1) Marie Knight

July 11

Heralded as the best contralto of her time, Louise Homer entered the hit list with the pop recording "The Old Folks at Home (Swanee River)," reaching

No. 6. Louise would run off a string of ten pop-chart hits through 1925 and recorded with such legends as Geraldine Farrar, Enrico Caruso, and Alma Gluck.

August 9

Famous black contralto Marian Anderson charted for the first and only time with "Nobody Knows the Trouble I've Seen," reaching No. 15. In 1939, the operatic great sang at the Lincoln Memorial in front of 75,000 people.

Notable birthdays: (August 15) Rose Maddox

October

Notable birthdays: (October 21) Celia Cruz

November

Notable birthdays: (November 20) June Christy

1926

April

Notable birthdays: (April 28) Blossom Dearie

June

Notable birthdays: (June 1) Marilyn Monroe

July

Notable birthdays: (July 19) Sue Thompson

August

Notable birthdays: (August 26) Georgia Gibbs

September

Notable birthdays: (September 26) Julie London

November

Notable birthdays: (November 18) Dorothy Collins

December

Notable birthdays: (December 11) Willie Mae "Big Mama" Thornton

1927

February

Notable birthdays: (February 10) Gisele MacKenzie

July 2

Ruth Etting charted with "Hoosier Sweetheart" on its way to No. 10 pop. The Nebraska native got her start in Chicago nightclubs and had her first success in the Ziegfeld Follies in 1927.

Notable birthdays: (July 16) Mindy Carson

August 1

The Carter Family, featuring Sarah Carter and her cousin Maybelle Carter, recorded for the first time in Bristol, Tennessee. The First Family of original hillbilly music, which contained the roots of country music, had later incarnations, including Sarah and (bass vocalist of the group) A. P. Carter's daughter, June Carter, eventual wife of Johnny Cash.

September 10

The ultimate torch-song specialist, Helen Morgan made her chart debut with "A Tree in the Meadow" (No. 9) from the Broadway musical *Peggy-Ann*. Morgan was best known for her appearance in *Show Boat* and her show-stopping performance of "Can't Help Lovin' Dat Man of Mine" (No. 7). Helen originated the sex-symbol pose: stretched out, singing on top of a piano.

October

Notable birthdays: (October 25) Barbara Cook

November

Notable birthdays: (November 8) Chris Connor, Patti Page

1928

January

Notable birthdays: (January 26) Eartha Kitt, (January 30) Ruth Brown

April

Notable birthdays: (April 4) Maya Angelou

May

Notable birthdays: (May 23) Rosemary Clooney

October

Notable birthdays: (October 27) Cleo Lane

1929

March

Notable birthdays: (March 16) Betty Johnson

April

Notable birthdays: (April 1) Jane Powell

June 22

Torch-song specialist Ruth Etting charted with "Deep Night," which would reach No. 17. Ruth scored sixty-two hits from 1926 through 1937. She had sixty hits before "Life Is a Song" in 1935 gave Ruth her first and only No. 1 song. In 1955, Doris Day starred in Etting's filmography, *Love Me or leave Me.* The song "Love Me or Leave Me" was a 1929 No. 2 hit and a signature piece for the songbird.

Notable birthdays: (June 23) June Carter Cash

July

Notable birthdays: (July 30) Christine McGuire (McGuire Sisters)

September 7

Broadway star Libby Holman, who was featured in musicals between 1927 and 1938, made her chart debut with the classic "Am I Blue." The recording reached No. 4 pop for the tempestuous torch-song singer, who was nicknamed the Dark Purple Menace.

November

Notable birthdays: (November 11) LaVern Baker (the Gliders)

1930

February

Notable birthdays: (February 13) Dorothy McGuire (McGuire Sisters)

March

Notable birthdays: (March 13) Jan Howard, Liz Anderson

May

Notable birthdays: (May 16) Betty Carter

June

Notable birthdays: (June 30) June Valli

July

Notable birthdays: (July 25) Annie Ross

August

Notable birthdays: (August 5) Damita Jo

September 27

A soprano star of dozens of movie musicals (including eight with Nelson Eddy), gorgeous Jeanette MacDonald made her pop-chart debut with "Beyond The Blue Horizon" (No. 9) from the film *Monte Carlo.*

Notable birthdays: (September 22) Joni James

December

Notable birthdays: (December 31) Odetta

More Moments in 1930

American composer Kay Swift was the first woman to score a complete musical, *Fine and Dandy,* debuting this year. Two of her most enduring songs are "Fine and Dandy" and "Can This Be Love?" (both from that show).

1931

February

Notable birthdays: (February 14) Phyllis McGuire (McGuire Sisters)

March

Notable birthdays: (March 16) Shirley Collie

May

Notable birthdays: (May 7) Teresa Brewer

June
Notable birthdays: (June 3) Dakota Staton

July
Notable birthdays: (July 6) Della Reese

August
Notable birthdays: (August 16) Eydie Gorme

October 10
Hailing from New Orleans, the legendary jazz-pop group the Boswell Sisters slid onto the singles hit list with "(With You on My Mind I Find) I Can't Write the Words," rising to No. 20. It was their fifth of seven straight hits that year.

November
Notable birthdays: (November 23) Gloria Lynne

December
Notable birthdays: (December 3) Jaye P. Morgan, (December 30) Skeeter Davis

1932

January 30
Jazz and swing singer supreme Mildred Bailey charted with her debut disc, "Georgia on My Mind," reaching No. 19 in a career of twenty-two hits through 1947.

March
Notable birthdays: (March 4) Miriam Makeba, (March 9) Keely Smith

April
Notable birthdays: (April 1) Debbie Reynolds, (April 27) Maxine Brown

May 2
Seven-year-old Rose Marie charted with "Say That You Were Teasing Me," reaching No. 19. The child star known as Baby Rose Marie would become better known in the 1960s for her role as Sally on the *Dick Van Dyke TV Show.*

Notable birthdays: (May 4) Tammy Wynette

September

Notable birthdays: (September 8) Patsy Cline

October 10

Jazz vocalist Connee Boswell, lead singer of the Boswell Sisters, made her solo debut with "Say It Isn't So," reaching No. 10. Considered one of the greatest female jazz vocalists, she was thought to be a major influence on Ella Fitzgerald.

Notable birthdays: (October 11) Dottie West

November 5

Ethel Merman made her singles debut on the pop chart with "How Deep Is the Ocean," rising to No. 14. The mesmerizing Merman performed in thirteen musicals, including *Annie Get Your Gun,* which included her signature song, "There's No Business Like Show Business."

November 15

Gifted vocalist Petula Clark was born today. Though well known in America for more than twenty hits, including "Downtown," "My Love," and "Don't Sleep in the Subway," she's also an accomplished actress, having appeared in over twenty British films. Her chart career started in 1954 with "The Little Shoemaker" and spanned four decades. Ironically, her last British hit in 1988 was a remix of her first American hit, "Downtown" (1964).

1933

February

Notable birthdays: (February 3) Betty Foley, Varetta Dillard, (February 21) Nina Simone

April 1

Broadway comedy and film star Mae West sashayed onto the pop chart for her first and only time with "I Like a Guy What Takes His Time" (No. 5). It was from the film *She Done Him Wrong.*

September

Notable birthdays: (September 30) Cissy Houston

October

Notable birthdays: (October 17) Jeanine Deckers (the Singing Nun)

November

Notable birthdays: (November 21) Jean Shepard

1934

January

Notable birthdays: (January 24) Ann Cole

April 14

Country Music Hall of Famer Loretta Lynn (Loretta Webb) was born. She went on to have seventy-seven hits between 1960 and 1981. Sources list differing year of birth for her, including 1940, as she stated: "When I was born, Franklin Delano Roosevelt was the president for several years. That's the closest I'm gonna come to telling my age . . ."

August

Notable birthdays: (August 16) Ketty Lester

October

Notable birthdays: (October 13) Nana Mouskouri, (October 9) Shirley Gunter

November 10

The Boswell Sisters "rocked" onto the charts with their legendary recording of "Rock & Roll" (No. 7). It was the first time the term had been used in a song and almost a decade before disc jockey Alan Freed coined the term. The recording was from the film *Transatlantic Merry-Go-Round* and was not about sex, as the term meant among the black community, or about music à la Freed but about rockin' and rollin' to the waves on a boat.

1935

January 5

The Boswell Sisters topped the pop charts today with their 78-rpm hit single "The Object of My Affection." It was the first No. 1 song by a girl group in music history and was from the film *Times Square Lady.* The Boswells were pioneering female vocalists who were the forerunners and influence for groups like the Andrews Sisters. The New Orleans ladies charted twenty times from 1931 to 1938. No mean feat in the early days of a man's music world.

January 12

Sexy torch-song specialist Libby Holman charted with the last of her nine hits when "You and the Night and the Music" weaved its way onto the popularity parade, reaching No. 11.

September

Notable birthdays: (September 28) Koko Taylor, (September 30) Jill Corey

October

Notable birthdays: (October 1) Julie Andrews, (October 5) Margie Singleton, (October 16) Sugarpie DeSanto

December

Notable birthdays: (December 12) Joan Weber, (December 23) Little Esther Phillips (Esther May Jones)

1936

March

Notable birthdays: (March 6) Sylvia Robinson (born Sylvia Vanderpool) (Mickey and Sylvia)

April

Notable birthdays: (April 4) Margo Sylvia (the Tune Weavers), (April 29) April Stevens

June

Notable birthdays: (June 19) Shirley Goodman (Shirley and Lee), (June 28) Cathy Carr

July 25

Ella Fitzgerald bounced onto the singles charts with "Sing Me a Swing Song" (No. 18). It became the first of fifty-three pop hits through 1963 for the all-time jazz great, who was discovered after a winning performance on the *Harlem Amateur Hour* in 1934.

November 14

The legendary Billie Holiday charted not once but twice today with two different singles. "The Way You Look Tonight" (No. 3) from the film *Swing Time* and "Who Loves You" (No. 4). It was her eleventh and twelfth hit in less than two years.

Musical film star Frances Newbern Langford slid easily onto the hit list with "Easy to Love" from the movie *Born to Dance*. Francis endeared herself to Americans with her numerous trips to entertain troops during World War II and the Korean War, accompanying the toastmaster of travel, Bob "If This Is Tuesday I Must Be Lost" Hope.

December 26

Jeanette MacDonald and Nelson Eddy, the sweethearts of the silver screen, charted with "Indian Love Call" from the movie *Rose Marie*. It reached No. 8.

1937

January

Notable birthdays: (January 6) Doris Troy, (January 8) Shirley Bassey, (January 14) Billy Jo Spears, (January 30) Jeanne Pruitt

February 27

Sultry actress Dorothy Lamour (born Dorothy Stanton) had her first of five hits when "Moonlight and Shadows" from the film *The Jungle Princess* debuted, rising to No. 10. Dorothy starred throughout the 1930s and 1940s in films, including the "road" movies with Bob Hope and Bing Crosby.

Notable birthdays: (February 20) Nancy Wilson

March 27

Jazz great Billie Holiday charted with "(This Is) My Last Affair" from the Broadway musical *New Faces of 1934*. Billie was discovered by Jazz critic John Hammond, who went on to head the A&R department at Columbia Records. The film *Lady Sings the Blues* was based on her life.

July

Notable birthdays: (July 10) Sandy Stewart, (July 31) Bonnie Brown (the Browns)

September 26

"Empress of the Blues" Bessie Smith died today. The Tennessee orphan was tutored by Ma Rainey while in The Rabbit Foot Minstrels Revue circa 1912.

Most remembered for "Tain't Nobody's Business If I Do" and "Careless Love Blues," Bessie was simply the best of the classic blues singers. Her first recording in 1923, "Down Hearted Blues," sold over 750,000 copies in a few months. She was known to have influenced many latter-day stars, including Billie Holiday, Mahalia Jackson, Ella Fitzgerald, and Janis Joplin. In fact, though there were over seven thousand people at her funeral, her grave laid without a marker until the 1960s when Janis Joplin paid for one. Bessie died when her car hit a truck near Clarksdale, Mississippi. She was only forty-three years old.

October

Notable birthdays: (October 20) Wanda Jackson

November

Notable birthdays: (November 7) Mary Travers (Peter, Paul and Mary)

1938

January 1

The Andrews Sisters charted with their first single, "Bei Mir Bist du Schoen," which soared to No. 1 for five weeks. It was their first of an astounding ninety-one pop hits through 1953. As if that wasn't enough, they had an additional thirteen more with Bing Crosby.

Notable birthdays: (January 25) Etta James, (January 30) Norma Jean

March 26

The Andrews Sisters charted today with two different single releases on the same day, "Ti-Pi-Pin" and "Shortenin' Bread." The first record reached No. 12 while the second single went to No. 16 for the Minneapolis trio, the most popular female singing group of the pre-rock era.

Notable birthdays: (March 13) Erma Franklin

June 18

Ella Fitzgerald stormed onto the hit list with "A-Tisket, A-Tasket." It settled in at No. 1 for an amazing ten weeks, becoming her biggest hit.

Notable birthdays: (July 20) Jo Ann Campbell, (July 26) Darlene Love (the Blossoms)

August

Notable birthdays: (August 8) Connie Stevens

"Less than a year ago, Patty, LaVerne, and Maxene Andrews were obscure vocalists in an overcrowded entertainment world—but today—as if by magic, the name Andrews Sisters is a household word throughout the nation." —Decca Records, 1938

November

Notable birthdays: (November 26) Tina Turner, (November 29) Bobbi Martin

December

Notable birthdays: (December 3) Jody Reynolds, (December 12) Connie Francis

More Moments in 1938

Gospel-turned-blues singer and guitar virtuoso "Sister" Rosetta Tharpe, appeared on John Hammond's 1938 extravaganza *From Spirituals To Swing*, at the famed New York venue Carnegie Hall (with Cab Calloway and Benny Goodman).

1939

February

Notable birthdays: (February 10) Roberta Flack

April 20

Billie Holiday recorded the acid-tongued ode to slavery "Strange Fruit," a song about a Southern lynching. Though it was banned by many radio networks as being too controversial, it still made No. 16 on the pop charts later that year and was a hit among the white liberal community.

Notable birthdays: (April 16) Dusty Springfield

May

Notable birthdays: (May 1) Judy Collins

June

Notable birthdays: (June 11) Wilma Burgess

July

Notable birthdays: (July 16) Denise LaSalle

September 9

Judy Garland's classic "Over the Rainbow" charted, soaring to No. 5. The standard from the film *The Wizard of Oz* has been recorded hundreds of times over the years, including more than sixty times as a single release, but only the Demensions' 1960 version came close to the success of the original, reaching No. 16. It was named the "Song of the Century" around the turn of the millennium.

Notable birthdays: (September 17) Shelby Flint

October

Notable birthdays: (October 13) Shirley Caesar, (October 14) Melba Montgomery, (October 28) Koko Taylor, (October 30) Grace Slick (Grace Barnett Wing) (Jefferson Airplane)

November

Notable birthdays: (November 12) Ruby Nash (Ruby and the Romantics), (November 23) Betty Everett

December

Notable birthdays: (December 15) Cindy Birdsong (Patti LaBelle and the Blue-Belles), (December 30) Kim Weston

Doris Day.

THE FEARFUL FORTIES

The first half of the 1940s featured the second world war in twenty-three years. When they needed it most, Americans and their music took a one-two punch. In 1940, a nine-month blackout of ASCAP-licensed songs left radio with little popular music to play, and in 1942, a thirteen-month musicians strike, which prevented bands from recording, left a huge gap in recorded output. The "fix" for the former was the establishment of a competing licensing society, BMI, and an effect of the latter was the advent of vocal artists, including many females, recording a cappella, thus altering popular-music tastes from big-band instrumentals back to vocals.

Big bands continued to provide a proving ground for new and exciting female vocalists, who would go on to achieve pop success as solo artists after the war. Just some of the multitude included Jo Stafford, Kay Starr, Kitty Kallen, Connie Haines, Dinah Shore, Bea Wain, Helen Forest, Doris Day, and Paula Kelly, who was the lead vocalist of the Modernaires when they fronted the Glenn Miller Orchestra on the first recognized gold record, "Chattanooga Choo-Choo."

The enormous popularity of jazz continued with a solid core of established 1930s stars and exciting newcomers, such as Savannah Churchill, Connee Boswell, the sultry Peggy Lee, Sarah Vaughan, Anita O'Day, Ella Mae Morse, and the amazing Dinah Washington. Broadway's enduring popularity continued with Carol Channing, Mindy Carson, Fran Warren, Pearl Bailey, and Lena Horne. Meanwhile, jazz, blues, and gospel artists were experimenting with a new, raw sound that would become rhythm and blues, and the early exponents included Blu Lu Barker, Savannah Churchill, Nellie Luther, and jazz vocalist Dinah Washington. The gospel genre saw the likes of Rosetta Howard and Mahalia Jackson taking the fervor from the church to the stadium. Foreign artists gained a foothold in the American music scene when France's Edith Piaf and Britain's Vera Lynn and Grace Fields became popular Stateside. Numerous actresses emerged from film to reach pop stardom, including Betty Grable, the King Sisters (Donna, Yvonne, Luise, and Alyce), and Carmen Miranda.

A musically diverse decade, the forties started with big bands at their peak only to dissolve by mid-decade, displaced by jazz and the emerging sounds of rhythm and blues. Pop, film musicals, and Broadway shows would reign supreme, and all styles would show the growth, development, and perseverance of women artists.

1940

March 30
The former lead singer of the legendary Boswell Sisters, Connee Boswell made her solo chart debut with "On the Isle of May," reaching No. 3. Connee, who had survived polio, performed from a wheel chair throughout her life.

August 10
Judy Garland charted with "I'm Nobody's Baby," reaching No. 3. It was the follow-up to her chart debut—the legendary version of "Over the Rainbow" from the film *The Wizard of Oz*. Making her film debut at age fourteen, the Grand Rapids, Michigan, miss hit the pop Top 30 seventeen times through 1954. Academy Award–winning actress and singer Liza Minelli is the icon's daughter.

October 12
The former vocalist for the Xavier Cugat Orchestra, Dinah Shore charted with "Maybe" (No. 17), her first of sixty-nine hits through 1957.

1941

January 4
Ella Fitzgerald's "Five O'clock Whistle" charted, rising to No. 9. Ella, who had a career forty-nine hits through 1954, was discovered after winning *The Harlem Amateur Hour* in 1934.

Notable birthdays: (January 9) Joan Baez, (January 14) Katerina Valente

"I've always taken The Wizard of Oz *very seriously, you know. I believe in the idea of the rainbow. And I've spent my entire life trying to get over it."—Judy Garland*

February

Notable birthdays: (February 18) Irma Thomas, (February 20) Buffy Sainte-Marie, (February 24) Joanie Sommers

March 15

Dinah Shore's fifth single, "I Hear a Rhapsody," charted today, rising to No. 9. Dinah went on to have two popular TV shows, *The Dinah Shore Show* (1951–1957) and *The Dinah Shore Chevy Show* (1956–1963).

March 22

Connie Haines and the Pied Pipers charted with "You Might Have Belonged to Another," reaching No. 16. The B-side to the Tommy Dorsey hit "Oh! Look at Me Now" (No. 2) was a contest winner on Dorsey's *Fame and Fortune* radio program.

Notable birthdays: (March 18) Margie Bowes, (March 27) Brenda Knight (Gladys Knight and the Pips)

April 12

Bea Wain reached the pop list with "Do I Worry?"—an eventual No. 20 hit. Bea was voted the No. 1 female band vocalist of 1939 by *Billboard*'s college poll, having been the vocalist with Larry Clinton and His Orchestra on such standards as "My Reverie" and "Deep Purple."

Notable birthdays: (April 9) Kay Adams, (April 26) Claudine Clark, (April 28) Ann-Margaret

May

Notable birthdays: (May 15) K. T. Oslin, (May 22) Jackie Landry (the Chantels)

June

Notable birthdays: (June 14) Julie Felix, (June 21) Mitty Collier

July

Notable birthdays: (July 18) Martha Reeves, (July 24) Barbara Love (Friends of Distinction)

August

Notable birthdays: (August 2) Doris Kenner (Shirelles), (August 3) Beverly Lee (Shirelles), (August 4) Timi Yuro, (August 14) Connie Smith

September

Notable birthdays: (September 15) Signe Toly Anderson (Jefferson Airplane), (September 19) Cass Elliot (the Mammas and the Papas)

October 11

Dinah Shore moved onto the singles survey with "Jim," rising to No. 5, her fourth hit in a year. Dinah was married for twenty years to actor George Montgomery.

Notable birthdays: (October 4) Arlene Smith (the Chantels), (October 25) Helen Reddy

November

Notable birthdays: (November 8) Laura Webb (the Bobbettes), (November 13) Carol Connors (born Annette Kleinbard) (the Teddy Bears), (November 13) Odia Coates, (November 29) Jody Miller

December

Notable birthdays: (December 6) Helen Cornelius

1942

January 31

Dinah Shore (born Frances Rose Shore) reached the pop list with "I Got It Bad and That Ain't Good" (No. 19). One of America's musical sweethearts through the 1940s and 1950s, Dinah amassed seventy-five chart singles through 1954. She started out as a band singer with bandleader Xavier Cugat.

Notable birthdays: (January 16) Barbara Lynn, (January 29) Claudine Longet

February

Notable birthdays: (February 9) Carole King

March

Notable birthdays: (March 25) Aretha Franklin

April

Notable birthdays: (April 9) Margo Smith, (April 24) Barbra Streisand, (April 28) Emma Pought (the Bobbettes)

May

Notable birthdays: (May 5) Tammy Wynette, (May 20) Jill Jackson (Paul and Paula)

June

Notable birthdays: (June 19) Elaine "Spanky" McFarlane (Spanky and Our Gang)

July

Notable birthdays: (July 17) Gale Garnett, (July 19) Vickie Carr, (July 23) Madeline Bell

August

Notable birthdays: (August 24) Fontella Bass

September

Notable birthdays: (September 9) Inez Foxx, (September 24) Linda McCartney (Wings), (September 24) Phyllis Allbut (the Angels)

October 10

The Andrews Sisters charted with the risqué-sounding title "Strip Polka," rising to No. 6

October 24

Billie Holiday hit the R&B hit parade with "Trav'lin' Light" as vocalist with the Paul Whiteman Orchestra. The record spent three weeks at No. 1.

Notable birthdays: (October 4) Helen Reddy, (October 22) Annette Funicello

December

Notable birthdays: (December 21) Carla Thomas

1943

January

Notable birthdays: (January 19) Janis Joplin, (January 26) Jean Knight

February

Notable birthdays: (February 9) Barbara Lewis

March

Notable birthdays: (March 18) Helen Gathers (the Bobbettes)

April

Notable birthdays: (April 13) Eva Graham (the New Seekers), (April 25) Leslie Uggams

May 27

British vocalist Cilla Black (actually Priscilla White) was born today. A coat-check girl at Liverpool's now famous Cavern Club, she was discovered by Beatles manager Brian Epstein in the early 1960s. She became hugely popular in Britain, charting twenty-one times, including with covers of "Anyone Who Had a Heart," "You've Lost That Lovin' Feelin'," and Lennon and McCartney's "It's for You."

Notable birthdays: (May 8) Toni Tennille (Captain and Tennille), (May 13) Mary Wells

June

Notable birthdays: (June 29) Little Eva, (June 30) Florence Ballard (the Supremes)

July

Notable birthdays: (July 3) Judith Durham (the Seekers), (July 4) Annette Sterling (Martha and the Vandellas), (July 6) Jan Bradley, (July 12) Christine McVie (Fleetwood Mac)

August

Notable birthdays: (August 5) Sammi Smith, (August 7) Lana Cantrell, (August 18) Sara Dash (LaBelle), (August 21) Clydie King

September 4

Broadway and musical film star Lena Horne charted with "Stormy Weather" from the film of the same name. It would reach No. 21 as her debut disc.

Notable birthdays: (September 2) Rosalind Ashford (Martha and the Vandellas), (September 12) Maria Muldaur, (September 22) Toni Basil, (September 30) Marilyn McCoo (the 5th Dimension)

October

Notable birthdays: (October 23) Barbara Ann Hawkins (the Dixie Cups)

November

Notable birthdays: (November 7) Joni Mitchell

December

Notable birthdays: (December 21) Gwen McCrea

1944

January 1

The Andrews Sisters' "Shoo Shoo Baby" jumped onto the pop hit list and eventually reached No. 1 for nine weeks. The song was from the film *Three Cheers for the Boys* and was one of numerous films the "Musical Queens of the War Era" would star in.

January 8

Jo Stafford, formerly of the Pied Pipers, had her first of seventy-eight Top 100 singles. "Old Acquaintance" first appeared on the popularity list on its way to No. 14. Her seventy-eight hits were compiled in only thirteen years (1944 through 1957).

January 17

Françoise Hardy, the French pop vocalist who introduced the world to the term "chanteuse," was born.

Notable birthdays: (January 11) Janice Pought (the Bobbettes), (January 14) Linda Jones, (January 19) Shelly Fabares

February

Notable birthdays: (February 4) Florence LaRue (the 5th Dimension), (February 28) Barbara Acklin, Barbara Peters

March

Notable birthdays: (March 6) Mary Wilson (the Supremes), (March 26) Diana Ross

April 29

Helen Forrest reached the pop chart with "Long Ago (And Far Away)" (No. 2), her second of nine solo hits through 1946. Helen earned her reputation having been the featured singer with the bands of Harry James, Artie Shaw, and Benny Goodman.

Originally popular in England, Wisconsin-born Hildegarde made her U.S. chart debut with "Suddenly It's Spring," rising to No. 15. She would have six hits by 1946, including the classic "June Is Bustin' Out All Over."

The four siblings of the King Sisters scored a hit with the standard "I'll Get By (As Long as I Have You)" (No. 12), a 1929 No. 3 smash for Ruth Etting. The girls named themselves after their father's middle name, William King Driggs. They would later have success with their own TV show (1965—1966), *The King Family Show.*

May

Notable birthdays: (May 1) Rita Coolidge, Reather Dixon (the Bobbettes), (May 4) Peggy Santiglia (Angels), (May 21) Marcie Blaine, (May 23) Rosetta

Hightower (the Orlons), (May 24) Patti LaBelle, (May 28) Gladys Knight

July

Notable birthdays: (July 15) Millie Jackson, (July 22) Estelle Bennett (the Ronettes), (July 27) Bobbie Gentry

August 12

Dinah Shore strode onto the bestseller's list with "I'll Walk Alone," a recording that spent four weeks at No. 1.

Notable birthdays: (August 21) Jackie DeShannon

September

Notable birthdays: (September 14) Joey Heatherton, (September 16) Betty Kelly (Martha and the Vandellas), (September 24) Rosa Lee Hawkins (the Dixie Cups), (September 27) Janie Grant

October 4

Dinah Shore became the first woman in history to top the American singles chart with "I'll Walk Alone."

October 26

Considered by many to be "the world's worst female singer" Pennsylvania-born Florence Foster Jenkins used her inestimable wealth to stage her own performances, which didn't start until she was forty, beginning in 1904. At the age of eighty, she reached the peak (though critics would say valley) of her "chutzpah" when she leased the use of Carnegie Hall in New York City to stage a performance in her chosen style, opera.

Notable birthdays: (October 1) Barbara Parritt (the Toys), (October 4) Marlena Davis (the Orlons), (October 8) Susan Raye, (October 24) Bettye Swann

November

Notable birthdays: (November 8) Bonnie Bramlett (Delaney and Bonnie), (November 26) Jean Terrell (the Supremes)

December

Notable birthdays: (December 9) Shirley Brickley (the Orlons), (December 11) Brenda Lee, (December 27) Tracy Nelson (Mother Earth), (December 29) Patti Drew

1945

January 13

The Andrews Sisters charted with "Corns for My Country" (No. 21) from the World War II classic film *Hollywood Canteen*.

Notable birthdays: (January 12) Maggie Bell (Stone the Crows), (January 15) Joan Johnson (the Dixie Cups)

February 17

Martha Stewart (no, not the TV home-shopping guru) charted with her only hit, "(All of a Sudden) My Heart Sings," from the Frank Sinatra movie *Anchors Aweigh.*

Notable birthdays: (February 25) Elkie Brooks

March 24

Former Benny Goodman vocalist Martha Tilton charted with "I Should Care," en route to No. 11 on the pop chart. It was her fourth of eight solo hits between 1944 and 1950.

Notable birthdays: (March 1) Arlene Harden, (March 9) Laura Lee, (March 21) Rosemary Stone (Sly and the Family Stone)

April

Notable birthdays: (April 29) Tammie Terrell, (April 30) Mimi Farina (née Baez)

May 12

Known as Lady Day, Billie Holiday charted (No. 5 R&B) with "Lover Man (Oh, Where Can You Be?)." It was her first and only R&B hit, but the last of her thirty-nine pop hits, beginning in 1935. The film *Lady Sings the Blues,* starring Diana Ross, was based on Billie's life.

Notable birthdays: (May 23) Misty Morgan

June

Notable birthdays: (June 1) Linda Scott, (June 4) Michelle Phillips, (June 20) Anne Murray, (June 25) Carly Simon

July 7

Jo Stafford danced onto the pop chart with "On the Sunny Side of the Street," reaching No. 17. The former lead singer of the Pied Pipers (1942–1944) was aided on this single with vocal support by her former Pipers.

Notable birthdays: (July 1) Deborah Harry (Blondie), (July 20) Kim Carnes, (July 21) Rosie Hamlin (Rosie and the Originals)

August 18

The "First Lady of Jazz" Ella Fitzgerald teamed up with the Legendary Delta Rhythm Boys on "It's Only a Paper Moon," which entered the R&B hit parade, with eventual stops at No. 4 and No. 9 pop. The song was originally titled "If You Believe in Me," which is a line from the chorus.

Notable birthdays: (August 10) Ronnie Spector (the Ronettes), (August 18) Barbara Harris (the Toys), Nona Hendryx (LaBelle), (August 23) Rita Pavone

September 29

Judy Garland moved onto the singles hit list with one of her most famous recordings, "On the Atchison, Topeka and the Santa Fe" (No. 9) from the film *The Harvey Girls,* in which she starred. The vocal backups were done by the Merry Macs.

Notable birthdays: (September 8) Cathy Jean (Cathy Jean and the Roommates), (September 9) Dee Dee Sharp, (September 19) Freda Payne

October 13

Vivacious film musical star of the 1940s and 1950s Betty Hutton charted with "What Do You Want to Make Those Eyes at Me For," reaching No. 15.

October 27

Margaret Whiting's "It Might as Well Be Spring" swept onto the bestseller list, reaching No. 6. It became her first of thirty-six hits through 1967.

Notable birthdays: (October 19) Jeannie C. Riley, (October 21) Kathy Young (Kathy Young and the Innocents), (October 29) Melba Moore

November 10

Peggy Lee rode onto the bestseller list with "Waitin' for the Train to Come In" (No. 4), her debut hit in a career thirty-four winners through 1969.

Notable birthdays: (November 15) Anni-Frid Lyngstad (ABBA)

December

Notable birthdays: (December 1) Bette Midler

1946

January

Notable birthdays: (January 11) Naomi Judd, (January 12) Cynthia Robinson (Sly and the Family Stone), (January 19) Dolly Parton, (January 27) Nedra Talley (the Ronettes), (January 30) Jackie Ross

February

Notable birthdays: (February 17) Dodie Stevens

March

Notable birthdays: (March 8) Carole Bayer Sager, (March 12) Liza Minelli, (March 19) Ruth Pointer (the Pointer Sisters)

April

Notable birthdays: (April 18) Hayley Mills

May 25

Sultry Peggy Lee charted with her second solo single, "I Don't Know Enough About You," reaching No. 7. Due to Disney Films' apparent shenanigans, she was awarded almost $4 million for singing in the animated film *Lady and the Tramp.*

Notable birthdays: (May 2) Lesley Gore, (May 7) Thelma Houston, (May 20) Cher (Cherilyn Sarkisian)

June 29

Ella Fitzgerald and Louis Jordan charted with their rousing duet "Stone Cold Dead in the Market (He Had It Coming)," reaching No. 1 R&B for five weeks and No. 7 pop.

Notable birthdays: (June 21) Brenda Holloway

July 27

Ella Fitzgerald and Louis Jordan entered the R&B hit list with "Petootie Pie," reaching No. 3, pretty good for a B-side. The A-side was the huge No. 1 hit "Stone Cold Dead in the Market (He Had It Coming)."

Notable birthdays: (July 1) June Montiero (the Toys), (July 15) Linda Ronstadt

August 10

Atlantic City, New Jersey's Helen Forrest reached the pop list with her tenth and last hit, "In Love in Vain," rising to No. 12. Helen had a successful radio show in the mid-1940s with vocalist Dick Haymes.

The legendary Andrews Sisters had their sixty-fourth chart hit with "Get Your Kicks on Route 66," reaching No. 14.

Notable birthdays: (August 6) Judy Craig (the Chiffons), (August 26) Valerie Simpson

September

Notable birthdays: (September 28) Helen Shapiro (Bethnal Green), (September 30) Sylvia Peterson (the Chiffons)

October

Notable birthdays: (October 3) Andrea Carroll, (October 13) Lacy J. Dalton

December

Notable birthdays: (December 14) Jane Birkin, Joyce Vincent Wilson (Tony Orlando and Dawn), Patty Duke, (December 29) Marianne Faithful, (December 31) Patti Smith

1947

January 6

Sandy Denny, the lead singer of British folk-rock pioneers Fairport Convention, was born today. She sang with the band from 1968 through 1970, went solo, and then returned from 1973 through 1976. Sandy did the original version of "Who Knows Were the Time Goes" later made popular by Judy Collins.

January 18

Jo Stafford charted with "Sonata," reaching No. 10 pop, her first of six hits during the year.

Judy Garland (Francis Gumm) breezed onto the hit list with "For You, for Me, Forevermore" (No. 19) from the film *The Shocking Miss Pilgrim.*

Peggy Lee reached the pop hit parade with the bouncy "It's a Good Day," rising to No. 16. Peggy starred in several famous films, including *The Jazz Singer* and *Pete Kelly's Blues.*

Notable birthdays: (January 3) Zulema, (January 6) Shirley Brown

February

Notable birthdays: (February 3) Melanie, (February 4) Mary Ann Ganser (the Shangri-Las), (February 26) Sandie Shaw (born Sandra Ann Goodrich)

March

Notable birthdays: (March 6) Kiki Dee, (March 24) Peggy Sue

April 12

Ella Fitzgerald charted with "Guilty," rising to No. 11. It was originally a hit for torch-song celeb Ruth Etting in 1931 (No. 4).

Notable birthdays: (April 2) Emmylou Harris, (April 7) Patricia Bennett (the Chiffons), (April 24) Ann Kelly (Hues Corporation), (April 27) Ann Peebles

May 24

The Hadda Brooks Trio charted with "That's My Desire," reaching No. 4 R&B. Hadda, often billed as "Queen of the Boogie" for her rollicking boogie-woogie piano style, was later presented the Prestigious Pioneer Award in 1993 by Bonnie Raitt on behalf of the Smithsonian-based Rhythm and Blues Foundation. She was in her 80s!

Notable birthdays: (May 16) Barbara Lee (the Chiffons), (May 25) Jesse Colter

June 7

Jo Stafford hit the pop list with "A Sunday Kind of Love" (No. 15), which would become a doo-wop standard after the Harptones recorded their version in 1954.

June 14

Country and western performers Louise Massey and the Westerners hit the charts with "My Adobe Hacienda," eventually reaching No. 16.

June 28

Ella Fitzgerald and the Andy Love Quintet (a vocal group) charted with a beautiful version of "That's My Desire," reaching No. 3 R&B.

Notable birthdays: (June 5) Laurie Anderson

July

Notable birthdays: (July 18) Linda Gail Lewis

August

Notable birthdays: (August 9) Barbara Mason

September

Notable birthdays: (September 26) Lynn Anderson

October 11

The Dinning Sisters charted with "I Wonder Who's Kissing Her Now," reaching No. 12 while becoming the second of their four hits through 1948. The Chicago sisters, Lou, Ginger, and Jean's biggest hit was their last, "Buttons and Bows" from the Bob Hope comedy *The Paleface.* Jean wrote a song called "Teen Angel' for her brother Mark that went to No. 1 in 1960.

October 25

America's answer to Britain's pop females of the forties like Vera Lynn was Dinah Shore, who reached the singles survey with "You Do," topping off at No. 4. The recording was from the film *Mother Wore Tights,* starring Betty Grable.

Notable birthdays: (October 6) Millie Small, (October 13) Dorothy Moore, (October 18) Laura Nyro

November

Notable birthdays: (November 8) Minnie Ripperton (Rotary Connection)

December

Notable birthdays: (December 19) Janie Fricke

1948

January 3

Jazz sensation Peggy Lee (Norma Jean Egstrom) danced onto the pop hit list with "I'll Dance at Your Wedding," reaching No. 11. She would chart thirty-four times through 1969.

Vocalist/pianist Rose Murphy hit the charts with the old standard "I Can't Give You Anything but Love," reaching No. 13 while becoming her sole hit.

January 24

Peggy Lee hit the charts with the rhythmic "Manana Is Good Enough for Me." The Latin-flavored smash stayed at No. 1 for nine weeks.

January 31

British singer/comedian Gracie Fields charted with "Now Is the Hour," rising to No. 3 in the States.

Notable birthdays: (January 23) Anita Pointer (the Pointer Sisters)

February 20

Ever popular Kate Smith charted with "Now Is the Hour" (No. 12), her last of twenty-seven hits from 1927 to 1948. Kate is best known for her stirring rendition of "God Bless America," which amazingly climbed the pop chart three times between 1939 and 1942 (Nos. 10, 5, and 23, respectively).

March 20

"Queen of the Blues" Dinah Washington charted with Fats Waller's "Ain't Misbehavin'," reaching No. 6 R&B. The song was originally used in Waller's 1929 Broadway musical *Hot Chocolates*. She is credited as a major influence on Aretha Franklin.

Notable birthdays: (March 8) Little Peggy March

April

Notable birthdays: (April 4) Gail Davies, (April 7) Carol Douglas, (April 27) Kate Pierson (B-52s)

May 29

Doris Day made her chart debut with "Love Somebody," rising to No. 1 for five weeks. It was the start of a superstar career for the Cincinnati miss, who chalked up forty-six hits through 1962 along with numerous starring roles in films and her own TV show from 1968 to 1973.

Notable birthdays: (May 6) Mary MacGregor, (May 17) Penny DeHaven, (May 26) Stevie Nicks (Fleetwood Mac)

June 5

The Pied Pipers, with June Hutton on lead, reached the pop hit list with "My Happiness," rising to No. 3.

June 26

Patti Page's "Confess" ran up the charts to No. 12. It was her first of an amazing eighty-one hits from 1948 through 1968.

Notable birthdays: (June 12) Lyn Collins

July 3

Sarah Vaughan reached the Top 100 with "Nature Boy," eventually hitting No. 9. It was the first of thirty-three hits through 1966 for the jazz vocalist known as "The Divine One."

Sarah Vaughan.

July 17

Margaret Whiting hit the bestseller lists with "A Tree in the Meadow," a No. 1 smash for five weeks and the biggest of her career thirty-six hits. She was the daughter of composer Richard Whiting ("Till We Meet Again").

July 24

The Marlin Sisters (Gloria and Trudy) charted with "My Happiness," rising to No. 24. The song would later be a hit for Connie Francis in 1959.

August

Notable birthdays: (August 10) Patti Austin

September 18

Dinah Shore ascended the Hot 100 with "Buttons and Bows," her biggest success of a career sixty-nine hits. The bouncy tune spent ten weeks at No. 1.

Notable birthdays: (September 13) Nell Carter, (September 26) Olivia Newton-John

October 2

Nellie Lutcher charted with "Alexander's Ragtime Band," reaching No. 13 R&B. The song was originally a No. 1 pop hit in 1911 for Arthur Collins and Byron Harlan.

October 9

Brazilian film star Carmen Miranda with the Andrews Sisters charted with "Cuanto la Gusto," eventually reaching No. 12. It was from the Jane Powell film *A Date with Judy*.

Notable birthdays: (October 28) Telma Hopkins (Tony Orlando and Dawn)

November 13

Jo Stafford charted with "My Darling, My Darling," her fifty-seventh hit and fourth No. 1 in just five years.

Notable birthdays: (November 16) Chi Coltrane

December 4

Oklahoma-born Kay Starr found her way onto the bestseller list with "You Were Only Foolin'" (No. 16), her first of forty hits through 1962.

Notable birthdays: (December 10) Jessica Cleaves (Friends of Distinction),

(December 25) Barbara Mandrell, (December 31) Donna Summer

1949

February

Notable birthdays: (February 16) Lynn Paul (the New Seekers)

March 19

Dinah Shore charted with "So in Love," from the Broadway musical *Kiss Me Kate*.

Jo Stafford's "A Your Adorable" charted, on its way to No. 4, becoming her fifty-ninth of seventy singles on the national hit parade. Jo originally sang with the Tommy Dorsey Band from 1940 to 1943.

Notable birthdays: (March 4) Carroll Baker

April 30

Kitty Kallen's debut 78-rpm disc, "Kiss Me Sweet," charted, reaching No. 30. She would have six more through 1954.

May

Notable birthdays: (May 4) Stella Parton, (May 26) Vickie Lawrence

June 11

Ella Fitzgerald and Louis Jordan charted with their duet, "Baby It's Cold Outside," reaching No. 6 R&B and No. 9 pop. It was from the film *Neptune's Daughter* starring 1940s swimming star Esther Williams.

July 30

Evelyn Knight (known as the "Lass with the Delicate Air") charted with "A Wonderful Guy" (from the film *South Pacific*), reaching No. 22. "A Wonderful Guy" was stuck in the middle of a consistent trend for Evelyn. It was the third of seven straight singles that reached no higher than No. 20 and no lower than No. 29, from 1949 through 1951.

Notable birthdays: (July 27) Maureen McGovern

August 13

Evelyn Knight charted with "Be Goody, Good Good to Me," reaching No. 29.

Jo Stafford reached the charts with "Homework," rising to No. 11.

August 20

Dinah Washington entered the R&B hit list with "Long John Blues," peaking at No. 3.

September

Notable birthdays: (September 7) Gloria Gaynor

October 1

"The Divine One" Sarah Vaughan hit the pop list with "Make Believe (You Are Glad When You Are Sorry)," reaching No. 20. It was a No. 1 hit in 1921 for Broadway star Nora Bayes. Sarah's career started when she won an amateur-night contest at New York's Apollo Theater in 1942.

The Andrews Sisters charted with "The Wedding of Lili Marlene," rising to No. 20 pop. Twenty-five years later, Patty and Maxene (sister LaVerne died in 1967) would star in the Broadway musical *Over There.*

November

Notable birthdays: (November 8) Bonnie Raitt, (November 10) Donna Fargo

December 24

Jo Stafford bounced onto the singles hit list with two sides today, "Bibbidi-Bobbidi-Boo" and "Echoes." The former reached No. 13 and the latter No. 18.

Paula Kelly and the Modernaires charted with "The Old Master Painter," reaching No. 13. The group began its career with the Glenn Miller Orchestra and sang on the huge hit "Chattanooga Choo Choo" (1941), which became the first record certified as a million seller.

December 31

The Andrews Sisters danced onto the hit list with "Merry Christmas Polka," rising to No. 18.

LaVern Baker.

THE FABULOUS FIFTIES

The decade that established the 45-rpm single as the preferred format for delivering music to the masses also gave the "platters" the perfect style to go with it: rock 'n' roll. With that, female performers had a new and exciting vehicle to tie their talents to. Though Doris Day and many other top stars of the decade and their producers stubbornly clung to a waning style and remained pop crooners, female artists were also some of the first ones to adopt the new backbeat. Connie Francis, LaVern Baker, Georgia Gibbs, Brenda Lee, Gogi Grant, Gail Storm, and the Mickey Mouse Club's Annette became idols of teens in the mid-to-late 1950s while inadvertently reducing the popularity of early to mid-1950s pop icons like Jay P. Morgan, Rosemary Clooney, Jane Morgan, Joni James, Kay Starr, and Jo Stafford.

Many of them, including Patti Page, Teresa Brewer, and Dinah Shore, were carryover song stylists from the 1940s, though their dominance during the early to mid-1950s cannot be denied. The birth of rock 'n' roll was probably the most significant development since the record was created, and by the end of the decade, the nascent genre had elbowed its way to the top of popular music styles. Rock 'n' roll also helped establish the golden age of vocal groups in the '50s. All-female groups such as the incredible Chantels, the Hearts, the McGuire Sisters, the Fontane Sisters, the Ponytails, the Quintones, the Chordettes, the Dreamers, and the first female rock 'n' roll group to have a Top 5 hit, the Bobbettes, were major contributors. Chugging along with a full head of steam, the golden age of girl groups would arrive soon after in the 1960s.

Jazz was newly refined and sophisticated, and its interpreters included femmes fatales Peggy Lee, Nina Simone, Carmen McRae, Lena Horne, and

> *"At what point did rhythm and blues start becoming rock 'n' roll? When the white kids started to dance to it."*
>
> —*Ruth Brown*

Julie London. Meanwhile, contemporary country broadened its audience, thanks to legends-to-be like Kitty Wells, Patsy Cline, Jean Shepard, the Davis Sisters, and the trio's solo singing sister, Skeeter Davis.

R&B also came into its own, thanks to the incomparable Ruth Brown, LaVern Baker, Faye Adams, Little Esther, Willie Mae "Big Momma" Thornton, Etta James, and the female-led duos Shirley and Lee and Mickey and Sylvia.

Truly an age for the ages, the 1950s were the start of a musical revolution.

1950

January

Notable birthdays: (January 24) Becky Hobbs, (January 28) Barbie Benton

February 4

The Robins' "Double Crossing Blues" (Savoy) charted, reaching No. 1 R&B, with Little Esther (Phillips) singing lead.

February 28

Rio de Janeiro's "Brazilian Bombshell," as she was known, Carmen Miranda had the second of her only two hit singles as "The Wedding Samba" charted, en route to No. 23. Backup vocals were by the Andrews Sisters.

Notable birthdays: (February 5) Ann Sexton, (February 6) Natalie Cole

March 25

Musical theater icon Mary Martin charted with "Go to Sleep, Go to Sleep, Go to Sleep," reaching No. 8. Mary had starred in such classics as *South Pacific* and the perennial children's classic *Peter Pan.*

Notable birthdays: (March 1) Connie Eaton, (March 2) Karen Carpenter, (March 10) Beverly Bremers

April 8

The Johnny Otis Orchestra, featuring Little Esther and Mel Walker on vocals, charted with "Mistrustin' Blues," reaching No. 1 for four weeks on the R&B

charts. Otis' previous hit was "Double Crossing Blues" with Little Esther and the Robins.

April 15

The Johnny Otis Orchestra with Little Esther on vocals charted with "Misery," reaching No. 9 R&B.

April 29

Broadway musical icon Ethel Merman (Ethel Zimmerman) charted with "(If I Knew You We're Comin') I'd've Baked a Cake," reaching No. 15. The recording was a duet with actor/singer Ray Bolger (best known for his portrayal as the Scarecrow in *The Wizard of Oz*).

The lovely Mindy Carson, formerly of the Paul Whiteman Orchestra in the 1940s, charted with "My Foolish Heart," rising to No. 6 while becoming the biggest of her seven solo hits.

Notable birthdays: (April 5) Agnetha Faltskog (ABBA)

May

Notable birthdays: (May 3) Mary Hopkin, (May 29) Rebbie Jackson

June

Notable birthdays: (June 1) Charlene, (June 3) Suzi Quatro, (June 19) Ann Wilson (Heart)

July

Notable birthdays: (July 6) Phyllis Hyman

October 21

French legend Edith Piaf recorded "La Vie en Rose" in French and had such huge success with it that she recorded an English-language version. That version charted in America and rose to No. 23.

Notable birthdays: (October 4) Patti Cathcart (Tuck and Patti)

November 18

Ella Fitzgerald and Louis Armstrong charted with "Can Anyone Explain? (No, No, No!)," reaching No. 30.

Patti Page's career maker, "The Tennessee Waltz," danced onto the bestseller list, rising to No. 1 and taking root there for thirteen weeks.

Singer, songwriter, and pianist Nellie Lutcher charted with "For You My Love," reaching No. 8 R&B. The last of the songstress' eleven hits, the song was a duet with Nat King Cole.

November 24

Petula Clark's *Pets Parlour* BBC-TV show aired for the first time. The show would run through July 1953, winning Clark the award for Most Outstanding Artist on British TV.

Notable birthdays: (November 12) Barbara Fairchild, (November 22) Delphine Reeves (Martha and the Vandellas), (November 22) Tina Weymouth (Talking Heads), (November 25) Jocelyn Brown

December 30

Les Paul and Mary Ford charted with "Tennessee Waltz," rising to No. 6.

More Moments in 1950

"Queen of the Boogie" Hadda Brooks hosted her own primetime TV variety show, *The Hadda Brooks Show,* in Los Angeles in the 1950s, making her the first African American to do so (and preceding Oprah by more than four decades!).

Notable birthdays: (December 9) Joan Armatrading

1951

January 6

Jazz diva Dinah Washington charted with "Harbor Lights," reaching No. 10 R&B. The Platters would take it to No. 15 R&B (No. 8 pop) in 1960, having carefully studied Dinah's version.

January 13

Jo Stafford, former lead singer of the Pied Pipers, had her 41st charter in just seven years when "If" waltzed onto the hit parade, reaching No. 8.

The legendary folk group the Weavers with female lead Ronnie Gilbert charted with "So Long (It's Been Good to Know Yuh)," rising to No. 4 on the pop list. The group was blacklisted in the McCarthy era, nearly ruining their career, but their 1955 Carnegie Hall concert helped bring on the folk music revolution of the late 1950s and early 1960s.

January 26

Little Esther Phillips recorded "Heart to Heart," singing lead for the Dominoes and in duet with Clyde McPhatter.

Notable birthdays: (January 9) Crystal Gayle, (January 15) Martha Davis (the Motels)

February 10

Evelyn Knight charted with her last of thirteen pop hits, "My Heart Cries for You." The recording was a duet with country great Red Foley. Evelyn was best known for her seven-week stay at No. 1 with "A Little Bird Told Me" in 1948.

February 24

Rosemary Clooney's "Your Just in Love" charted, peaking at No. 24. It was the first of twenty-eight hits for the Maysville, Kentucky, miss between 1951 and 1960.

Notable birthdays: (February 15) Melissa Manchester

March 17

Famous as the featured vocalist for the Jimmy Dorsey Orchestra, Helen O'Connell debuted on the pop charts on her own with "Would I Love You," rising to No. 16.

Notable birthdays: (March 14) Zella Lehr

April

Notable birthdays: (April 7) Janis Ian

May

Notable birthdays: (May 23) Judy Rodman

June 23

TV actress and blond bombshell Dagmar hit the chart, singing with Frank Sinatra on a Mitch Miller–produced novelty single on Columbia, "Mama Will Bark," reaching No. 21.

Notable birthdays: (June 3) Deniece Williams, (June 11) Lynsey De Paul

July 7

Dinah Shore entered the pop-chart competition with "Sweet Violets," reaching No. 3.

Les Paul and Mary Ford reached the pop hit list with "Josephine," rising to No. 12. It was the ninth of thirty-three hits for couple. Mary Ford (aka Colleen

Summers), who was born today, was a superlative country singer who combined Les Paul's jazz influence to create numerous pop hits in the 1950s, like "Vaya Con Dios" and "How High the Moon." Paul's innovative electric-guitar sound and double tracking of Mary's voice made for a most identifiable hit sound.

One of the 1950s most popular singers, Rosemary Clooney charted with "Come on a My House." The 45-rpm single spent eight weeks at No. 1 and became the first of six career No. 1 records.

Notable birthdays: (July 11) Bonnie Pointer (the Pointer Sisters)

September 8

Film and musical star Gloria DeHaven charted for the first and only time with the standard "Because of You" (No. 11), from the film *I Was an American Spy.*

Notable birthdays: (September 7) Chrissie Hynde (the Pretenders)

October 27

Les Paul and Mary Ford charted with "Just One More Chance," rising to No. 5.

November 3

The Fontane Sisters (Bea, Geri, and Marge) charted with "Cold, Cold Heart," reaching No. 16. The trio would amass twenty-four hits in their nine-year chart career, from 1950 to 1958, not including singing backup on numerous hits with Perry Como.

December

Notable birthdays: (December 17) Wanda Hutchinson (the Emotions), (December 29) Yvonne Elliman, (December 30) Nancy LaMott

1952

January 5

The Bell Sisters (eleven-year-old Kay and sixteen-year-old Cynthia) hit the charts with their debut, "Bermuda," reaching No. 7. It was the biggest of their three hits, all in 1952.

February 16

Kay Starr landed on the Top 100 with "The Wheel of Fortune," her biggest record (No. 1 for ten weeks) of forty hits.

Notable birthdays: (February 18) Randy Crawford

March 15

Doris Day (born Doris Kappelhoff) charted with "A Guy Is a Guy," eventually reaching No. 1. It was the twenty-second hit in less than four years for the former Les Brown Band singer, who went on to be the No. 1 film box-office star of the late 1950s and early 1960s.

March 22

Margaret Whiting reached the pop hit list with "I'll Walk Alone," rising to No. 29. The recording was featured in the film *A Song in My Heart,* starring Susan Hayward.

March 29

Clara Ann Fowler charted with "Whispering Winds," reaching No. 16 pop. She began her career singing on Tulsa, Oklahoma, radio station KTUL, replacing a singer sponsored by the Page Milk Company with the stage name Patti Page. When Patti left, Clara not only took her spot, she also took her name, becoming one of the biggest female stars of the 1940s and 1950s.

Notable birthdays: (March 17) Susie Allanson

May 3

Broadway musical star Jane Froman had her chart debut with "I'll Walk Alone," reaching No. 14. Froman miraculously recovered from severe injuries in a 1943 plane crash to bravely continue her career. The recording was featured in Jane's biographical film, *With a Song in My Heart,* starring Susan Hayward as Jane.

Notable birthdays: (May 19) Cyndi Grecco, Grace Jones

June 7

Ella Mae Morse charted with the last of nine hits, from 1943 to 1952, "Oakie Boogie," reaching No. 23. Ella Mae was Capitol Records' first female hit act.

July 4

British songstress Vera Lynn had the distinction of having the first British No. 1 record on the American charts when her single "Auf Wiedersehen, Sweetheart" hit the top spot.

July 15

An eight-year-old girl won $2,000 and a gold cup for her rendition of "Too Young" on Ted Mack's *Amateur Hour.* The child was Gladys Knight.

Notable birthdays: (July 17) Nicolette Larson, Phoebe Snow, (July 23) Janis Siegel (the Manhattan Transfer)

August 2

Doris Day charted with the standard "When I Fall in Love" (No. 20), from the movie *One Minute to Zero.* It would later be a No. 7 hit for the Lettermen in 1962.

Former Benny Goodman songstress Peggy Lee scored a hit with the standard "Just One of Those Things," reaching No. 14.

Gloria Hart hit the pop list with "I Would Rather Look at You," reaching No. 18. The melody would later wind up in the Elvis Presley song "Tonight Is So Right for Love," from his *G.I. Blues* album in 1960.

August 9

Former Pied Pipers lead singer Jo Stafford reached the hit list today with "You Belong to Me." The standard spent an incredible twelve weeks at No. 1 and was the biggest of seventy-eight hits for the No. 1 female vocalist of the pre-rock era.

August 13

Willie Mae "Big Mama" Thornton, an early R&B howler who played drums and harmonica, recorded Leiber and Stoller's original "Hound Dog" in Los Angeles, backed by the Johnny Otis Orchestra. By mid-1953, it was a smash, holding down the No. 1 spot on the R&B charts for seven weeks. It was her only hit in a more than twenty-year career. It also was only a prelude to the song's success. Three years later, Elvis Presley took the song to No. 1 on the pop charts for eleven weeks, after hearing a bar band play the song!

August 23

Actress Marlene Dietrich teamed up with Rosemary Clooney for the novelty song "Too Old to Cut the Mustard," which charted today, rising to No. 12. Though the glamour girl popularized the song "Falling in Love Again" from her film *The Blue Angel* in 1931, Marlene (born Maria Magdalene Dietrich Von Losch) never charted in America again.

September 4

Gladys and Brenda Knight, along with their brother Merald and cousins William and Eleanor Guest, performed at Merald's tenth birthday party and decided they should become a group. They named themselves after the nickname of another cousin, James "Pips" Woods. It would be ten years before they became known as Gladys Knight and the Pips.

September 27

The iconic Pearl Bailey charted for the first and last time with "Takes Two to Tango," reaching No. 7. Pearl starred in the Broadway-musical version of *Hello Dolly* during the sixties.

October 25

Britain's answer to American pop females of the forties like Dinah Shore, Vera Lynn stormed the U.S. pop lists with "Yours," rising to No. 7. She was England's most popular female vocalist of World War II and recorded the hit "We'll Meet Again," which was used tongue-in-cheek at the now-famous finale of the Peter Seller's black comedy *Dr. Strangelove* in 1964.

Karen Chandler (born Eve Nadauld) charted with "Hold Me, Thrill Me, Kiss Me," reaching No. 5. She originally sang with the Benny Goodman Orchestra under the name Eve Young on the hit "A Gal in Calico" (No. 6) in 1947.

November 29

Patti Page's smooth ballad "Why Don't You Believe Me" sailed onto the hit list, reaching No. 4 for the Tulsa, Oklahoma, sweetheart, who was one of eleven kids.

Notable birthdays: (November 2) Maxine Nightingale

December 6

TV's *Your Hit Parade* star Gisele MacKenzie charted with "Don't Let the Stars Get in Your Eyes," reaching No. 11 for the biggest of her three hits.

December 13

Teresa Brewer charted with "Til I Waltz Again with You." It was her biggest of thirty-five hits from 1950 through 1961, reaching No. 1 for seven weeks. The Toledo, Ohio, miss began her career at the age of five on Major Bowes' *Amateur Hour.*

Notable birthdays: (December 27) Karla Bonoff

1953

January 3

Joni James (Joan Carmello Babbo) charted with "Have You Heard," reaching No. 4. It was her sophomore hit, coming on the heels of her debut charter "Why Don't You Believe Me," reaching No. 1 for six weeks. Both songs became hits for the Doo Wopping Duprees in 1963.

Les Paul and Mary Ford's "Bye Bye Baby" said hello to the hit list, eventually reaching No. 5, as their twenty-fifth of a career thirty-three hits between 1945 and 1954.

January 20

The McGuire Sisters' first of fifty-nine singles, "Pickin' Sweethearts," was released.

January 31

Patti Page (born Clara Ann Fowler) reached the hit parade with "How Much Is That Doggie in the Window" and surged to No. 1 for eight weeks, creating one of the biggest (and cutest) hits of the year.

Pop vocalist Sunny Gale (born Selma Segal) charted with "A Stolen Waltz" (No. 18).

Notable birthdays: (January 10) Pat Benatar, (January 12) La Wanda Linsey, (January 17) Sheila Hutchinson (the Emotions)

March 28

Willie Mae "Big Mama" Thornton charted with "Hound Dog," reaching No. 1 for seven weeks on the R&B hit parade.

Notable birthdays: (March 23) Chaka Khan

April 18

Willie Mae "Big Mama" Thornton hit No. 1 on the *Cashbox* R&B chart with "Hound Dog," which the magazine described as a "once in a lifetime" event.

April 30

The McGuire Sisters' "Goodnight, Sweetheart Goodnight" was released and became their first Top 10 hit (No. 7). The group would amass thirty-three Top 100 singles by 1961.

Notable birthdays: (April 6) Dottsy

June

Notable birthdays: (June 8) Bonnie Tyler, (June 22) Cyndi Lauper

July 11

Les Paul and Mary Ford charted with "Johnny (Is the Boy for Me)," reaching No. 15. It was the follow-up to their biggest hit, "Vaya con Dios," which stayed at No. 1 for eleven weeks.

Notable birthdays: (July 6) Nancy Griffith, (July 15) Alicia Bridges

August

Notable birthdays: (August 5) Samantha Sang, (August 16) Kathy Lee Gifford

September 5

Ella Fitzgerald and the Ray Charles Singers charted with a cover of the Orioles' classic "Crying in the Chapel." Ella and company raced up the bestseller list to No. 15 while the Orioles won the competition, reaching No. 11.

Notable birthdays: (September 21) Betty Wright, (September 30) Deborah Allen

October 10

The Davis Sisters' one and only single, "I Forgot More Than You'll Ever Know," charted, reaching No. 16. The "sisters" were Mary Frances "Skeeter" Davis and Betty Jack Davis, who were not related. After Betty died in a car accident in 1953, Skeeter went solo, having her biggest success with 1963's "The End of the World" (No. 2). She went on to have forty-one country hits through 1976, and from the Davis Sisters days through 1974 was with RCA.

Notable birthdays: (October 21) Charlotte Caffey (the Go Go's)

November 28

Patti Page popped onto the hit listings with "Changing Partners," reaching No. 3.

December

Notable birthdays: (December 21) Betty Wright

More Moments in 1953

Rhythm and blues pioneer Ruth Brown's "(Mama) He Treats Your Daughter Mean" was released on Atlantic Records. Brown's two dozen hit records helped Atlantic secure its stature, and is often referred to as the "House That Ruth Built."

1954

March

Notable birthdays: (March 16) Nancy Wilson (Heart)

April 17

Former Jimmy Dorsey Big Band vocalist Kitty Kallen flew onto the Top 100 with "Little Things Mean a Lot" and perched at No. 1 for nine weeks!

Notable birthdays: (April 29) Karen Brooks

May

Notable birthdays: (May 4) Pia Zadora

June 5

Patti Page charted with "Steam Heat" (No. 8) her thirty-fifth hit in just six years.

June 19

Betty Hutton and Tennessee Ernie Ford hit with "The Honeymoon's Over," reaching No. 16.

Notable birthdays: (June 15) Terri Gibbs

July 2

Lillian Leach, one of the premier R&B lead singers of the fifties, and her group, the Mellows, signed to Jay Dee Records.

July 10

The epitome of sex symbols and a legend of the silver screen, Marilyn Monroe (born Norma Jean Baker) and her wispy voice made her one and only chart encounter with "River of No Return," from the movie of the same name. It reached No. 30. If anyone had had the foresight to issue her smoldering recording of "Happy Birthday" that she sang to President Jack Kennedy in the early sixties, it probably would have gone Top 10 (especially if accompanied by a picture sleeve).

July 14

Lillian Leach and the Mellows recorded the Doo-Wop standard "Smoke from Your Cigarette," now a $125 collectors item.

July 24

Petula Clark's cover of the American hit "The Little Shoemaker" reached No. 7 on the British charts. Her chart debut, it was recorded while she was still in shock following a car accident on the way to the studio. The British thrush would go on to have twenty-nine British hits through 1988 on thirty-three chart entries.

Notable birthdays: (July 9) Debbie Sledge (Sister Sledge), (July 13) Louise Mandrell

August 7

Rosemary Clooney raced onto the charts with "This Old House," eventually embracing the top spot. It became her last of six No. 1s.

Ruth Brown charted with "Oh What a Dream," reaching No. 1 for eight weeks!

August 25

Elvis Presley attended a star-studded rhythm-and-blues concert in Memphis that included Big Maybelle, LaVern Baker, the Drifters, the Spaniels, and Roy Hamilton. The early show was for "whites only" and the late show was for "colored."

September 9

Raised on their father's sugar plantation in Cuba, the DeCastro Sisters ascended the hit list with "Teach Me Tonight," an eventual No. 2.

Notable birthdays: (September 6) Stella Barker (the Belle Stars), (September 30) Patrice Rushen

October 9

Shirley Gunter and the Queens, a Los Angeles female quartet, hit the R&B singles survey with "Oop Shoop" (No. 8). By the time "Oop Shoop" was released, Shirley (sister of Coasters member Cornel Gunter) was legally blind.

October 20

LaVern Baker recorded her rock 'n' roll classic "Tweedle Dee" at New York's Atlantic Studios.

October 30

The Chordettes hit the Hot 100 with "Mr. Sandman" (No. 1), their first of fourteen hits through 1961.

November 13

Rosemary Clooney bounced onto the hit list with "Mambo Italiano," reaching No. 9. One of the fifties' most popular singers, she and her sister, Betty, began singing with the Tony Pastor Orchestra in the 1940s.

November 20

Known as "Little Miss Share Cropper," LaVern Baker (born Delores Williams) had her debut disc, "Tweedlee Dee," released today. It reached No. 4 R&B and No. 14 pop while beginning her string of twenty-one hits through 1966.

December 27

Colorado-born Jaye P. Morgan charted with "That's All I Want from You" (No. 3). It was her initial hit, followed by nineteen more through 1960.

Sarah Vaughan reached the coveted hit list with "Make Yourself Comfortable" (No. 6), her biggest single of thirty-three hits.

Notable birthdays: (November 8) Ricki Lee Jones, (November 19) Annette Guest (First Choice), (November 30) June Pointer (the Pointer Sisters)

December 18

Teresa Brewer sprinted onto the hit list with "Let Me Go Lover," reaching No. 6.

December 25

The DeJohn Sisters jumped onto the bestseller list with "(My Baby Don't Love Me) No More," an eventual No. 6 hit.

Notable birthdays: (December 25) Annie Lennox (the Eurythmics)

1955

January 7

Marion Anderson debuted at the Metropolitan Opera House in New York City. She was the first black singer to become an alumni of the Met.

January 8

The McGuire Sisters' cover record of the Moonglows' "Sincerely" charted, on its way to No. 1 for ten weeks.

January 15

LaVern Baker charted with "Tweedlee Dee" (No. 14), her first of twenty pop Top 100 45s between 1955 and 1966. She also had twenty-one R&B hits and was inducted into the Rock and Roll Hall of Fame in 1991.

January 27

Lillian Leach and the Mellows' third and fourth singles, "I Still Care" and "Yesterdays Memories" were recorded. The Jay-Dee singles cost 69 cents each. Today they're collectibles, priced at $100 each.

Notable birthdays: (January 4) Kathy Forester (the Forester Sisters)

February 12

The McGuire Sisters' biggest hit, "Sincerely," reached No. 1.

February 19

Etta James charted with "The Wallflower" (sometimes called "Roll with Me Henry"), reaching No. 1 R&B for four weeks. The song was an answer record to Hank Ballard's "Work with Me Annie" while Georgia Gibbs copied Etta's version for a pop version called "Dance with Me Henry." Etta would go on to have thirty R&B hits, with her last one being a cover of Big Brother and the Holding Company's (aka Janis Joplin and band's) "Piece of My Heart."

March 26

Georgia Gibbs' "Dance with Me Henry" (a cover of Etta James' "Roll with Me Henry") charted, on its trip to No. 1. It was her second of thirteen Top 100 singles through 1958.

The Hearts, one of the first female rock 'n' roll groups stormed the R&B charts with their scintillating, powerhouse performance of "Lonely Nights," reaching No. 8. The record was also one of the first to have a talking bridge, and anyone who's heard that smokin' line "You great big lump a sugar" will never forget the first in-your-face "attitude" hit. The group included Jeanette "Baby" Washington and Zell Sanders. Zell went on to have her own J&S label and produced the hit "Over the Mountain, Across the Sea" for Johnnie and Joe.

Notable birthdays: (March 10) Bunny DeBarge (DeBarge), (March 16) Nancy Wilson (Heart), (March 28) Reba McEntire

"Etta [James] is earthy and gritty, ribald and out there in a way that few performers have the guts to be. From the first time I heard her as a teenager, with songs like 'Tell Mama,' 'At Last,' 'I'd Rather Go Blind'—there was just something about that ache I heard that got me bad. Still does."—Bonnie Raitt

April

Notable birthdays: (April 29) Karen Brooks

May

Ruth Brown's hit "(Mama) He Treats Your Daughter Mean" was banned in Britain. The BBC felt it might encourage wife beating.

Notable birthdays: (May 4) Pia Zadora, (May 16) Hazel O'Connor, (May 24) Roseanne Cash

June 1

Patsy Cline recorded "A Church, a Courtroom and Then Goodbye" at her first recording session in Nashville at Owen Bradley's Barn. It became her debut single.

Notable birthdays: (June 15) Terri Gibbs

August 20

A vocal trio from New Milford, New Jersey, the Fontane Sisters charted with "Seventeen," en route to No. 3. It was their fifth of eighteen hits between 1954 and 1958.

September 17

Ella Fitzgerald and Peggy Lee's album *Songs from Pete Kelly's Blues* ascended the album hit list, leveling off at No. 7. It became Ella's biggest of eleven charters through 1969.

September 26

Singer/actress Debbie Reynolds married singer Eddie Fisher.

September 30

Another Petula Clark TV show *Pet's Parade* (not to be confused with her earlier 1950–1953 *Pet's Parlour*) aired for the first time on BBC-TV, running through February 1957.

Notable birthdays: (September 6) Stella Barker (the Belle Stars), (September 26) Carlene Carter, (September 30) Patrice Rushen

October 9

Wanda Jackson performed at the Cherry Springs Dance Hall in Cherry Spring, Texas, along with a guy named Elvis Presley, Johnny Cash, and future star Porter Wagoner. Often hailed as the "Queen of Rockabilly," Jackson got her start on the Decca label in 1954, thanks to the encouragement of "friend" Elvis

"If it had not been for people like Patsy [Cline], it wouldn't be possible for women like me to do what I do today." —k. d. lang

and her dad. She later switched to Capitol Records, where she later scored a Top 40 pop hit in 1960 with the re-release of her rendition of "Let's Have a Party" (also covered earlier by Elvis).

October 22

TV star Gale Storm (born Josephine Cottle) blew onto the singles charts with a cover of Fats Domino's "I Hear You Knocking" (No. 2). It was her first of twelve hits through 1957.

October 29

The first R&B show held at Carnegie Hall in New York included Etta James, the Peaches, the Five Keys, Gene and Eunice, the Clovers, and Big Joe Turner.

Notable birthdays: (October 12) Jane Siberry

November 12

Dorothy Collins' novelty hit "My Boy Flat Top" charted, en route to No. 16. Dorothy was one of the stars of TV's *Your Hit Parade*.

Sultry songstress/actress Julie London stormed onto the bestseller list with "Cry Me a River" (No. 9), the only hit for the wife of Sgt. Joe Friday (Jack Webb) of TV's *Dragnet*.

November 19

The Fontane Sisters' cover of the Drifters' "Adorable" charted, but only reached No. 71.

Notable birthdays: (November 8) Ricki Lee Jones, (November 19) Annette Guest (First Choice), (November 30) June Pointer (the Pointer Sisters)

December 31

Kay Starr's "Rock and Roll Waltz" charted today, on its way to No. 1 for six weeks.

Notable birthdays: (December 25) Alannah Myles

1956

January 10

Publicist Mae Axton contributed to the legend that would become Elvis Presley when her original "Heartbreak Hotel" was recorded by the King among his first sides for RCA at its Nashville studio. Mae was the mother of singer Hoyt Axton.

Notable birthdays: (January 1) Diane Warren

February 11

The first rock 'n' roll stage show in the Bronx was held at the Opera House Movie Theater, featuring the Bonnie Sisters, the Cadillacs, and Heartbeats and Valentines.

February 18

The Bonnie Sisters charted with "Cry Baby." The trio were not sisters, but they were all nurses at New York's Bellevue Hospital.

February 20

Detroit's Riviera Theater hosted a show, featuring the Jewels, the Bonnie Sisters, Frankie Lymon and the Teenagers, and the 5 Keys.

March 31

Brenda Lee made her professional performing debut on Red Foley's *Ozark Jubilee* on ABC-TV at the age of eleven. It led to a five-year management deal with Dub Albritton of Top Talent.

"She [Brenda Lee] has the greatest rock 'n' roll voice of them all."
— John Lennon

Notable birthdays: (March 5) Teena Marie, (March 26) Charley McClain, Stephanie Mills

March

Singer/actress Gale Storm assaulted the hit list with a cover of Frankie Lymon and the Teenagers' No. 6 smash "Why Do Fools Fall in Love."

April 21

Eydie Gorme charted with "Too Close for Comfort" (No. 39), her first of seventeen Top 100 singles through 1972.

April 28

Gogi Grant's "The Wayward Wind" blew onto the charts, eventually topping the hit list for eight weeks.

May 2

The Joytones, one of rock 'n' roll's first girl groups, recorded "Gee, What a Boy." The 79-cent single is a $75 collectable today.

June 1

Doris Day signed a five-year recording agreement with Columbia for $1 million dollars.

June 23

Shirley and Lee's immortal "Let the Good Times Roll" was issued (No. 20).

July 1

Eleven-year-old Brenda Lee signed with Decca Records.

July 12

Shirley and Lee sang at the Carrs Beach Amphitheater in Maryland, along with the Teenagers, Carl Perkins, the Cleftones, and the Spaniels. Over 8,000 lucky fans got in to see them while an unlucky 10,000 were turned away!

August 5

Doris Day hit No. 1 in England with "Que Sera Sera," her second chart topper there. It was also No. 2 Stateside.

August 6

Filming began on Alan Freed's classic flick *Rock, Rock, Rock,* featuring LaVern

Baker, along with Frankie Lymon and the Teenagers, the Flamingoes, the Moonglows, and Chuck Berry.

August 11

New Orleans schoolmates Shirley Goodman and Leonard Lee as Shirley and Lee charted with their soon-to-be rock 'n' roll classic "Let the Good Times Roll," which hit No. 1 on the R&B chart and No. 20 on the *Billboard* Hot 100. In the mid-1960s, Goodman worked on sessions with Sonny and Cher and Dr. John, and sang background vocals on the Rolling Stones' *Exile on Main Street*.

August 31

Before the British Invasion, Americans had their own version in England, when the top nine records on the U.K. singles chart were all by Yanks. No. 1 was "Que Sera, Sera, (Whatever Will Be, Will Be)" by Doris Day.

September 22

Brenda Lee's first single at age eleven, "Jambalaya," was issued by her career-long record company, Decca (MCA).

Notable birthdays: (September 22) Debby Boone, June Forester (the Forester Sisters), (September 30) Basia

October 19

The world premier of the rhythm-and-blues film *Rockin' the Blues* was held at New York's Apollo Theater. The cast included the Miller Sisters, the Harptones, the Wanderers, and the Hurricanes. The flick was followed by a stage show featuring the Wheels.

November 8

After pop vocalist Kay Starr rejected a new song, it was given to Patsy Cline, who reluctantly recorded it today at Bradley's Barn in Nashville and commented, "It's nothin' but a little ol' pop song." Patsy's version of that "little ol' pop song," "Walkin' After Midnight," reached No. 2 country and No. 12 pop in early 1957.

November 24

LaVern Baker's "Jim Dandy" was released. It soared to No. 1 R&B and No. 17 pop.

December 1

Pat Cordel and the Crescents' "Darling Come Back" was released, becoming an instant collectible ($800). The Crescents (minus Pat) went on to become the Elegants of "Little Star" fame. Pat's father didn't want her touring with a group of rambunctious, testosterone-filled teen boys, and that ended her musical career.

December 22

Mickey and Sylvia charted with their rock 'n' roll classic "Love Is Strange," reaching No. 1 R&B and No. 11 pop. Sylvia Vanderpool had a dozen hits in the 1970s and 1980s, including the No. 1 "Pillow Talk" while Mickey "Guitar" Baker went on to become one of the music business' most sought after session musicians.

Notable birthdays: (December 1) Julee Cruise, (December 9) Sylvia, (December 30) Suzy Bogguss

More Moments in 1956

Guitarist and performer Mary Kaye, dubbed the "First Lady of Rock and Roll," appeared in a promotional ad for Fender guitars with her combo, the Mary Kaye Trio, featuring a new Stratocaster electric guitar. The light-colored guitar outfitted with gold hardware later became popularly known as the "Mary Kaye Strat." Decades later, in 2005, Fender reissued the Custom Shop Mary Kaye Tribute Strat, just a few years before her death in February 2007.

1957

January 21

Patsy Cline performed on *Arthur Godfrey's Talent Scouts,* winning with "Walkin' After Midnight." Godfrey told her, "You are the most innocent, the most nervous, most truthful and honest performer I have ever seen." Soon after, she became a regular on his weekly TV show.

Notable birthdays: (January 4) Patty Loveless

February 15

LaVern Baker and Ann Cole began a U.S. tour with Chuck Berry, Fats Domino, Clyde McPhatter, the 5 Keys, the Moonglows, Charles Brown, the Schoolboys, and the 5 Satins in Irving Feld's *Greatest Show of 1957* rock review. The extravaganza would run through May 5, starting in Pittsburgh, for eighty straight days and nights.

February 23

Patsy Cline moved onto the Top 100 with "Walkin' After Midnight," an eventual No. 12 hit and the first of thirteen pop charters over six years (1957–1963).

Notable birthdays: (February 28) Cindy Wilson (B-52s)

March 2

Brenda Lee charted with "One Step at a Time" (No. 43). The thirteen-year-old country icon went on to have fifty-five Top 100 hits through 1973.

March 7

The Tune Weavers' standard "Happy, Happy Birthday Baby," with Margo Sylvia on lead, was recorded in a Boston studio.

March 16

The Mellows' "Moon of Silver" (now a $100 collectors item) was released (don't you wish you'd kept those old 45's!).

Notable birthdays: (March 11) Cheryl Lynn, Gloria Lynn, (March 22) Stephanie Mills

April 17

An all-star show was held at the Regal Theater in Chicago, including Big Maybelle, Little Esther (Phillips), the Sensations, Annie Laurie, the Dells, and the Spaniels, among others.

May 25

Patsy Cline embarked on her first tour, with Brenda Lee.

Notable birthdays: (May 12) Janna Allen, (May 27) Susan Dallion (Siouxsie and the Banshees)

June 10

The Bobbettes' immortal "Mr. Lee" (No. 6) was released today, along with rock 'n' roll standard "Happy, Happy Birthday Baby" by Margo Sylvia and the Tune Weavers.

Notable birthdays: (June 26) Patti Smyth (Scandal)

July 1

A Philadelphia radio station with only 250 watts of power began repeat plays of Margo Sylvia and the Tune Weavers' new release "Happy, Happy Birthday Baby." By October it was No. 1.

Notable birthdays: (July 24) Pam Tillis, (July 31) Laura Branigan

August 5

The Bobbettes roared onto the Top 100 with "Mr. Lee," a song about their public school teacher that reached #6, making them the first female group in the rock era to have a Top 10 hit (and a No. 1 R&B record).

The Chordettes were the first guests on Dick Clark's *American Bandstand* after it began airing on ABC-TV nationally. The show would go on to be a national institution for more than thirty years and was always hosted by Dick Clark.

August 13

The Five Royales recorded the original version of "Dedicated to the One I Love," which was covered two years later by the Shirelles, who turned it into a bottom-of-the-charts single (No. 83). Two years later, after the girl group had achieved success, the single was reissued, rising to No. 3.

August 19

The Chantels' debut 45, the harmony standard "He's Gone," was released.

Notable birthdays: (August 21) Kim Sledge (Sister Sledge), (August 22) Holly Dunn, (August 31), Gina Schuck (the Go Go's)

September 9

Ivy Records formed and signed the Deltairs. Their debut disc was "Lullaby of the Bells."

September 28

Having ended her management relationship with her father and moved out of the family home into an apartment in London's West End earlier in the year, Petula Clark's cover of Jodi Sands' American hit "With All My Heart" reached No. 4 in Britain.

September 30

Four siblings from Middletown, Ohio, the Shepherd Sisters had their lone hit when "Alone" reached the bestseller list today, rising to No. 18.

Legendary girl group the Chantels' first single, "He's Gone," written by lead singer Arlene Smith, debuted on the charts, reaching No. 71.

Notable birthdays: (September 1) Gloria Estefan, (September 10) Siobahan Fahey (Bananarama)

October 7

The Crests' first single, "My Juanita," was released. The record reached No. 86 pop, and the five group members each earned $17.50. The only girl member, Patricia Vandross, was the older sister of later-to-be heartthrob Luther Vandross.

October 16

The Chantels recorded their now-legendary hit "Maybe" in a New York studio that was actually a refurbished church!

November 15

Patsy Cline won *Billboard*'s Most Promising Country and Western Female Artist of 1957 Award.

December 2

Connie Francis began her rise to stardom when "The Majesty of Love" charted (No. 93). It was her first of fifty-six Hot 100 entries through 1969.

"They don't make pop stars like Connie Francis anymore. The most prolific and popular female singer of the late '50s and early '60s, Francis had a powerful voice that could sound like a sob while staying on key."—Neva Chonin, critic at large, San Francisco Chronicle

The Chantels' classic-to-be "Maybe" (No. 15 pop, No. 2 R&B) was released.

December 13

The Chantels, the Paragons, and the Clovers performed at the Apollo Theater.

December 14

In a cover battle with American artists the Sheppard Sisters (No. 14) and British group the Southlanders (No. 17), Petula Clark's version of "Alone" reached No. 8 in England.

December 30

The McGuire Sisters bounced onto the national singles survey with "Sugartime," ultimately spending four weeks at No. 1.

More Moments in 1957

Mary Kaye, the "First Lady of Rock and Roll," was awarded the Certificate of Merit in *Playboy* magazine's All-Star Jazz Poll Awards in 1957 and later in 1962.

One of the first female lead guitarists in rock 'n' roll, Peggy Jones (aka Lady Bo) joined up with Bo Diddley as a guitarist and backing vocalist. She worked full-time with Bo until 1961, when she formed her own group, the Jewels.

Notable birthdays: (December 1) Gloria Estefan, (December 20) Anita Baker

1958

January 10

New York's St. Nicks Sports Center hosted a rock 'n' roll show and dance, featuring girl groups the Chantels and the Deltairs, along with the 5 Satins and the Dubs.

January 13

The original version of "Dedicated to the One I Love" by the 5 Royales was released. It only reached No. 81 pop and took three years and two releases to do that, but it became a trademark hit three years later for the Shirelles (No. 3) and again in 1967 for the Mamas and the Papas (No. 2).

January 20

The Chantels' classic "Maybe" charted, eventually reaching No. 15.

January 22

The Chantels recorded five sides, including their hit follow-up to "Maybe," "Every Night" (No. 16 R&B, No. 39 pop).

Notable birthdays: (January 6) Kathy Sledge (Sister Sledge), (January 10) Shawn Colvin, (January 21) Anita Baker

February 3

The Blossoms, a girl group of professional backup singers who had worked with literally hundreds of artists from Elvis Presley, Paul Anka, and Dionne Warwick to Bobby Darin, the Beach Boys, and the Mamas and the Papas, finally had their own single released, "Have Faith in Me." When it didn't chart, they went back to the lucrative world of session singing.

February 10

The Shirelles (originally called the Poquellos) had their first single issued today. The Song, "I Met Him on a Sunday," reached No. 49 and was also their first of twenty-six hits over the next nine years.

Notable birthdays: (February 21) Mary Chapin Carpenter

March 3

The Chantels' "Every Night" was released. It reached No. 39 pop and No. 16 R&B

March 10

Operatically trained Lynn Nixon and the Aquatones' "You" was released. The doo-wop ballad rose to No. 21, making the Valley Stream, Long Island, New Yorkers, one-hit wonders.

March 24

One of the most influential gospel singers of all time, Mahalia Jackson contributed several gospel songs to the seminal film *St. Louis Blues,* released this year. Jackson had two important performances at the Newport Jazz Festival in both 1958 and 1959 and sung at the 1961 inauguration of U.S. President John F. Kennedy. In 1963, she sang at the March on Washington in 1963 with friend Martin Luther King Jr. (and at his funeral several years later, in April 1968). In 1964, accompanied by "wonderboy preacher" Al Sharpton, she performed at the New York World's Fair. Posthumously, in 1997, Jackson was inducted into the Rock and Roll Hall of Fame and was the first gospel artist to receive a star on the Hollywood Walk of Fame.

April 5

The Chordettes' "Lollipop" peaked at No. 2 and became their second million seller.

April 21

The Shirelles charted for the first time with "I Met Him on a Sunday," reaching No. 49 pop. They originally formed in junior high school as the Poquellos. The New Jersey teens renamed themselves the Shirelles, probably after lead singer Shirley Owens Alston.

April

Teen songwriter Sharon Sheeley wrote "Poor Little Fool," which became a No. 1 hit for Ricky Nelson this year. Sheeley went on to write songs for Glen Campbell, Ricky Nelson, Brenda Lee, and her former fiancé, Eddie Cochran—to whom she was introduced by former flame Don Everly (of the Everly Brothers).

May 5

Well before her first hit as a songwriter and recording artist, Carole King had her first 45. "The Right Girl" was released today.

May 12

The legendary Chantels' "I Love You So" (No. 42 pop) was released.

May 16

Connie Francis' "Who's Sorry Now" began a six-week run at No. 1 in Britain. A child accordionist at four, Concetta Rose Maria Franconero began appearing on local television at age ten, having appeared on Arthur Godfrey's network talent show. It was Godfrey who suggested she change her name.

Notable birthdays: (May 21) Jane Wiedlin (the Go Go's), (May 23) Shelly West, (May 30) Marie Fredricksson (Roxette)

June 9

The Shirelles' "My Love Is a Charm" was released.

June 23

A trio from Lyndhurst, Ohio, the Poni-Tails released their first single, "Born Too Late" No. #7). It became their first and biggest hit 45.

June 30

Connie Francis' "Stupid Cupid" (No. 14) and Peggy Lee's "Fever" (No. 8) were both released today.

Peggy Lee.

July 14

Sultry jazz singer Norma Jean Egstrom, better known as Peggy Lee, heated up the hit list with "Fever," her eventual signature song and a No. 8 winner.

The Drinkard Singers' spiritual 45 "Rise, Shine" was issued. The group consisted of Dionne Warwick, Cissy Houston (Whitney's mother), Dee Dee Warwick (Dionne's sister), and Judy Clay.

July 28

The Quintones' quintessential doo-wop classic "Down the Aisle of Love" was issued. It reached No. 18 pop and No. 5 R&B.

Notable birthdays: (July 30) Kate Bush

August 28

The Chantels and the Quintones performed at the Apollo Theater in New York, along with the Spaniels, the Coasters, and the Olympics.

Notable birthdays: (August 16) Madonna (Madonna Louise Ciccone), (August 17) Belinda Carlisle (the Go Go's)

September 1

The Clara Ward Singers broke up, forming two groups, the Gay Charmers and the Stars of Faith.

September 6

The Quintones performed their hit "Down the Aisle of Love" (No. 18 pop, No. 5 R&B) on Dick Clark's *American Bandstand.*

September 22

The Quintones, one of the best of the one-hit-wonder doo-wop groups, charted with their classic "Down the Aisle of Love," stopping at No. 5 R&B and No. 18 pop.

The Teddy Bears (with Carol Connors on lead) released their first No. 1 single, "To Know Him Is to Love Him," written by group member Phil Spector. It reached No. 1 while launching Spector's production career.

September 26

A major star not just in America but in England as well, Connie Francis topped the British chart for week one of a six-week run with "Stupid Cupid."

October

Notable birthdays: (October 10) Tanya Tucker

November 10

LaVern Baker's "I Cried a Tear" was issued. It became her biggest hit (No. 6) of twenty charters between 1955 and 1966.

November 17

Brenda Lee's Christmas classic "Rockin' Around the Christmas Tree" was first released today and has been a holiday radio and department store staple for over forty years. In 1960, it actually reached No. 14 pop.

November 24

Ruth Brown's "(Mama) He Treats Your Daughter Mean" was released for the second time. The fiery tune had reached No. 1 R&B in 1953.

December 15

Actress/singer Polly Bergen charted with "Come Prima" (No. 67), her only Top 100 single.

More Moments in 1958

Elizabeth "Libba" Cotten's *Folksongs and Instrumentals with Guitar* was released on Folkways Records. Cotten, in her sixties, was discovered by the folk-singing Seeger family (she was their cleaning lady). The LP resulted from recordings made by Mike Seeger and contains what would become her signature song, "Freight Train," written as a preteen and covered by many artists, including Peter, Paul and Mary, and Bob Dylan.

1959

January 5

Annette (Funicello), one of the original and the most popular *Mickey Mouse Club* TV regulars, starting in 1955, had her debut single, "Tall Paul," chart, reaching No. 7 pop. It would become her biggest hit as she went on to have ten pop charters through 1961. She then went on to co-star with Frankie Avalon in a series of popular beach party movies in the 1960s, including *Beach Blanket Bingo, Beach Party, Muscle Beach Party, Bikini Beach,* and who could forget *How to Stuff A Wild Bikini.* Her last, *Back to the Beach,* in 1987, was the same year the "Queen of Teens" was diagnosed with multiple sclerosis.

Notable birthdays: (January 7) Kathy Valentine (the Go Go's), (January 16) Sade, (January 17), Susanna Hoffs (the Bangles), (January 30) Jody Watley (Shalamar)

February 16

Dodie Stevens became a one-hit wonder when "Pink Shoe Laces" charted and charged up the hit list to No. 3. She was thirteen years old at the time and was discovered while singing on the Art Linkletter TV show at age eight.

March 9

The Fleetwoods debut disc, "Come Softly to Me," charted, en route to No. 1.

Notable birthdays: (March 18) Irene Cara

April 11

The Fleetwoods performed on Dick Clark's Saturday-night show, singing their No. 1 hit "Come Softly to Me."

April 20

Dolly Parton, all of thirteen-years-old, released her first 45, "Puppy Love."

Notable birthdays: (April 27) Sheena Easton

May 3

Florence Greenberg, a Passaic, New Jersey, housewife who discovered the Shirelles, opened her own Scepter Records in New York, signing the girls after they charted on Decca with "I Met Him on a Sunday." The Shirelles would go on to have twenty-five more pop hits and twenty R&B charters, all on Scepter, which would also become the home of Dionne Warwick.

May 18

Connie Francis reached the Hot 100 with "Lipstick on Your Collar," one of seven hits she would have that year.

May 25

Dinah Washington made her pop-chart debut with "What a Difference a Day Makes" (No. 8). By 1963, she would have twenty more.

Notable birthdays: (May 30) Ann Hampton Calloway

June

Notable birthdays: (June 21) Kathy Mattea, (June 26) Terri Nunn (Berlin), (June 27) Lorrie Morgan

July 17

"Lady Day" Billie Holiday died of a heroin overdose at the age of forty-four in New York.

Notable birthdays: (July 11) Susanne Vega

August 3

The Shirelles charted pop with "Dedicated to the One I Love," only reaching No. 83 with the Five Royales original. The group first heard the song while performing on a bill at the Howard Theater in Washington, D.C., where the

Five Royales sang it. It would be reissued in 1961, reaching No. 3 pop and No. 2 R&B for the girls.

September 2

Los Angeles radio disc jockey Art Laboe created the first rock 'n' roll compilation album, *Oldies but Goodies*. It was inspired by his girlfriends' complaints about the stack of 45s that failed to drop properly onto her record player.

September 7

The Fleetwoods' second No. 1, "Mr. Blue," charted.

September 28

"Sweet Nothin's," Brenda Lee's first Top 5 hit, was released today. Though it reached No. 4, it was actually the B-side of "I'm Sorry," which would spend three weeks at No. 1.

Notable birthdays: (September 23) Lita Ford

October

Notable birthdays: (October 13) Marie Osmond (the Osmonds)

December

Notable birthdays: (December 12) Sheila E., (December 30) Tracy Ullman

More Moments in 1959

The Mary Kaye Trio's first rock 'n' roll hit, "You Can't Be True Dear," climbed the *Billboard* charts. Mary Kaye, armed with her iconic Fender Stratocaster, was one of the first females on the rock scene to stand out from her predominantly male peers. Her illustrious recording career included thirteen albums and twenty-one singles!

Michelle Phillips.

THE TURBULENT SIXTIES

From an Age of Innocence to the Protest Era

The 1960s was a decade that came in like a lamb and went out like a lion. It featured the death of a president and the birth of a new attitude in music, ending with the nation split over a war that created the first widespread peace movement.

The sixties began innocently enough—the country was prospering, and popular music was polite. Light pop ruled the airwaves, and rock 'n' roll was still in its naïve infancy, served up by the likes of Shelley Fabares, Marcie Blaine, Ketty Lester, Lil' Peggy March, Haley Mills, and Linda Scott. The only music with any "sock" at the time was early R&B and its developing offshoot, soul music, as enthusiastically delivered by Gladys Knight, Aretha Franklin, the amazing Tina Turner, Darlene Love, Mary Wells, Dee Dee Sharp, Inez Foxx, Maxine Brown, Esther Phillips, and the four Barbaras—George, Lewis, Lynn, and Mason—among many others.

Then came the horrifying assassination of beloved President Kennedy. The age of innocence was over, and popular music quickly reflected it. Beats became more powerful and urgent, and lyrics would soon mirror a spectrum of complex feelings. Songwriters began to question everything, reflecting the uneasy mood of the public and society, which felt lost and betrayed. Through it all, the girl-group sound entered its glory days, full of syrupy-sweet, hopeful, and dance-happy tunes by groups like the Chiffons ("He's So Fine"), the Crystals ("He's Sure the Boy I Love"), the Blue-Belles ("I Sold My Heart to the Junkman"), the Cookies with Little Eva ("The Loco-Motion"), the Marvelettes ("Please Mr. Postman"), the Orlons ("The Wah-Watusi"), the Paris Sisters ("I Love How You Love Me"), Ruby and the Romantics ("Our Day Will Come"), and the Shirelles ("Will You Love Me Tomorrow").

After the assassination, in November 1963, girl-group music became a powerful reflection of the times, emanating the ladies' own special flair. Phil Spector's "wall of sound" was made for the beseeching powerhouse vocals of the Ronettes ("Be My Baby"), the Crystals ("He's a Rebel"), and Darlene Love with the Ronettes and Crystals ("Wait Til' My Bobby Gets Home"). Music with drive and urgency was also coming from the girl groups of Motown, including the Supremes ("You Keep Me Hangin' On") and Martha and the Vandellas ("Dancin' in the Streets"). The girl-group population in general created a broad spectrum of music, from the soft voices of the Dixie Cups, the Jaynettes, and the Toys to the introspection of the Mamas and the Papas, melodrama queens the Shangri-Las, the carefree Cowsills, and the gospel soul of the Staple Singers. On the schizophrenic cusp of the era were the Angels, who went from the "angelic" hit ballad "Til," in 1961, to the brash and "in your face" rocker "My Boyfriend's Back," in 1963.

Female solo artists also found an age of enlightenment in the mid-to-late '60s, questioning authority and singing with a newfound freedom of expression that was driven by the force and power of rock 'n' roll. The daring Grace Slick (Jefferson Airplane) urgently insisting "You better find somebody to love," the mind-blowing Janis Joplin howling "Break another little piece of my heart," the defiantly retaliatory Timi Yuro asking "What's a matter baby, is it hurtin' you," the sensational neophyte Linda Ronstadt declaring the start of a new era with the women's anthem "Different Drum," the powerhouse provocateur Mariska Veres (Shocking Blue) enflaming listeners with "I'm your Venus, I'm your fire, what's your desire," and the rock 'n' roll reincarnation of Ethel Merman Spanky McFarlane (Spanky and Our Gang) soul-searchingly lamenting "Sunday Will Never Be the Same" all added energizing fuel to a decade racing into chaos.

Even pop artists proved to be unexpected vocal and lyrical forces, like Cher ("Half-Breed"), Nancy Sinatra ("These Boots Were Made for Walking"), Leslie Gore ("You Don't Own Me"), the Mamas and the Papas' Cass Elliott, and the incredible Barbra Streisand. Country music flourished in the sixties as women were emboldened to voice their feelings. Brenda Lee, Skeeter Davis, Bobbie Gentry, Tammy Wynette, Jody Miller, Sandy

Posey, Jeannie C. Riley, and country queen Dottie West led the charge for feminine change. But the biggest calls for universal transformation came from the re-emerging folk field and its antiwar messages. Artists like Joan Baez, Judy Collins, Mary Travers, and Buffy Sainte-Marie sang about everything from pollution to peace. You couldn't help listening to the frustrated females without reliving the line from the famous Marlon Brando film *The Wild One,* when a man asked him, "What are you protesting?" and Brando dryly responded, "Whaddaya got?"

1960

January 15

Etta James was the only female invited to perform tonight at the Regal Theater in Chicago. The guys were Little Junior Parker, Bo Diddley, Bobby Bland, Bill Doggett, and the Isley Brothers.

January 28

Dinah Washington performed at San Francisco's Facks No. 2 Club.

Notable birthdays: (January 11) Vicki Peterson (the Bangles)

February 1

Actress/singer Connie Stevens charted with "16 Reasons," eventually rising to No. 3. She was starring in TV's *Hawaiian Eye* at the time.

March 11

Dinah Washington performed at the Regal Theater in Chicago.

March 24

Tommy Sands, appearing on the *Tennessee Ernie Ford Show,* performed the song "That's Love," dedicated to his future bride, Nancy Sinatra.

March 25

Dinah Washington, Ray Charles, and jazzmen Horace Silver and Art Blakely performed at the Opera House in Chicago. Down the road, Etta James, Big Maybelle, Jerry Butler, the Spaniels, Harvey (of the Moonglows), and Wade Flemons would bring down the house at the Regal Theater.

April 2

Connie Francis won the Bestselling Female Artist Award at the first annual NARM (National Association of Recording Merchandisers) Awards. She went on to win again in 1961 and 1962.

April 15

Etta James, the Clovers, the Olympics, Robert and Johnny, Santo and Johnny, and Ben E. King (in his first appearance after leaving the Drifters) performed at the Apollo Theater's *Dr. Jive Rhythm and Blues Revue.*

April 16

The latest installment of the Biggest Show of Stars '60 tour, including the lone female LaVern Baker, with Joe Turner, Lloyd Price, Little Anthony and the Imperials, Clyde McPhatter, the Coasters, Jimmy Jones, Sammy Turner, and Jimmy Reed began their travels at the Municipal Auditorium in Norfolk, Virginia.

April 17

Songwriter Sharon Sheeley and rock star Gene Vincent were injured, and legendary rockabilly artist Eddie Cochran was killed while touring England. The three were on their way to London's airport after their last performance of the tour, when the chauffeured car they were in blew a tire and slammed into a lamppost, throwing Eddie onto the pavement, killing him. Ironically, the driver was not injured at all.

April 22

Improvisational jazz stylist and singer Betty Carter joined Tarheel Slim, Little Ann, and Ray Charles to perform at the Apollo Theater. As a youngster, Carter traveled in circles that included jazz greats like Charlie Parker, Dizzy Gillespie, Sarah Vaughan, and Billy Eckstine and was hired as a featured vocalist by Lionel Hampton (who nicknamed her "Betty Bebop") in 1948.

April 25

The Angels' debut disc, *P.S. I Love You,* was released under their original name, the Starlets.

May 2

Etta James reached the Hot 100 with "All I Could Do Was Cry" (No. 33), her first of twenty-eight hits over the next ten years.

"He'll Have To Stay," Jeannie Black's answer record to Jim Reeves' "He'll Have to Go," charted, climbing to No. 4.

May 3

Cathy Jean and the Roommates recorded "Please Love Me Forever" (No. 12), though the lead singer hadn't ever met the group! Cathy did her vocals and left the studio before the group arrived to do its backgrounds.

May 9

Connie Francis charted with "Everybody's Somebody's Fool" (No. 1). Of her fifty-six Hot 100 hits, it turned out to be her biggest.

May 13

Irma Thomas, Shirley and Lee, Frankie Lymon (without the Teenagers), Robert and Johnny, Billy Bland, Major Lance, and Barrett Strong performed on the bill at the Regal Theater in Chicago.

May 23

Ella Fitzgerald charted with "Mack the Knife," reaching No. 6 R&B. The song was recorded in West Berlin with the Paul Smith Quartet doing backup vocals. Despite the huge success of the Bobby Darin pop version, which hit the Top 100 nine months ahead of Ella's pop chart debut, her version still impressively reached No. 27.

First recorded by the Spaniels in 1958, "A Rockin' Good Way" bounced onto the Hot 100 for Dinah Washington in a duet with Brook Benton while rockin' its way to No. 7.

May 28

LaVern Baker performed on the nighttime version of Dick Clark's *American Bandstand.* Also appearing were Johnny Tillotson, Jimmy Jones, and Harold Dorman.

May 30

Brenda Lee's first No. 1, "I'm Sorry," charted. She went on to have fifty-two Top 100 charters in sixteen years.

Notable birthdays: (May 20) Susan Cowsill (the Cowsills)

June 7

Polly Bergen and Betty Grable backed up Bobby Darin, singing "Buttons and Bows" on George Burns' NBC-TV show.

June 27

Connie Francis' "Everybody's Somebody's Fool" arrived at No. 1, giving the songstress her sixth million seller. The B-side, "Jealous of You," rose to No. 19.

Notable birthdays: (June 24) Siedah Garrett, (June 29) Evelyn "Champagne" King

July 4

The Demensions' magnificent cover of "Over the Rainbow" with Marisa Martelli's startling falsetto hit the Top 100 (No. 16). Their version was the first since Judy Garland's 1939 recording to chart, even though sixty different versions had been issued during that twenty-one-year span.

July 22

Annie Laurie (who had an R&B hit with "Since I Fell for You" in 1947) and Faye Adams, along with Screamin Jay Hawkins, the Five Satins, Joe Turner, and Ben E. King appeared at Chicago's Regal Theater.

August 1

Aretha Franklin recorded her first mainstream songs upon signing with Columbia Records. The Songs included "Over the Rainbow," "Today I Sing the Blues," Right Now," and "Love Is the Answer." She was eighteen years old, but had begun recording gospel music at age fourteen for Checker Records of Chicago.

When the originally scheduled vocalist didn't show, producer Ike Turner took his twenty-two-year-old wife, Tina, and recorded her on "A Fool in Love," which was released today. It rose to No. 27 and became the first of twenty Hot 100 hits for the volatile couple.

August 5

The Regal Theater in Chicago hosted a great show, with Big Maybelle, the Sheppards, the Isley Brothers, Dee Clark, Bill Doggett, Buster Brown, and Little Jimmy Scott performing.

Notable birthdays: (August 7) Jacqui O'Sullivan (Bananarama)

September 11

Singer, and daughter of Frank Sinatra, Nancy Sinatra married teen idol Tommy Sands. They were divorced in 1965.

September 12

The Chiffons, locked in a cover battle with the Shirelles, charted today with "Tonight's the Night." Though the New Jersey Shirelles out paced the Bronx, New York, quartet (No. 39 to No. 76), the recording was memorable as the Chiffons' first Hot 100 offing of a career twelve hits through 1966.

September 19

Seventeen-year-old Mary Wells played a song for producer Berry Gordy Jr., and on the basis of "Bye Bye Baby," she was signed to his newly formed Motown label. The song (which she originally wrote for Jackie Wilson) was released on this day, reaching No. 45 pop and No. 8 R&B.

September 22

The Bobbettes, Hank Ballard and the Midnighters, Bo Diddley, Sam Cooke, the Olympics, Marv Johnson, and Dion and the Belmonts performed at the Veterans Memorial Auditorium in Columbus, Ohio, as part of the ongoing Biggest Show of Stars '60 tour.

September 26

Connie Francis became the first female singer to ever have two consecutive No. 1s, when her recording of "My Heart Has a Mind of Its Own" topped the singles charts. The first was "Everybody's Somebody's Fool."

Notable birthdays: (September 22) Joan Jett

October 19

The Shirelles appeared on *American Bandstand,* performing what was their first R&B charter nine days earlier, "Tonight's the Night."

October 22

Ike and Tina Turner's chart debut, "A Fool in Love," reached No. 2 R&B and No. 27 pop.

October 24

Aretha Franklin charted with her first single release for Columbia Records, "Today I Sing the Blues," which reached No. 10 R&B. "The Queen of Soul" decided on a career in singing after hearing her mentor Clara Ward sing "Peace in the Valley" at a funeral. She would go on to have an astounding ninety-eight R&B chart singles through 2003.

Brenda Lee's "I Want to Be Wanted" reached No. 1, giving "Little Miss Dynamite" three million seller's in a row.

Notable birthdays: (October 19) Jennifer Holiday

November 11

Savannah Churchill, Sonny Boy Williamson, Little Willie John, and the Sheppards played the Regal Theater in Chicago.

November 14

The Shirelles (formerly known as the Poquellos) with songwriter Carole King playing drums had their soon-to-be standard "Will You Love Me Tomorrow" released today.

November 16

Patsy Cline, recently signed to Decca Records, began recording her first session for them, including her standard "I Fall to Pieces."

Notable birthdays: (November 4) Kim Forester (the Forester Sisters), (November 18) Kim Wilde, (November 25) Amy Grant

December 1

Sixteen-year-old actress Sandra Dee and twenty-four-year-old Bobby Darin married in a secret ceremony in Elizabeth, New Jersey. They met three months earlier on the set of the film they both starred in, *Come September.* The same day, one of Darin's former girlfriends pined away by debuting at New York's Copacabana for a two-week engagement. The heart broken miss was Connie Francis.

December 11

Aretha Franklin performed at a folk club, the Village Vanguard in Greenwich Village, New York City, not singing gospel or rhythm and blues but doing standards. She was still thirteen days away from her first R&B chart single, "Today I Sing the Blues."

December 24

The Christmas Eve edition of Merv Griffin's *Saturday Prom* TV show (NBC) featured Kathy Young and the Innocents singing their hit "A Thousand Stars."

December 26

Brenda Lee's "Emotions" (No. 7) was released.

The Shirelles, the Drifters, the Coasters, Chubby Checker, Little Anthony and the Imperials, Bo Diddley, and the Blue Notes, among others, appeared at the Paramount Theater in Brooklyn's all-star Christmas show.

December 31

Former gospel vocalist in the Manhattans and the Royaltones, Maxine Brown reached the hit list with "All in Your Mind," her first of fifteen charters through 1969.

The standard-to-be "Will You Love Me Tomorrow" by the Shirelles entered the charts on this last day of the year, rising to No. 2 R&B and No. 1 pop.

Notable birthdays: (December 28) Kathy Burch (the Burch Sisters)

1961

January 2

Eighteen-year-old Aretha Franklin began her pursuit of a mainstream music career, with heavy emphasis on the blues, with her performance in Philadelphia at the Showboat.

January 15

The Supremes were signed to Motown Records.

"The Supremes were the epitome of the Motown sound. . . . Diana Ross's voice would come on the air and give you chill bumps. It had such presence, terrific tone, and was so identifiable. She didn't sing like Aretha Franklin—she wasn't a gospel singer—but she was a stylist, and you always believed her." —Producer Antonio "LA" Reid

January 21

Patsy Cline performed at the Grand Ole Opry two weeks before giving birth to a son, Randy.

January 30

Carole King had her first songwriting No. 1 when the Shirelles' "Will You Love Me Tomorrow" reached the top spot (with Carole playing drums). It would be almost ten years before she would have a No. 1 as an artist ("It's Too Late").

February 6

Memphis soul queen Carla Thomas charted with the eventual Top 10 R&B and pop hit "Gee Whiz (Look in His Eyes)" on the Stax label—one of the first Memphis soul records to garner national attention. Over the next decade, she'd score an additional twenty-two singles on the national charts. Her vocal banter with Otis Redding on *King & Queen* produced the sassy "Tramp" single. Thomas later received a Pioneer Award from the Rhythm and Blues Foundation in 1993.

February 17

Brook Benton headlined at the Apollo Theater in New York. Aretha Franklin, a newcomer to R&B, was his opening act.

February 21

The Shirelles appeared on *American Bandstand*, singing "Dedicated to the One I Love" and "Will You Love Me Tomorrow."

February 23

Petula Clark had her first British No. 1 with "Sailor." The pert Brit songstress would go on to have twenty-three Top 40 hits through 1988 in her homeland.

February 27

Aretha Franklin made her pop-chart debut with "Wont Be Long" on Columbia Records. It reached No. 76, the same number of pop hits for the "Queen of Soul" over the next thirty-seven years.

Kathy Jean and the Roommates' "Please Love Me Forever" charted, en route to No. 12.

March 13

Pop singer Linda Scott debuted on the charts with her first single, "I've Told Every Little Star" (No. 3). She had ten more charters over the next three years, including 1963's "Who's Been Sleeping in My Bed," one of the first collaborations between the legendary writing duo of Hal David and Burt Bacharach.

March 31

The Brooklyn Fox's Easter Extravaganza included performances by the Shirelles, Carla Thomas, Rosie (formerly of the Originals), the Marcels, Little Anthony and the Imperials, Maurice Williams and the Zodiacs, Ben E. King, the Olympics, Chuck Jackson, the Capris, and the Isley Brothers. All that for a couple of dollars.

April 2

The Shirelles began a major tour in Irving Feld's Biggest Show of Stars, 1961, starting in Philadelphia. Other acts included the Drifters, Fats Domino, Chubby Checker, and Bo Diddley.

April 11

Joan Baez met Bob Dylan for the first time at Gerde's Folk City in Greenwich Village, New York. She would frequently introduce the twenty-year-old folk singer/songwriter and future boyfriend onstage during her concert appearances over the next few years.

April 28

Maxine Brown, the Flamingos, the Vibrations, the Miracles, Shep and the Limelites, and Jerry Butler played Philadelphia's Uptown Theater.

Notable birthdays: (April 19) Alexus Korner

May 8

Darlene Love and the Blossoms, who were the premier vocal backup singers for everyone from Elvis to Dionne Warwick, finally earned some attention with a single of their own when "Son-in-Law" charted, reaching No. 79. It was their only Top 100 single and the answer record to Ernie K-Doe's "Mother-in-Law."

May 15

Gladys Knight and the Pips became the first act in history to have two different versions of the same song on the charts at the same time when "Every

Beat of My Heart" hit the Top 100. First recorded for Huntom and licensed to VeeJay (No. 6), they rerecorded it for Fury (No. 45), and both raced up the hit list starting today.

Notable birthdays: (May 29) Melissa Etheridge

June 2

Carla Thomas appeared on *American Bandstand.*

June 25

Brenda Lee, the Shirelles, Etta James, B. B. King, Jerry Lee Lewis, the Diamonds, Gene McDaniels, and Clarence "Frogman" Henry, among others, performed in Alan Freed's spectacular at the Hollywood Bowl in Los Angeles. A front-row seat set you back $4.00!

Notable birthdays: (June 6) Teri Nunn (Berlin), (June 18) Alison Moyet

July 3

Damita Jo charted with "I'll Be There" (No. 12), the answer record to Ben E. King's "Stand by Me."

The Chantels' biggest hit, "Look in My Eyes," charted today, on its way to No. 14.

July 17

The Shirelles' "What a Sweet Thing That Was" charted a week after its A-side, "A Thing of the Past," did the same thing, and consequently the songs killed each other off on the race up the charts, with "What" reaching No. 54 and "Thing" halting at No. 41.

The Supremes' first single on Motown, "Who's Lovin' You," was issued. It did not chart, and it would be more than a year before their first charter, "My Heart Belongs to You," hit the Top 100.

July 21

The Supremes' second single, "Buttered Popcorn," was released, with Florence Ballard singing lead. The group was still more than a year away from its first chart 45, "Your Heart Belongs to Me."

July 24

Timi Yuro reached the bestseller list with the scorching ballad "Hurt" (No. 4). It was the first of eleven hits through 1965 for the Chicago native.

August 14

The Marvelettes' first single, "Please Mr. Postman," was released. It delivered a No. 1 record, their only No. 1 of a twenty-three-hit-record career.

August 21

Patsy Cline recorded her all-time classic "Crazy" while on crutches. She was still recuperating from a car crash in which she was thrown through the windshield.

Notable birthdays: (August 2) Apollonia, (August 22) Debbie Peterson (the Bangles)

September 4

The Paris Sisters moved onto the singles survey with "I Love How You Love Me" (No. 5). The trio began recording for Decca in 1954, and it took them almost eight years to achieve their first hit.

The Shirelles' "Baby It's You" was issued, soon becoming one of their biggest hits (No. 8). It was the B-side to "The Things I Want to Hear" (which never charted).

September 7

The Shirelles, Chubby Checker, Chuck Jackson, and Bobby Lewis performed at Palisades Amusement Park, in Ft. Lee, New Jersey.

September 11

Aretha Franklin's "Rock-a-Bye Your Baby" was released. It became her only Top 40 single of nine pop charters (No. 37) while on Columbia and in the misguided hands of Mitch Miller, who never knew what to do with her soul potential.

Judy Garland began a historic chart run of thirteen weeks at No. #1 with her album *Judy at Carnegie Hall.*

September 16

"Please Mr. Postman" by the Marvelettes was issued and took fifteen weeks to reach the top of the national charts.

October 2

The Crystals' debut disc, "There's No Other," was released. The B-side ballad in a Chantels styling went on to No. 20 pop and No. 5 R&B. Produced by Phil

Spector, it was the first successful single on the now-legendary Philles label.

October 6

The Apollo Theater in New York billed their show as an all-girl revue, featuring the Chantels, Big Maybelle, the Bobbettes, Tiny Topsy, and Gladys Knight (with the Pips, who we guess didn't count).

October 20

LaVern Baker, Johnnie and Joe, the Starlets, the Halos, Little Caesar and the Romans, the Mar-Keys, and Wade Flemons performed at the Regal Theater in Chicago.

November 6

The Chantels only up-tempo hit, "Well, I Told You" (No. 29), was issued today.

November 20

The Crystals debut single, "There's No Other" charted (#20) as the first of their eight hits.

November 27

Joan Baez, Vol. 2, (distinguished by her sparsely accompanied, pristine vocal style) became her first chart album, reaching No. 13, thus confirming the popularity of the rising folk-music scene, which Baez would help pioneer.

Notable birthdays: (November 2) k. d. lang

December 22

New York disc jockey Murray "The K" Kaufmann hosted the Brooklyn Paramount's Christmas show, featuring top girl groups the Crystals and the Chantels, and Timi Yuro, alongside Johnny Mathis, the Isley Brothers, the Vibrations, Bobby Lewis, and Gary U.S. Bonds.

December 24

The holiday revue at Chicago's Regal Theater included Erma Franklin, Mittie Collier, the Spaniels, the Dukays, Lloyd Price, and the Sheppards.

December 25

Gladys Knight and the Pips charted with their doo-wop classic "Letter Full of Tears," reaching No. 3 R&B and No. 19 pop. The group began in the 50s, performing on tours with the likes of Jackie Wilson, Sam Cooke, and B. B. King.

Their first single was in 1959, a cover of the Moonglows' rocker "Whistle My Love."

December 31

Janis Joplin made her first public singing engagement at the Halfway House in Beaumont, Texas.

More Moments in 1961

Betty Carter (on the recommendation of Miles Davis) teamed with Ray Charles on a legendary duet album, *Ray Charles and Betty Carter,* which produced the standout single "Baby, It's Cold Outside," and topped the R&B charts that year.

1962

January 15

The Shirelles performed their current hit, "Baby It's You," on *American Bandstand.*

January 18

Ike and Tina Turner performed their current chart 45, "Poor Fool," on *American Bandstand.*

February 9

The Ronettes, the Vibrations, Bobby Lewis, the Capris, and Tommy Hunt, along with his former group, the Flamingos, performed at the Apollo Theater in New York.

February 16

The Sensations ("Let Me In"), the Crystals ("There's No Other"), and Erma Franklin (sister of Aretha) played the Apollo in New York.

Notable birthdays: (February 11) Sheryl Crow

March 3

Actress Shelly Fabares (niece of actress Nanette Fabares) charted with "Johnny Angel," a dreamy teeny-bopper tune that soared to No. 1 with the backup vocal help of the Blossoms.

March 5

The twist was still the world's biggest music craze, and the Marvelettes made their contribution by singing "Twistin' Postman" on Dick Clark's *American Bandstand.*

March 19

Barbara George performed her one and only self-penned R&B chart record, "I Know (You Don't Love Me No More)," on *American Bandstand.* The song, issued the previous year, has since been covered by many artists, including Bonnie Raitt. Barbara was one of the few artists in music history to have her only chart single make its way to No. 1. With her, it was all or nothing.

March 23

The Regal Theater in Chicago presented a dynamite lineup of the Crystals, Aretha and Erma Franklin, Lloyd Price, Eddie Holland, Gene Chandler, Jimmy McCracklin, and Solomon Burke.

March 31

Connie Francis' "Don't Break the Heart That Loves You" became the New Jersey miss' third No. 1.

The Crystals' "Uptown" charted and became their only single featuring six members, as La La Brooks joined to replace a pregnant Merna Girard, who held on long enough to record at the session.

Notable birthdays: (March 7) Taylor Dayne

April 7

Decca Records released Brenda Lee's "Everybody Loves Me but You." Within a week, it was on the pop charts, rising to No. 6 while becoming her ninth Top 10 hit in only two and a half years.

April 14

The Shirelles' "Soldier Boy" charted, becoming their biggest pop hit at No. 1 for three weeks and No. 3 R&B. The song, written in a country-and-western vein, was put together by the writers (Greenberg and Dixon) in a few minutes and tagged on at the end of a recording session. The track, done in about ten minutes, was instantly disliked by the group.

April 21

Patti LaBelle and the Blue-Belles hit the Hot 100 with a song they hadn't recorded! "I Sold My Heart to the Junkman" was actually done by the Starlets (a female group featuring Dynetta Boone), who were signed to Chicago-based Pam Records. While touring in Philadelphia, they recorded "Junkman" for a used-car dealer, who issued the rocker as a recording by his own unsuspecting Blue-Belles. It rose to No. 15 as Patti and company rose to stardom while the Starlets drifted into obscurity.

May 9

Dionne's sister, Dee Dee Warwick, singing lead with the Dixie Flyers, sailed onto the Hot 100 with "She Didn't Know" (No. 70).

May 11

In a blockbuster show put on by legendary Pittsburgh disc jockey Porky Chedwick, the Civic Arena was rocked by Patti LaBelle and the Blue-Belles (then only known as the Blue-Belles), the Marvelettes, Ketty Lester, Big Maybelle, the Carousels, along with male counterparts the Skyliners, the Drifters, Jerry Butler, Jackie Wilson, the Flamingos, the Jive Five, Bo Diddley, the Coasters, Gene Pitney, and Bobby Vinton. The average ticket price for the spectacular was under $3.00. with 13,000 fans in attendance.

May 12

Connie Francis' "Second Hand Love" (written by Phil Spector) hit the Hot 100, on its way to No. 7.

May 26

Miss Toni Fisher made her last of three chart appearances with "West of the Wall" (No. 37), a song inspired by the Berlin Wall crisis in Germany. The name on her records actually read "Miss Toni Fisher."

June 2

In an interesting evening, mixing R&B, jazz, and big-band swing, LaVern Baker, the Dave Brubeck Quartet, and Lionel Hampton and His Orchestra performed in Atlanta, Georgia.

June 9

Carole King's babysitter, Little Eva, had her first single released. It became the rock 'n' roll standard "Locomotion," a worldwide No. 1.

The Orlons leaped onto the Hot 100 with "The Wah-Watusi," rising to No. 2 and becoming their third straight Top 5 hit.

Notable birthdays: (June 19) Paula Abdul

July 5

Little Eva introduced "The Locomotion" to a national TV audience via *American Bandstand,* helping to take the record to No. 1. Previous to the recording, Eva had been the babysitter for songwriter Carole King.

July 14

One of the most powerful vocalists of the '60s, Timi Yuro rocked onto the Hot 100 with "What's a Matter Baby" (No. 12). Unfortunately for her fans, the petite powerhouse lost her voice in 1980 and underwent several throat operations.

July 21

The Ronettes' "I'm on the Wagon" was released. It was their first single under their hit name, as they had previously recorded one single for Colpix Records, "I Want a Boy," as Ronnie and the Relatives.

July 23

The Shirelles charted with "Welcome Home Baby," a logical continuation of their last hit "Soldier Boy." The single made it to No. 20 R&B and No. 22 pop. Soon after, a publisher offered the groups manager, Florence Greenberg, a new tune as a follow-up called "He's a Rebel," but Florence turned it down. The Crystals went on to have a No. 1 hit with it.

July 27

Ketty Lester began a week's engagement at Chicago's Regal Theater, along with the Flamingos, Chuck Jackson, Sam Cooke, and the Falcons.

July 28

Having established herself on the charts in Britain by covering American hits, Petula Clark did it again, this time doing Lee Dorsey's "Ya Ya" (the British recording was called "Ya Ya Twist") in French, reaching No. 14 in England. She would later record a song called "Chariot" in French, which would become a million seller in Europe, though never charting in England, while the American version by Little Peggy March would be a huge hit as "I Will Follow Him."

Notable birthdays: (July 28) Rachel Sweet

August 2

American Bandstand welcomed newcomer Aretha Franklin, who was making her national-TV debut, singing "Try a Little Tenderness" and "Don't Cry Baby." She was still four years away from the soul style she would become famous for.

"She [Aretha Franklin] is blessed with an extraordinary combination of remarkable urban sophistication and the deep blues feeling that comes from the Delta. The result is maybe the greatest singer of all time." —Ahmet Ertegun, co-founder, Atlantic Records

August 11

Carole King's "It Might as Well Rain Until September" was issued. It became her first chart single (No. 22) of an eighteen-hit career.

Formerly known as the Primettes, the newly named Supremes hit the Hot 100 with "Your Heart Belongs to Me," their first of 47 hits through 1976.

August 24

Bob B. Soxx and the Blue Jeans recorded the Phil Spector–produced "Zip-a-

Dee Doo Dah" (No. 8). The group was really the Blossoms with Darlene Love and studio singer Bobby Sheen on lead.

August 31

Dee Dee Sharp, the Marvelettes, the Ronettes, the Shirelles, Little Eva, the Majors, Chuck Jackson, Ben E. King, the Del-Satins, and Tony Orlando (years before Dawn) performed at Murray the K's annual New York Labor Day Rock 'n' Roll show at the Brooklyn Fox Theater.

September 1

Carol Burnett and Julie Andrews' album *Julie and Carol at Carnegie Hall* reached the album charts, peaking at No. 85.

September 8

Thirteen days after it's release, the Crystals' "He's a Rebel" charted, on its way to No. 1 for two weeks. The Gene Pitney song was rush-released to beat out a competing version by Vikki Carr.

September 16

The Angels began a British tour with Dion, Del Shannon, and Buzz Clifford.

September 22

The Springfields became the first British vocal group to reach the American Top 20 when their single "Silver Threads and Golden Needles" hit No. 20. The group's lead singer was Mary O'Brien, who changed her name to Dusty Springfield. Coming full circle, the song was originally a hit in 1950 for American artist Dinah Shore.

Notable birthdays: (September 18) Joanne Cathecall (Human League)

October 13

Carole King's recording of "It Might as Well Rain Until September" reached No. 22 (for the second week in a row) in the States and became a huge No. 3 charter in Great Britain.

October 16

Mary Wells and the Supremes began a two-month tour, starting in Washington, D.C., along with a slew of other Motown acts, including the Miracles, Little Stevie Wonder, and Marvin Gaye.

October 20

Eighteen-year-old Brooklynite Marcie Blane charted with "Bobby's Girl," which ultimately peaked at No. 3.

October 26

The first Motortown Revue began in Washington, D.C., at the Howard Theater. The tour ran for three months and included only acts from the Motown stable, including the Supremes, Mary Wells, Martha and the Vandellas, the Marvelettes, Little Stevie Wonder, Smokey Robinson and the Miracles, the Temptations, Marvin Gaye, and the Contours.

October 27

Dionne Warwick's debut disc, "Don't Make Me Over," was released (No. 21), beginning a streak of thirty-three chart hits sung by Dionne and written and produced by Burt Bacharach and Hal David. It was the start of one of the most successful long-term careers for a female artist in music history.

November 3

The Crystals' smash "He's a Rebel" hit No. 1 for the first of two weeks. Unfortunately for the New York–based Crystals, it wasn't them singing on the hit. Producer Phil Spector used a West Coast backup group, the Blossoms, featuring Darlene Wright (later Darlene Love), when he needed to rush-release the 45 so as to beat Vickie Carr's rival version to the marketplace. The Crystals' only saving grace was that their name, not the Blossoms, was on the hit single.

November 19

Influential blues star of the 1950s Savannah Churchill made a comeback performance at the Room at the Bottom Line in New York's Greenwich Village, after being badly injured when a fan fell on top of her after falling out of the balcony of a Brooklyn nightclub several years earlier.

December 1

In the first package tour featuring only one record organization's artists, Motown's Motortown Revue set down in Memphis at the Ellis Auditorium. The revue included Martha and the Vandellas, Mary Wells, the Supremes, the Marvelettes, Little Stevie Wonder, the Temptations, and Marvin Gaye.

December 18

The Shirelles charted with "Baby It's You," one of their best recordings, reaching No. 8 pop and No. 3 R&B. The song was originally titled "I'll Cherish You."

December 21

Tamla/Motown Records issued the Marvelettes' single "Playboy," an eventual No. 7 pop hit. A year earlier, the high school students, calling themselves the Marvels, auditioned for Motown boss Berry Gordy, singing Chantels and Shirelles songs and were told to go home and come back when they graduated.

December 29

The Crystals charted with "He's Sure the Boy I Love" (No. 11). Unfortunately, as with their previous hit, "He's a Rebel," it wasn't the Crystals singing on the record but Darlene Love and the Blossoms, thanks to the decision-making shenanigans of producer Phil Spector.

The Supremes charted with "Let Me Go the Right Way," reaching No. 26 R&B (No. 90 pop). It was their first of forty-three R&B hits through 1977.

December 30

Brenda Lee was mildly injured in a fire at her Nashville home as she tried to save her poodle, Cee Cee, who died of smoke inhalation.

Notable birthdays: (December 17) Sarah Dallen (Bananarama)

More Moments in 1962

Patti LaBelle and the Blue-Belles, Little Esther Phillips, Etta James, Erma Franklin, Lloyd Price, the Dells, and the Radiants performed at Chicago's Regal Theater for the start of their annual Christmas shows.

1963

January 2

Dionne Warwick sang her debut single, "Don't Make Me Over," on *American Bandstand.*

January 5

Jan Bradley had her biggest hit when "Mama Didn't Lie" charted, eventually reaching No. 14. When other hits failed to follow, Jan went on to be a social worker.

January 25

Janis Joplin began singing in North Beach (San Francisco) coffeehouses, passing her hat for beers.

January 26

Skeeter Davis hit the Top 100 with "The End of the World" (No. 2), her biggest of eight career charters.

February 2

Sixteen-year-old Helen Shapiro and the Honeys began a British tour in Gaumont Cinema, Bradford, England, with the Beatles. The bill had the Beatles' name listed last. The Mop Tops set included hit songs by female artists such as "Keep Your Hands off My Baby" (Little Eva) and "Chains" (the Cookies). John and Paul wrote "Misery" on the bus for Helen, but she passed on recording it.

February 9

Ruby (Nash) and the Romantics' day came when "Our Day Will Come" charted, storming to No. 1. It was their first of eight hits through 1965.

February 15

Girl groups the Exciters, the Orlons, and the Debonairs, along with the Jive Five, Little Anthony, Jackie Wilson, and the 5 Royales performed at the Syria Mosque in Pittsburgh.

February 22

LaVern Baker headlined a show at Chicago's Regal Theater.

February 23

The Chiffons' mega hit "He's So Fine" was the first vocal-group No. 1 record in rock history to be produced by another vocal group, the Tokens.

Notable birthdays: (February 2) Eva Cassidy

March 2

The Crystals performed at Chubby Checker's "Limbo Party" at San Francisco's Cow Palace, along with Marvin Gaye, Dee Dee Sharp, and the 4 Seasons.

March 13

"Foolish Little Girl" by the Shirelles hit the charts, reaching No. 9 R&B and No. 4 pop while becoming their last of six Top 10 hits. During the group's 1963 performances, they would often call upon a label mate to fill in when one of the girls couldn't be available. The backup vocalist was Dionne Warwick.

March 21

Little Esther Phillips began a two-week engagement at Baltimore's Royal Theater.

March 30

Lesley Gore's pop standard-to-be "It's My Party" was recorded at Bell Sound Studio, New York, produced by relative newcomer Quincy Jones. It was rush-released after Jones encountered Phil Spector that same evening on the steps of Carnegie Hall (where the two were attending a performance by Charles Aznovour) and learned that Spector was intent on recording the song with the Crystals. In a story that could only happen in the sixties, the record was recorded on Monday, manufactured on Tuesday, and on the air by Wednesday!

The Chiffons reached No. 1 with "He's So Fine." The single spent four weeks in the top spot, becoming a million seller.

Notable birthdays: (March 10) Nenah Cherry, (March 18) Vanessa Williams

April 6

Sixteen-year-old Lesley Gore heard her March 30 recording of "It's My Party" on New York's WINS radio while driving home from school.

Martha and the Vandellas charted with "Come and Get These Memories," reaching No. 6 R&B and No. 29 pop, becoming their first of twenty-four pop hits through 1974. The group was first called the Del Phis, but became the Vandellas after backing Marvin Gaye on "Hitch Hike." "Vandellas" came from a combination of Detroit's Van Dyke Street and Martha's favorite singer, Della Reese.

April 13

Barbra Streisand's *The Barbra Streisand Album* debuted on the pop hit list and rose to a million-selling No. 8. It was the first of forty-six albums she would place on the Top 200 over the next thirty-two years while winning the 1963 Grammy for Best Album of the Year.

April 27

The Crystals soared onto the pop hit list with "Da Doo Ron Ron," an eventual No. 3 classic.

May 3

Dionne Warwick, the Crystals, Little Esther, the Drifters, Sam Cooke, Jerry Butler, Dee Clark, and Solomon Burke performed at Pittsburgh's Syria Mosque.

May 8

Darlene Love made a rare TV appearance when she performed on Dick Clark's *American Bandstand,* singing her current hit, "(Today I Met) The Boy I'm Gonna Marry."

May 12

The Raeletts and Ray Charles began their first British tour in London's Finsbury in Astoria.

May 17

Joan Baez headlined the first Monterey Folk Festival in Monterey, California, along with her protégé Bob Dylan. Joan was the second of three daughters of a Mexican physicist father and a Scottish mother who taught English drama. She was raised in California, New York, Iraq, and finally Massachusetts, where her father worked at MIT. Joan Studied at Boston University's School of Drama, having played local coffeehouses Golden Vanity and the Ballad Room in Cambridge.

May 18

Jackie DeShannon charted with a Phil Spector–styled production, entitled "Needles and Pins," arranged, written, and produced by Spector protégées Sonny Bono and Jack Nitzsche. Though it only reached No. 84, the British band the Searchers heard her version and less then a year later had a No. 13 hit with it.

May 25

The Chiffons' "One Fine Day" was released, eventually reaching No. 5 pop and No. 6 R&B.

May 27

Ruth Brown appeared at the Café Tia Juana in Cleveland. Ruth was once asked by a reporter, "At what point did rhythm and blues start becoming rock and roll?" Without hesitation she fired back: "When the white kids started to dance to it."

June 1

Lesley Gore's "It's My Party" topped the pop chart today, on its way to million-selling status. She was only seventeen at the time. Written by Tin Pan Alley pros John Gluck Jr., Wally Gold, and Herb Weiner, the song would go on to receive a Grammy nomination for Best Rock 'n' Roll Record in 1964 and would become a staple of American radio for the next forty-five years.

The Chiffons, a quintet of teenagers from the Bronx, New York, charted with "One Fine Day," which went on to No. 5 pop. The recording was originally done by Little Eva, of "Locomotion" fame, and produced by the song's composers, Gerry Goffin and Carole King for the Tokens, who were the Chiffons' producers. The Tokens decided to erase Little Eva's vocal, replacing it with the Chiffons.

June 6

Little Miss and the Muffets (originally called the Meltones) topped the Hot 100 with "Chapel of Love," but thanks to a last-minute name change, they became known to the world as the Dixie Cups.

June 14

Dionne Warwick, the Chiffons, the Shirelles, and Little Peggy March headlined a night at Pittsburgh's Civic Center, along with Dion, Freddy Cannon, and the Impressions.

June 22

The Four Pennies charted, en route to No. 67 pop, with a Chiffons-styled takeoff of the Crystals' "Uptown," titled "My Block." One reason for the style similarity was because the Four Pennies were the Chiffons! With their current hit, "One Fine Day," riding up the charts, the group's producers were so enamored with "My Block" they didn't want to wait months to release it as another Chiffons song, so they just renamed the group, at least for the one release.

July 3

LaVern Baker performed at the Riviera Hotel in Las Vegas. It was her first Vegas booking after fifteen years in show business and eighteen pop-chart singles.

July 6

Anita Humes and the Essex, a vocal group made up of five U.S. Marines, topped the singles chart with "Easier Said Than Done."

Lesley Gore's follow-up to her monster hit "It's My Party," "Judy's Turn to Cry" hit the singles survey (No. 2), becoming her second of nineteen eventual hits in only four years.

The Cookies' "Will Power" charted (No. 72 pop). Though the female trio had four pop and four R&B charters, they were mostly a backup group for the likes of Neil Sedaka, Carole King, and Little Eva's monster hit "Locomotion." An earlier incarnation in the 1950s became Ray Charles' background vocalists, the Raeletts, but as the Cookies they reached No. 9 R&B with "In Paradise" in 1956.

The Percells, Dee Dee Sharp, Chubby Checker, and the Earls performed at New York's Polo Grounds prior to a Mets baseball game.

July 13

Lesley Gore's "It's My Party" reached No. 9 in Great Britain.

July 15

Dick Clark's Caravan of Stars began their cross-country tour with Barbara Lewis, the Crystals, Ruby and the Romantics, the Orlons, Bob B. Soxx and the Blue Jeans, Big Dee Irwin, the Tymes, Gene Pitney, and the Dovells, among others.

July 20

The Essex's "Easier Said Than Done" hit No. 1 R&B (and eventually pop). Led by Anita Humes, the quintet were all active marines and needed Marine Corps approval to perform off the base or to tour.

July 26

The Newport Folk Festival featured Joan Baez and Peter, Paul and Mary, along with a host of folkies such as Bob Dylan, who duetted on "With God on Our

Side" with his girlfriend, Joan Baez, an astute reader of character who, unknown to the tense troubadour, would put Librium in his coffee to calm him down.

Notable birthdays: (July 4) Ute Lemper, (July 7) Vonda Shepard, (July 17) Regina Belle

August 3

The Angels' "My Boyfriend's Back" charted, en route to No. 1.

August 17

The Crystals charted with "Then He Kissed Me" (No. 6).

August 22

The Shangri-La's teen-angst standard "Remember" charted, en route to No. 5. It was their first of eleven hits in less than two years.

August 28

Joan Baez sang "We Shall Overcome" at the Civil Rights March in Washington, D.C. Her version was recorded at Miles College in Birmingham, Alabama, and would become Joan's and the '60s peace movement's theme song.

August 30

New York disc jockey Murray the K held his annual Labor Day spectacular at the Brooklyn Fox Theater, featuring the Chiffons, the Shirelles, the Tymes, the Drifters, Ben E. King, Little Stevie Wonder, Jay and the Americans, the Miracles, Randy and the Rainbows, and many others.

August 31

The Ronettes charted with "Be My Baby," a single the Beach Boys' Brian Wilson called, "The most perfect pop record of all time." It peaked at No. 2 for three weeks, becoming their first of eight hits. The "Bad Girls in Bouffant" started as $10-a-night dancers at New York's famed Peppermint Lounge, performing and touring with Joey Dee and the Starlighters as the Dolly Sisters.

Notable birthdays: (August 1) Cindy Burch (the Burch Sisters), (August 9) Whitney Houston, (August 22) Tori Amos, Emily Saliers (Indigo Girls)

September 7

The Angels' "My Boyfriend's Back" reached No. 1, becoming their only chart topper.

September 10

Doris Troy, Inez Foxx, the Crystals, Martha and the Vandellas, Ruby and the Romantics, Marvin Gaye, the Drifters, James Brown, Jimmy Reed, and Major Lance began The Biggest Show of Stars for '63 package tour.

September 14

Patti LaBelle and the Blue-Belles charted pop with "Down the Aisle (Wedding Song)," reaching No. 37 and becoming their first of eleven R&B charters (No. 14) for them as both the Blue-Belles and later LaBelle. The group formed in 1961 from two school groups, the Del Capris and the Ordettes.

September 21

Martha and the Vandellas' "Heatwave" peaked at No. 4 pop while reaching No. 1 R&B for four weeks and selling over a million copies. Martha started out as a $35-a-week secretary at Motown for the writers of "Heatwave," Eddie Holland, Lamont Dozier, and Brian Holland, as well as Smokey Robinson.

September 24

The British folk group the Springfields announced they were breaking up. Their lead singer would soon go on her own as Dusty Springfield. Dusty's real name was Mary Isabel Catherine Bernadette O'Brien, and with a name like that, it's not surprising that she was educated in a convent.

September 26

Baby Washington, Sam Cooke, Freddie Scott, the Tymes, Little Willie John, and Bobby "Blue" Bland performed in New Orleans.

September 28

San Francisco's Cow Palace hosted a surf party, including Dionne Warwick, Dee Dee Sharp, the Coasters, Bobby Freeman, the Drifters, the Righteous Brothers, and the Beach Boys.

The Angels' album *My Boyfriend's Back* (No. 33) became their only chart LP despite six hit singles over a four-year period.

October 6

The Angels appeared on *The Ed Sullivan Show,* performing their current (and only) No. 1 million seller, "My Boyfriend's Back."

October 11

Edith Piaf (Edith Giovanna Gassion) was born into poverty and raised in a brothel. "The Little Sparrow," as she became known, began singing for French francs (pennies) in the streets of Normandy. Through drug abuse, a suicide attempt, and a marriage cut tragically short, she rose to become one of France's greatest singers. Her biggest hit, "La Vie en Rose," even charted in America, reaching No. 23 in 1950 (English version). Among those influenced by her were Nana Mouskouri, Judy Garland, and Liza Minelli. The legendary French chanteuse died at age forty-eight today.

October 19

Timi Yuro and Lesley Gore began what was billed as the Greatest Record Show of 1963 British tour, along with Dion, Trini Lopez, and Brook Benton. The tour's first stop was at Finsbury Park, in Astoria, London.

October 20

Dusty Springfield made her solo debut after the breakup of the Springfields. The performance was at a show for British troops stationed in what was then West Germany.

November 4

The Exciters, known for their 1962 hit "Tell Him," released their newest single, "Do Wah Diddy," which would only reach No. 78. The song would go on to be a quintessential part of the British invasion less than a year later, when it reached No. 1 as done by Manfred Mann.

November 8

Dusty Springfield began her first solo tour as the only female act among Freddie and the Dreamers, the Searchers, Dave Berry, and Brian Poole and the Tremeloes in Halifax, Yorks, England.

November 9

Joan Baez charted with "We Shall Overcome" (No. 90), her first of nine Hot 100 singles through 1975.

The Shirelles began their first British tour, starting at the Regal Cinema in Edmonton, London, along with Duane Eddy and Little Richard.

November 13

The Ronettes opened in Teaneck, New Jersey, as part of Dick Clark's Caravan of Stars.

November 22

Mary Wells and Sam Cooke performed their first of two concerts today at New York's Apollo Theater. Between shows, word came through that President Kennedy had been assassinated. Sam immediately canceled his performance and flew back to Los Angeles.

November 23

The Ronettes' "Be My Baby" reached No. 4 in England. It was the first of four British hits for the New York teen trio.

November 30

The Supremes charted with "When the Lovelight Starts Shinning Through His Eyes," reaching No. 23 and becoming their first pop hit record.

December 7

Dionne Warwick charted with the haunting "Anyone Who Had a Heart," reaching No. 8. It was her first pop Top 10 hit.

Lesley Gore's "She's a Fool" reached No. 5. (By the end of the year, Lesley was voted the Most Promising Female Vocalist of 1963 by the National Association of Record Merchandisers (NARM) and 16 magazine voted her Best Female Vocalist at their third annual Gee-Gee Awards.)

The first female foreign-language No. 1 record in America was "Dominique" by Sister Sourire. The famous Belgium "Singing Nun" apparently could not handle her celebrity status and committed suicide in 1985.

December 14

Dinah Washington, known to many as the "Queen of the Blues," died of an overdose of sleeping pills. At the time, she had been married to the Detroit Lions' Dick "Night Train" Lane, who was her seventh husband. She was only thirty-nine years old.

The Ronettes' "wall of sound" gem "Baby, I Love You" was released, on its journey to No. 24.

December 22

Scheduled for an earlier release but held up due to the assassination of President Kennedy, Darlene Love's epic Christmas classic "Christmas, Baby Please Come Home" was finally issued. Background vocals on rock's greatest holiday recording were by the Ronettes, the Crystals, and Cher.

December 28

Lesley Gore's fourth Top 5 charter in a row, "You Don't Own Me" began its run up the Hot 100 today, en route to No. 2.

Notable birthdays: (December 7) Barbara Weathers (Atlantic Starr)

1964

January 1

Dusty Springfield's "I Only Want to Be with You" became the first record played on Britain's new pop-music TV show *Top of the Pops*.

January 2

The Rolling Stones backed Cleo Sylvestri, a British backup singer on the Teddy Bears' 1958 hit written by Phil Spector, "To Know Him Is to Love Him." The recording never charted.

January 4

Betty Harris' second of three Top 100 singles, "His Kiss," charted today. Betty was originally a maid for blues singer Big Maybelle. Her career started when Maybelle brought her onstage for duets.

Patti LaBelle and the Blue-Belles charted with the standard "You'll Never Walk Alone," reaching No. 34.

January 11

Dusty Springfield's solo debut, "I Only Want to Be with You," peaked at No. 4 in Great Britain. It would go on to reach No. 12 in America. Dusty was formerly a member of the vocal trio the Lana Sisters and later the folk trio the Springfields.

The Sapphires, a Philadelphia-based R&B trio led by Carol Jackson, charted, en route to their biggest hit with "Who Do You Love" (No. 25).

January 25

Dusty Springfield charted with "I Only Want to Be with You" (No. 12). It became her first of nineteen hits through 1987.

February 1

Lesley Gore's smoldering ballad "You Don't Own Me" became her second million seller, reaching No. 2. She was kept from the top spot for three weeks by the Beatles' "I Want to Hold Your Hand."

February 8

The Ronettes greeted the Beatles in New York, asking them questions in a radio interview.

February 9

Dusty Springfield went on tour to South Africa while stating that she would only perform in front of non-segregated audiences.

February 11

The Chiffons were the opening act on the Beatles' historic first American concert at Washington Coliseum in Washington, D.C.

February 14

The Crystals performed on the British teen show *Ready Steady Go*, which was the English equivalent of *Soul Train* and *American Bandstand* rolled into one.

February 16

The Crystals embarked on a British tour backed by Manfred Mann.

February 27

Twenty-one-year-old Cilla Black hit No. 1 in England with a cover of Dionne Warwick's "Anyone Who Had a Heart." Not bad for a former coatroom attendant and hairdresser.

February 29

Betty Everett charted with "The Shoop Shoop Song," which rose to No. 6.

Dusty Springfield started a twice-nightly tour for twenty-nine days at the Adelphi Cinema in Slough, England, with Bobby Vee and the Searchers.

March 5

Country music's version of "The day the music died": Patsy Cline, Cowboy Copas, and Hawkshaw Hawkins were killed in a plane crash in Camden, Tennessee. They were returning from a Kansas City benefit concert for the widow of a local disc jockey.

March 21

The Ronettes' "Best Part of Breakin' Up" was released. It would reach No. 39 pop in the U.S. and No. 43 on the British pop charts. Particularly popular in Britain, the group had toured with the Rolling Stones and were the first female act to induce mass hysteria among teen boys.

Notable birthdays: (March 20) Tracy Chapman

April 3

Joan Baez, in the infancy of her protest days, refused to appear on ABC-TV's *Hootenanny* because the program refused to book blacklisted artists. She also refused to pay 60 percent of her income tax to protest U.S. government expenditures on arms and then joined a picket line in Texas, supporting young people opposing racial discrimination in employment.

April 4

Barbra Streisand's "People" charted, en route to No. 5. It was the first of her forty-two hit 45's over the next thirty-two years.

Mary Wells' "My Guy" debuted on the Hot 100, rising to the top spot and making Mary the first Motown artist to have a No. 1.

April 12

New York disc jockey Murray the K's package tour opened at Brooklyn's Fox Theater, with a host of acts including the Chiffons, the Shirelles, and Dionne Warwick.

April 20

Dusty Springfield's "Wishin' and Hopin'" wished its way to No. 6. The background singers on the single were Martha Reeves and the Vandellas.

April 25

Dionne Warwick's classic pop/R&B ballad "Walk on By" charted, reaching No. 6. It would also become a standard in England, reaching No. 9.

May 4

The Marvelettes reached the R&B charts for the eighth time in less then two years with "Locking up My Heart" (No. 25).

May 10

Dusty Springfield performed her hit "I Only Want to Be with You" on TV's *The Ed Sullivan Show*

May 16

Lulu and the Lovers debuted on Britain's ITV show *Thank Your Lucky Stars.* Sixteen-year-old lead singer Lulu (Marie Lawrie) would go on to have ten hits in America and twenty-four in the U.K., including the No. 1 "To Sir with Love."

May 23

Ella Fitzgerald became the first artist to have a hit with a Beatles cover in England when "Can't Buy Me Love" hit the British charts, eventually rising to No. 34 pop.

Millie Small charted with her soon-to-be hit "My Boy Lollipop" (No. 2 U.S. and U. K.). The harmonica part was played by a nineteen-year-old folksinger named Rod Stewart.

May 30

Dionne Warwick made her debut in England, appearing on BBC-TV's *Top of the Pops.*

Notable birthdays: (May 30) Wynonna Judd

June 1

Dolly Parton moved to Nashville the day after her high school graduation, staying with relatives. Soon after, she would be signed to Monument Records, with Ray Stevens producing her as a pop artist. Having made her own guitar at age five and already having appeared on a Knoxville, Tennessee, radio show at age ten, Dolly and her uncle Bill Owens took a Greyhound bus to Lake Charles, Louisiana, to record her first single, "Puppy Love," for the local Gold Band label.

June 5

The Chiffons began a tour, starting in San Bernardino, California, as the opening act for the Rolling Stones on their debut American tour.

June 13

One of the Ronettes' most powerful pieces of pop, "Do I Love You" was released (No. 34).

June 20

Lesley Gore's "I Don't Wanna Be a Loser" made it to No. 37, just as the eighteen-year-old Gore graduated from high school.

June 22

Former student at St. Joseph's Convent School in England and the daughter of an Austrian baroness and a British university lecturer, eighteen-year-old Marianne Faithfull met Rolling Stones manager Andrew Loog Oldham at a London party. He was so impressed with her looks that he offered her a recording contract. Within three months, she was on the charts with a cover of the Stones' As Tears Go By" (No. 9 U.K.).

June 26

The Supremes, the Shirelles, and the Crystals, among others, performed at the Fairgrounds Grandstand in Allentown, Pennsylvania, on Dick Clark's Caravan of Stars tour.

July 14

A new duo, Caesar and Cleo, debuted with the release of their first single, "The Letter." Though it received little attention, they would soon become known worldwide when they changed their name to Sonny and Cher.

July 18

The Dixie Cups charted with "People Say," an eventual No. 12 pop hit. Though the black trio had five hit singles in the mid-'60s, their music was considered so popish that they never charted R&B.

July 31

In one of their early appearances, the Who performed at the Goldhawk Social Club in Shepherd's Bush, England. In order to get their ten-minute performance, they grudgingly agreed to back unknown female vocalist Valerie McCullam.

August 8

Gale Garnett was on her way to her biggest hit when "We'll Sing in the Sunshine" charted, becoming a million-selling No. 4 record.

August 15

Martha and the Vandellas' exciting dance classic "Dancing in the Streets" was released, on its way to No. 2.

August 19

The Beatles started their American tour at San Francisco's Cow Palace. Also on the bill were the Exciters, Jackie DeShannon, the Righteous Brothers, and the Bill Black Combo.

August 22

Martha and the Vandellas' "Dancing in the Streets" charted, eventually reaching No. 2.

August 26

The Supremes' "Where Did Our Love Go" became their first No. 1 this week. Before Diana Ross left in 1969, they would have eleven more.

Notable birthdays: (August 12) Amy Ray

September 12

Marianne Faithfull, daughter of a British university lecturer and an Austrian baroness, peaked at No. 9 in Britain with her cover of the Rolling Stones ballad "As Tears Go By."

The Butterflys' "Goodnight Baby" charted, en route to No. 51. The trio was actually singer/writer Ellie Greenwich multi-tracking her voice.

September 13

The Ronettes, the Shangra-Las, Martha and the Vandellas, the Supremes, the Temptations, the Miracles, and Marvin Gaye, among others, performed in Murray the K's ten-day Rock 'n' Roll Spectacular at the Brooklyn Fox Theater.

September 19

Marianne Faithfull made her live-performance debut at the Adelphi Cinema in Slough, Bucks, England. She was previously signed by Rolling Stones manager Andrew Loog Oldham after meeting him at a party in London. He was so impressed by her beauty that after learning she had a desire to be a folksinger, he offered to sign and record her, having never heard her sing.

Notable birthdays: (September 19) Trisha Yearwood

October 3

The Shangri-Las soap-opera single "Leader of the Pack" was issued today. It would chart within a week and go on to be their biggest hit (No. 1) of eleven Top 100 singles in their three-year chart career (1964–1966).

October 9

The Supremes made their first visit to England and performed on the British TV show *Ready Steady Go.*

October 17

"Walking in the Rain," the classic Ronettes ballad, was released today, ultimately reaching No. 23. It gave producer Phil Spector his only Grammy . . . and it was for sound effects!

Martha and the Vandellas' scintillating "Dancing in the Streets" hit No. 2 pop. The song was written by producers Mickey Stevenson and Marvin Gaye and was originally turned down by Motown artist Mary Wells.

The Ronettes' "Do I Love You" peaked at No. 35 in Britain and became their last hit there.

October 22

The Shangri-Las arrived in London for a round of TV shows to promote their new single, "Leader of the Pack." However, three major shows, *Ready Steady Go, Thank Your Lucky Stars,* and the *Eamonn Andrews Show,* all banned the group from performing the song. Despite that, the single reached No. 14 in England.

October 28

The Supremes and Lesley Gore performed in the TAMI (Teenage Awards Music International) Show at the Civic Auditorium in Santa Monica, California, along with the Beach Boys, Chuck Berry, James Brown, and the Rolling Stones, among others. Meanwhile, Gore's "Maybe I Know" reached No. 20 in Great Britain. In a little over a month, trade magazines *Cashbox, Music Business,* and *Record World* would all name Lesley the year's Best Female Vocalist.

October 31

Marianne Faithfull appeared on BBC-TV's *Juke Box Jury,* commenting on one record, "I'd like it at a party if I was stoned."

Notable birthdays: (October 10) Neneh Cherry

November 4

Jackie DeShannon took the place of Marianne Faithfull during a twenty-six-date British tour with Gene Pitney, Gerry and the Pacemakers, and the Kinks, after Marianne collapsed and was confined to bed.

Martha and the Vandellas visited Britain and performed on the popular TV show *Top of the Pops.*

November 19

The Supremes became the first all-girl group to reach No. 1 in Britain when "Baby Love" hit the coveted top spot.

November 28

Dionne Warwick performed on British TV show *Thank Your Lucky Stars.*

Marianne Faithfull's "As Tears Go By" charted in America, on its way to No. 22 and her biggest of five hits in the States.

The Shangri-Las' "Leader of the Pack" hit No. 1. Taking sound effects to the extreme, engineer Joe Veneri brought his Harley chopper into the studio and recorded the record's trademark revved-up-engine sound right in the booth.

Notable birthdays: (November 16) Diana Krall

December 14

Dusty Springfield sang to a multi-racial audience at a cinema near Cape Town, South Africa, during the height of apartheid.

December 15

Dusty Springfield, who earlier stated she would only play to non-segregated audiences in South Africa, was served with deportation orders by officials from the South African minister of the interior. The defiant Dusty left South Africa the next day.

December 19

Patti LaBelle and the Blue-Belles charted with the old standard "Danny Boy" (based on the 1855 Irish tune "Londonderry Air"). It was their third of six Hot 100 singles (No. 75), before they became LaBelle in 1975 and garnered hits like the No. 1 "Lady Marmalade."

Petula Clark's "Downtown" went uptown to No. 2 in England, right behind the Beatles' "I Feel Fine." (Warner Bros. A&R executive Joe Smith, on vacation in London, heard the song and signed Petula to the label in America.) Tony Hatch, Petula's producer, originally wrote the song for the Drifters but gave it to Petula instead. It would soon reach No. 1 Stateside. The pert Brit had already had sixteen hits in England before the U.S. discovered her.

December 24

Elkie Brooks performed at the Hammersmith Odeon in London, doing two shows a night for the annual Beatles' Christmas show. Also on the bill were the Yardbirds, Freddie and the Dreamers, Georgie Fame, and of course the Beatles.

December 26

Red Bird Records made the unusual move of releasing two singles by the Shangri-Las at the same time, and both "Give Him a Great Big Kiss" (No. 18) and "Maybe" (No. 91) (a remake of the Chantels hit) charted today.

December 27

The Supremes made their TV debut on *The Ed Sullivan Show.*

1965

January 23

Petula Clark became the first British female to reach the top of the American pop charts since Vera Lynn (1952) when "Downtown" hit No. 1.

January 30

Shirley Bassey charted with "Goldfinger," from the James Bond movie of the same name, on her way to No. 8. It was her first of four Top 100 singles.

February 13

LaVern Baker charted with "Fly Me to the Moon," reaching No. 31 R&B. It was the last solo hit for "Little Miss Sharecropper," as she was known, though she did have one more chart single on a duet with Jackie Wilson, "Think Twice" (No. 37 R&B). In all, she had twenty-one hits, starting in 1955, and was considered one of the finest female R&B singers of the 1950s.

Petula Clark.

March 11

Janis Joplin's made her debut performance as a member of Big Brother and the Holding Company at the Avalon Ballroom in San Francisco.

March 13

The Ikettes, a female trio that spent most of its performance life as the back-up singers/dancers for Ike and Tina Turner, charted with their own single, "Peaches 'n' Cream" (No. 36).

March 20

Martha and the Vandellas and the Supremes, along with the Miracles, the Temptations, and Stevie Wonder began a twenty-one-date, twice-nightly tour of England as the Tamla Motown package.

March 27

Five months after Marianne Faithfull was replaced on a tour by Jackie DeShannon due to illness, Marrianne's "Come and Stay with Me," written by DeShannon, became her biggest British hit, reaching No. 4.

March 29

Dionne Warwick performed at London's Savoy Hotel in the intimate setting of a cabaret.

April 2

Dionne Warwick performed on Britain's *Ready Steady Go* live-TV-show debut.

April 6

Marianne Faithfull began a U.S. tour with Gene Pitney (with whom she was rumored to be having an affair with).

April 10

England's popular TV show *Juke Box Jury* welcomed Dionne Warwick as a guest panelist.

May 1

Petula Clark's "I Know s Place" reached No. 3, making Clark the only female vocalist to chart her first two singles in the U.S. top three. It would be nineteen years before her record was reached by Cyndi Lauper, in 1984.

The Supremes leaped onto the charts with "Back in My Arms Again," their fifth No. 1 in a row!

May 15

Barbara Mason's Hot 100 debut, "Yes I'm Ready" (No. 5), was followed by ten more soulful singles over the next ten years.

Connie Francis made her twenty-fifth appearance (reportedly a record) on CBS-TV's *The Ed Sullivan Show*.

The "Queens of Musical Melodrama" The Shangri-Las' "Give Us Your Blessings" was issued, reaching No. 29.

May 23

Joan Baez's "We Shall Overcome" peaked at No. 26 in England as she performed at London's Royal Albert Hall.

June 5

Joan Baez founded the Institute for the Study of Non-Violence in Carmel, California, giving her the motivation to withhold another 10 percent of her taxes from the U.S. government. (They must have loved her!)

June 19

Marianne Faithfull performed at Uxbridge, Middlesex, England, with several acts, including the Who and Solomon Burke.

June 26

Oscar-winning actress Patty Duke hit the Hot 100 with "Don't Just Stand There," her debut chart climber (No. 8) while still starring in the hit TV series *The Patty Duke Show.*

Sonny and Cher's "I Got You Babe" was released. It was their first chart record and only No. 1 together.

June 28

The Ronettes, Dionne Warwick, the Supremes, Martha and the Vandellas, the Temptations, and the Four Tops performed on the *It's What's Happening Baby* special on CBS-TV.

July 3

Cher technically had her first Hot 100 entry today when "All I Really Want to Do" started its climb to No. 15. It was the beginning of her thirty-one hit singles streak between 1965 and 1999. It was on a technicality because her soon-to-be ex-partner, Sonny Bono, sang backup on the single.

Joan Baez's five-year-old album *Joan Baez* finally charted and peaked at No. 9.

July 6

The Jefferson Airplane played their debut gig at the Matrix in San Francisco, a club owned by the group's Marty Balin.

July 17

Joan Baez #5 stopped at No. 3 in England and would become her biggest British album.

July 24

The California folk quintet the We Five, with Beverly Bivens singing lead, charged onto the pop survey with "You Were on My Mind" (No. 3).

July 29

The Supremes performed at the world-famous Copacabana in New York at the start of a three-week stay. It would be recorded for a future album.

Notable birthdays: (July 9) Courtney Love

August 1

Marianne Faithfull collapsed during a concert in England and had to cancel her engagements, including an American tour set for the end of the month.

August 7

Both Joan Baez's album *Joan Baez in Concert, Part 2,* and her cover single of Phil Ochs' "There but for Fortune" reached No. 8 in England. The album's slow climb eventually had its peak more than a year after initially charting.

Lesley Gore's "Sunshine, Lollipops and Rainbows," co-written by newcomer Marvin Hamlisch (from the Frankie Avalon movie *Ski Party,* in which Gore had a cameo role), reached No. 13. Meanwhile, the TAMI show movie *Gather No Moss,* in which she was featured, had its British premiere at Birmingham's Futurist Cinema.

Martha and the Vandellas' "You've Been in Love Too Long" was released. It was their ninth hit (No. 36) in just two years.

August 9

A band from Hull, England, called the Silkie was discovered by Brian Epstein. The four-piece group fronted by Silvia Tatler recorded "You've Got to Hide Your Love Away" today, with John Lennon overseeing. George Harrison played tambourine while Paul McCartney played guitar on a record that eventually reached No. 10 in America and No. 28 in Britain.

August 11

Janis Joplin performed with Big Brother and the Holding company for the first time. She had begun singing as part of the Waller Creek Boys trio in Texas circa 1960.

August 13

Petula Clark's "Downtown" won the Best Rock 'n' Roll Recording of 1964 Award at the seventh annual Grammy Awards.

Jefferson Airplane (with original lead singer, Signe Toly Anderson) made their performance debut at San Francisco's Matrix Club.

August 14

Dusty Springfield, who had just had a hit with Burt Bacharach's "Wishin' and Hopin'," performed on British TV's tribute *The Bacharach Sound*, with Dionne Warwick and the Searchers, among others.

Petula Clark sang "Downtown" and "I Know a Place" on *The Ed Sullivan Show* during her first visit to America.

The Ronettes began a fourteen-city tour in Chicago as the opening act for the Beatles, though lead singer Ronnie Bennett was kept behind by her jealous and paranoid boyfriend (and soon to be husband), producer Phil Spector.

August 17

Gospel singer Marie Knight prayed her way onto the R&B charts with the Julie London–penned pop hit "Cry Me a River," reaching No. 35. Marie had four hit singles from 1948 through 1965, a rare accomplishment for a gospel artist. Her biggest single was "Up Above My Head, I Hear Music in the Air" with Sister Rosetta Tharpe (No. 6) in 1948.

August 21

Dusty Springfield hosted the British TV special *The Sound of Motown*, featuring the Supremes, Martha and the Vandellas, the Miracles, the Temptations, and Stevie Wonder.

August 24

Actress/singer Julie Andrews charted with her only Top 100 single, "Super-cali-fragil-istic-expi-ali-docious" (No. 66). God knows what she could possibly have followed that with!

Notable birthdays: (August 28) Shania Twain, (August 29) Pebbles

September 4

Judy Garland and Liza Minelli's album *Live at the London Palladium* charted (No. 41). The mother-and-daughter hit reached the Top 200 again in 1963 (No. 164), becoming Garland's last of eleven hit LPs.

September 11

A New York trio, the Toys hit the big time with "A Lovers Concerto" (No. 2). The song's melody was based on Bach's *Minuet from the Anna Magdalena Notebook*.

Notable birthdays: (September 26) Cindy Heron (En Vogue)

October 2

Fontella Bass charted with "Rescue Me," her eventual No. 4 pop hit and biggest of her six charters. The song, thanks to her version, has gone on to legendary status, used in commercials and films for decades.

October 16

Jefferson Airplane (with original lead singer Signe Toly Anderson) headlined the first Family Dog commune's "A Tribute to Dr. Strange" dance at Longshoreman's Hall in San Francisco, where they met Grace Slick (Grace Barnett Wing), who was singing with another band that day, the Great Society.

October 23

Dusty Springfield's "Some of Your Lovin,'" with vocal support from Doris Troy and Madeleine Bell topped out at No. 8 in Great Britain. The single never charted in America.

Notable birthdays: (October 14) Karen White

November 1

Petula Clark was offered the chance to co-star in the film *Paradise Hawaiian Style* with Elvis Presley but turned it down.

November 6

The historic theater Fillmore West opened, with Grace Slick and Jefferson Airplane, and the Grateful Dead. Bill Graham rented the Fillmore Auditorium in New York for $60 and then proceeded to become the premier music promoter of the rock era.

November 13

The Crystals embarked on their second Dick Clark's Caravan of Stars tour that year with the Supremes, Dee Dee Sharp, the Drifters, Lou Christie, Bobby Freeman, and Brian Hyland.

November 27

Connie Francis eventually hit the Top 50 singles survey for the last time when "Jealous Heart" (No. 47) started its climb today.

Petula Clark's "You're the One" reached No. 23 in England, but was not released as a single in the U.S., giving the Vogues' cover version a chance to reach no. 4 without competition.

The Royalettes, a Baltimore vocal group in the image of the Chantels/Shirelles, charted with "I Want to Meet Him," peaking at No. 26 R&B. The group was better known for their scintillating recording of "It's Gonna Take a Miracle" from earlier in the year.

Notable birthdays: (November 12) Bjork

December 6
The Ronettes performed on NBC-TV's *Hullabaloo.*

December 10
Signe Toly Anderson and Jefferson Airplane, and Grace Slick and the Great Society both performed at the inaugural concert at Bill Graham's Fillmore Auditorium in San Francisco.

December 16
Signe Toly Anderson and Jefferson Airplane, who had recently signed with RCA for $25,000, cut their first tracks ("High Flyin' Bird," "It's No Secret," "It's Alright," "Runnin' Round the World," and "Run Around") in Los Angeles.

December 25
The Mamas and the Papas' classic "California Dreamin'" was released.

1966

January 1
The Marvelettes' "Don't Mess with Bill" charted, reaching No. 7. It became the last of three Top 10 hits for the ladies.

The Supremes reached No. 11 on the pop charts with their *Supremes at the Copa* album, recorded live the previous year.

The Three Degrees barely scrapped the bottom of the Top 100 with "Look in My Eyes" (No. 97), a song originally recorded by the Chantels in 1961. Both records were produced by Richard Barrett, who was also manager of the girl groups.

January 9
Joan Baez's "Farewell Angeliou" (written by Bob Dylan) made it to No. 35 as its associated album, *Farewell Angelina,* rose to No. 10. A nice birthday present for the twenty-five-year-old.

January 11

Patti LaBelle and the Blue-Belles began a tour of England, starting at the Cromwellian Club in London.

January 14

Patti LaBelle and the Blue-Belles performed on British TV's *Ready Steady Go* while promoting their new single, "Over the Rainbow."

January 22

Frank Sinatra's daughter, Nancy, hit the Top 100 with "These Boots Are Made for Walking" They "walked" all the way to No. 1.

January 29

Three classic folk albums, *Joan Baez, Joan Baez Vol. #2,* and *Joan Baez in Concert,* were all certified gold by the Recoding Industry Association of America.

Notable birthdays: (January 16) Maxine Jones (En Vogue), (January 25) Stacy Lattisaw

February 5

Though Petula Clark disliked and tried to sabotage the release of "My Love," her label prevailed, and the single reached No. 1. It became her second American million seller and made her the first British female artist to have two U.S. No. 1s.

February 17

Nancy Sinatra reached No. 1 in England with "These Boots Are Made for Walking." Nine days later, it would be No. 1 in America.

February 19

Janis Joplin and Big Brother and the Holding Company played San Francisco's Avalon Ballroom with Grace Slick and Jefferson Airplane.

March 8

Lulu became the first British female singer to perform behind the Iron Curtain when she began a Polish tour with the Hollies in Warsaw.

March 12

Cher's "Bang Bang" charted and would become her first solo Top 5 hit (No. 2).

March 24

Marianne Faithfull started a four-week engagement at the Paris Olympia, France, before appearing at the Golden Rose Festival in Montreux, Switzerland.

April 2

Sarah Vaughan's cover of the Toys' hit "A Lover's Concerto" charted, reaching No. 63 pop. It was the last of her thirty-three singles to reach the charts.

April 9

The Mamas and the Papas' only No. 1, "Monday, Monday," charted.

April 23

Cher's "Bang Bang" stopped at No. 2 and became her first solo million seller.

April 28

Dusty Springfield's "You Don't Have to Say You Love Me," an Italian ballad (which had been that country's entry for the San Remo Song Festival) topped the British chart and became her bestselling single of twenty-five English charters through 1993 (not including five more with her former group, the Springfields).

Notable birthdays: (April 11) Lisa Stansfield, (April 15) Samantha Fox

May 7

After going without a Top 10 hit for almost three years, the Chiffons came back strong when "Sweet Talking Guy" charted, on its way to No. 10 pop. The song was co-written by Doug Morris, who went on to become president of Universal Music Group.

Tina Turner recorded her legendary vocal on Phil Spector's crowning achievement, "River Deep, Mountain High." Spector had already spent over $22,000 creating the backing track, and that didn't include the $20,000 he paid Ike Turner to stay out of the studio!

May 13

Karen Carpenter signed on with musician Joe Osborn's micro label Magic Lamp Records. Five hundred copies of the single "Looking for Love" were issued. Her brother, Richard, and Wes Jacobs were also on the recording. They went on to be signed by RCA as the Richard Carpenter Trio, four years before their first success with "Ticket to Ride," in 1970.

May 30

Dolly Parton married Carl Dean in Catoosa County, Georgia. They met at the Wishy Washy Laundromat on the first day she came to Nashville as an eighteen-year-old singing hopeful.

May 31

Lulu began filming *To Sir with Love* with Sidney Poitier at England's Pinewood Studios.

Notable birthdays: (May 16) Janet Jackson

June 18

Ike and Tina Turner's (actually only Tina's) thundering "River Deep, Mountain High" only reached No. 88 pop. Even though the British had a much greater appreciation of it (No. 3 U.K.), its failure in America so demoralized producer Phil Spector that he withdrew from producing for several years.

June 24

Patti LaBelle and the Blue-Belles, Percy Sledge, Sam and Dave, and Otis Redding began a grueling one-nighter tour schedule of forty-six performances with a show in Greensboro, North Carolina.

July 2

Dionne Warwick had her first charter after a draught of three and a half years when "Trains, Boats and Planes" drove onto the hit survey (No. 22).

July 8

Michelle Gilliam Phillips was fired from the Mamas and the Papas by her husband, John Phillips, and replaced by Jill Gibson, girlfriend of Jan and Dean's Jan Berry. Michelle returned within a month.

July 28

Janis Joplin and Big Brother and the Holding Company were discovered playing at California Hall by Mainstream Records President Bob Shad. He offered them a recording contract, but they turned him down.

July 31

Joan Baez's "Pack Up Your Sorrows" (written by Baez's brother-in-law, Richard Farina, who had died in a motorcycle crash two months earlier), reached No. 50 in Britain.

Notable birthdays: (July 29) Martina McBride

August 6

The Supremes' "You Can't Hurry Love" was issued and raced to No. 1.

August 12

The Ronettes, Bobby Hebb, and the Cyrkle all joined the Beatles, who started their 1966 U.S. tour at the International Amphitheater in Chicago.

August 18

Dusty Springfield's British TV series *Dusty* aired for the first time.

August 23

Broke and desperate in Chicago, Janis Joplin and Big Brother and the Holding Company reconsidered and signed with Bob Shad's Mainstream Records. Their album was recorded (with Shad not allowing the group in the studio during the final mix), but was not issued until their successful performance at the Monterey Pop Festival the following year.

August 29

The final broadcast of TV's *Hullabaloo* featured Lesley Gore, Paul Anka, the Cyrkle, and Peter and Gordon.

Notable birthdays: (August 19) Lee Ann Womack

September 5

Martha and the Vandellas performed at the Fillmore Auditorium in San Francisco.

September 23

Gladys Knight and the Pips, Martha and the Vandellas, the Temptations, Jimmy Ruffin, Stevie Wonder, and a host of lesser acts started a week's engagement at Detroit's Fox Theater, in what is historically known as the Motortown Revue.

Ike and Tina Turner toured England with the Rolling Stones and the Yardbirds, starting in the Royal Albert Hall in London.

Notable birthdays: (September 5) Terry Ellis (En Vogue)

October 1

Cher, who recorded as Bonnie Jo Mason and Cherilyn in 1964, hit the Top 200 album charts with the self-titled *Cher* (No. 59).

"For me—and I imagine for millions of others—Tina [Turner] now stands as an enduring symbol of survival and of grace. Her music is a healing thing. . . . Tina has the ability to dream, get out, get over, and get on with it. She's transformed herself into an international sensation—an elegant powerhouse."—Janet Jackson

October 8

Joan Baez performed at a peace festival with the Grateful Dead and Quicksilver Messenger Service at the Outdoor Theater in Mt. Tamalpais State Park, California.

October 14

The Mamas and the Papas performed at New York's prestigious Carnegie Hall.

October 15

Signe Toly Anderson (original lead singer of Jefferson Airplane), being unable to cope with the demands of being a new mother and playing in the band, made her final appearance with them in the middle of a three-day stint at the Fillmore Auditorium.

October 16

Joan Baez and 123 of her closest antidraft demonstrators were arrested for blocking the entrance to the Armed Forces Induction Center in Oakland. Joan and her army were jailed for ten days.

One day after Jefferson Airplane's original lead singer, Signe Toly Anderson, left to raise her new child, Grace Slick joined the band, bringing with her two songs she had performed with her previous group, the Great Society. The songs were "Somebody to Love" and "White Rabbit." (The Great Society recorded two live albums for Columbia that the label did not release until Slick clicked with Jefferson Airplane.)

October 23

The first female vocal group to top the U.S. album charts were the Supremes, with *Supremes a Go Go*.

October 27

Ike and Tina Turner's "A Love Like Yours" charted in England, reaching No. 16. The song, produced by Phil Spector, was originally a B-side for Martha and the Vandellas.

November

Notable birthdays: (November 14) Jeanette Jurado (Exposé), (November 25) Stacy Lattisaw

December 3

The Mamas and the Papas' "Words of Love" began its run up the singles survey, on its way to No. 5.

December 23

Dusty Springfield's stage career started when she starred in *Merry King Cole* at the Empire Theater in Liverpool, England.

December 24

Lulu performed in Murray the K's Christmas show at New York's Brooklyn Fox Theater.

December 27

Ike and Tina Turner performed at the Galaxy in Los Angeles for Christmas week.

December 28

Martha and the Vandellas, Gladys Knight and the Pips, Jimmy Ruffin, the Temptations, and Stevie Wonder performed at the Fox Theater in Detroit, in what became known worldwide as the Motortown Revue.

Notable birthdays: (December 8) Sinead O'Connor

1967

January 6

The Supremes recorded an album of Disney songs; however, the collection was never released. Only the song "When You Wish upon a Star" ever saw the light of day, when it was issued on their thirty-fifth, and last, chart album, *Diana Ross and the Supremes 25th Anniversary* (No. 112 pop), in 1986.

January 7

Kim Weston, duetting with Marvin Gaye, charted with "It Takes Two" (No. 14). It was her biggest of six Top 100 singles, starting in 1963.

January 14

Blues great Big Maybelle had her only pop-chart single when "96 Tears" hit the Top 100 today, eventually reaching (you guessed it!) No. 96.

Jefferson Airplane, with new lead singer Grace Slick (having replaced Signe Toly Anderson), played at the first "Be-In" in Golden Gate Park, San Francisco, before starting their first East Coast tour.

The 5th Dimension hit the Top 100 with "Go Where You Wanna Go" (No. 16), their first of thirty charters through 1976.

January 19

Lesley Gore appeared on the *Batman* TV show as Catwoman's assistant, Pussycat, singing, "California Nights," which would eventually rise to No. 16. By June, Lesley would make her theatrical debut in *Half a Sixpence*.

January 21

Dolly Parton's first chart 45 was the stereotypical but totally unfounded

"Dumb Blonde," which hit the country chart, eventually reaching No. 24. It was taken from her debut album, *Hello I'm Dolly*.

January 27

Aretha Franklin recorded her first sides for Atlantic Records at Rick Hall's Florence, Alabama, Music Emporium (FAME) studios in Muscle Shoals. The day's work produced the classic "I Never Loved a Man (The Way I Love You)."

January 31

Janis Joplin performed at the Matrix in San Francisco, doing her "Amazing Grace/High Heel Sneakers" Medley.

Notable birthdays: (January 15) Lisa Velez (Lisa Lisa and Cult Jam)

February 12

Marianne Faithfull was with Mick Jagger at Keith Richard's house when police raided the place, but, unlike the Stones' Jagger and Richard, she was not arrested for drug possession.

February 24

Martin Luther King Jr. presented Aretha Franklin with the Southern Christian Leadership Award at Cobo Hall in Detroit as the city declared it Aretha Franklin Day.

March 3

Princess Margaret attended a performance at the London Palladium to hear Petula Clark sing.

March 4

Aretha Franklin's Atlantic Records debut, "I Never Loved a Man (The Way I Love You)" charted, en route to No. 1 R&B for seven weeks and No. 9 pop, becoming her first of seventeen Top 10 pop hits. Atlantic had outbid Columbia for her contract with an offer of $25,000, after Columbia tried to break out the artist doing standards, jazz, and soul-less R&B from 1960 through 1965. Playing piano on many of her recordings, Aretha learned by listening to Eddie Heywood records.

March 11

The Supremes reached No. 1 for the ninth time when "Love Is Here and Now You're Gone" hit the top spot today.

March 25

Aretha Franklin's album *I Never Loved a Man (The Way I Love You)* reached No. 2, garnering Lady Soul her first gold album.

April 8

Peaches and Herb charted with their cover of the Five Keys' 1955 classic No. 5 R&B hit "Close Your Eyes," reaching No. 4 R&B and No. 8 pop.

April 25

"Society's Child" by Janis Ian (born Janis Fink, she took her brother's first name as her last,) was featured on orchestra leader Leonard Bernstein's TV special *Inside Pop—The Rock Revolution*" after *New York Times* music critic Robert Shelton gave Bernstein's TV producer a copy. Ian's controversial song, dealing with teenage interracial love, was turned down by twenty-two record companies before it came out on Verve. Atlantic Records, who paid for the session, refused to release it. Thanks to the TV performance, the recording that was marred in controversy charted by May, topping off at No. 14.

April 27

British songstress Sandi Shaw hit No. 1 with "Puppet on a String" in England, making it her third No. 1 and that year's Eurovison Song Contest winner.

April 28

Petula Clark performed before President Johnson at the annual White House Press Correspondents Dinner in Washington, D.C.

April 29

Cindy Birdsong (Patti LaBelle and the Blue-Belles) made her stage debut as a replacement for Florence Ballard with the Supremes at the Hollywood Bowl, in a Benefit concert for the UCLA School of Music.

May 6

Hit songwriter and former lead singer of the Raindrops ("The Kind of Boy You Can't Forget") Ellie Greenwich made her only solo chart appearance with "I Want You to Be My Baby" (No. 83).

May 7

Grace Slick and Jefferson Airplane appeared on CBS-TV's *The Smothers Brothers Comedy Hour.*

May 13

Philly soul singer Tammi Terrell (born Thomasina Winifred Montgomery) was signed to the Motown label while in her twenties and achieved some success through a couple of Top 30 R&B singles in 1966. But it wasn't until she was paired with Marvin Gaye in '67 that her star rose, thanks to classic duets like "Ain't No Mountain High Enough" (which charted today), "Ain't Nothing Like the Real Thing," and "You're All I Need to Get By." She was diagnosed with a brain tumor, resulting in her death at the age of twenty-four on March 16, 1970.

May 17

Grace Slick and Jefferson Airplane were the sixth band to appear on the second evening of the Monterey Pop Festival at the County Fairgrounds in Monterey, California. Meanwhile, "Somebody to Love," written by Grace's brother-in-law, Darby Slick, peaked at No. 5.

May 27

Sixteen-year-old Janis Ian charted with "Society's Child," a song about interracial romance that was ahead of its time in 1967. She wrote it when she was fourteen years old!

June 3

The 5th Dimension charted with "Up, Up and Away," which became their first million seller, reaching No. 7. The light, lilting feel of the recording was such that it never got near the R&B charts. In fact, the all-black group charted almost twice as many pop (thirty times) as R&B (seventeen) during their ten-year hit-list career.

The Staples Singers charted with "Why? (Am I Treated So Bad)," reaching No. 95 pop. It was the first Top 100 single for the family of gospel-turned-R&B vocalists, who would have eighteen charters through 1992.

June 8

LaVerne Andrews, of the pioneering 1940s vocal group the Andrews Sisters, died.

June 9

Latino popster Vickie Carr (born Florencia Martinez Cardona) charted with "It Must Be Him," her first and biggest hit (No. 3).

June 16

The Mamas and the Papas, and Laura Nyro, along with Simon and Garfunkel, the Grateful Dead, Otis Redding, the Association, Canned Heat, and Buffalo Springfield were among the acts who performed at the Monterey Pop Festival, the first legendary pop and rock festival.

June 17

Janis Joplin and Big Brother and the Holding Company's appearance at the seminal Monterey Pop Festival in Monterey, California, was a breakthrough performance for the band. Grace Slick and Jefferson Airplane were the sixth act to perform on the festival's second night.

June 18

D. A. Pennebaker filmed the legendary Monterey Pop Festival. Artists included Janis Joplin, the Byrds, the Who, the Blues Project, and Jimi Hendrix. The Mamas and the Papas were the closing act. Unbeknownst to them at the time, it became the last live performance by the original quartet.

June 24

Grace Slick and Jefferson Airplane hopped on the Top 100 with their classic "White Rabbit" (No. 8).

June 25

Marianne Faithfull sang in the chorus of the Beatles' "All You Need Is Love," recorded live during the "One World" global TV broadcast.

July 1

Petula Clark's "Don't Sleep in the Subways," reached No. 2 in Britain and would eventually peak at No. 5 in America. The song was created by writer/producer Tony Hatch from unfinished portions of three other songs.

July 3

Lulu and Dusty Springfield attended a party for the Monkees at the Speakeasy in London. Among the guests were the Beatles (minus Ringo, who was out of town), Eric Clapton, the Who, Procol Harum, Manfred Mann, and Monkees Micky Dolenz, Mike Nesmith, and Peter Tork (Davy Jones was also absent).

July 15

Janis Ian's "Society's Child" reached No. 14 while her debut album, *Janis Ian*, ascended to No. 29.

July 29

Jefferson Airplane's "White Rabbit," a surreal interpretation of *Alice in Wonderland* written by lead singer Grace Slick reached No. 8, becoming a million seller.

July 31

Janis Joplin played a benefit for the Free Clinic with Blue Cheer and the Charlatans (with Bill Cosby playing drums).

August 8

Joan Baez was refused permission to perform live at Constitution Hall, Washington, D.C., by the Daughters of the American Revolution because of her vehement opposition to the Vietnam War.

August 12

Aretha Franklin headlined the first New York Jazz Festival at Downing Stadium.

August 26

Thanks to the wife of the Duke of Bedford, the first British hippie pop festival was held on the grounds of her home in Woburn Abbey, England, though the festival, called the Festival of Flower Children was not what she expected, as she exclaimed in shock to a local newspaper: "I thought it was going to be a flower show, with competitions, prizes and lots of flowers."

September 3

Aretha Franklin's "Respect" topped the pop charts for two weeks and the R&B list for six, giving Aretha her second million seller.

September 23

Aretha Franklin's "A Natural Woman" was released, eventually reaching No. 8.

Notable birthdays: (September 21) Faith Hill

October 7

"Dolly Parton Day" was celebrated in Sevier County, Tennessee, where she was born as the fourth of twelve kids. Seven thousand locals attended her concert at the courthouse to celebrate her signing with RCA. She also replaced Norma Jean on *The Porter Wagoner TV Show,* to whom she had earlier sent songs to record.

The Mamas and the Papas' British tour and TV appearances were canceled when Mama Cass Elliot was jailed for a night, accused of stealing items from a hotel.

The Staples Singers charted with a cover of Buffalo Springfield's "For What It's Worth," reaching No. 66 pop.

October 14

Carla Thomas, Sam and Dave, Eddie Floyd, Otis Redding, Percy Sledge, Arthur Conley, and Booker T. and the MGs brought the Soul Explosion Tour to England, performing at Finsbury Park in Astoria, London.

Gladys Knight and the Pips' "I Heard It Through the Grapevine" was released and quickly rose to No. 2.

October 17

Cilla Black, the Beatles, Gerry Marsden of Gerry and the Pacemakers, Billy J. Kramer, and the Fourmost (all clients of Brian Epstein) attended a memorial service for Brian at the New London Synagogue.

October 21

Lulu's "To Sir with Love," which was issued simultaneously with the release of the movie, reached No. 1 today and stayed there for five weeks. It became her only million seller.

November 4

The Supremes' "In and Out of Love" (No. 9) was released today.

November 23

Aretha Franklin appeared in New York's Thanksgiving Day parade on the Lady in the Show float.

December 9

Judy Collins performed at New York's Carnegie Hall. Fourteen years earlier, at the age of thirteen, after studying classical piano in Denver, she made her public debut with the Denver Businessmen Symphony Orchestra.

December 16

Gladys Knight and the Pips reached No. 2 pop and No. 1 R&B (for six weeks) with "I Heard It Through the Grapevine," which would later become a Marvin

Gaye signature song. "Grapevine" would become Gladys' biggest of sixty-eight R&B hits, from 1961 through 1996.

December 20

Joan Baez and her mother were sentenced to forty-five days in prison for taking part in another of her countless antiwar demonstrations.

December 31

Grace Slick and Jefferson Airplane performed a New Year's Eve concert, with Janis Joplin and Big Brother and the Holding Company, at the Fillmore West.

Judy Collins guested on the New Year's Eve broadcast of *The Smothers Brothers Show*. Her early-'60s days included a regular engagement at Chicago's Gate of Horn, billed second to poet Lord Buckley.

1968

January 12

Talk about hysterical casting, an episode of TV's *Tarzan* featured the Supremes . . . as nuns!

January 20

Commemorating the death of recently deceased folksinger Woody Guthrie, Judy Collins appeared with Bob Dylan, the Band, and others in a concert at Carnegie Hall, New York,

January 22

The Supremes sang at the Talk of the Town club in London. Taking in the performance were Paul McCartney and actor Michael Cain.

Notable birthdays: (January 28) Sarah McLachlan

February 1

In the '50s, a two-sided hit was a common occurrence, though it had all but vanished in the highly competitive '60's until Dionne Warwick pulled it off with "I Say a Little Prayer," which peaked at No. 4 pop and No. 8 R&B, while its flip, "(Theme from) The Valley of the Dolls," reached No. 2 pop and No. 13 R&B. Dionne recorded the film's song at the request of the movie's female lead, Barbara Parkins.

February 3

The Supremes were so big in England that a performance they made in a London club the month before was recorded, and aired tonight as a British TV special called *The Supremes Live at the Talk of the Town*.

February 17

Janis Joplin appeared in New York for the first time, playing the Anderson Theater.

February 29

The 5th Dimension's "Up, Up and Away" demolished the competition at the tenth annual Grammy Awards, grabbing Record of the Year, Song of the Year, Best Contemporary Single, Best Performance by a Vocal Group, and Best Contemporary Group Performance, Vocal or Instrumental award categories. Aretha Franklin held her own when she won Best R&B Recording (for "Respect") and Best R&B Solo Vocal Performance, Female.

Notable birthdays: (February 1) Lisa Marie Presley, (February 12) Chynna Phillips (Wilson-Phillips, daughter of the Mamas and the Papas' Michelle Phillips)

March 8

Big Brother and the Holding company, featuring Janis Joplin, debuted at the Fillmore East, which was a converted movie theater on New York's Second Avenue. Soon after, Columbia Records would buy the group's Mainstream Records contract and sign Janis and company.

Notable birthdays: (March 11) Lisa Loeb, (March 30) Celine Dion

April 12

Dusty Springfield duetted with Jimi Hendrix on "Mockingbird" during her British TV show *It Must Be Dusty*.

April 28

The eventual trend-setting musical *Hair* debuted at New York's Biltmore Theater. Among the cast of new faces was Beverly Bremers, who went on to have the 1971 hit "Don't Say You Don't Remember" and later won the American Song Festival with her co-writer Jackie English for Jackie's hit "Morning Music."

April 30

Grace Slick and Jefferson Airplane debuted at the Kaleidoscope Club on the Sunset Strip in Los Angeles with Canned Heat.

The Cilla Black Show debuted on BBC TV in England. Her theme song, "Inside Love," was written by Paul McCartney.

Notable birthdays: (April 5) Paula Cole, (April 29) Carnie Wilson (Wilson-Phillips)

May 4

Jefferson Airplane with lead singer Grace Slick performed at the Fillmore East in New York. They went on to headline there eighteen times over the next three years.

May 5

Mary Hopkin's success with "Those Were the Days" (No. 1 U.S. and U.K.) came about thanks to famed model Twiggy, who saw the pert songstress perform on Britain's TV talent show *Opportunity Knocks,* called friend Paul McCartney, and insisted he sign her. He did, and she went on to have one of the biggest hits of the year worldwide.

May 7

Aretha Franklin made her first tour of Europe. While at the Olympia Theater in Paris, her performance was recorded for a future album.

May 8

Dusty Springfield's second TV series in two years, *It Must Be Dusty,* debuted for the first time on British television. The show ran for nine weeks.

May 11

The Raeletts entered the R&B charts with "I'm Gett'n' Long Alright," reaching No. 23. The group was originally called the Cookies and were Ray Charles' backing vocalists through the mid-'60s. Some of the outstanding vocalists in the group at various times included Merry Clayton, Clydie King (Brown Sugar), and Mabel John.

May 19

The 5th Dimension performed on *The Ed Sullivan Show,* singing "Stone Soul Picnic."

Notable birthdays: (May 6) Cynthia, (May 28) Kylie Minogue

June 17

Lulu sang with an eye patch at Issy's Club in Vancouver, Canada, due to a boating accident that morning.

June 20

The Blossoms, led by Darlene Love, began working with Elvis Presley on his first TV special in Hollywood. The Blossoms were the actual, un-credited voices on the Crystals' early '60s hits "He's a Rebel" and "He's Sure the Boy I Love."

June 28

Grace Slick and Jefferson Airplane appeared on the cover of *Life* magazine.

Grace Slick.

Three and a half years after they formed, the Mamas and the Papas members John Phillips, Cass Elliot, and Denny Doherty wrote a letter to Michelle Phillips (John's wife), firing her for the second time in three years.

June 29

Dolly Parton's RCA debut, "Just Because I'm a Woman," entered the country survey, eventually reaching No. 17. During the year, Parton became a regular on *The Grand Ole Opry.*

Cass Elliot's "Dream a Little Dream of Me" was released, rising to No. 12. It was credited as her first solo record on the Dunhill label, even though she was backed by the rest of the Mamas and the Papas.

July 25

Janis Joplin's immortal album, *Cheap Thrills,* was released, earning a gold album on just advance sales. Janis' original title and album-cover idea was to call it *Cheap Thrills, Drugs and Sex,* and she was vehemently miffed when the label vehemently opposed it.

July 26

Country singer Jeannie C. Riley was inadvertently responsible for the sale of the legendary Sun Records label, thanks to her recording on this day of "Harper Valley P. T. A." The record was the first hit for Shelby Singleton's Plantation label, selling over 2 million copies and fortifying his cash flow, enabling him to buy Sun from Sam Phillips the next year.

Notable birthdays: (June 2) Merrill Bainbridge, (June 13) Deniece Pearson (5 Star)

August 4

Grace Slick and Jefferson Airplane performed at the Newport Pop Festival in Costa Mesa, California, with Sonny and Cher, Steppenwolf, Canned Heat, the Byrds, and the Grateful Dead, among others.

August 11

Apple Records issued its first promotional releases today, including the Beatles' "Hey Jude," Mary Hopkin's "Those Were the Days," Jackie Lomax's "Sour Milk Sea," and the Black Dyke Mills Band's "Thingumybob."

August 27

Mary Hopkin's Paul McCartney-produced "Those Were the Days," based on the melody of the traditional Ukranian folksong "Darogio Dlimmoyo," was released to the general public as the first of two singles on the Beatles' Apple label in Great Britain. The other simultaneous release was the Beatles' "Hey

Jude." Hopkin was discovered by British model Twiggy when she saw the folk-singer on TV and recommended her to her friend McCartney. Her recording would sell over 8 million copies worldwide.

The Staple Singers performed at San Francisco's Fillmore West with Santana and Steppenwolf.

August 29

Grace Slick and Jefferson Airplane made their British debut appearance at the Revolution Club in London while on their first European tour, which included an appearance at the Isle of Wight Festival.

August 30

Janis Joplin performed at the Palace of Fine Arts Festival in San Francisco.

August 31

Big Brother and the Holding Company's "Piece of My Heart" tore onto the Hot 100, peaking at No. 12. It was the first chart 45 for lead singer Janis Joplin and company.

September 7

Grace Slick and Jefferson Airplane played the second of two nights at London's Roundhouse, along with the Doors.

September 15

Martha and the Vandellas performed on the initial edition of NBC-TV's music show *Soul* with Lou Rawls.

September 25

As if according to a preordained script, Mary Hopkin's "Those Were the Days" replaced the Beatles' "Hey Jude" at No. 1 in Great Britain, topping the hit list for the first of six weeks. She was the first female to hit No. 1 that year. "Days" and "Hey Jude" were released the same day on the same label, as the first two issues on the Beatles' Apple label.

September 27

Gladys Knight and the Pips, the Jackson Five, Bobby Taylor and the Vancouvers, and Shorty Long performed at a benefit for the mayor of Gary, Indiana, at the Gilroy Stadium in Gary.

September 28

Joni Mitchell, Al Stewart, and Fairport Convention performed at London's Festival Hall in "An Evening of Contemporary Song." Joni was born Roberta Joan Anderson but took her middle name and the sir name from her short-lived marriage to musician Chuck Mitchell to become Joni Mitchell in 1965.

Manager Albert Grossman announced that Janis Joplin was leaving Big Brother and the Holding Company at the end of the year.

October 8

Three months after the Mamas and the Papas disbanded, Mama Cass opened as a solo act at Caesar's Palace in Las Vegas, but collapsed with a throat hemorrhage, necessitating a major operation, thus canceling the six-week stint. She was back recording by early 1969.

Notable birthdays: (October 7) Toni Braxton

November 2

Mary Hopkin's hit "Those Were the Days" peaked at No. 2 for three weeks, unable to dislodge the Beatles' "Hey Jude" from No. 1. Mary went on to record the song in Hebrew, Italian, French, Spanish, and German. By early 1969, the worldwide sales topped 8 million copies.

November 17

Jennifer Warnes, billed as Jennifer Warren, made her first appearance on *The Smothers Brothers Comedy Hour,* singing with folk hit-maker Donovan.

November 19

The Supremes performed at the Royal Variety Show in London before Queen Elizabeth.

November 25

The 5th Dimension performed on the TV special *Francis Albert Sinatra Does His Thing.*

Notable birthdays: (November 28) Dawn Robinson (En Vogue)

December 6

Janis Joplin made her last appearance with Big Brother and the Holding Company as their tour ended in Hawaii.

December 15

Grace Slick appeared wearing blackface during Jefferson Airplane's performance of "Crown of Creation" on *The Smothers Brothers* TV show.

December 18

Yoko Ono and John Lennon staged a performance at the Royal Albert Hall in London wearing a large white paper bag.

December 21

Janis Joplin performed at the Stax/Volt convention in Memphis for the first time with her new band, the Kozmic Blues Band.

Judy Collins' exquisite version of Joni Mitchell's "Both Sides Now" became her biggest single, reaching No. 8 today.

December 28

Judy Collins' *Wildflowers* album, made up of her own compositions along with interpretations of songs by Jacques Brel, Brecht/Weill, and new writers Joni Mitchell and Randy Newman, reached No. 5 after fifty-two weeks on the chart and would become the biggest of her sixteen hit albums through 1982.

The third major rock/pop festival, and first on the East Coast, was held in Miami, Florida. Known as the Miami Pop Festival, many of the acts were really folk artists such as Buffy Sainte-Marie and Ian and Sylvia. The rock and pop side were represented by Joni Mitchell, the Turtles, the Grateful Dead, Chuck Berry, the Box Tops, Iron Butterfly, Joe Tex, and Marvin Gaye.

1969

January 3

New Jersey police were having a field day confiscating over 30,000 copies of John and Yoko's *Two Virgins* album, justifying it by stating the nude cover was pornographic. The highlight (or lowlight, depending on how you looked at it) was a full-frontal nude photo of the couple. The LPs were only allowed in the U. S. after the record label agreed to wrap them in plain brown paper.

January 4

Dolly Parton became a member of the Grand Ole Opry. She made her debut at the Opry in 1958 at the age of twelve. Dolly was originally a drummer for her Sevier County High School marching band.

February 1

Joni Mitchell made her debut at Carnegie Hall in New York. In 1967, she'd moved to Los Angeles to record an album produced by David Crosby, who had discovered her singing at Coconut Grove, Florida's Gaslight Club.

February 15

Vickie Jones was arrested on fraud charges after impersonating Aretha Franklin at a concert in Fort Myers, Florida. Apparently the charade was impressive. No one in the audience asked for their money back.

March 3

The Post Card album by Mary Hopkin was issued in America, ten days after its U.K. release and with one cut the British album didn't contain, a song that would go on to be a worldwide No. 1 hit, "Those Were the Days."

March 7

Gladys Knight and the Pips performed in Amsterdam, Holland, at the Grand Gala du Disque, along with British legends the Moody Blues.

March 8

Featuring Florence LaRue and Marilyn McCoo, the 5th Dimension's "Aquarius/Let the Sun Shine" charted, becoming the group's first No. 1 and ninth hit single in two years.

March 12

Dionne Warwick won Best Contemporary Pop Vocal Performance, Female at the eleventh annual Grammy Awards with "Do You Know the Way to San Jose."

Linda Eastman and Paul McCartney were married at the Maryleybone Register Office in London. The reception guests included Princess Margaret, Lord Snowdon, and George Harrison.

March 15

Rolling Stone magazine decimated Janis Joplin's Fillmore concerts with the cover story "Janis: The Judy Garland of Rock?"

March 18

Janis Joplin appeared on *The Ed Sullivan Show.*

March 21

Mary Hopkin began her first British tour with headliner Engelbert Humperdink at the Gaumont Cinema in Worcester, England.

March 29

Connie Francis' "The Wedding Cake" (No. 91) was her final of fifty-six chart singles in just twelve years. It was taken from her last album of the decade, *The Wedding Cake*. She continued to headline on the nightclub circuit, along with doing charity shows, notably with UNICEF, and entertaining U.S. troops in Vietnam.

April 12

The 5th Dimension's "Aquarius/Let the Sun Shine In" topped the pop charts for six weeks while reaching No. 6 R&B. It became their biggest hit, selling over three million copies, two million of those in just three months. Producer Bones Howe saw the separate songs performed in the Broadway show *Hair* and joined the two tracks together, with the group adding their vocals while performing in Las Vegas with Frank Sinatra.

Country artist Lynn Anderson's *With Love from Lynn* album hit the pop charts today (No. 197). It was her first of ten Top 200 LPs through 1973.

April 14

The Clara Ward Singers, along with a load of stars, including Little Richard, Fats Domino, Buddy Miles, and Jerry Lee Lewis performed on the NBC-TV special hosted by the Monkees, *33 1/3 Revolutions per Monkee*.

April 16

The 5th Dimension's "Aquarius/Let the Sun Shine In" charted in England, on its way to No. 11. The original American release, which was shortened for radio play and which omitted most of "Aquarius," was accidentally issued in England. The radio edit became the British hit and was never corrected!

April 18

Lulu married Maurice Gibb of the Bee Gees at Gerrards Cross in Bucks, England. The best man was his Bee Gees brother Robin.

April 19

Mary Hopkin's "Goodbye," written and produced by Paul McCartney, reached

No. 19 in America and No. 2 in Great Britain. Hopkin soon met her future husband, record producer Tony Visconti, while recording foreign-language versions of the song. By 1972, her solo career seemingly over, she would be recording with the group Hobby Horse.

April 21

Janis Joplin performed at London's famed Royal Albert Hall.

April 22

The Carpenters signed with A&M Records. Two years earlier, they had recorded as part of a group called Spectrum, who recorded eleven sides for RCA, though they were never released.

April 26

Dorothy Morrison and the Edwin Hawkins Singers hit the pop charts with the pure gospel song "Oh Happy Day," which broke all barriers on its way to No. 4 and million selling status.

May 1

Joni Mitchell appeared on ABC-TV's *The Johnny Cash Show* that would air on June 7. She wrote her first song at age twenty-one, a blues number, "Day After Day," on her way to perform at the Mariposa Folk Festival in Ontario, Canada, in 1964.

May 24

Marianne Faithfull's home in London (which she occupied with Mick Jagger) was raided by British bobbies, who promptly arrested the couple for marijuana possession. When the smoke cleared (literally), they were released on a £50 bond each.

The Emotions charted with "So I Can Love You," their debut disc on both the pop (No. 39) and R&B (No. 3) charts. The trio of Hutchinson sisters went on to have thirty R&B hits through 1984.

Notable birthdays: (May 18) Martika

June 13

Trumpeted as the biggest-ever soul music festival to date, Aretha Franklin, Clara Ward, the Staple Singers, Sam and Dave, along with Ray Charles, Percy Sledge, Reverend James Cleveland, Johnny "Guitar" Watson, and more performed at Soul Bowl '69 at the Houston Astrodome.

June 21

Pop-rock trio the City had its first single, "Why Are You Leaving," released. (The lead singer was Carole King.)

June 22

Ike and Tina Turner and the Impressions performed at the Fillmore West in San Francisco, a venue known for hosting mostly rock bands.

Legendary entertainer Judy Garland died of a drug overdose.

July 5

Comedienne Moms Mabley charted with her version of "Abraham, Martin and John," reaching No. 18 R&B and No. 35 pop. Probably the oldest artist to ever have a hit that wasn't posthumous, Moms was seventy-five years old at the time.

July 8

Marianne Faithfull was discovered in a coma caused by an overdose on the Australian set of the film *Ned Kelly,* in which she was to co-star with Mick Jagger. She was sent to a hospital for treatment of heroin addiction and promptly fired from the movie.

July 22

Aretha Franklin was arrested and fined $50 for creating a disturbance in a Detroit parking lot. The "Queen of Soul" was so upset that upon leaving, she ran over a road sign.

July 26

Bill Davis and Marilyn McCoo of the 5th Dimension married, a week after their tenth pop hit, "Workin' on a Groovy Thing," charted (No. 20 pop, No. 15 R&B). Marilyn had originally been in a group called the Hi Fi's, where two of its members later formed the Friends of Distinction. Billy was originally with a St. Louis doo-wop group called the Versatiles.

Dionne Warwick charted two albums: *Odds and Ends* (No. 43, 1969) and *No Night So Long,* (No. 23, 1980), the same day, eleven years apart.

August 1

Grace Slick and Jefferson Airplane, Joni Mitchell, and Janis Joplin, among others, performed at the Atlantic City Pop Festival in Atlantic City, New Jersey, in front of an audience in excess of 110,000.

August 3

Janis Joplin sang a duet with Little Richard at the Atlantic City Pop Festival.

August 11

Diana Ross invited 350 guests to the Daisy Club in Beverly Hills to unveil her new discovery, the Jackson Five.

August 15

The Woodstock Festival began its first of three memorable days of concerts amid torrential rains. Females were well represented at that historic gathering as Melanie, Janis Joplin, Joan Baez, and Grace Slick of Jefferson Airplane performed.

August 16

Melanie performed at the now-legendary Woodstock Festival in Bethel, New York, during a rainstorm. She was so moved by the audience appreciation that the experience inspired her to write her hit "Lay Down (Candles in the Rain)."

The Supremes performed at the Great Western forum in Inglewood, California, with the Jackson Five, who were making their performance debut as a Motown group. Though the press releases touted Diana Ross as the one who discovered of the group, it was actually Gladys Knight who first saw them perform and alerted Motown's Berry Gordy Jr.

August 17

The Woodstock Festival ended. Performers included Janis Joplin, Joan Baez, Jefferson Airplane, Crosby, Stills and Nash, Sha Na Na, John Sebastian, Joe Cocker, Santana, Richie Havens, Blood, Sweat and Tears, Iron Butterfly, and Creedence Clearwater Revival. Over a half a million people attended, three died, two were born, and their were six miscarriages. Not bad for $7.00!

August 18

Joni Mitchell appeared on Dick Cavett's TV talk show. Because of that scheduled appearance, her agent, David Geffen, had convinced her to pull out of her planned performance at the Woodstock Festival. In tribute to the monumental event, she then wrote the hit "Woodstock."

August 30

A major pop festival Texas-style was held in Lewisville, drawing over 120,000 people for the three-day doings that encompassed fifteen acts, including Janis

Joplin, Rotary Connection (with Minnie Ripperton), Delaney and Bonnie, Chicago, Led Zeppelin, Sam and Dave, Santana, and Grand Funk Railroad.

September 20

Janis Joplin performed at the Hollywood Bowl in Los Angeles.

September 21

The 5th Dimension performed on the *Woody Allen TV Special* on CBS.

Notable birthdays: (September 6) Ce Ce Penniston, (September 29) Jennifer Rush

October 4

"You've Lost That Lovin' Feelin'," a remake of the Righteous Brothers hit by Dionne Warwick charted, reaching No. 13 R&B and No. 16 pop.

October 18

Ella Fitzgerald's album *Ella* scratched the Top 200 (No. 196), becoming her last of eleven chart LPs. She went on to become the most honored jazz vocalist in history.

October 25

Gladys Knight and the Pips' "Friendship Train" (No. 17 pop, No. 2 R&B) became their lucky thirteenth of sixty-six pop charters, from 1961 through 1994.

Notable birthdays: (October 3) Gwen Stefani, (October 12) Martie Macquire (Dixie Chicks), (October 16) Wendy Wilson (Wilson-Phillips)

November 7

Ike and Tina Turner were the opening act on a Rolling Stones tour that started in Denver.

November 8

The Supremes' swan song as an entity including Diana Ross, "Someday, We'll Be Together," was the last of the group's twelve No. 1s. However, it was technically not the Supremes at all. Diana wound up recording the song with the vocal-backing professionals the Waters, along with Johnny Bristol on bass.

November 14

Petula Clark's *An Evening with Petula* aired, becoming the first BBC-1 show to be transmitted in color in England.

November 15

Janis Joplin was arrested while performing in Tampa, Florida, for arguing with a policeman and refusing to request that the audience sit down (tough cops in Florida!).

November 16

Janis Joplin was charged with two counts of using vulgar and obscene language during a show at Curtis Hall in Tampa, Florida.

November 22

Jazz diva Nina Simone charted with "To Be Young, Gifted and Black," which obviously had a more receptive audience among R&B listeners as it reached No. 8 R&B while only making it to No. 76 pop. Nina's first chart single ten years earlier was the passionate "I Loves You, Porgy," which reached No. 2 R&B and was from George Gershwin's *Porgy and Bess*.

November 26

Grace Slick and Jefferson Airplane performed at the Fillmore East, with Slick dressed as Hitler and actor Rip Torn guesting as Richard Nixon.

November 27

Janis Joplin and Tina Turner sang together at the Rolling Stones concert in Madison Square Garden.

November 29

Jane Birkin and Serge Gainsbourg charted in America with the French song "Je T'Aime . . . Moi Non Plus" (No. 58), a sexual recording banned on many stations worldwide, yet it managed to reach No. 1 in England.

December 13

Mariska Veres and her band, Shocking Blue, hurtled onto the Hot 100 with "Venus," which would become the first Dutch group No. 1 on the American hit list.

December 15

Yoko Ono and hubby, John Lennon, performed the "War Is Over" concert at the Lyceum Theater in London, along with Delaney and Bonnie.

December 21

Diana Ross and the Supremes made their final TV appearance together when they performed "Someday We'll Be Together" on *The Ed Sullivan Show.*

More Moments in 1969

Guitarist June Millington and her sister, Jean, found the band Fanny this year—the first all-girl rock band to be signed to a major record label! They only had two hits—"Charity Ball," in 1971, and "Butter Boy," in 1975—peaking at No. 40 and No. 29, respectively.

"*Janis Joplin was absolutely a barnstormer and a complete groundbreaker. She wasn't just a great woman in rock—at the time she was* the *woman in rock. Janis really created this whole world of possibility for women in music: Without Janis Joplin, there would be no Melissa Etheridge. Without Janis, there would be no Chrissie Hynde, no Gwen Stefani. There would be no one. . . . She was a very fierce, very beautiful bright light that burned out way, way too quickly.*" —Rosanne Cash

THE CYNICAL SEVENTIES

On the positive side, the seventies featured the end of the Vietnam War, the Supreme Court ruling that states cannot deny women the opportunity to serve on a jury, and the introduction, in 1973, of airport passenger screenings to prevent hijackings (there were twenty-nine in 1972, none after screenings began that year). On the negative side, we had the Arab oil embargo that created an energy crisis, polyester clothes, and President Nixon's

> *"Onstage I make love to 25,000 people, then I go home alone."*
> —*Janis Joplin*

dangerous and costly attempt at creating a dictatorship, which culminated with the Watergate scandal. Depending on whether you considered it a positive or a negative, the biggest thing in music was disco, and seemingly everyone got on the 112-beats-per-minute bandwagon. Women contributed greatly as Vicki Sue Robinson, Taste of Honey, Gloria Gaynor, Freda Payne, Evelyn "Champagne" King, and queen of disco Donna Summer all took old and new songs in a disco direction. Even porn star Andrea True stripped down to the hypnotic, basic-drum-and-bass rhythm with a Top 5 hit, "More, More, More" (How Do You Like It?)."

Rock 'n' roll and pop-rock acts dominated as Carly Simon, Janis Joplin (until her untimely death), ABBA, Blondie, Fanny, Heart, Bette Midler, Bonnie Raitt, Bonnie Tyler, Nicolette Larson, Suzy Quatro (who played Leather Tuscadero on TV's *Happy Days*), and the across-the-

> *"I think it's an asset to a performer to be sexually attractive."*
> — *Carly Simon*

board favorite Joni Mitchell gave the public what it wanted. So, too, did a militant version of rock 'n' roll known as punk rock, with its foremost female exponent being the gaunt, toothpick-like punk poet Patti Smith.

Pure pop still had its influence, including Captain and Tennille, Debby Boone, Beverly Bremers, Kim Carnes, Rita Coolidge, Vicky Lawrence, Mary MacGregor, Melanie, Melissa Manchester, Maureen McGovern, and three of the decade's biggest female stars—Helen Reddy, Olivia Newton-John, and the Carpenter's Karen Carpenter.

> *"I'd rather have ten years of super-hyper most than live to be seventy by sitting in some god-damn chair watching TV."*
> —*Janis Joplin*

There may have been an energy crisis, but there was no lack of energy in the dominating R&B genre, where Natalie Cole, the Emotions, Thelma Houston (Whitney's mother), the bawdy Millie Jackson, Chaka Khan, Stephanie Mills, the exciting Pointer Sisters, Candy Staton, and Sister Sledge kept the fans fueled all decade long, even if their cars' gas tanks read empty. Carryovers from the '60s, such as Diana Ross, Aretha Franklin, Labelle (formerly Patti LaBelle and the Blue-Belles), and Gladys Knight made R&B a continually strong force in popular music. A more sophisticated style of R&B fused with jazz was delivered by acts like Roberta Flack, Rikki Lee Jones, Manhattan Transfer, and Melba Moore.

> *"There are moods I'm in when I can't stand to listen to some of my own music."*
> —*Joni Mitchell*

While the country was riding the roller coaster of economic recession and political change (highlighted by President Nixon's resignation), country music was in anything but a recession as Barbara Mandrell, Lynn Anderson, Debby Boone, Sammi Smith, Crystal Gayle, Donna Fargo, Emmylou Harris, Loretta Lynn, Anne Murray, Marie Osmond, Tanya Tucker, and the one-of-a-kind Dolly Parton kept music sales booming and women in the forefront of tours, TV, and recordings. Tammy Wynette's huge '60s success carried over to the '70s, illustrating country fans' loyalty to their artists.

A decade that reached new musical heights, the 1970s also reached a new low in the cynicism of politics and politicians. Throughout, the female creative community would make its very vocal commentary as well as artistic contributions.

1970

January 3

The 5th Dimension, featuring Marilyn McCoo and Florence LaRue, reached the Top 100 with "Blowing Away" (No. 21), their fourth hit from the *Age of Aquarius* album.

January 14

Diana Ross performed in her last show as a Supreme at Las Vegas' Frontier Hotel. She would go on to have a hugely successful solo career, encompassing forty-one hits through 1986.

January 23

Judy Collins, testifying at the trial of the "Chicago Seven," was denied permission to sing her testimony!

February 14

The Carpenters' "Ticket to Ride" charted. Though it only reached No. 54, it was the first of twenty-nine pop charters for the brother-sister team over the next twelve years.

February 17

In the shortest severance of a career on record, Joni Mitchell announced onstage at London's Royal Albert Hall that she was retiring. Even by music industry standards, it was brief since . . . it never happened. She'd gotten her musical start only eight years earlier, when she learned how to play from a Pete Seeger teach-yourself record on her $36 baritone ukulele.

February 27

Grace Slick and Jefferson Airplane were fined $1,000 for obscenity in Oklahoma City.

March 8

Diana Ross made her solo debut in Framingham, Massachusetts, after leaving the Supremes.

March 11

Joni Mitchell won the Best Folk Performance Award for "Clouds" at the twelfth annual Grammy Awards. The 5th Dimension's "Aquarius/Let the Sun Shine In" won the Best Contemporary Vocal Performance by a Group and Record of the Year categories.

March 14

Brooklyn-born Bobbi Martin, who toured the Far East with Bob Hope's Christmas shows, charted with "For the Love of Him" (No. 13). It was her biggest of five Top 100 singles.

March 16

Tammi Terrell, who had ten chart hit duets with Marvin Gaye, died of a brain tumor onstage, in Marvin's arms. She was only twenty-three.

Notable birthdays: (March 9) Roxanne Shante, (March 18) Queen Latifah, (March 27) Mariah Carey

April 2

Janis Joplin got a tattoo over her heart that read: "One for the boys."

April 4

Janis Joplin reunited with Big Brother and the Holding Company for a concert at San Francisco's Fillmore West.

April 13

Dionne Warwick performed at London's Royal Albert Hall.

April 18

The "New" Supremes, with Jean Terrell replacing Diana Ross, reached No. 10 pop and No. 5 R&B with their first release, "Up the Ladder to the Roof."

April 25

Diana Ross touched the Hot 100 with "Reach Out and Touch (Somebody's Hand)." It reached No. 20 and was her first solo success since leaving the Supremes.

June 13

Joni Mitchell, who charted today, struck it big in England when "Big Yellow Taxi" eventually reached No. 11 while its companion album, *Ladies of the*

Canyon, peaked at No. 8. It would turn out to be her only chart single in Great Britain.

The Three Degrees chart debut, "Maybe," reached No. 4 R&B and No. 29 pop. The recording was a remake of the Chantels' 1958 standard.

June 20

The *Andy Williams Presents Ray Stevens* NBC-TV show premiered with regular guests Mama Cass Elliot and Lulu.

The Carpenters' "Close to You" charted, en route to No. 1.

June 27

Grace Slick and Jefferson Airplane headlined the Bath Festival of Blues and Progressive Music at the Royal County Fairgrounds in Shepton Mallet, Somerset, England, with Led Zeppelin.

July 12

Janis Joplin played her first show with her last group, the Full Tilt Boogie Band, in Louisville, Kentucky.

"I was demanding of myself a deeper and greater honesty, more and more revelation in my work in order to give it back to the people, where it goes into their lives and nourishes them and changes their direction and makes light bulbs go off in their head and makes them feel."—Joni Mitchell

July 18

Canadian songbird Anne Murray charted with "Snowbird" (No. 8). It was her first of twenty-eight U.S. hits through 1986, along with fifty-four country winners.

July 25

Dawn's "Candida" charted (No. 3 pop), becoming their first of twenty-five Top 100 hits.

The Carpenters' "(They Long to Be) Close to You," a little-known Bacharach/David composition recorded by Dionne Warwick seven years earlier, reached No. 1 for the first of four weeks. In 1968, the duo, then a soft-pop foursome known as Spectrum, actually was the opening act for hard rockers Steppenwolf!

Notable birthdays: (July 24) Jennifer Lopez

August 2

Janis Joplin played a concert in Forest Hills, New York.

August 8

Having released her maiden solo album, *Christine Perfect,* in June, Perfect flew to the U.S. to join Fleetwood Mac, after announcing that she was quitting the music business for good. (She was voted Britain's *Melody Maker*'s [magazine] Female Vocalist of the Year in 1969 and would subsequently go under the surname McVie, having married John.) Obviously Christine McVie's retirement was short lived.

Janis Joplin bought a headstone for the grave of Bessie Smith, whom she considered her greatest influence. Bessie died in 1937, when she was refused admission to a hospital for whites only.

August 12

Janis Joplin gave her last performance at Harvard Stadium in Cambridge, Massachusetts.

August 26

Joni Mitchell and Joan Baez were among numerous superstars who performed at the third annual Isle of Wight festival, including the Doors, the Who, the Moody Blues, and Chicago.

August 27

Pop group Tomorrow (put together by record producer Don Kirshner) had a musical-comedy film, also titled *Tomorrow,* open in theaters throughout Great Britain, and RCA simultaneously released a soundtrack album by the group. Both failed miserably despite intense promotion. One of the members was twenty-one-year-old Olivia Newton-John. Soon after, the quintet of four guys and Olivia disbanded.

August 29

Joni Mitchell performed on the fourth day of the famous Isle of Wight Festival. During her set, to her amazement and amusement, a man jumped onstage and yelled, "This is just a hippie concentration camp."

August 30

Thirteen days after performing at the historic Woodstock Festival, Joan Baez played the final day of the Isle of Wight Pop Festival.

Notable birthdays: (August 25) Jo Dee Messina, (August 31) Debbie Gibson

September 1

Blondie, led by Deborah Harry, signed with Chrysalis Records, which, in an unusual move, bought their contract from Larry Uttal's Private Stock label.

September 12

Joan Baez, among others, performed at the Woody Guthrie Memorial Concert at L.A.'s Hollywood Bowl.

September 14

Syreeta Wright married Stevie Wonder. Syreeta, previously a secretary at Motown Record, would have the hit "With You I'm Born Again" (No. 4), in 1980, with Billy Preston.

September 19

Diana Ross' "Ain't No Mountain High Enough" reached No. 1 and became her first chart topper without the Supremes. It was originally a hit (No. 19) in 1967 for Tammi Terrell and Marvin Gaye.

September 25

The Partridge Family TV show, featuring Shirley Jones, debuted on ABC. It ran for ninety-six episodes through September 1974 and was modeled on the real-life vocal group the Cowsills.

Notable birthdays: (September 9) Macy Gray

October 3

Janis Joplin listened to the final track to be included on her album *Pearl.* She planned to record her vocals the next day on that song, titled "Buried Alive in the Blues." It never happened. (See October 4).

October 4

Alone in her room at the Landmark Hotel in Los Angeles at 1:40 a.m., Janis Joplin died of a drug overdose combined with alcohol. Janis was only twenty-seven years old.

October 10

The Carpenters' "(They Long to Be) Close to You" peaked at No. 6 in Britain. It was already No. 1 Stateside. In 1968, the duo, as part of Spectrum, were playing one-off gigs at the local Troubadour and Whisky a Go-Go clubs in Los Angeles.

October 25

During the month, Joan Baez would co-organize and perform at the Big Sur Folk Festival in Big Sur, California, along with Linda Ronstadt, the Beach Boys, Kris Kristofferson, and Country Joe McDonald.

October 31

Michelle Phillips, formerly of the Mamas and the Papa's and just divorced from Papa John Phillips, married actor Dennis Hopper. The happily married couple lasted through eight days of wedded bliss.

Notable birthdays: (October 31) Linn Berggren (Ace of Base)

November 14

Gladys Knight and the Pips' "If I Were Your Woman" (No. 9) was released on this day.

November 26

Pearl Bailey, Dionne Warwick, and the Supremes appeared on the Andy Williams NBC-TV special.

December 5

Judy Collins' recording of "Amazing Grace" charted in England, reaching No. 5. That was not the most impressive aspect of her ride up the charts. The amazing part was that it charted another seven times through 1972 and spent a total of sixty-seven weeks in the British Top 50.

1971

January 9

The Supremes and the Four Tops (thanks to the incredible Motown marketing machine) reached No. 14 pop and No. 7 R&B with a competent (though lesser by comparison) remake of the Tina Turner classic "River Deep, Mountain High."

January 25

Grace Slick of Starship gave birth to a baby girl. She toyed with the idea of calling the child "God" before opting for the only slightly less awesome name of China.

Notable birthdays: (January 11) Mary J. Blige

February 20

Helen Reddy reached the Top 100 today with "I Don't Know How to Love Him" from the rock opera *Jesus Christ, Superstar.* It was the first of twenty-one hits for the Australian vocalist.

Notable birthdays: (February 26) Erykah Badu, (February 27) Rozonda "Chilli" Thomas (TLC)

March 5

Aretha Franklin and Ray Charles performed at the Fillmore West, along with King Curtis and His Orchestra. The performance was captured on a seminal (and essential) recording, *Live at Fillmore West.*

March 16

Dionne Warwick earned her second Grammy for Best Contemporary Vocal Performance, Female, for her rendition of "I'll Never Fall in Love Again."

March 27

Ike and Tina Turner's raucous remake of Creedence Clearwater Revival's

"Proud Mary" reached No. 4 pop and No. 5 R&B, giving the tempestuous duo their first Top 5 hit.

Kiki Dee had her first American charter with "Love Makes the World Go Round" (No. 87). The Yorkshire, England, rocker went on to have five more through 1993, including the No. 1 duet with Elton John, "Don't Go Breaking My Heart."

April 3

Margie Joseph debuted on the charts with her revision of the Supremes' "Stop! In the Name of Love" (No. 96). Six years earlier to the day, the Supremes version was No. 1.

April 17

"Want Ads" by the Honey Cone charted, on its way to No. 1 pop and R&B. The female trio from Los Angeles consisted of a former Ikette, a former member of Bob B. Soxx and the Blue Jeans, and the sister of Blue Jeans/Blossoms lead singer Darlene Love.

Aretha Franklin's "Bridge over Troubled Waters" charted, on it's way to No. 1 R&B and No. 6 pop. Writer Paul Simon had previously stated that he wrote the song with Aretha in mind, though Simon and Garfunkel had the original hit a year earlier.

Carly Simon's mesmerizing "That's the Way I've Always Heard It Should Be" charted, eventually reaching No. 10. It became the first of twenty-three hits through 1989 for the daughter of Richard Simon of the Simon and Schuster publishing empire.

April 24

Her debut album, *Carly Simon,* entered the pop chart, eventually reaching No. 30. Carly's career took off after she met Bob Dylan's manager, Albert Grossman, who wanted to turn her into a female Dylan. Simon went on to have twenty-five hits through 2001.

May 1

Carole King's "It's Too Late" was released today. The multimillion-selling single would reach No. 1 for five weeks.

May 8

Ronnie Spector breached the Hot 100 with "Try Some, Buy Some" (No. 77), produced by George Harrison and Phil Spector. It was her only chart 45 without the Ronettes.

May 13

Grace Slick crashed her Mercedes into a wall near the Golden Gate Bridge in San Francisco and was briefly hospitalized.

May 29

Olivia Newton-John jumped on the Hot 100 with "If Not for You," her first of thirty-eight hits through 1992.

June 6

Gladys Knight and the Pips were the last pop act to appear on *The Ed Sullivan Show.*

June 12

Roberta Flack first charted with "You've Got a Friend" (No. 29). She reached the Top 100 a total of eighteen times over the next twenty years.

June 19

Carole King's double A-side "Its Too Late/I Feel the Earth" peaked at No. 1, beginning a five-week run at the top. Its parent LP, the now-legendary *Tapestry* album, also reached No. 1. It would remain there for fifteen weeks, including a 302-week chart ride, and would eventually sell over 15 million copies worldwide.

June 26

Country artist Jody Miller slid onto the pop charts with her version of the Chiffons' hit "He's So Fine" (No. 53). Her arrangement of the song was similar to George Harrison's "My Sweet Lord," which was a plagiarized version of "He's So Fine."

July 10

Carly Simon's hauntingly exquisite ballad "That's the Way I've Always Heard It Should Be" peaked at No. 10. Carly and her older sister, Lucy, started as a singing duo, the Simon Sisters, playing the college and folk club circuit, including New York's Bitter End and Gaslight. The were "discovered" at the Bitter End by record prexy Dave Kapp. They had a minor hit (U.S. No. 73) in 1964 with "Winkin' Blinkin' and Nod," which was based on a children's song.

July 17

Agnetha Faltskog married Bjorn Ulvaeus in Verum, Sweden. Less then three years later, they would have their first hit, "Waterloo," as half of the internationally successful ABBA.

July 24

Carole King's landmark *Tapestry* album, already No. 1 in America for five weeks, entered the British chart and would reach No. 4 (on September 4) while having a ninety-week chart run. At about this time, Carole became the first pop artist to perform at New York's traditionally classical Philharmonic Hall at Lincoln Center.

Notable birthdays: (July 1) Missy Elliott, (July 23) Allison Krause

August 1

The Sonny and Cher Comedy Hour began its run on CBS-TV today. It would run for sixty-one episodes through May 1974.

August 14

Joan Baez stunned the pop world when the folk protest singer charted with "The Night They Drove Old Dixie Down" and ascended to No. 3. Her pop efforts before and after never rose higher than No. 35.

August 17

Five months after they performed together at San Francisco's Fillmore West, Aretha Franklin was singing at the funeral of King Curtis, who had been murdered on a street corner four days earlier. Also joining Aretha in prayer and song were Cissy Houston and Stevie Wonder.

August 21

Diana Ross reached No. 1 with "I'm Still Waiting" in England, though the single wasn't well received in America, reaching only No. 40 R&B and No. 63 pop.

Grace Slick was sprayed with mace when a scuffle ensued, after the Jefferson Airplane's equipment manager called police "pigs" during a show at the Rubber Bowl in Akron, Ohio.

August 23

Diana Ross hit No. 1 in England with "I'm Still Waiting," her first British solo chart topper.

August 30

Olivia Newton-John appeared on BBC1-TV, performing in Cliff Richard's holiday special (the closest thing to Elvis that Britain had), *Getaway with*

Cliff. Cliff's original backup group, the Shadows, included Bruce Welch, who Olivia met in 1966 at a concert in Bournemouth, England. He offered her the chance to star in Cliff Richard and the Shadows' London Palladium pantomime *Cinderella.* She turned him down in order to return to Australia for Christmas, but wound up moving in with him two years later.

September 18

Cher jumped on the hit list with "Gypsies, Tramps and Thieves," an eventual No. 1. Among the superstar's quirks: she demanded a separate security room for her wigs backstage for concerts.

September 22

Grace Slick and Jefferson Airplane's tour ended at Winterland. It turned out to be the last Jefferson Airplane performance for seventeen years. (The band would, however, make six more albums before disbanding in 1978.)

October 2

Joan Baez's recording of the Band's Civil War song "The Night They Drove Old Dixie Down" was a surprise pop hit, reaching #3, becoming a million seller. It was taken from *Blessed Are,* her thirteenth Top 100 album for Vanguard Records, giving Joan her first Top 15 album in six years as it rose to No. 11.

October 16

The Carpenters' hit "Superstar" reached No. 2. The song was heard by Richard Carpenter via a Bette Midler performance on NBC-TV's *The Tonight Show.*

October 30

Melanie leaped onto the singles survey with "Brand New Key," a runaway No. 1 hit. Misinterpretations of its overtly innocent lyrics caused the song to be banned by numerous radio stations.

Notable birthdays: (October 2) Tiffany (aka Tiffany Darwish)

November 6

Joan Baez's American hit "The Night They Drove Dixie Down" rose to No. 6 in England.

November 11

BBC-TV in London celebrated it 400th show with performances by Cher, Cilla Black, Clodagh Rogers, and Dana, along with Tom Jones and the Newbeats.

November 27

The nine-member, female-dominated vocal group the Hillside Singers, featuring Lorri Marsters Hamm, bounced onto the Hot 100 with "I'd Like to Teach the World to Sing" (No. 13). The hit was known more for its worldwide exposure as a Coke commercial than for its hit status.

December 2

Martha and the Vandellas played their farewell concert at the Cobo Hall in Detroit. Martha Reeves then went on to a solo career while her sister, Lois, joined the soul group Quiet Elegance.

December 11

Brenda Lee Eager and Jerry Butler's duet "Ain't Understanding Mellow" charted, reaching No. 3 R&B (No. 21 pop). It was Brenda's first and biggest hit of six charters (four of them with Butler). Brenda, who was discovered in a Chicago choir run by the Reverend Jesse Jackson, would go on to become a member of his backing group, the Peaches.

December 18

Beverly Bremers' "Don't Say You Don't Remember" ascended the singles survey, on its way to No. 15.

December 25

In an unusual recording move, LaBelle did all the backup vocals on Laura Nyro's album *It's Gonna Take a Miracle*, which was a collection of doo-wop and rock 'n' roll standards, including "Desiree," "The Wind," "I Met Him on a Sunday," "You've Really Got a Hold on Me," and the title song. The album reached No. 46 pop and No. 41 R&B. Nyro, best known as a composer and lyricist, wrote a string of hits for artists including the 5th Dimension ("Wedding Bell Blues," "Stoned Soul Picnic"), Blood, Sweat and Tears ("And When I Die"), and Barbra Streisand ("Stoney End").

Melanie's "Brand New Key" reached No. 1 and stayed there for three weeks. She originally wrote the song as a simple ditty for use in between songs at concerts. It took her all of fifteen minutes to create it.

The Staples Singers reached No. 12 pop and No. 2 R&B with "Respect Yourself" their breakthrough hit 45.

1972

January 23

Big Maybelle (Mabel Smith) died in Cleveland, Ohio. The blues singer weighted in at 260 pounds, with a heroin addiction of mammoth proportions. Best known for her 1953 hits "Gabbin' Blues" and "My Country Man," the portly pianist/vocalist passed on at age forty-eight.

January 27

Mahalia Jackson, the giant of gospel music, died at age sixty-one of heart failure.

February 1

Aretha Franklin sang "Take My Hand, Precious Lord" at the funeral of her mentor and old friend Mahalia Jackson in Chicago.

February 12

Carly Simon's "Anticipation" peaked at No. 13. It was taken from her second album of the same name, which was recorded at Morgan Studios in Willesden, North London.

February 26

The Carpenters' "Hurting Each Other," originally recorded by Ruby and the Romantics, rose to No. 2.

March 9

Barbra Streisand and Carole King performed at a benefit for presidential candidate George McGovern at the Great Western Forum in Inglewood, California. Acting as ushers were Mama Cass, Carly Simon, and actresses Julie Christie and Britt Eckland.

March 14

Carly Simon won the Best New Artist category, and Aretha Franklin received the Best R&B Vocal Performance, Female, trophy for "Bridge over Troubled Waters" at the fourteenth annual Grammy Awards.

April 15

Roberta Flack's "The First Time Ever I Saw Your Face" reached No. 1 and stayed there for six weeks. It was the longest-running No. 1 by a female solo artist since Gogi Grant's "The Wayward Wind" in 1956.

May 6

Carly Simon's powerful "Legend in Your Own Time" reached only No. 50 pop. It was tons better than its promotion.

Notable birthdays: (May 19) Jenny Berggren (Ace of Base), (May 21) Angelica

June 2

Shirley and Lee, the Exciters, Lloyd Price, Little Richard, Danny and the Juniors, and a reunited Dion and the Belmonts performed a rock 'n' roll spectacular at New York's Madison Square Garden.

June 3

The Staples Singers had their first of two No. 1 pop hits and three No. 1 R&B smashes when "I'll Take You There" reached the top spot today. Nineteen years later, lead singer Mavis Staples would have a hit with it, this time as the lead, with Bebe and Cece Winans, reaching No. 1 R&B once again.

July 15

Martha and the Vandellas charted with "Tear It Down" (No. 37), their last of twenty-four R&B hits over nine years.

August

Notable birthdays: (August 6) Geri Halliwell (Ginger Spice of the Spice Girls), (August 16) Emily Erwin (the Dixie Chicks)

September 8

The Ann Arbor Jazz and Blues Festival was held. The event played out in a Michigan field to honor the memory of blues great Otis Span. Performers included Bonnie Raitt, Muddy Waters, Junior Walker, Otis Rush, Bobby "Blue" Bland, and numerous others.

September 30

Country star Donna Fargo reached the Hot 100 with "Funny Face" (No. 5). It was her only Top 10 pop hit.

November 3

Carly Simon married singer-songwriter James Taylor in her Manhattan apartment. That evening, she joined him onstage at his performance, where he told the world of their nuptials.

December 2

Carly Simon stormed onto the hit list with "Your So Vain," a single that spent three weeks at No. 1 and included the backing vocals of Mick Jagger.

December 3

Bette Midler performed at Philharmonic Hall in Lincoln Center, New York. She was now doing mainstream cabaret and signed to Atlantic Records. It would be twenty days before her first single "Do You Want to Dance" charted, reaching No. 17 pop.

December 16

Joan Baez arrived in Hanoi, North Vietnam, to distribute Christmas gifts and mail to American prisoners of war.

December 23

Hawaiian-raised Bette Midler hula'd her way onto the singles survey with the 1958 Bobby Freeman hit "Do You Wanna Dance" (No. 17). It was her first of eighteen hits through 1991.

December 31

Bette Midler performed at the Philharmonic Hall in Lincoln Center, New York

1973

January 6

Carly Simon's standard-to-be "You're So Vain" topped the chart (and would hit No. 3 in Britain). The song took on a separate life as fans wondered who she was singing about that was "so vain." Though most thought the obvious choice was guest vocalist Mick Jagger, it turned out to be Kris Kristofferson.

Dolly Parton reached the country hit list with "My Tennessee Mountain Home" (No. 15), one of ninety-nine charters for the country charmer through 1990.

January 13

Carly Simon's album *No Secrets* rocketed to No. 1 for the first of five weeks while also reaching No. 3 in Britain. With a harder rock edge than her previous works, it would become her most successful album.

February 10

After composing the song "The Night the Lights Went Out in Georgia," Bobby Russell offered the tune to Cher, who turned it down. Russell then gave it to his wife, Vickie Lawrence, who had the No. 1 hit.

February 24

Roberta Flack's "Killing Me Softly with His Song" topped the U.S. charts for the first of five weeks. Roberta first heard the song as sung by Lori Lieberman on a TWA flight from Los Angeles to New York.

March 3

Roberta Flack dominated the fifteenth annual Grammy Awards, winning Song of the Year and Record of the Year for "The First Time Ever I Saw Your Face," as well as Best Pop Vocal Performance by a Duo for "Where Is the Love" with Donny Hathaway.

March 10

The Philadelphia girl group First Choice attacked the Top 100 with their disco hit "Armed and Extremely Dangerous" (No. 28). It became their biggest hit of five Top 100 singles.

April 4

Joan Baez performed at the Empire Pool in Wembley, London.

April 7

Gladys Knight and the Pips reached No. 2 pop and No. 1 R&B (for four weeks) with "Neither One of Us (Wants to Be the First to Say Goodbye). Their fourth No. 1 R&B charter, the song was actually a country tune by Mississippi writer/ artist Jim Wetherly.

April 22

Tina Turner began filming for the motion picture *Tommy* in her role as the Acid Queen. The former Annie Mae Bullock began singing at nightclubs with husband, Ike (who renamed her Tina because she reminded him of the star of the TV series, *Sheena, Queen of the Jungle*), while working in a hospital by day.

Notable birthdays: (April 4) Kelly Price

May 19

The Joan Baez album *Where Are You Now My Son* placed on the Top 200, reaching No. 138. Her eighteenth chart LP, it contained actual war sounds taped in Vietnam.

May 25

Carole King performed a free concert in New York's Central Park for an audience of over 100,000!

Notable birthdays: (May 14) Natalie Appleton (All Saints), Shanice Wilson

June 2

Diana Ross' "Touch Me in the Morning" ascended the charts, on its way to No. 1.

August 6

Blues great Memphis Minnie (Lizzie Douglas) died in (where else!) Memphis, Tennessee. The prolific (she had over 250 recordings) powerhouse vocalist/guitarist/banjo player influenced numerous blues artists, including J. B. Hutto and J. B. Lenoir. She was seventy-six years old.

August 9

Lillian Roxon, author of the highly acclaimed *Rock Encyclopedia,* died in New York City. She was only forty-one and passed away from an asthma attack.

August 18

The Pointer Sisters charted with "Yes You Can Can," reaching No. 12 R&B and No. 11 pop, with their debut Top 100 disc. The four sisters began as studio singers for the likes of San Francisco stars Dave Mason, Elvin Bishop, and Boz Scaggs.

August 19

Rita Coolidge married singer/actor Kris Kristofferson in Malibu, California.

September 29

Former New York City model Millie Jackson nudged her way onto the Top 200 album list with *It Hurts So Good* (No. 175), her second of fourteen hit LPs.

Notable birthdays: (September 3) Jennifer Paige

October 15

Patsy Cline became the first female solo performer to be inducted into the Country Music Hall of Fame. The induction finally came ten years after she died.

October 18

Marianne Faithfull appeared—dressed as a man—on NBC-TV's *The Midnight Special,* headlined by David Bowie performing "I Got You Babe."

October 27

Gladys Knight and the Pips reached No. 1 pop (for two weeks) and No. 1 R&B (for four weeks) with "Midnight Train to Georgia." The song, written by country writer Jim Weatherly, was originally recorded by him as "Midnight Plane to Houston."

Notable birthdays: (October 11) Charlie Baltimore

December 15

Bette Midler performed (with her musical director, Barry Manilow, from her days of performing at the Continental Baths, the legendary New York gay Turkish bath establishment) at Broadway's Palace Theater. At about this time, she was No. 1 on Mr. Blackwell's Worst Dressed Women of the Year list, though it bothered her little.

Melanie's version of the Shirelles' "Will You Love Me Tomorrow" (No. 82) became her last of nine charters that started with "Lay Down (Candles in the Rain)" in 1970.

December 29

Olivia Newton-John hit the Top 200 with "Let Me Be There" (No. 71), her second of seventeen chart albums between 1971 and 1992.

1974

January 2

The Pointer Sisters performed at the annual music industry festival MIDEM in Cannes, France.

January 5

Diana Ross' "Last Time I Saw Him" hit the Top 100 today, peaking at No. 14.

January 23

The Staples Singers performed at the eighth annual MIDEM festival in Cannes, France. The gathering is the music publishing business equivalent of the Cannes Film Festival, which is held in the same place, The MIDEM attracts over 7,000 music publishers and related business people from around the world.

Notable birthdays: (January 12) Melanie Chisholm (Sporty Spice of the Spice Girls)

February 2

Barbra Streisand hit No. 1 with the film theme song "The Way We Were." It went on to win both a Grammy and an Oscar for Song of the Year.

"At her best, Barbra Streisand is probably the greatest singing actress since Maria Callas."
—Grammy Award–winning classical pianist Glenn Gould

Carly Simon and James Taylor charted with "Mockingbird," which peaked at No. 5. The song was adapted from the same traditional folk lyrics as the song "Bo Diddley."

February 14

Carole King joined Bob Dylan on the last gig of his thirty-nine-date tour in Los Angeles.

Toni Tennille and Daryl Dragon married in Virginia City, Nevada, while driving through twenty-two states, promoting their debut disc, "The Way I Want to Touch You." It was also Valentines Day.

February 19

The Carpenters won the Favorite Duo category at the inaugural American Music Awards in Hollywood.

February 20

Cher filed for divorce from husband and former singing partner, Sonny Bono.

February 23

Suzi Quatro's "Devil Gate Drive" hit No. 1 in Great Britain for the first of two weeks. The Detroit native's recording never charted in the States. Suzi's sister, Patti, was in the all-girl rock band Fanny.

March 2

Gladys Knight and the Pips won Best Pop Vocal Performance by a Group for "Neither One of Us" and Best R&B Vocal Performance for "Midnight Train to Georgia" at the sixteenth annual Grammy Awards. Bette Midler won the Best New Artist category. She was named by her movie-loving mother after Bette Davis. Olivia Newton-John won the Best Country Vocal Performance, Female, category for "Let Me Be There."

March 19

Grace Slick's Jefferson Airplane officially became Jefferson Starship.

April 6

Australian Olivia Newton-John represented Great Britain in the Eurovision Song Contest, held in Brighton, England, with "Long Live Love" (the song lost in the competition won by ABBA with "Waterloo," but her recording peaked at No. 11 in Great Britain). The record was never issued in the States.

April 9

Janet Jackson, youngest of the nine Jackson family siblings, and older sister La Toya made their performance debuts with the Jackson Five at the MGM Grand Hotel in Las Vegas. Janet was seven years old and La Toya seventeen.

April 20

Diana Ross peaked at No. 5 in Britain with a remake of the Stylistics hit "You Are Everything." However, her American fans never got to consider it as Motown didn't issue it Stateside.

April 21

The Pointer Sisters became the first pop act to ever perform at the San Francisco Opera House. The night's work was recorded for a live album, which eventually reached No. 96 pop.

Notable birthdays: (April 17) Victoria Beckham (née Adams, aka Posh Spice of the Spice Girls)

May 1

The Carpenters performed at a White House state dinner at the request of President Nixon, in honor of West German Chancellor Willy Brandt.

May 6

Joan Baez's album *Gracias a la Vida!* was issued. It was recorded entirely in Spanish, with Joni Mitchell duetting on the cut "Dida."

May 9

Melanie performed with Bob Dylan and Pete Seeger at New York's Felt Forum in the Friends of Chile benefit concert to aid Chilean refugees.

June 1

ABBA, featuring Frida Lyngstad and Agnetha Faltskog, charted with "Waterloo." It would reach No. 6, become an international hit, and launch the career of one of the most successful worldwide acts of all time. The group would eventually have twenty hits in America through 1982.

June 8

Joni Mitchell's "Help Me" reached No. 7 while its companion album, *Court and Spark,* peaked at No. 2 for four weeks. It would be her biggest single hit (for the predominantly album-oriented artist) of eleven chart singles through 1997. Not bad for a girl who grew up in an apartment above a drug store in Fort McLeod, Canada, having been stricken with polio at the age of nine.

The Dolly Parton–penned "I Will Always Love You" raced to No. 1 country (and would be an international mega-million seller for Whitney Houston in 1992). She then formed the Traveling Family Band, which included four siblings and two cousins. (With her startlingly-voluminous-bust-and-big-wig image well established, Dolly said of her appearance, "When I wear fancy outfits and hairdos and sparkling jewelry, people might think I'm showing off. But I'm not. When I was a little girl I liked toys but I didn't have any, I was always very impressed when I saw someone dressed real fine; I used to sigh and say *someday girl, someday.*"

June 15

The jazz/funk group Rufus charted, reaching No. 3 pop with "Tell Me Something Good," which was originally recorded by Stevie Wonder. The group was first called Ask Rufus, and their lead singer would go on to stardom as a solo act. It was Chaka Khan.

June 22

Carly Simon's "I Haven't Got Time for the Pain" had time to reach No. 14, her seventh chart hit in three years, six of which reached the Top 20.

June 26

Sonny and Cher were divorced.

Notable birthdays: (June 1) Alanis Morissette

July 13

Gladys Knight and the Pips' "On and On" became their fourth consecutive gold 45 when it peaked at No. 5 pop. It reached No. 2 R&B, the first of their last four singles to not be No. 1 R&B.

July 27

Dionne Warwick teamed with the Spinners on "Then Came You," which charted today. It became her first No. 1 after forty hits and twelve years!

July 29

Cass Elliot (born Ellen Naomi Cohen) was a great vocalist with the '60s trend-setters the Mamas and the Papas. She had sixteen hits with the quartet, including "California Dreamin'" and "Monday, Monday." She also had seven solo charters, including "Dream a Little Dream of Me." She died in singer Harry Nilsson's London flat from a heart attack, brought on by choking on a ham sandwich. She was only thirty-two. It was the same apartment Keith Moon of the Who would die in four years later.

Notable birthdays: (July 13) Deborah Cox

August 3

Anne Murray headlined a Schaefer Festival concert in New York. The opening act was Bruce Springsteen's E Street Band.

September 14

Suzi Quatro's American chart debut, "All Shook Up," stopped at No. 85.

October 5

Olivia Newton-John's "I Honestly Love You" became her first No. 1, selling over a million copies.

The Pointer Sisters' single "Fairytale" charted, reaching No. 13 pop and No. 37.

October 12

Alice Coltrane, wife of famed musician John Coltrane, reached the Top 200 with her jazz keyboard album *Illuminations* (No. 79).

Gladys Knight and the Pips charted with the Tony Camillo–produced and penned "I Feel a Song in My Heart," attaining No. 21 pop, No. 1 R&B, and another gold disc for the Atlanta quartet.

Olivia Newton-John's album *If You Love Me, Let Me Know* topped the chart for a week. The lively Australian got her first break when she won a Johnny O'Keefe national talent contest, with the prize being a trip to England, where she would sing in pubs with her Melbourne friend Pat Carroll as Pat and Olivia.

October 26

Dionne Warwick teamed with the Spinners and struck gold when their recording of "Then Came You" reached No. 1 today. It was the first No. 1 single for both acts, even though Dionne had thirty-nine previous pop charters over twelve years, and the Spinners had broached the Top 100 thirteen times since 1961.

Notable birthdays: (October 14) Natalie Maines (the Dixie Chicks)

November 1

Chrissie Hynde, the Ohio native living in Paris, France, as part of a pre-Pretenders band called the Frenchies, performed her first gig on vocals, supporting the Flamin' Groovies at the Olympia, Paris. The following year, Hynde moved to Cleveland and joined R&B group Jack Rabbit, before returning to Britain in 1976 to play in the short-lived Berk Brothers. The Pretenders would not come into being until 1978.

November 8

Connie Francis was attacked at knifepoint and raped in a second-floor room at a Howard Johnson's Motel after an appearance at the Westbury Music Fair in

Westbury, New York. Emotionally distraught, she would not perform live again for fourteen years, when she made a comeback in Los Angeles and Las Vegas.

December 3

Christine McVie was invited to join Fleetwood Mac, making it the tenth line-up since 1967. In 1970, she stated she was quitting the music business for good, a year after she was voted Melody Maker's Female Vocalist of the Year under the name Christine Perfect.

December 24

Carly Simon, Joni Mitchell, Linda Ronstadt, and James Taylor enjoyed Christmas Eve by singing Christmas carols door to door in Los Angeles.

December 28

A rare live version of Joni Mitchell's "Big Yellow Taxi" hit the charts, eventually making it to No. 24, four and a half years after the studio version charted.

A song turned down by Cher became a career maker for Helen Reddy as her recording of "Angie Baby" went to No. 1 today.

Notable birthdays: (December 7) Nicole Appleton (All Saints)

More Moments in 1974

Blues and gospel singer Linda Hopkins stars in her self-penned, one-woman homage to Bessie Smith, *Me and Bessie,* which premiered in Los Angeles this year. Her numerous theatrical appearances earned her a Tony Award in 1972 for *Inner City.* The New Orleans–born Hopkins was discovered at age eleven by Mahalia Jackson.

1975

January 1

Patti Smith performed in the "New Year's Day Extravaganza," a New York poetry reading project, with Yoko Ono.

January 4

LaBelle's "Lady Marmalade" charted today, on its way to No. 1, the only chart topper the group would ever achieve. LaBelle was actually Patti LaBelle and the Blue-Belles transformed for the glam-rock era.

January 5

Phoebe Snow's "Poetry Man" rhymed his way onto the hit list, up to No. 5. It was the first (and biggest) of five Top 100 singles for Phoebe.

January 18

Minnie Riperton, former member of the rock-R&B sextet Rotary Connection charted, on the way to No. 1, with "Lovin' You."

February 16

Bette Midler was a guest with Elton John on the debut of Cher's weekly CBS-TV series. Bette got her start in the Broadway production of *Fiddler on the Roof,* in which she had a long-running chorus-line part. It was Cher's second starring variety series in four years and would run for twenty-six episodes.

February 18

Olivia Newton-John won in four categories, Favorite Album Country, Favorite Female Artist Country, Favorite Female Artist Pop/Rock, and Favorite Single Pop/Rock, at the second annual American Music Awards at Santa Monica's Civic Auditorium.

Notable birthdays: (February 4) Natalie Imbruglia

March 1

Aretha Franklin won her tenth Grammy Award with "Ain't Nothing Like the Real Thing" for Best R&B Vocal Performance. It was her eighth win in a row in that category. Unexpectedly, the Pointer Sisters won Best Country Vocal Performance by a Duo or Group for their hit "Fairytale." Olivia Newton-John's "I Honestly Love You" was named Record of the Year, and Olivia won the Best Pop Vocal Performance, Female, category. She was also voted Female Vocalist of the Year by the Country Music Association, the first British performer to win.

Carole King's "Nightengale" peaked at No. 9. The backing vocals featured her daughters, Louise and Sherry Goffin.

March 22

Janis Ian, who was discovered by classical conductor/composer Leonard Bernstein, charted with her LP *Between the Lines.* It became her only No. 1 of eight Top 200 albums.

March 23

Joan Baez performed in an all-star SNACK (Students Need Athletics, Culture & Kicks) benefit at San Francisco's Kezar Stadium before a crowd of 60,000 to raise money to make up for a shortfall in the San Francisco School System's budget.

March 29

LaBelle's "Lady Marmalade" reached No. 1 and became a million seller. The group was formerly known as Patti LaBelle and the Blue-Belles.

April 12

Folk great Judy Collins' album *Judith* charted, reaching No. 17. It was her eleventh Top 200 hit collection since 1964 and contained "Suite: Judy Blue Eyes," written for her by Stephen Stills.

April 19

Captain and Tennille charted with "Love Will Keep Us Together," reaching #1 and holding the top spot for four weeks. It became the first of fourteen hits (six were Top 5) over the next five years.

Emmylou Harris charted country for the first time with "Too Far Gone" (No. 73). She would go on to have fifty-one country charters through 1993, be named 1980s Country Female Vocalist of the Year by the CMA Awards, and eventually win *Billboard* magazine's Century Award in 1999. Not bad for a girl who started out as a sax player in her high school marching band and later became a waitress.

May

Notable birthdays: (May 25) Lauryn Hill, (May 29) Melanie Brown (Scary Spice of the Spice Girls)

June 7

Olivia Newton-John's "Please Mr. Please" charted (No. 3), becoming her fifth Top 10 hit in a row.

June 21

Captain and Tennille's "Love Will Keep Us Together" reached No. 1 and held the top spot for four weeks.

June 30

Cher and the Allman Brothers' Greg Allman were married four days after she and Sonny Bono were divorced. The Cher and Greg combine lasted ten days.

July 10

Gladys Knight and the Pips began their own four-week summer replacement TV show on NBC.

July 19

Esther Phillips charted with "What a Difference a Day Makes," reaching No. 10 R&B and No. 20 pop. It was her first Top 10 rhythm-and-blues hit in thirteen years and her biggest of nineteen hits since "Release Me" hit No. 1 (No. 8 pop).

July 26

Jazz stylist Nancy Wilson hit the Top 200 with her LP *Come Get to Thee* (No. 119). It was the thirty-first of thirty-four chart albums for the veteran vocalist between 1962 and 1984.

Joan Baez's *Diamonds and Rust*, featuring songs by Janis Ian and Jackson Browne, became her biggest-selling album in four years, peaking at No. 11.

Notable birthdays: (July 11) Lil' Kim (born Kimberly Jones)

August 2

Evie Sands hit the Hot 100 with "I Love Makin' Love to You" (No. 50), her last of three entries that all peaked between No. 50 and No. 53.

August 9

Olivia Newton-John's "Please Mr. Please," written by boyfriend Bruce Welch of the Shadows, hit No. 3, becoming her fifth million-selling single in a row.

August 10

The Manhattan Transfer began a four-week run with their own CBS-TV comedy variety show.

August 30

Natalie Cole bounced onto the Hot 100 with "This Will Be" (No. 6), her first of seventeen hits through 1991.

September 6

Grace Slick and Jefferson Starship's *Red Octopus* album began a four-week run at No. 1 while selling two million copies.

September 13

Janis Ian's "At Seventeen," her first chart single in twelve years, peaked at No. 3, becoming a million seller. The parent album, the Brooks Arthur–produced *Between the Lines,* would reach No. 1, earning a gold record for half a million copies sold.

Less than three months after "Love Will Keep Us Together" by Captain and Tennille hit No. 1, the duo rerecorded the song in Spanish as "Por Amor Viviremos"—and amazingly reached No. 49.

September 27

Captain and Tennille's second hit, "The Way I Want to Touch You," charted, reaching No. 4. It had been previously released three times in 1974 on three different labels and bombed each time, but being the follow-up to their No. 1 1975 hit, "Love Will Keep Us Together," gave it new attention.

October 11

Janis Ian and Billy Preston performed on the first-ever *Saturday Night Live* TV show.

November 1

Karen Carpenter, weighting only ninety pounds, fell ill due to an excessive diet (that would later turn out to be anorexia) and took two months off to recuperate, forcing the cancellation of a scheduled British tour. She had spent the previous five years on a constant recording and touring binge.

November 13

British songstress Joan Armatrading began a thirty-city U.K. tour, along with label mates Supertramp, at Colston Hall in Bristol, England. Joan was a self-taught musician on piano and guitar and was influenced by the first album she bought at nineteen, Van Morrison's *Astral Weeks.*

November 15

Joan Baez's "Diamonds and Rust" single, an autobiographical number about her romance with Dylan, reached No. 35, becoming her last of nine Top 100 singles, from 1963 to 1975. She took part in Dylan's Rolling Thunder Revue tour this year.

November 22

Natalie Cole peaked at No. 6 pop while reaching No. 1 R&B with her dazzling recording of "This Will Be." Daughter of legendary pop-jazz vocalist Nat "King" Cole, Natalie started out in a jazz group called, of all things, the Malibu Music Men, which included keyboard player Daryl Dragon (later of Captain and Tennille).

December 1

Bette Midler was hospitalized on her birthday while undergoing an emergency appendectomy.

December 6

Donna Summer's sex-saturated single "Love to Love You Baby" (No. 2) became her first of thirty-four charters today, spanning twenty-five years through 2000. The seventeen-minute version done in Germany was originally released to discos before a radio edit was shipped. It also reached No. 3 R&B and No. 4 in England.

December 8

Roberta Flack performed at Madison Square Garden in New York during Bob Dylan's Rolling Thunder Revue tour. The particular night's concert was a benefit for convicted murderer and boxer Rubin "Hurricane" Carter. Guess there was no world hunger or homelessness that night.

December 10

Bette Midler began a twenty-city, eighty-performance tour of the U.S.

December 27

The Staple Singers reached No. 1 pop and R&B with "Let's Do it Again," having just signed to Curtis Mayfield's Curtom label.

December 29

Grace Slick and Jefferson Airplane guitarist Paul Kantner broke up, after living together for seven years. (Grace would later marry the group's twenty-four-year-old lighting engineer, Skip Johnson, in November 1976.)

1976

January 3

Chaka Khan's "Sweet Thing" charted, going on to No. 5 pop and becoming her third Top 10 hit in eighteen months.

Linda Ronstadt and Emmylou Harris did a duet on "The Sweetest Gift," entering the Country chart on its way to No. 12.

January 23

The Donny and Marie Show debuted on ABC-TV tonight. It ran for three years and fifty-seven episodes.

Notable birthdays: (January 21) Emma Bunton (Baby Spice of the Spice Girls)

February 2

Although the Patti Smith Group's debut album, *Horses*, only reached No. 47 on the charts, its legacy continues on. It is considered one of the greatest rock albums of all time by the media, from Rolling Stone to VH1.

"Instead of Messiahs, we always had big rock 'n' roll stars. We'd like to see who we're worshipping." —Patti Smith

February 17

Winning the Harvard University Hasty Pudding Theatrical Society honors as their Woman of the Year, Bette Midler stated in her acceptance speech that the award "characterizes what the American male wants in a woman—brains, talent, and gorgeous tits."

February 22

Florence Ballard, the original lead singer of the Supremes, died of a heart attack, nine years after being forced out of the trio. Though she sang on numerous hits, including nine No. 1 singles, Flo passed away penniless while living on welfare with her three children. The eulogy at her funeral was given by Reverend C. L. Franklin, Aretha Franklin's father and the pall bearers were the Four Tops and Marv Johnson. She was only thirty-two years old.

February 25

Joni Mitchell participated in the Band's farewell concert, "The Last Waltz," in San Francisco, singing "Helpless" with Neil Young.

February 28

Janis Ian won the Best Pop Vocal Performance, Female, category at the eighteenth annual Grammy Awards while Captain and Tennille won Record of the Year with "Love Will Keep Us Together."

March 6

Stevie Nicks sang lead on Fleetwood Mac's charter "Rhiannon," which reached No. 11 and became their third of twenty-three hits between 1970 and 1990.

March 13

Former Nashville-born porn star Andrea True seduced the charts today on her way to a No. 4 disco smash with "More, More, More."

April 3

Diana Ross' "Love Hangover" sprinted onto the Hot 100, eventually settling in the top spot. It was her fourth solo No. 1 in six years.

April 10

Emmylou Harris' cover of the Beatles' "Here There and Everywhere" made it to No. 65. At about the same time, she had greater success as a featured vocalist on Bob Dylan's No. 1 album *Desire*.

April 17

Ann Wilson and Heart charted, on their way to No. 35 and their first of thirty hits through 1993, when "Crazy on You" jumped on the Hot 100 today.

May 16

The Patti Smith Group made their British debut at the Roundhouse in Chalk Farm, London, among a cadre of punk lovers that unnerved Patti with their religious fervor for the soon-to-be star of the punk movement. Patti started a small local newspaper in 1969 before working for *Creem* magazine at the age of twenty-three.

May 22

Donna Summer reached No. 52 pop with "Could It Be Magic," originally recorded by Barry Manilow.

June 14

An Evening with Diana Ross began its performance tour at the Palace Theater in New York.

July 4

Born Pauline Mathews, Kiki Dee ascended the charts in a duet with Elton John on "Don't Go Breaking My Heart" (No. 1).

July 10

Captain and Tennille's remake of the Miracles' "Shop Around" peaked at No. 4, becoming their fourth Top 5 hit in a year.

July 17

Ann and Nancy Wilson with their group Heart charted, on their way to No. 9, with "Magic Man." Ann started as a member of a group, Ann and the Daybreaks, and later joined the Seattle-based band, the Army, formed in 1963 when she was only twelve years old.

July 31

Natalie Cole secretly married her producer, Marvin Yancey Jr. However, they did not announce it until seven months later (on Valentines Day), when she also announced she was pregnant.

Notable birthdays: (July 12) Tracie Spencer

August 31

A U.S. judge found George Harrison guilty of "subconscious plagiarism" when he lifted the Chiffons' "He's So Fine" melody for his "My Sweet Lord." Taking advantage of the publicity, the Chiffons then recorded their own version of "My Sweet Lord."

September 4

Fifteen months after Fleetwood Mac's self-titled album entered the chart, it reached No. 1, going platinum. It would stay on the charts for 148 weeks, going five times platinum.

September 18

Diana Ross and Alice Cooper (now that's an interesting pairing!) co-hosted Don Kirshner's Rock Awards.

September 27

The Runaways were held by bobbies in London after the theft of a hair dryer from a hotel during their first British tour.

October 9

Warm-voiced West Indian vocalist Joan Armatrading hit the album Top 200 for the first time with her self-titled collection, eventually reaching No. 67. She would go on to have eleven more albums chart in America through 1990.

October 15

More than three months after escaping years of abuse from husband/producer Ike Turner, Tina Turner announced their professional association was over after nineteen years.

October 30

After an arduous trip up the charts, Heart, led by Ann and Nancy Wilson, saw their *Dreamboat Annie* album peak at No. 7. It would eventually spend a hundred weeks on the Top 200, selling over two million units.

November 10

Olivia Newton-John's first American TV special, *A Special Olivia Newton-John*, was aired on ABC-TV, with guest Lynda Carter.

"Music conveys both the source of my anguish and my relief. It is what exorcises—and exercises—your demons. You've just got to go out there and sing your guts out."—Linda Ronstadt

November 25

Joni Mitchell, Emmylou Harris, and the Staple Singers, among others, performed in the Band's farewell concert, "The Last Waltz," at the Winterland Ballroom in San Francisco. Joni sang "Helpless" with Neil Young and joined an all-star group on "I Shall Be Released."

December 2

Linda Ronstadt graced the cover of *Rolling Stone* magazine.

December 4

The Carpenters received twenty-one gold records while visiting London. Unfortunately, they had to leave them behind at the airport because they were too heavy to take on as excess baggage.

December 8

The Carpenters appeared on their first television special with John Denver.

December 18

LaBelle's sixth and last R&B Top 100 entry, "Isn't It a Shame," charted, reaching No. 18, less than two months after the group had broken up. Lead singer Patti LaBelle would go on to stunning success as one of rock and R&B's legendary divas.

December 25

Karen Lawrence and the L.A. Jets charted with "Prisoner" (No. 86). The obscure tune was later a hit for Barbra Streisand and was the title song from the film *Eyes of Laura Mars*" when music publisher Jay Warner placed the song with Streisand.

The Supremes' "You're My Driving Wheel" reached No. 85 pop, becoming their last of forty-seven singles to hit the Top 100. The last original member, Mary Wilson, then left the group, forming her own Mary Wilson & the Supremes.

1977

January 7

Gladys Knight and the Pips performed at the New Victoria Theater in London.

January 19

Aretha Franklin sang "God Bless America" a cappella at Jimmy Carter's Inaugural Eve Gala in Washington, D.C.

January 23

Poet/vocalist Patti Smith fell offstage while performing in Florida and plummeted fifteen feet. Her spine and neck were so severely injured (requiring twenty-two stitches) that she whiled away the coming months in veritable traction while confined to a straight up-and-down brace. She was opening for Bob Seger at the time.

January 29

Jennifer Warnes' "Right Time of The Night" charted, reaching No. 6. It was the first of her nine Top 100 singles through 1987.

Natalie Cole charted with "I've Got Love on My Mind," reaching No. 5 pop and No. 1 R&B for five weeks. It would be her biggest hit of a career eighteen pop hits and thirty-one R&B winners through 1997. The record was also her fourth No. 1 of her first five chart singles.

February 4

The Pointer Sisters performed on Dick Clark's twenty-fifth anniversary edition of *American Bandstand.*

February 5

Ann and Nancy Wilson and Heart's "Dreamboat Annie" reached No. 42. The song was written at the girls' parents' house, on a coffee table.

February 14

Janis Ian received 461 Valentine's Day cards after indicating she had never received any in the lyrics to her million seller "At Seventeen."

February 19

Fleetwood Mac's *Rumours* album was released. It went on to spend an amazing thirty-one weeks at No. 1.

Linda Ronstadt won the Best Female Pop Vocal Performance for "Hasten Down the Wind" at the nineteenth annual Grammy Awards while Emmylou Harris received the Best Country Vocal Performance for "Elite Hotel."

February 20

Pat Benatar married her guitarist, Neil Geraldo, on the island of Maui, Hawaii.

March 5

The Supremes' "Let Yourself Go" (No. 83) became their last of forty-three R&B chart singles.

March 6

A ninety-minute extravaganza, *An Evening with Diana Ross* aired on American TV. Most of the show was built around her stage act.

April 2

Suzi Quatro's "Tear Me Apart" reached No. 27 in Britain. The producers of the TV series *Happy Days,* having seen her on the cover of *Rolling Stone,* cast her as female rocker *Leather Tuscadero* on the show. She was offered a spin-off series, but she refused, wanting to stay in England with her husband.

May 7

Rita Coolidge charted with her smoldering version of Jackie Wilson's hit "Higher and Higher." It was her biggest single (No. 2) of fifteen career Top 100 entries.

May 8

Olivia Newton-John made her New York live-performance debut at the Metropolitan Opera House. She was then asked to play the lead role of Sandy in *Grease*, a movie version of the Broadway '50s-nostalgia hit musical.

May 21

Blues and folk artist Bonnie Raitt hit the pop charts today with a remake of Del Shannon's 1961 rock 'n' roll classic "Runaway." It would only go to No. 57. Though her real fan base was album buyers, the single served to provide a wider audience for the gifted performer, who would still make the pop singles charts eleven times through 1995.

May 28

Heart, with Ann and Nancy Wilson, rocked the Oakland-Alameda County Stadium to the delight of an audience 100,000 strong. Also on the bill were the Eagles, Foreigner, and Steve Miller.

Olivia Newton-John stared in "The Big Top Show" at Windsor Castle, in Windsor, England, with Elton John and Leo Sayer, as part of Queen Elizabeth's Queen's Silver Jubilee Celebration.

June 15

Marilyn McCoo and Billy Davis, formerly of the 5th Dimension, began co-hosting a summer TV variety show, titled *The Marilyn McCoo and Billy Davis Jr. Show*. It would run for six weeks.

July 9

Fleetwood Mac's "Don't Stop" charted, en route to No. 3. The hit was later used without permission by the Dole for President campaign in 1996.

July 14

Bonnie Raitt, who was a Quaker that espoused a strong pacifist political stance, performed with James Taylor, the Doobie Brothers, Santana, and several Russian acts in the July 4th Disarmament Festival in the Soviet Union.

July 16

Heart's album *Little Queen* shot to No. 9, becoming their second million seller.

July 21

Linda Ronstadt did a duet with Mick Jagger on "Tumbling Dice" at a Rolling Stones concert in Tucson, Arizona.

July 22

Tony Orlando announced during a show with his act, Dawn, that he was retiring from performing, which shocked the girl group since he never told them.

July 23

Carly Simon ascended the Hot 100 with "Nobody Does It Better" (No. 2) from the James Bond film *The Spy Who Loved Me.*

Donna Summer's "I Feel Love" reached No. 1 in England and would soon be No. 3 pop in America. The "Queen of Disco" started out in the German productions of *Hair* and *Godspell* before being discovered by producer Giorgio Moroder at a Blood, Sweat and Tears demo session.

August 13

Cherrie Currie quit the Runaways and was replaced as lead singer by Joan Jett.

August 27

Connie Francis' *20 All Time Greats* soared to No. 1 in England for the first of two weeks and earned a platinum record.

September 3

Former member of the Boone Gospel Quartet and daughter of singer Pat Boone, Debby Boone assaulted the charts with her soon-to-be No. 1, "You Light Up My Life."

Heart's powerful rocker "Barracuda" swam to No. 11.

September 10

Linda Ronstadt charted with "Blue Bayou" (No. 3), her eighteenth hit since she first reached the pop listings with "Different Drum" as lead singer of the Stone Poneys ten years earlier.

September 17

Diana Ross and the Supremes' *20 Golden Greats* compilation reached No. 1 in England and stayed there for seven weeks.

September 20

Thirty-one-year-old Linda Ronstadt performed at the Universal Amphitheater decked out in a Cub Scout uniform!

Notable birthdays: (September 13) Fiona Apple

October 8

Patti LaBelle had her first R&B solo chart single with "Joy to Have Your Love" (No. 31). She would have thirty-six more solo R&B winners through 2004.

The Emotions' (the three Hutchinson sisters—Wanda, Sheila, and Jeanette) "Don't Ask My Neighbors" (No. 44 pop, No. 7 R&B) charted as the follow-up to their huge hit "Best of My Love" (No. 1 pop and R&B). It was the seventeenth of thirty R&B hits they would have between 1969 and 1984.

October 13

Orlons member Shirley Brickley was shot to death. One of the hottest dance music groups of the early '60s, she was a member through all nine of their Top 100 hits. Shirley was only thirty-two years old.

October 15

Debby Boone rocketed to No. 1 with "You Light Up My Life," which held the top spot for a record ten weeks, the longest stay at the pinnacle since Guy Mitchell's "Singing the Blues" twenty-one years earlier.

October 22

Carly Simon's "Nobody Does It Better," bolstered by its inclusion as the theme song to the James Bond movie *The Spy Who Loved Me*, peaked at No. 2, behind another female artist, Debby Boone, whose "You Light Up My Life" practically owned the top spot at that time.

October 29

The disco group Chic charted for the first time, with "Dance, Dance, Dance (Yowsah, Yowsah, Yowsah)," on their way to No. 6 both pop and R&B. The group was originally a '60s rock band called New World Rising and then a rock-fusion aggregation, the Big Apple Band, before freaking out all together as *Allah and the Knife-Wielding Punks* (no kidding!) for a short time. Obviously a return to sanity soon followed with the much more acceptable Chic.

December 3

Twenty-nine-year-old Patti Austin's debut album, *Havana Candy,* charted, reaching No. 116. God-daughter of jazz great Dinah Washington, Patti had been performing since she took the stage at the Apollo Theater at the age of four.

December 11

Joni Mitchell's *Hejira* charted, eventually reaching No. 13, becoming her seventh consecutive gold album. She would eventually have seventeen Top 200 albums, from 1968 through 1994.

December 17

Showing the developing power of TV on music in the '70s, Gladys Knight and the Pips' K-Tel double-album collection *30 Greatest Hits* reached No. 3 in England.

1978

January 14

Dolly Parton's "Here You Come Again," hit No. 3 pop. At first, Dolly didn't want to record the song, but her publishers convinced her to. Lord knows what would have happened if she'd found out at the time that the song had been recorded several times previously and bombed.

Natalie Cole charted, reaching No. 10 pop, with "Our Love," but more importantly, it reached No. 1 R&B. In doing so, she had her fifth chart topper in a little over two years.

January 16

Natalie Cole co-hosted the fifth annual American Music Awards, held at the Civic Auditorium in Santa Monica, California, where she also walked off with the Favorite Female Artist, Soul/Rhythm and Blues, honor. Meanwhile, Fleetwood Mac, led by Stevie Nicks and Christie McVie, won the Favorite Band, Duo or Group, Pop/Rock, and Favorite Album, Pop/Rock, categories.

January 20

English songstress Kate Bush debuted with the single "Wuthering Heights," topping the U.K. charts for four weeks. Signed by EMI at the young age of sixteen (on the recommendation of Pink Floyd's David Gilmour), Bush went on to accept a BRIT Award for Best British Female Solo Artist in 1987.

January 28

Yvonne Elliman hit it big with "If I Can't Have You" (No. 1, from *Jesus Christ Superstar*), which first charted today.

March 18

Blondie, featuring Miami-born Deborah Harry, had their initial break in Britain, reaching No. 2 with "Denis" ("Denee"), a punk/pop cover of Randy and the Rainbows' 1963 No. 10 hit. Harry, a former beautician and Playboy bunny waitress, had also worked the bar at New York's Max's Kansas City club.

Heart (with Ann and Nancy Wilson), Santana, Aerosmith, and Ted Nugent, among others, performed at the California Jam 2 festival in Ontario, California, in front of over 250,000 people.

April 1

Former Stevie Wonder backup singer (with Wonderlove) Deniece Williams teamed with Johnny Mathis on "Too Much, Too Little, Too Late," which debuted on the pop listings today and eventually reached No. 1.

Patti Smith performed at the first of three sellout shows at London's Rainbow Theater.

April 19

Patti Smith's "Because the Night" was issued. It reached No. 13, becoming her only hit single.

April 21

Sandy Denny was a smooth and tender-voiced folk vocalist and member of the British group Fairport Convention. Originally a member of the folk band the Strawbs in 1967, Denny recorded the original version of "Who Knows Where the Time Goes" with Fairport (later made popular by Judy Collins) during her tenure, between 1968 and 1970. She died by accident after falling down a flight of stairs at a friend's home at age thirty-one.

May 6

Diana Ross performed at the London Palladium.

May 17

Donna Summer's film *Thank God It's Friday* premiered in Los Angeles.

May 20

Quincy Jones hit the music charts with "Stuff Like That," reaching No. 1 R&B and No. 21 pop. Similar to his predecessor Johnny Otis, Quincy used guest vocalists on the recordings with his orchestra, and the vocals for "Stuff" were by Chaka Khan and (Nicholas) Ashford and (Valerie) Simpson.

June 16

Olivia Newton-John's movie *Grease* opened in theaters across America.

June 17

Grace Slick's alcohol problem prevented her from performing at the Lorelei Festival in Hamburg, West Germany. When the word got out, fans rioted, stealing or destroying a large part of the band's equipment.

Kim Carnes rolled onto the charts with "You're a Part of Me" (No. 36), her first of nineteen hits over the next twelve years.

Olivia Newton-John's duet with John Travolta, "You're the One That I Want," hit No. 1 in England for the first of nine weeks, selling over 1.8 million singles, making it the third best-selling single in British pop-music history to date. The soundtrack album also became a multi-million seller.

June 18

Grace Slick took to the Hamburg, Germany, stage at the Lorelei Festival in an obviously drunk and fowl mood and insulted the audience with taunts about World War II.

June 21

Aretha Franklin performed in Las Vegas for the first time in eight years.

June 24

Carly Simon's "You Belong to Me" (written with Michael McDonald of the Doobie Brothers over the telephone) peaked at No. 6. That must have been some phone bill!

Janice Marie Johnson led A Taste of Honey onto the charts with "Boogie Oogie Oogie." It finally stopped boogeying at No. 1.

Patti Smith's "Because the Night," co-written with Bruce Springsteen, peaked at No. 13 Stateside and No. 5 in Great Britain.

July 1

Martha and the Vandellas reunited for the first time in ten years for a benefit concert for actor Will Geer in Santa Cruz, California.

July 9

The No. 1 record in England became Olivia Newton-John's duet with John Travolta, "You're the One That I Want," from the film *Grease*.

July 29

Barbra Streisand charted with "Prisoner (Captured by Your Eyes)," the theme song from the film *Eyes of Laura Mars* (No. 21). The song was originally recorded by Karen Lawrence and the L.A. Jets and brought to Streisand's attention by music publisher Jay Warner.

August 12

Donna Summer's "Last Dance" reached No. 3 pop and No. 5 R&B. It would go on to earn an Academy Award for Best Film Song in 1979.

August 26

Singing and songwriting duo (Nick) Ashford and (Valerie) Simpson entered the R&B hit list with "It Seems to Hang On," peaking at No. 2 on Valerie's birthday. Though the duo had thirty-five R&B chart singles through 1997, they're best known for the songs they've written for others, including "Let's Go Get Stoned" (Ray Charles), "Ain't No Mountain High Enough" (Marvin Gaye), and "Ain't Nothing Like the Real Thing" (Marvin Gaye and Tammi Terrell), among many others.

August 27

The Patti Smith Group played on the final day of the eighteenth National Jazz Blues and Rock Festival, "Reading Rock '78."

September 1

Gloria Fajardo married musician Emilio Estefan on her twenty-first birthday after a two-year romance. By year's end, Gloria Estefan would earn a BA degree in psychology from the University of Miami, Coral Gables, Florida. It would be more than seven years before Gloria would have here first hit, "Conga," as a member of the Miami Sound Machine.

September 3

Bette Midler's British TV special aired on ITV and was appropriately called *Old Red Hair Is Back.*

September 16

Deborah Harry and Blondie performed at London's Hammersmith Odeon Theater. She originally fronted a female vocal group, the Stilettos, in the '60s.

September 18

Emmylou Harris performed at London's Hammersmith Odeon Theater.

September 21

Bette Midler's debut British tour started with a concert at the London Palladium.

October 6

Anni-frid Lyngstad and Benny Anderson (both of ABBA) finally married in an unpublicized ceremony at their local church after nine years of living together.

October 23

Maybelle Carter died on October 23. She was the matriarch of the famous Carter Family, pioneers of country music. The group started singing in 1927 and included Maybelle on guitar and vocals. The original group disbanded in 1943 and reorganized later with Maybelle and daughters Anita, Helen, and June (who went on to marry Johnny Cash). In 1993, her image graced a U.S. postage stamp honoring the Carter Family.

October 28

Chic's "Le Freak" charted, on its way to No. 1 pop for five weeks and No. 1 R&B for six weeks. The disco hit of the age would go on to be one of the largest-selling singles of the '70s.

The Barbra Streisand and Neil Diamond hit collaboration "You Don't Bring Me Flowers" was not their first performance encounter. In fact, they sang together at New York City's Erasmus Hall High School in the school choir during the '60s.

Turning everything she could get her hands on into a disco recording, Donna Summer reached No. 5 in Britain with the 1968 Richard Harris epic "MacArthur Park." It would also make No. 1 pop and No. 8 R&B in the U.S.

November 11

Donna Summer's disco version of the 1968 Richard Harris hit "MacArthur Park" climbed to No. 1 and stayed there for three weeks.

The Pointer Sisters' "Fire" charted, reaching No. 2 pop and No. 14 R&B.

November 20

Dolly Parton finished a three-week European tour with a performance at London's Hammersmith Odeon.

November 25

Bette Midler hosted *Rolling Stone—the 10th Anniversary* TV special on CBS.

December 16

Originally a member of the Soul Satisfiers (1971), Gloria Gaynor attacked the singles survey with "I Will Survive," a No. 1 anthem for women and the sixth of her seven hits from 1974 through 1979.

December 23

Chic's *C'est Chic* album reached No. 4 and would become a milestone among dance albums, defining the disco age.

The Carpenters' second hit collection, *The Singles 74–78,* a British-only release, reached No. 2.

Notable birthdays: (December 2) Nelly Furtado

1979

January 12

Donna Summer became the "Queen of Disco" at the sixth annual American Music Awards, when she won the Favorite Single Disco, Favorite Album Disco, and Favorite Female Artist Disco trophies.

Notable birthdays: (January 16) Aaliyah

February 3

Deborah Harry and Blondie's "Heart of Glass," disco/rock-styled third single, topped the British charts for four weeks, selling over a million copies in England alone, making it the band's biggest British hit of seventeen chart entries through 1994.

February 15

Donna Summer won the Best R&B Vocal Performance, Female, category for "Last Dance" at the twenty-first Grammy Awards, and Dolly Parton won the Best Country Female Vocal Performance category.

February 17

Deborah Harry and Blondie hit the charts with "Heart of Glass" (No. 1), their first of nine hits in a little over three years.

Dolly Parton became the first country artist to have a disco hit, with the self-written "Baby I'm Burnin'," which made No. 25 pop and No. 1 country.

Notable birthdays: (February 11) Brandy

March 10

The disco and fem anthem "I Will Survive" by Gloria Gaynor reached No. 1, both in the U.S. and across the pond. The hit was originally a B-side!

March 16

Bonnie Bramlett (Delaney and Bonnie), while singing backup for Stephen Stills in Columbus, Ohio, got into a race-related/music-related argument with Elvis Costello and belted him in the face!

April 3

British popster Kate Bush made her live-performance debut at the Liverpool Empire in Liverpool, England. She went on to have twenty-seven hits in the United Kingdom between 1978 and 1994. Her debut single, "Wuthering Heights," was her only No. 1.

April 9

Donna Summer's "Last Dance" won an Oscar for Best Original Song at the Grammy's fifty-first annual awards.

April 28

Deborah Harry and Blondie blitzed the American charts when their disco/rock-styled third single, "Heart of Glass," leaped to No. 1. The song was originally called "Once I Had a Love" when it was written five years earlier. Their album *Parallel Lines* would soon reach No. 6. The album would eventually sell over 20 million copies around the world.

Deborah Harry.

May 5

"We Are Family" by Sister Sledge charted, reaching No. 1 R&B and No. 2 pop. Background vocals were added by Luther Vandross, who watched and learned how his older sister did it when Patricia Vandross was a member of the '50s hit group the Crests.

May 12

Originally known as the gospel group the Heavenly Sunbeams, the Emotions (paired with Earth, Wind and Fire) charted with "Boogie Wonderland," (No. 6) their last of nine Hot 100 discs.

Suzi Quatro's "Stumblin' In," peaked at No. 41 in England. The Detroit native had more success in Great Britain than in America as she charted sixteen times through 1982 over there while reaching the Stateside Top 100 only seven times through 1981.

May 17

Joan Baez became one of eighty-four signatories of an open letter to the Socialist Republic of Vietnam, calling for an end to torture in Vietnam and release of political prisoners. Baez lobbied President Carter to rescue Vietnamese boat people from drowning, and the celebrity of her antiwar stature being so great, the president sent the Seventh Fleet to expedite Baez' plea.

May 19

Former lead of the R&B/rock group Rotary Connection, Minnie Ripperton hurdled the Top 200 with "Minnie" (No. 29), the fifth of six solo album successes between 1974 and 1980.

Tenna Marie, the quintessential white funkster, charted with her debut single, "I'm a Sucker for Your Love," reaching No. 8 R&B.

May 26

British-born Maxine Nightingale, who starred in *Jesus Christ Superstar* and *Godspell*, hit the Top 100 with "Lead Me On" (No. 5).

June 15

Joni Mitchell appeared at the Playboy Jazz Festival at the Hollywood Bowl.

June 20

The Blues Brothers film opened throughout America. One of the movie's highlights was Aretha Franklin's portrayal of a crusty waitress singing her 1968 hit "Think."

June 23

Donna Summer's "Hot Stuff" became the No. 1 record in America. The same day, Chic's "Good Times" charted, on its way to No. 1 R&B for six weeks and No. 1 pop for one week.

July 7

Distinctively-styled jazz/folk artist Rickie Lee Jones' "Chuck E's in Love" reached No. 4 nationally and No. 18 in Great Britain. At about the same time, her self-titled debut album soared to No. 3 Stateside and No. 18 in the United Kingdom. Not bad for a girl who ran away from home for the first time at age fifteen, stole a car, and had been asked to leave three schools in succession in Washington State for bad behavior.

July 28

Dolly Parton's "You're the Only One" became her tenth solo country No. 1.

August 4

Bonnie Raitt, Emmylou Harris, Linda Ronstadt, and Nicolette Larson, among others, performed at the Great Western Forum in Inglewood, California, at a benefit concert in aid of Lowell George's widow. The 25,000-plus audience raised over $230,000.

August 25

Joan Baez's album *Honest Lullaby,* produced by Barry Beckett in Muscle Shoals Sound Studios, reached No. 113, and became Baez's last of twenty-five chart-making albums, from 1961 through 1979.

September 10

The Patti Smith Group played their last gig before 85,000 fans in Florence, Italy. She was once a writer for rock monthly *Creem* magazine in New York.

September 19

Carly Simon performed, along with Bonnie Raitt (who was one of the organizers), at the Musicians United for Safe Energy (MUSE) antinuclear concert at Madison Square Garden in New York. The event included performances by the Doobie Brothers, Bruce Springsteen, and Jackson Browne.

September 29

Genya Raven reached the album survey with "And I Mean It" (No. 106). It was the second, and last, solo charter for the former Goldie Zelkowitz of Brooklyn, who had driven the rock act Ten Wheel Drive as lead vocalist.

Notable birthdays: (September 6) Foxy Brown, (September 8) Pink (Alicia Moore)

October 6

Deborah Harry and Blondie's "Dreaming," featuring legendary songwriter Ellie Greenwich on backup vocals, reached No. 2 in England. It would soon reach No. 27 across the pond.

Stevie Nicks and Fleetwood Mac rocked onto the charts with "Tusk" (No. 8), a single recorded with the USC Marching Band at Dodger Stadium in Los Angeles.

October 7

Chaka Khan's "I'm Every Woman" charted, rising to become her first of four R&B No. 1s. Chaka (born Yvette Stevens) assumed her new first name while working for the Black Panther's breakfast program in Chicago (*Chaka* meaning "fire") and her second name after marrying musician Hassan Khan at age seventeen.

October 10

The motion picture *The Rose,* starring Bette Midler, opened in America. The story of a Janis Joplin–like performer earned Midler an Academy Award nomination.

October 20

Donna Summer teamed with Barbra Streisand and rolled onto the bestseller list with "No More Tears (Enough Is Enough)" (No. 1). It would become Donna's fourth chart topper in two years.

Notable birthdays: (October 10) Mya

November 1

Jennifer Warnes' "I Know a Heartache When I See One" peaked at No. 19. Her real name was Jennifer Jeane Warner, and she made an impressive performing debut in 1966 in high school: wrapped in the American flag, singing the "Star-Spangled Banner" accompanied by 300 accordions.

November 10

Fleetwood Mac's *Tusk* album, which reportedly cost over $1 million to record, topped the British chart.

November 23

Marianne Faithful was arrested at the airport in Oslo, Norway, for possession of marijuana. The police would not let her proceed on her tour of the country unless she signed a confession, which she did. Considering she wasn't deported, fined, or jailed, it's a novel way to get a singer's autograph.

December 22

Pat Benatar (born Patricia Andrzejewski) rocked onto the hit list with "Heartbreaker," her first of seventeen hits through 1988.

December 31

Deborah Harry and Blondie's show at the Apollo Theater in Glasgow, Scotland, was broadcast live on BBC-2 TV's *The Old Grey Whistle Test.*

More Moments in 1979

Marianne Faithfull's definitive recording, *Broken English,* was released. Her place in music history is often overshadowed by her association with the Rolling Stones (in particular, her relationship with Mick Jagger).

"Being on tour sends me crazy. I drink too much and out comes the John McEnroe in me."—Chrissie Hynde, the Pretenders

THE EVER-CHANGING EIGHTIES

The eighties saw an actor in the White House, 20 percent interest rates, the fall of the Berlin Wall, and the "me" mentality of a new American generation. Technological changes allowed for more musical offshoots, such as techno and electro-pop. Much of these sounds developed first in the European marketplace and eventually crossed into the American musical mainstream.

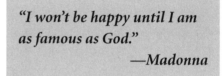

"I won't be happy until I am as famous as God."
—*Madonna*

Rock and pop were still the main forces in popular music, and many rock bands featured female vocal leads, including Deborah Harry (Blondie), Annie Lennox (the Eurythmics), Terri Nunn (Berlin), Joan Jett (the Blackhearts), Stevie Nicks and Christine McVie (Fleetwood Mac), Chrissie Hynde (the Pretenders), Rindy Ross (Quarterflash), and Patti Smyth (Scandal). Of course, that still left plenty of solo hard-charging women rockers, such as Laura Branigan, Kim Wilde, Pat Benatar, Belinda Carlisle (formerly of the Go-Go's), and Martika, not to mention all-girl bands like the Go-Go's, Bananarama, and Fanny.

"The only people who can express anything new in rock are girls and gays."
—*Deborah Harry (Blondie)*

Country music evolved into a powerhouse format that was no longer confined to Nashville, or for that matter the South. The typical male dominance of decades past had been eroding since the 1970s. New acts like the Judds, Kathy Mattea, Roseanne Cash, Reba McEntire, K. T. Oslin,

> *"I taught Madonna how to fuckin' wear tights, man. I'm so happy someone else is doing it. Now maybe they won't look at the color of my panties, and they can concentrate on my singing."*
> —*Pat Benatar*

Christy Lane, Juice Newton, Janie Fricke, the Forrester Sisters, Shelley West, and Marie Osmond together with greats from the '60s and '70s, such as Dolly Parton, Anne Murray, Lynn Anderson, and Emmylou Harris, competed favorably with their male country counterparts. Eighties R&B launched a new generation of divas, including Whitney Houston, Jennifer Holliday, Tracy Chapman, Janet Jackson, Teena Marie, the Mary Jane Girls, and Vanessa Williams. Bouncing between jazz and R&B, stalwarts such as Anita Baker, Patti Austin, Basia, Sade, and Patrice Rushen kept the musical art form flourishing.

Though many artists from the fields of rock, R&B, and country made regular forays into pop, the '80s featured some truly notable pop stars and superstars, including Madonna,

> *"I'm not trying to sell sex. I just don't like wearing a lot of clothes onstage."*
> —*Sheila E.*

Paula Abdul, Debbie Gibson, and Cyndi Lauper, while Latin pop was the almost exclusive domain of Gloria Estefan. Techno-pop and the music videos featured on MTV brought success to the likes of Toni Basil, among others, and a commercially viable form of gospel and Christian music fused, creating contemporary Christian, the pop version of "spreading the word" as popularized by its early and foremost exponents, Amy Grant and Debbie Boone.

> *"People used to throw rocks at me for my clothes. Now they want to know where I buy them."*
> —*Cyndi Lauper*

A diverse musical period, the '80s would be the last purely musical decade before the oncoming melody killer—the age of rap.

1980

January 13

Grace Slick and Jefferson Starship, the Beach Boys, and the Grateful Dead headlined a Los Angeles benefit concert to aid the victims of the Khmer Rouge in Kampuchea.

January 19

Chrissie Hynde and the Pretenders topped the British chart for the first of two weeks with "Brass in Pocket." The group then started a thirty-date British tour while their debut album, *Pretenders*, entered the British chart at No. 1 and began a run to No. 9 in the States.

February 21

Janet Vogel was the queen of soprano vocalists in the late '50s. The Pittsburg native first sang with the Crescents and then the legendary Skyliners. Anyone remembering their classic hit "Since I Don't Have You" will remember her amazing ultra-high note finale that always brought the house down. The group charted pop six times, including with "This I Swear" and "Pennies from Heaven," but by 1961, Vogel had tired of touring and retired, though she did return for oldies concerts in the '70s. Sadly, Janet committed suicide today by inhaling carbon-monoxide fumes in the garage of her home in Pittsburgh.

February 27

Emmylou Harris won her second Best Country Vocal Performance, Female, award for the single "Blue Kentucky Girl" at the twenty-second annual Grammy Awards. Meanwhile, Rickie Lee Jones won the Best New Artist of 1979 Award, mostly due to her hit "Chuck E's in Love." The song was about Los Angeleno Chuck E. Weiss, whom Rickie met in the kitchen at the Tropicana Motel. Rickie Lee wrote her first song when she was only seven and began her road to success by waitressing in an Echo Park, Los Angeles-area Italian restaurant.

March 1

Patti Smith married MC5 rocker Fred "Sonic" Smith.

April 14

Jennifer Warnes sang "It Goes Like It Goes" (from the film *Norma Rae* starring Sally Fields) at the Academy Awards. When the film won the Oscar for Best Original Song, it became the first of three hits she would have from films that would go on to win Oscars over the next nine years.

April 19

Deborah Harry and Blondie's "Call Me," a track written and produced for the soundtrack of the Richard Gere movie *American Gigolo,* reached No. 1 in America.

For the first time in country music history, all five artists in the Top 5 were female: Tammy Wynette (No. 5), Emmylou Harris (No. 4), Debby Boone (No. 3), Dottie West (No. 2), and Crystal Gayle (No. 1).

April 26

Karen Carpenter did a duet with Ella Fitzgerald on "This Masquerade" during the Carpenters' *Music, Music, Music* TV special on ABC-TV.

May 31

Chrissie Hynde and the Pretenders' "Brass in Pocket" reached No. 14. Hynde decided on the name Pretenders in 1978, inspired by the Platters' 1956 hit "The Great Pretender."

June 7

Joan Armatrading hit the Top 200 album chart with her fifth, and biggest, success, *Me, Myself, I.* It reached No. 28. Though she charted twelve times on the album Top 200, Joan never had a single on the R&B charts, as lack of commercial product was her eventual undoing in America.

June 14

Singer/dancer/actress/pianist Irene Cara earned her first taste of stardom when "Fame" (from the film *Fame*) vaulted onto the Top 100. The No. 4 smash was the first of her eight hits through 1984.

June 19

Donna Summer became the first act signed to former William Morris Agency mailroom boy David Geffen and his Geffen Records.

July 12

Diana Ross bounced onto the Hot 100 with "Upside Down" (No. 1). It was her fifth solo chart topper in ten years.

Leaning ever more into bluegrass, Emmylou Harris' *Roses in the Snow* album rose to No. 26, becoming her seventh straight gold record.

Olivia Newton-John starred with Gene Kelly in the movie musical *Xanadu.*

August 1

British vocalist Hazel O'Connor had her biggest hit, "Eighth Day," released, reaching No. 5 in Britain. It was her first of seven hits through 1982.

August 15

Pat Benatar performed at the old Waldorf in San Francisco. She had originally been singing off-Broadway in *The Zinger* in 1975, before going on to perform in cabaret at New York City's Catch a Rising Star.

August 21

Linda Ronstadt opened on Broadway in the Gilbert and Sullivan stage classic *Pirates of Penzance,* playing the part of Mabel.

August 30

Pat Benatar's third chart single, "You Better Run," a revival of the Young Rascals' 1966 No. 20 hit (given to her by Rascals publisher Jay Warner), reached No. 42. Benatar studied classical singing in New York and worked as a bank clerk and waitress in Richmond, Virginia, before becoming a rock artist.

Sheena Easton's bouncy, commuter-themed pop composition "9 to 5" drove to No. 3 in Britain. The Scottish lass, the youngest of six children, spent her evenings performing on the local club and pub circuit in Glasgow during her student days, and then graduated as a teacher of speech and drama from the Royal Scottish Academy of Music and Drama, a month after a winning audition for EMI Records in London.

September 17

Bette Midler's film *Divine Madness,* based on one of her 1979 concerts, premiered in Los Angeles at the Civic Auditorium in Pasadena, California.

September 20

Sheena Easton's first single, "Modern Girl" (No. 56), re-charted to No. 8 in the U.K., giving Easton two simultaneous Top 10 hits ("9 to 5" being the other)—a rare achievement for a female Brit in Britain.

October 4

Carly Simon collapsed from exhaustion onstage in Pittsburgh during a nationwide tour to promote her current album, *Come Upstairs*. It was after that collapse that Carly developed a fear of performing live for several years.

October 25

Diana Ross had her twenty-sixth solo turn on the charts when "It's My Turn" sashayed onto the Hot 100 (No. 9).

Notable birthdays: (October 13) Ashanti

November 17

Sheena Easton appeared in the "Royal Variety Show" in London, in the presence of the Queen Mother.

November 22

Heart reached the bestseller list with "Tell It Like It Is" (No. 8), their biggest hit up to that time.

November 29

Manhattan Transfer's remake of the Videos' "Trickle, Trickle" charted (No. 73).

December 19

Dolly Parton's "9 to 5," written for the movie of the same name, topped the pop chart and became her second of five charters in England, reaching No. 47.

December 20

Jackie English, a white songwriter who became known for only having songs recorded by black artists like as Patrice Rushen, Eloise Laws, George Benson, and Ronnie Laws, among others, finally had her own hit record when she charted with "Once a Night" (from the movie *Hopscotch*).

Notable birthdays: (December 18) Christina Aguilera

More Moments in 1980

Lizzie "Memphis Minnie" Douglas, one of the most influential and pioneering female blues musicians and guitarists of all time, was inducted into the Blues Foundation's Hall of Fame. Reputedly one of the first blues musicians to don a strap and play standing—as well as one of the first to play electric guitar—she recorded for forty years, virtually unheard of for any woman at the time!

Singer-songwriters Wendy and Lisa joined Prince's band this year. Also known as the Girl Bros., Lisa Coleman and Wendy Melvoin share musical family legacies: both their fathers—Mike Melvoin and Gary Coleman (not the actor!)—were both in-demand session musicians. Although most known for their collaboration with Prince, Wendy and Lisa have gone on to become music producers and session artists, working with Seal, k. d. lang, and Sheryl Crow, and have scored music for NBC hit shows *Crossing Jordan* and *Heroes*.

1981

January 10

Heart's revision of Aaron Neville's 1967 smash "Tell It Like It Is" peaked at No. 8. It was their first Top 10 record since "Magic Man" five years earlier.

January 18

Wendy O'Williams, the brawny-belle leader of the Plasmatics, was arrested in Milwaukee after feigning masturbation with a sledgehammer while onstage. During the arrest, the police had to pin the divine Miss O'W to the floor in order to control her as a melee broke out. She received twelve stitches for her efforts from the cut above her eye.

January 19

Marie and Donny Osmond, along with Frank Sinatra and Dean Martin, performed at President Reagan's inaugural ball.

Notable birthdays: (January 25) Alicia Keyes

February 5

Canadian Prime Minister Pierre Trudeau inducted Joni Mitchell into Canada's Juno Hall of Fame.

February 14

Sheena Easton's "Morning Train" debuted on the Hot 100, on its way to No. 1. The song was originally called "9 to 5," but was changed to avoid confusion with Dolly Parton's hit.

Notable birthdays: (February 11) Kelly Rowland (Destiny's Child)

March 28

British beauty Kim Wilde's debut single, "Kids in America," a pop single written by her brother, Ricky, and produced by her father, Marty (who was a Brit hit maker in the late '50s and '60s) reached No. 2 in England while the kids in America would make it No. 25 a year later.

Deborah Harry and Blondie scored their fourth No. 1 in two years Stateside with "Rapture," holding off John Lennon's "Woman" from the top spot.

Kim Carnes, (a former member of the New Christy Minstrels with Kenny Rogers) charted with "Bette Davis Eyes," which roared to No. 1 for nine weeks. It became her biggest hit of nineteen Top 100 entries

Notable birthdays: (March 11) Latoya Luckett (Destiny's Child)

April 4

Heart's version of "Unchained Melody" became the eighth version of the song to make the Hot 100 when it rose to No. 83. It was recorded live at McNichols Arena in Denver.

April 25

Emmylou Harris' cover of the Chordettes' 1954 hit "Mister Sandman," featuring Dolly Parton and Linda Ronstadt on backup vocals, reached No. 37, becoming her last of only four pop Top 100 singles.

May 2

Over eight months after being a hit in England, Sheena Easton's "Morning Train (9 to 5)" topped the U.S. chart for the first of two weeks. It would eventually sell over a million copies. The title was changed for the American market to avoid confusion with Dolly Parton's then-current No. 1 song "9 To 5."

May 16

Kim Carnes' sixth chart single, "Bette Davis Eyes" (a remake of the obscure Jackie DeShannon 1974 album cut), topped the charts for week No. 1 of a nine-week run, kicking EMI America label-mate Sheena Easton ("Morning Train") off the pinnacle in the process. An international hit, it also reached No. 10 in England.

May 23

Kim Carnes turned down the Smokey Robinson song "Being with You," so he recorded it himself and it reached No. 2 pop today. He was kept from the top spot by (you guessed it) Kim Carnes' "Bette Davis Eyes."

May 28

Mary Lou Williams, the "Queen of Kansas City pianists" during the Roaring Twenties and thirties died at age seventy-one of cancer.

May 30

Kim Wilde's "Chequered Love" spent its second of two weeks at No. 4 in England. Admitting that she didn't have a strong enough voice yet for live performances, Kim concentrated on promoting her records via TV and video appearances.

June 16

Kim Carnes' "Bette Davis Eyes" was certified gold by the RIAA. Kim was originally a jingle and demo session singer and spent the late '60s in the folk group the New Christy Minstrels.

June 27

Kim Carnes' rock-orientated, synthesizer-driven *Mistaken Identity* album, featuring musical guest Wendy Waldman, topped the American chart for the first of four weeks and reached No. 26 in Britain.

July 4

Annie Lennox and Dave Stewart (the Eurythmics) debuted with "Never Gonna Cry Again," which stalled at No. 63 in Britain. They formed the duo a week after their love affair ended. (The name emanated from a 1990s dance-and-mime form by Emil Jacques Dalcrose, based on Greek formats of teaching children music by movement.)

July 25

Stevie Nicks, formerly of the band Fritz and Fleetwood Mac, leaped onto the Hot 100 with "Stop Draggin' My Heart Around" (No. 3). It was her debut solo hit of fourteen she would have through 1994.

"She's [Stevie Nicks] so tiny, and she has this big deep voice that comes rattling out, and I think that's very, very sexy." —Deborah Harry

August 1

Pat Benatar's "You Better Run" video was the first music video by a female and second music clip overall broadcast on the premiering MTV cable network, following the Buggles' "Video Killed the Radio Star."

August 5

Olivia Newton-John was honored with a star on Hollywood's Walk of Fame.

August 8

Sheena Easton became the only James Bond theme singer to be seen onscreen (singing the song during the credits) as her "For Your Eyes Only" peaked at No. 8 in England.

August 26

Patti Austin's Quincy Jones–produced *Every Home Should Have One* album charted, on its way to No. 36, becoming Patti's biggest of five Top 200 albums through 1990. Patti was more well known behind the scenes, having provided backing vocals on albums by such stars as Michael Jackson (*Off the Wall*), Paul Simon, Billy Joel, and George Benson, among many others.

August 29

The Pointer Sisters' "Slow Hand" reached No. 2 pop and No. 7 R&B, becoming their biggest pop hit. The song that kept it from No. 1 was Lionel Richie and Diana Ross' "Endless Love."

September 5

Stevie Nicks' "Stop Draggin' My Heart Around" peaked at No. 3 the same week as her debut solo album, *Bella Donna,* topped the American chart while reaching No. 11 in Britain in August. It would be the beginning of her dual career with Fleetwood Mac and as a solo artist.

September 25

After escaping with 36 cents and a Mobil gas credit card from a brutal relationship with husband Ike Turner, Tina Turner began her comeback as the supporting act for the Rolling Stones' tenth American tour, starting at JFK Stadium, Philadelphia. Prior to the performance, Tina was half a million dollars in debt and working anywhere she could, including less-than-exotic venues in Bahrain, Yugoslavia, and Poland.

Notable birthdays: (September 4) Beyoncé Knowles (Destiny's Child)

October 2

Ann and Nancy Wilson (Heart) performed, along with Joan Baez and Paul Simon at the Greek Theater in Berkeley, California, at the Bread and Roses Festival, a benefit for prisoners aid run by Baez's sister, folksinger Mimi Farina.

October 17

Sheena Easton's "For Your Eyes Only" (theme from the James Bond movie of the same name) reached No. 4 (and No. 8 in England). She became the only Bond-theme vocalist to be seen onscreen as she sung the song during the credits.

November 14

Australia's version of a U.S. invasion occurred when four of the Top 10 singles were from Down Under, led by technical Aussie Olivia Newton-John's

"Physical" (No. 3). The others were Little River Band, Air Supply, Rick Springfield.

November 21

A song that would become one of the first and most identifiable aerobic themes, "Physical" by Olivia Newton-John reached No. 1 for the first of a ten-week stay, equaling the second longest American chart topper in pop history behind Elvis Presley's eleven-week run with "Hound Dog." It also made it to No. 7 in England.

Notable birthdays: (November 1) LaTavia Roberson (Destiny's Child), (November 26) Natasha Bedingfield

December 12

Sheena Easton earned Britain's *Daily Mirror* "Nationwide" Rock and Pop Awards' Best Female Singer category and the *TV Times* Readers' Female Personality of the Year Award in Britain. She also garnered *Billboard*'s Top New Artist trophy in America.

December 18

Tina Turner and Kim Carnes performed at Rod Stewart's Great Western Forum gig in Inglewood, California. The show was broadcast live to over 35 million people.

December 19

Diana Ross' first RCA single after two decades with Motown, "Why Do Fools Fall in Love," a remake of the Frankie Lymon and the Teenagers' classic peaked at No. 7 pop, No. 6 R&B, and No. 4 in England.

December 20

The musical *Dreamgirls* opened on Broadway. It was based on the career of the Supremes. After four years and 1,522 performances, it closed, after garnering six Tony Awards in 1982. The musical was adapted into an award-winning film twenty-five years later.

Notable birthdays: (December 2) Britney Spears

More Moments in 1981

The single "O Superman" launched the recording career of performance artist and musician Laurie Anderson, rising to No. 2 on the British pop charts and subsequently appearing on *Big Science,* the first of her seven albums on the

Warner Bros. label. Anderson also created several of the unique instruments used on her recordings and performances.

1982

January 24

Diana Ross sang the national anthem at Superbowl XVI in Pontiac, Michigan's Pontiac Silverdome.

January 25

Pat Benatar received the Favorite Female Artist, Pop/Rock, Award at the ninth American Music Awards at the Shrine Auditorium in Los Angeles.

February 6

Joan Jett and the Blackhearts charted with "I Love Rock and Roll," an eventual No. 1 and the first of her ten Top 100 hits through 1990.

February 18

Cher began her Broadway acting debut in *Come Back to the Five and Dime, Jimmy Dean, Jimmy Dean.*

February 24

Having topped the charts in twenty-one countries, Kim Carnes' "Bette Davis Eyes" not surprisingly won both the Record of the Year and Song of the Year categories at the twenty-fourth annual Grammy Awards ceremonies.

Randy Crawford won the Best Female Artist Award at the first annual BRIT Awards in London. Crawford's initial notoriety came from her pairing with jazz-fusion group the Crusaders on 1979's "Street Life," included on the soundtrack for the Burt Reynolds flick *Sharky's Machine.*

March 6

The Go Go's debut album, *Beauty and the Beast,* topped the U.S. charts for the first of six weeks, receiving two platinum sales awards as their single "We Got the Beat" beat a path to No. 2. The all-female New Wave band originally called themselves the Misfits in 1977. A year later, they would change it to the Go Go's.

March 13

The British male trio Fun Boy Three brought in female trio Bananarama to add backup vocals to its second single, "It Ain't What You Do, It's the Way

That You Do It," which reached No. 4 in England. It was the female group's first hit. The trio were still working day jobs at the time, with Siobhan Fahey working in the Decca Records press department, Karen Woodward working for the BBC, and Sarah Dallin attending the London College of Fashion.

March 18

Punk rock star and actress Roxy Saint was born. Though brought up in Alabama, she became a sensation in England, becoming known as the Queen of Punk mostly due to a series of frenetic performances with Korn, Linkin Park, Green Day, the Offspring, and sixteen raunchy and raucous videos. Her newest film is *Zombie Strippers,* costarring with Jenna Jameson and Robert Englund, in 2008.

April 9

Tina Turner performed at the Hammersmith Odeon in London. During this period in her comeback, the tremendously energetic and talented artist, amazingly, did not have a recording contract.

April 10

Chrissie Hynde and Ray Davies were to be married, but were turned away by a registrar concerned that they were arguing too much.

April 24

Patti Austin, in a duet with James Ingram, "Baby Come to Me," reached the Top 100 for the second time today. The record was first released almost a year earlier, reaching only No. 73, but after being featured on the soap opera *General Hospital,* it was reissued and would eventually climb to No. 1. It would be Patti's only pop chart No. 1. Unlike in England, where reissued singles are a common practice, it's almost unheard of in America.

Notable birthdays: (April 24) Kelly Clarkson

May 1

Bananarama's moribund revival of the Velvelettes' oldie "Really Sayin' Somethin'" reached No. 5 in Britain. The group originally performed as an a cappella vocal trio in clubs and pubs.

May 28

Grace Slick and Jefferson Airplane took part in a benefit concert for the

Vietnam Veterans' Project at Moscone Center in San Francisco, with the Grateful Dead and Boz Scaggs.

June 10

Addie "Mickie" Harris of the Shirelles died of a heart attack after performing at a show in Atlanta. She died on the birthday of Shirelles lead singer Shirley Owens.

June 12

Never one to miss a good cause, Joan Baez with Linda Ronstadt and others performed for over 750,000 people at a rally for nuclear disarmament in Central Park, New York.

July 10

Former Leonard Cohen backup vocalist Laura Branigan hit the Hot 100 with "Gloria" (No. 2), her second of thirteen charters between 1982 and 1990. "Gloria" was originally a hit in Italian for its singer/composer, Umberto Tozzi.

August 7

Carly Simon's "Why," taken from the film *Soup for One,* with its pop/dance irreverence, reached No. 10 in Great Britain, though it would peak at only No. 74 in America. Carly had eight chart singles in Britain, with the biggest being "You're So Vain," reaching No. 3.

August 14

The Go Go's' second single, "Vacation," entered the pop chart, eventually rising to No. 8 and gold status.

August 15

Kim Wilde's "Kids in America" made it to No. 25 Stateside as her label announced she had sold over 6 million discs worldwide in just eighteen months. Interestingly that's more than both her father, Marty Wilde, who had a fourteen-hit British career, and her mother, Joyce (her manager), who was a member of the '60s Vernon Girls, combined.

August 21

Jennifer Warnes and Joe Cocker climbed onto the singles survey with "Up Where We Belong." The duet from the film *An Officer and a Gentlemen* spent three weeks in the top spot.

Notable birthdays: (August 28) LeAnn Rimes

September 4

Choreographer Toni Basil (*American Graffiti*) hit the bestseller list as a vocalist with "Mickey," which became a No. 1 smash. Talk about shortening your name, her stage name was a nom de guerre for Antonia Basilotta! The world-famous video for Mickey included real cheerleaders from Dorsey High School in Los Angeles.

September 9

Patti LaBelle opened on Broadway, co-starring with Al Green in the gospel musical *Your Arm's Too Short to Box with God.*" The Alvin Theater schedule called for thirty shows, but due to rave reviews, the show ran for eighty performances.

September 16

Dionne Warwick's "Heartbreaker" was issued. It became her eleventh Top 10 hit (No. 10) since she began recording in 1962.

September 25

Jennifer Holliday ascended the R&B charts with "I Am Changing" (No. 29), the song she sang in the Broadway play *Dreamgirls.*

October 9

Diana Ross charted with "Muscles," reaching No. 10 pop (No. 4 R&B). The song was written and produced by Michael Jackson, and it's no coincidence that Muscles was also the name of Michael's pet snake.

November 6

Donna Summer led an all-star backup group of Dionne Warwick, Stevie Wonder, Michael Jackson, James Ingram, Lionel Richie, and Kenny Loggins in the "State of Independence" single, but it wasn't enough as it only reached No. 41 pop and No. 31 R&B today.

Jennifer Warnes' duet with Joe Cocker "Up Where We Belong," from the film *An Officer and a Gentleman,* starring Richard Gere, topped the pop chart, staying on to the pinnacle for three weeks.

November 20

Suzi Quatro's "Heart of Stone" stopped at No. 60 in Britain, her last of sixteen charters there. The Detroit native then began hosting the British daytime program *Gas*. Suzi started out playing piano and drums, as taught by her father, and played bongos in her father's semi-professional Art Quatro Trio at age eight. She left school in 1964 and formed the Pleasure Seekers with her sisters, Patti, Arlene, and Nancy. In 1967, Quatro and her sisters traveled to Vietnam to tour casualty wards.

November 25

Carole King made her second appearance of the year on NBC-TV's *Late Night with David Letterman.*

November 26

Gladys Knight and Aretha Franklin performed at the Jamaica World Music Festival in Montego Bay, Jamaica, before more than 45,000 fans.

November 27

The Pointer Sisters contagious dance track "I'm So Excited" reached No. 30 pop, but would have a rebirth in a slightly different and more pulsating mix two years later, when it was reissued and reached No. 9.

December 17

Karen Carpenter made her last singing appearance, performing Christmas carols at the Buckley School in Sherman Oaks, California, a performance attended by her godchildren.

December 18

Janet Jackson's career started modestly when "Young Love" reached the hit list today (No. 64), becoming her first of forty-two charters through 2002.

December 31

Bette Midler and Barry Manilow appeared as Baby New Year and Father Time, respectively, at a New Years Eve concert at the Universal Amphitheater

More Moments in 1982

One of the most important jazz guitarists of the '80s, Emily Remler's unorthodox technique garnered raves from luminaries like guitar great Herb Ellis, who referred to her as "the new superstar of guitar." In an interview with *People* magazine this year, she said of herself: "I may look like a nice Jewish girl from New Jersey, but inside I'm a fifty-year-old, heavyset black man with a big thumb, like Wes Montgomery."

1983

January 8

Reba McEntire, who already had fifteen country chart singles, finally had her first No. 1, "Can't Even Get the Blues." She would go on to have seventeen more through 1993. Reba began her entertainment career as a singer and hometown rodeo performer (in barrel races), learning the tricks of the trade from her rodeo champion, steer-roping father.

Notable birthdays: (July 2) Michelle Branch

February 4

Karen Carpenter was the epitome of the soft rock/pop sound of the '70s. She (a rare case of a lead vocalist/drummer) and her brother, Richard, fashioned twenty-nine hits between 1970 and 1982, including "Close to You," "We've Only Just Begun," and "Rainy Days And Mondays." Karen was found unconscious in her parents' Downey, California, home and was rushed to Downey Community Hospital, where she died of cardiac arrest today. She was only thirty-two years old.

February 8

Kim Wilde was named Best British Female Artist at the second annual BRIT Awards at London's Grosvenor House Hotel. Obviously buoyed with confidence, the beautiful twenty-two-year-old would finally move from her family home to an apartment in London.

February 19

James Ingram and Patti Austin's "Baby Come to Me" reached No. 1 on the pop charts, after taking eighteen weeks to get their.

March 12

Bonnie Tyler, the Welsh powerhouse female version of Rod Stewart, hit No. 1 in England with "Total Eclipse of the Heart." Later in the year, she'd attain the same status in America.

March 19

Bananarama's update of Steam's 1969 American No. 1, "Na Na Hey Hey Kiss Him Goodbye," hit No. 5 in Britain.

Chrissie Hynde and the Pretenders' "Back on the Chain Gang," from the Martin Scorsese's film *King of Comedy*, peaked at No. 5. Hynde was heavily influenced by mid-'60s soul artists (having attended a Mitch Ryder and the Detroit Wheels concert at a local amusement park in 1965 when she was only years old). She learned to play a ukulele before playing guitar with the Akron, Ohio, band Saturday Sunday Matinee.

April 11

Jennifer Warnes and Joe Cocker performed their hit recording "Up Where We Belong" at the Academy Awards, and the song went on to win the Oscar for Best Original Song. Not bad for a girl who worked at the Bun and Cone hamburger stand in Fullerton, California, before becoming a sales assistant at the Shades and Blinds store.

April 20

Deborah Harry opened in the comedy *Teaneck Tanzi: The Venus Flytrap*, in which she starred as a wrestler, with Andy Kaufman. The show had its debut at the Nederlander Theater in New York and closed after its opening night.

May 14

The Eurythmics charted with "Sweet Dreams." The duo's debut on the American charts reached No. 1, followed by fourteen more hits through 1989.

May 16

The Supremes (Diana Ross, Mary Wilson, and Cindy Birdsong) reunited for Motown's twenty-fifth anniversary, which was televised on NBC-TV.

May 21

Anita Baker debuted on the R&B charts with "No More Tears," which reached No. 49. She would go on to have twenty-one R&B chart singles through 1995.

May 28

Gladys Knight's "Save the Overtime (for Me)" reached No. 1 R&B, giving Gladys her first No. 1 in almost nine years, not to mention a nice thirty-ninth birthday present.

June 4

Donna Summer entered the charts with the unofficial women's national anthem of the '80s, "She Works Hard for the Money," reaching No. 1 R&B for three weeks and No. 3 pop.

July 2

Bananarama, a girl trio from London, had their U.S. chart debut today with "Shy Boy," eventually peaking at No. 83. The group would chart eleven times Stateside with their biggest hit "Venus" (a remake of Shocking Blue's 1969 No. 1) reaching No. 1 in 1984. The group coined its name by combining the children's TV show *The Banana Splits* with the Roxy Music song "Pyjamarama."

July 9

Jerry Butler, who had a succession of hits duetting with females (Brenda Lee Eager, Betty Everett, and Thelma Houston), hit the R&B charts with Patti Austin on "In My Life" (No. 92).

July 16

The female version of Rod Stewart, Bonnie Tyler charted with "Total Eclipse of the Heart" (No. 1). Her distinctive, raspy sound was caused by a throat operation to remove nodules in 1976.

July 22

Diana Ross performed in Central Park in New York at a free concert to make up for the show she started the night before but was whipped out after only three tunes by high winds and a typical New York downpour.

July 23

"All Night Long" by the Mary Jane Girls charted, eventually reaching No. 11 R&B.

August 6

Bananarama's infectious single "Cruel Summer" peaked at No. 8 in England.

August 18

Joan Jett and the Blackhearts performed at Shea Stadium in Queens, New York, along with the Police.

August 21

Shirley Caesar, Andre Crouch, and Barry White performed in Jerusalem at the First Annual Gospel Festival.

September 3

Annie Lennox and Dave Stewart's (the Eurythmics') "Sweet Dreams (Are Made of This)" rose to No. 1 in America, eventually selling a million copies. Four years earlier, Lennox and Stewart were in a group called the Tourists, who performed at London's Lyceum Ballroom on a bill with the B-52's. They also had four chart singles in 1979-'80, including their biggest, a remake of Dusty Springfield's "I Only Want to Be with You," which reached No. 4 in the U.K.

Tony Award winner Jennifer Holliday (*Dreamgirls*) charted R&B with "I Am Love" (No. 2).

October 1

The postal system in Sweden issued an ABBA stamp.

October 2

Agnetha Faltskog of ABBA was hospitalized with a concussion after a car crash in Skane, Sweden.

October 29

Dolly Parton's "Islands in the Stream," a duet with Kenny Rogers, written by the Bee Gees, hit No. 1 pop, the only platinum-selling single of the year. It would eventually win a slew of awards, including Favorite Country Single and the Academy of Country Music's Single Record of the Year.

Madonna's "Holiday," which was passed on by Phyllis Hyman and Mary Wilson, charted, on its way to No. 16. Her break came at the Danceteria Club, when she gave DJ/producer Mark Kamins a tape of the dance material she made. Kamins introduced her to Sire Records' executive Michael Rosenblatt, who upon hearing her cassette agreed to sign her.

December 8

Annie Lennox traveled to Vienna, Austria, to see a throat specialist about a recurring voice problem.

"As part of the generation that's coming up, you look at Madonna and you don't want to let her down. That's such a motivation for me. I love doing what I do, but when Madonna comes around—like when we were making the video for 'Me Against the Music'—it's like, 'Everybody get your act together—the godmother is here.'"—Britney Spears

December 10

Pat Benatar's "Love Is a Battlefield" fought its way to No. 5 on the national pop charts. Meanwhile, her *Live from Earth* album landed at No. 13.

December 17

Former vocalist with the group Blue Angel, Cyndi Lauper ascended the charts with "Girls Just Wanna Have Fun," an eventual No. 2. It was her debut single and first of fourteen hits through 1995.

1984

January 14

Madonna's debut, "Holiday," charted, eventually reaching No. 6 in the U.K., helped by her performance on BBC-1 TV's *Top of The Pops*. Meanwhile, her self-titled album peaked at No. 6 in Great Britain.

January 16

Pat Benatar won the Favorite Female Artist, Pop/Rock, category for the second time at the eleventh annual American Music Awards at the Shrine Auditorium in Los Angeles.

February 4

Pat Benatar's eleventh American chart single, "Love Is a Battlefield," landed her on the British charts at No. 49 for the first time.

The Eurythmics reached No. 8 in Britain, on their way to No. 7 U.S. with "Here Comes the Rain Again." The song was recorded in a little-used church in Crouch End, London.

February 13

Donna Summer's remake of the Drifters' 1960 hit "There Goes My Baby" peaked at No. 21 pop and No. 20 R&B.

February 25

British jazz/R&B singer Sade charted in England with her debut, "Your Love Is King," reaching No. 6. It would be almost a year before she would become known in America, but for a different song, "Smooth Operator."

Pat Benatar.

March 3

The German group Nena, featuring alluring Nena Kerger, reached No. 1 in Holland, Germany, and England, and No. 2 in the U.S. The song had such a contagious pop melody that no one apparently cared that "99 Luft Ballons" (Red Ballons) was sung in German!

March 10

Madonna charted for the first time with "Borderline" (No. 10). She's since reached the Top 10 thirty-four times through 2002.

April 5

Cyndi Lauper's "Girls Just Wanna Have Fun" won the second annual Best Female Video at the American Video Awards.

May 26

Bananarama's "Robert De Niro's Waiting" only reached No. 95, but it reportedly caught the ear of De Niro, who loved the song and contacted the band to arrange a meeting. The song topped out at No. 3 in Britain.

June 2

Whitney Houston charted for the first time with "Hold Me," a duet with Teddy Pendergrass. The record reached No. 5 R&B (No. 46 pop) and would be the first of forty-five R&B charters through 2003. Before recording on her own, Whitney was a background singer for Chaka Khan and Lou Rawls.

June 9

Cyndi Lauper's "Time After Time" soared to No. 1, earning a gold disc, while reaching No. 3 in Great Britain. Lauper left her Queens, New York, home at seventeen in 1970 to hitchhike through Canada with her dog, Sparkle.

June 16

Tina Turner's *Private Dancer* album charted, reaching No. 3 (No. 1 R&B), becoming such a huge hit that it stayed in the Top 10 for ten months. It also sold over 10 million copies worldwide. In Britain, it reached No. 2. Not bad for her first album without ex-husband Ike.

July 25

Willie Mae "Big Mama" Thornton was a powerful blues singer who also played drums and harmonica. It must have been a sight to see a 350-pound woman pounding out drumbeats in the '40s. She's best known for her original, growling version of "Hound Dog" (later recorded by Elvis Presley) and "Ball and Chain" (later cut by Janis Joplin). She died of alcohol dependency in Los Angeles at age fifty-seven today.

July 29

British vocal group Bananarama's first major American chart success, "Cruel Summer," was released, after being featured in the film *The Karate Kid,* reaching No. 9.

August 4

The Pointer Sisters rocked the Hot 100 with "I'm So Excited" (No. 9). It was the second release for the single, and except for a slight remix, was the same recording that hit No. 30 in 1982.

September 1

Four years before her first success, Melissa Etheridge performed at the West Coast Women's Festival in Santa Barbara, California .

Tina Turner's "What's Love Got to Do with It" reached No. 1 pop (No. 2 R&B) on the same day she was offered a part in the third of the Mad Max series of movies.

September 7

Janet Jackson announced that she had secretly married DeBarge's James DeBarge. Seven months later, she was back in mama's arms.

September 8

Chaka Khan reached the Hot 100 with "I Feel for You," her biggest hit (No. 3).

Cyndi Lauper's "She Bop" reached No. 3, earning her a third gold disc.

September 18

Bette Midler co-hosted (with Dan Aykroyd) the first MTV Video Music Awards at Radio City Music Hall in New York. Tina Turner performed, and Cyndi Lauper won the Best Female Video category for "Girls Just Wanna Have Fun." Annie Lennox (the Eurythmics) received the Best New Artist Video category for "Sweet Dreams." Madonna also performed.

September 29

The Go Go's last of seven chart singles, "Yes or No," peaked at No. 84. Guitarist

Jane Wiedlin then decided to quit the band rather than continue to put up with vocalist Belinda Carlisle and bassist Kathy Valentine's ongoing drug problems.

October 8

The Pointer Sisters' "I Need You" (No. 48 pop, No. 13 R&B) charted. The group initially made a name by singing backup for Elvin Bishop, Grace Slick, and Boz Scaggs.

November 17

Madonna's "Like a Virgin" reached the singles survey today, on its way to No. 1. It was the first of eleven No. 1s for the "sexpose" expert.

November 25

Bananarama gathered with thirty-five other artists in SARM Studio in Notting Hill, London, to record the historic "Do They Know It's Christmas?"

December 1

Diana Ross moved onto the Hot 100 with "Missing You," a No. 10 hit, which was written and produced by Lionel Ritchie as a dedication to slain singer Marvin Gaye.

December 8

Cyndi Lauper's "All Through the Night" stopped at No. 5, becoming her fourth consecutive Top 5 smash in one year.

December 22

Madonna's "Like a Virgin" streaked to No. 1, perching there for the first of six weeks, the longest chart topper since another female (Olivia Newton-John) did it in 1981 with "Physical," which stayed on top for ten weeks.

More Moments in 1984

Folk senior Elizabeth "Libba" Cotton, discovered in her sixties, is bestowed with honors: a National Endowment for the Arts National Heritage Fellowship Award and a Grammy for Best Ethnic or Traditional Folk Recording for *Elizabeth Cotten Live!* She would later receive another Grammy nod for Best Traditional Folk Recording in 1986. She was in her nineties!

Sheila E's "The Glamorous Life," penned by friend Prince, becomes an '80s classic and launches her solo career.

1985

January 12

Madonna's "Like a Virgin" peaked at No. 3 in Britain. The femme fatale started out in a band in 1979 called the Breakfast Club, playing local clubs in Paris, originally as the group's drummer but soon moving to the mike.

January 15

Kim Carnes, in a duet with Barbra Streisand on "Make No Mistake, He's Mine," peaked at No. 51. Meanwhile, her participation in the one-off trio with Kenny Rogers and James Ingram on "What About Me" (No. 15) and Carnes' solo single "Invitation to Dance" (featured in the film *That's Dancing*) at No. 68 made Kim the only artist (male or female) ever to simultaneously hold positions on the American charts as a soloist, in a duet, and as a member of a trio.

January 28

The sign on the wall said, "Check Your Egos at the Door," and with that directive from Quincy Jones, forty-five major stars entered A&M Studios in Hollywood to record the song Michael Jackson and Lionel Richie had written (in only two hours) called "We Are the World." The recording was to act as a fund-raiser for the USA for Africa fund. Among the icons at the mike were Tina Turner, Diana Ross, Dionne Warwick, Cyndi Lauper, Kim Carnes, Ray Charles, Stevie Wonder, Michael Jackson, Lionel Richie, Bruce Springsteen, Paul Simon, and Bob Dylan. It took over ten hours to do the single recording. Prince was invited but didn't come.

January 29

Dolly Parton's duet with Kenny Rogers, "Islands in the Stream," won the Favorite Single, Country, category at the twelfth annual American Music Awards held at the Shrine Auditorium in Los Angeles. The record also went to No. 7 in England, becoming Dolly's biggest hit there.

January 31

Barbara Cowsill was the mom and background singer in the popular '60s folk/rock group the Cowsills, which was actually made up of members of her children. The Rhode Island mom and her brew were discovered by record producer Wes Farrell and subsequently charted eight times between 1967 and 1969, including the million sellers "Hair," "Indian Lake," and "The Rain, The Park and Other Things." ABC-TV chose them to sing the theme from *Love American Style,* but they balked at performing in a sitcom about themselves when told that the mother would be played by actress Shirley Jones. Instead, ABC, with Farrell producing the music, made its own Cowsills sitcom called the *Partridge Family,* and the rest, as they say, is history. By 1972, Barbara and the family were bankrupt. Barbara died today while working the graveyard shift at a Tempe, Arizona, nursing home of emphysema. She was fifty-sic years old.

February 9

Madonna's *Like a Virgin* album began a three-week visit to No. 1 and would become her most successful album, staying in the Top 200 for over two years and selling over 9 million domestic copies.

Patti LaBelle charted R&B with "New Attitude," from the movie *Beverly Hills Cop,* reaching No. 3 R&B and No. 17 pop.

February 11

Sade's "Diamond Life" won the Best British Album category at the fourth annual BRIT Awards at London's Grosvenor House Hotel.

February 13

Madonna and actor Sean Penn had their first date at the Private Eyes club in New York.

February 26

Tina Turner won Record of the Year, Song of the Year, and Best Female Vocal Performance, all for the million seller "What's Love Got to Do with It" at the twenty-seventh annual Grammy's. The Pointer Sisters won Best Performance by a Duo or Group with Vocal for "Jump (For My Love)" while Cyndi Lauper earned the Best New Artist category.

March 2

Sheena Easton became the first artist in history to achieve Top 10 hits on the pop, R&B, country, dance, and adult contemporary charts when "Sugar Walls" (written by Prince) reached No. 9 today.

March 8

Whitney Houston's self-titled debut album reached No. 1 on the pop charts and stayed there for fourteen weeks. The album sold over 12 million records

"With her looks and talent, she had all the credentials. Her success was something that was supposed to happen. And like all of us in the family, Whitney [Houston] was singing from the moment she came out." —Singer (and cousin) Dionne Warwick

worldwide, establishing her as a premier artist of the times, though it took the album twelve months to climb to the top.

April 1

The Singing Nun (Sister Luc-Gabrielle) had one of the all-time "surprise" hits when "Dominique" went to No. 1. The Belgian nun innocently record-ed an album at the Philips Records studio for her friends at the Fichermont Monastery when the execs heard the work and sent out a thousand copies for sale. A European hit, the album was issued in America, and "Dominique" spent two months at No. 1. By 1966, Sister Luc had left the monastery under her real name, Jeanine Deckers, to do charity work. Making the story even more unusual was her bizarre demise in a suicide pact with her female lover when the two overdosed on drugs and alcohol. She was fifty-two years old.

May 10

The short-lived all-female rock band the Go Go's announced at a press con-ference that they were formally breaking up after seven successful singles, in-cluding "We Got the Beat," and three hit albums. Jane Wiedlin would go on to have an acting career, appearing in *Clue, Sleeping Beauty, Bill and Ted's*

Excellent Adventure, and *Star Trek IV,* among other films. The breakup would last for all of five months (see October 8.)

May 11

Whitney Houston charted solo for the first time on the pop charts with "You Give Good Love," reaching No. 3 and becoming her first of eight R&B No. 1s. Whitney is the daughter of Cissy Houston and cousin of Dionne and Dee Dee Warwick. Before her solo career started, she was a model for *Glamour* magazine and had graced the front cover of *Seventeen.*

May 18

Annie Lennox's (the Eurythmics') *Be Yourself Tonight* album peaked at No. 3 in Britain and would soon reach No. 9 in America. Guest vocalists included Aretha Franklin, Elvis Costello, and Stevie Wonder.

Sade reached No. 5 pop and R&B with "Smooth Operator." The former model of English/Nigerian descent was a member of the eight-member funk band Pride before establishing her own group called Sade, though most people thought of her as a solo artist.

June 8

The Mary Jane Girls peaked at No. 7 pop for three straight weeks (No. 3 R&B) with the infectious dance hit "In My House."

June 29

Whitney Houston stormed onto the singles chart with "Saving All My Love for You," an eventual No. 1 pop and R&B hit. She would go on to have eleven pop No. 1 singles through 2002. The song was originally done in 1982 by Marilyn McCoo and Billy Davis, formerly of the 5th Dimension.

July 7

Aretha Franklin and Annie Lennox's "Sisters Are Doing It for Themselves," was already a hit in England. Meanwhile, Annie made her acting debut in the film *Revolution,* starring Al Pacino.

July 13

Annie Lennox's (the Eurythmics') "Would I Lie to You?" topped off at No. 5. Though Annie was scheduled to play at the Live Aid concert, she had to cancel when her voice problems recurred.

In the most ambitious rock and pop festival ever held, more than fifty legendary acts performed in two simultaneous events broadcast live from both Philadelphia, Pennsylvania, and London, England. Known as the Live Aid concert (to raise money for starving Africans), acts included Joan Baez, Madonna, Tina Turner, Patti LaBelle, Paul McCartney, Bob Dylan, Mick Jagger, the Beach Boys, Elton John, David Bowie, the Who, Queen, Santana, Little River Band, the Four Tops, Ozzy Osbourne, David Ruffin and Eddie Kendricks, the Pretenders, Tom Petty and the Heartbreakers, B. B. King, Men at Work, Black Sabbath, Jimmy Page, Robert Plant, Crosby, Stills, Nash and Young, and Duran Duran.

Madonna, performing at the Philadelphia part of the Live Aid concert at JFK Stadium, was introduced by Bette Midler, who stated that Madonna was "A woman who pulled herself up by her bra straps." About this same time, *Penthouse* and *Playboy* magazines featured early (1977) nude photos of her.

July 16

Madonna's "Crazy for You" was certified gold. It was her fifth Top 10 hit and second No. 1 in a year.

July 27

Whitney Houston's solo single debut, "You Give Good Love," peaked at No. 3. A year earlier, the then-unknown singer recorded a duet with Teddy Pendergrass, "Hold Me," which only reached No. 46.

August 16

Madonna married Sean Penn on her twenty-sixth birthday. News helicopters and paparazzi flew overhead as the cliffside wedding took place.

August 17

Whitney Houston stormed the Hot 100 with "Saving All My Love for You." It was her first of eleven No. 1s through 2002.

August 24

Heart's ballad "What About Love?" reached No. 10 on the pop charts.

August 31

Chrissie Hynde teamed with UB40 on a revival of Sonny and Cher's "I Got You Babe," which reached No. 28 pop while topping the British chart. The spirited vocalist spent three years at Kent State University, studying art, and later, while in London, modeled at St. Martin's School of Art.

September 13

Tina Turner won the Best Female Video trophy at the second annual MTV Video Music Awards at New York's Radio City Music Hall for "What's Love Got to Do with It." The famine-relief recording, "We Are the World," by USA for Africa won Best Group Video and the Viewers Choice Award.

September 18

Gladys Knight debuted in the sitcom *Charlie & Co.* with Flip Wilson, which would run for one season.

September 21

Madonna's "Like a Virgin" crawled to the top of the British charts after almost a year of being released.

Notable birthdays: (September 27) Avril Lavigne

October 8

The Go-Go's reformed to pose nude for a benefit poster for PETA (People for the Ethical Treatment of Animals)with the caption, "We'd rather go naked than wear fur." They then planned for an upcoming reunion tour.

October 12

Jennifer Rush reached No. 1 in England with "The Power of Love." It would stay there for five weeks and become the biggest hit of the year. The Queens, New York, sixteen-year-old (born Heidi Stern) only reached No. 57 in her homeland.

October 19

Gloria Estefan charted with "Conga" (No. 10), her first of thirty hits through 2001.

November 9

The Winans gospel group crossed over to secular music with the chart debut of "Let My People Go" (No. 42 R&B).

November 23

Aretha Franklin and Annie Lennox's "Sisters Are Doing It for Themselves" hit No. 9 in Britain.

December 7

With her mother, Cissy, singing backup vocals, Whitney Houston jumped onto the hit list with "How Will I Know," ultimately reaching No. 1.

December 12

Dionne Warwick received a star on the Hollywood Walk of Fame.

December 14

Madonna's "Dress You Up" peaked at No. 5 in Britain, becoming her eighth Top 10 hit of the year. She became the only woman to have three singles in the English Top 15 since Ruby Murray did it thirty years earlier.

December 21

Heart's self-titled new album, their first for Capitol Records, peaked at No. 1 for a week, eventually garnering platinum status.

1986

January 18

Dionne Warwick and her friends (Gladys Knight, Elton John, and Stevie Wonder) began a four-week stay at No. 1 with "That's What Friends Are For." It became a million seller and the biggest selling single of the year.

January 20

The Pointer Sisters, Stevie Wonder, Eddie Murphy, and Bill Cosby performed in concert to honor the first annual observance of Martin Luther King Jr.'s birthday as a national holiday.

January 29

Stevie Nicks married Warner Bros. Records promotion man Kim Anderson. That's one way to make sure your product gets priority.

February 1

Diana Ross married shipping tycoon Arne Naess in Geneva, Switzerland. Stevie Wonder sang at the reception.

The Bangles performed at the first of six British dates at Portsmouth Polytechnic.

February 8

Gloria Estefan and the Miami Sound Machine's "Conga," based on a traditional Cuban street dance, stepped its way to No. 10, their first American charter. Earlier, the city of Miami renamed the street on which the Estafans lived Miami Sound Machine Boulevard, in honor of the local group's success.

February 10

Annie Lennox was named Best British Female Artist for the second time at the fifth annual BRIT Awards at the Grosvenor House Hotel in London, England.

February 15

Whitney Houston's "How Will I Know" topped the pop charts.

February 25

Dionne Warwick presented her cousin Whitney Houston with the Best Pop Vocal Performance, Female, award at the twenty-eighth annual Grammys. Meanwhile, Amy Grant won the Best Gospel Performance, Female, category (for the fourth consecutive year) for "Unguarded." Amy was first signed at the age of fifteen to the Contemporary Christian Word label in 1975.

Notable birthdays: (February 21) Charlotte Church

March 15

The Bangles' single "Manic Monday," written by Christopher (Prince's pseudonym), was the group's chart debut in England and would eventually reach No. 2 in both America and Britain.

March 22

Heart's "These Dreams," a ballad dedicated to a twenty-one-year-old cancer victim, Sharon Hess, who had spent two weeks with the group prior to her death, reached No. 1, usurping the top spot from Starship's "Sara." "These Dreams" was recorded by Heart after being rejected by Stevie Nicks.

April 19

The Bangles reached No. 2 with "Maniac Monday," which was written by Prince, but it could not displace His Purpleness' "Kiss" from the No. 1 spot.

May 9

Belinda Carlisle made her first solo appearance after leaving the Go-Go's, in Cleveland, Ohio.

May 10

Gloria Estefan and the Miami Sound Machine's "Bad Boy" reached No. 8. At the same time, the group's first all-English album *Primitive Love,* containing both "Conga" and "Bad Boy," hit No. 23. It would eventually be a double-platinum smash.

May 17

Former Go-Go's member Belinda Carlisle charted for the first of her nine Top 100 singles with "Mad About You."

June 4

Joni Mitchell and Joan Baez added their talents to the two-week Amnesty International A Conspiracy of Hope concert tour, performing with Peter Gabriel, Bryan Adams, the Neville Brothers, Sting, and Lou Reed, which started at the Cow Palace in San Francisco.

June 14

Patti LaBelle, in a duet with Michael McDonald, topped the pop charts with "On My Own." The song was recorded by each singer in separate studios 3,000 miles apart. In fact, the two did not meet until they performed the song together on Johnny Carson's *The Tonight Show.*

June 15

Joni Mitchell sang three songs at the Amnesty International Concert at Giants Stadium in East Rutherford, New Jersey.

June 20

Tina Turner performed in the "Prince's Trust" concert in London, along with Elton John, Bryan Adams, and Eric Clapton.

June 21

Berlin, featuring Terri Nunn, leaped onto the Hot 100 with "Take My Breath Away," an eventual No. 1. Terri was a teen TV actress, having appeared in shows such as *Lou Grant.*

June 28

Sade performed at an anti-apartheid concert in London. Also appearing were Sting, Boy George, Elvis Costello, Peter Gabriel, and Hugh Masekela, among others.

July 5

Janet Jackson's *Control* album soared to No. 1, making the twenty-year-old the youngest artist since thirteen-year-old Little Stevie Wonder topped the album Top 200.

July 12

Madonna's *True Blue* entered the British album chart at No. 1 and stayed there for five more weeks, earning multi-platinum status on the same day her "Papa Don't Preach" single topped the British singles survey.

August 9

Janet Jackson breached the bestseller list with "When I Think of You," the first of ten eventual No. 1s through 2002 for the youngest member of the Jackson family.

August 16

"Papa Don't Preach" by Madonna topped the Hot 100 singles list the same day her *True Blue* album started a five-week stay at No. 1. It would eventually sell more than 7 million copies in America alone.

The former lead singer of Chapter 8, Anita Baker swept onto the bestseller list with "Sweet Love." After leaving Chapter 8 in 1980, she took an office job in Detroit until her chance to record solo came in 1983. "Sweet Love" was her first pop hit.

August 28

Tina Turner was honored with a star on the Hollywood Walk of Fame in front of Capitol Records, the company she recorded for.

September 2

Sixteen-year-old Debbie Gibson signed with Atlantic Records while still attending high school, beginning a string of eleven chart singles.

September 6

Actress/singer Melba Moore together with Freddie Jackson entered the R&B charts with "A Little Bit More," reaching No. 1, for her career best of thirty-two R&B hits, from 1975 to 1990.

Bananarama's "Venus" topped the charts, as did Shocking Blue's original some sixteen years earlier.

September 20

Gloria Estefan's first ballad in English, "Words Get in the Way," peaked at No. 5 on the Top 100 singles chart.

Though mainly a contemporary Christian artist, Amy Grant (with Peter Cetera) charted with "Next Time I Fall." The No. 1 recording was the first of seven Top 20 pop hits for the Augusta, Georgia, native.

September 27

The Bangles' "Walk Like an Egyptian" ran onto the Hot 100, finally stopping at No. 1. The group survived only three more years before disbanding.

October 11

Madonna's "True Blue" topped the British charts, tying Britisher Sandie Shaw's record of most U.K. No. 1s (three) by a female act.

When Janet Jackson's "When I Think of You" reached No. 1, she and her brother Michael became the first siblings to have solo No. 1s in the rock era. Michael's No. 1 was "Ben," in 1972.

October 13

Reba McEntire received the Entertainer of the Year Award from the Country Music Association.

October 18

Christine McVie of Fleetwood Mac married Portuguese composer Eduardo Quintela de Mendonca in London.

Hard to believe it never happened before, but for the first time in rock history, females held the top three spots on the charts, Janet Jackson ("When I Think of You"), Tina Turner ("Typical Male"), and Cyndi Lauper ("True Colors").

November 1

Anita Baker's "Sweet Love" peaked at No. 8 on the pop charts today. Anita started her career as lead singer of the Detroit group Chapter 8, which had five R&B chart singles, starting in 1979. An international bestseller, "Sweet Love" also reached No. 13 in England.

Sippie Wallace (born Beaulah Thomas) was a gospel singer turned blues vocalist of the 1920s, who was influential among latter-day artists such as Bonnie Raitt. Sippie was best known for recordings like "Bedroom Blues" and "Up the

Country Blues." She died on the same date she was born while on tour in Germany at the age of eighty-eight!

November 15

All of the top five spots on the British singles chart were held by women for the first time. They were Terri Nunn (Berlin), Kim Wilde, Susannah Hoffs (the Bangles), Mel and Kim, and Corinne Drewery (Swing Out Sisters).

Kim Wilde's remake of the Supremes' 1966 smash "You Keep Me Hanging On" reached No. 2 in England. During her tour of Europe, she picked up the nickname "the Bardot of Rock," a reference to France's sex symbol Brigitte Bardot.

The Bangles' "Walk Like an Egyptian" reached No. 3 in Great Britain. The song was originally turned down by Tony Basil. The origin of the all-girl band came about when Los Angeles resident Vickie Peterson formed her first band in ninth grade and, needing a drummer, bought a drum kit and drafted her sister Debbi to play it.

November 29

Cyndi Lauper's "Change of Heart" charted, eventually reaching No. 3.

December 2

In a fit of performance euphoria more akin to American rockers, Annie Lennox while performing "Missionary Man" in Birmingham, England, ripped off her bra before the astounded and ecstatic (male members, anyway) audience.

December 6

Amy Grant's "The Next Time I Fall," a pop-ballad duet with Peter Cetera, topped the pop chart as her album *The Collection,* comprising the majority of her inspirational hits, made it to No. 66 on the pop charts, an astounding accomplishment for an inspirational album.

December 13

Madonna's "Dress You Up" reached No. 5 in England, becoming her eighth Top 10 hit of the year in the British Isles.

December 20

Rebbie Jackson paired with rocker Robin Zander of Cheap Trick to chart with "You Send the Rain Away," reaching No. 50 pop. The song was intended for Barbra Streisand and Neil Diamond by publisher Jay Warner, but an A&R exec sent the song to Rebbie by mistake.

The Bangles' "Walk Like an Egyptian" became the group's biggest U.S. hit, topping the chart for the first of four weeks, helped in no small measure by a "King Tut" parody-styled video. Lead singer Sussanah Hoffs formed the band after placing a classified ad in a local paper: "Band members wanted: Into the Beatles, Byrds and Buffalo Springfield." The group would become first the Supersonic Bangs, then the Bangs, and finally the Bangles.

December 31

Melba Moore and Gladys Knight performed on CBS-TV's *Happy New Year America* show.

More Moments in 1986

June Millington, of the all-girl rock band Fanny of the late '60s/early '70s, co-founds the Institute for the Musical Arts, an organization that educates and empowers female musicians.

Heart gets their first No. 1 hit with "These Dreams," released as the third single from their eponymous 1985 album. Sung by guitarist Nancy Wilson, it features lyrics penned by Elton John collaborator Bernie Taupin.

1987

January 10

Cyndi Lauper's "Change of Heart," with the Bangles singing backup, stopped at No. 67 in the U.K. She had better luck Stateside as it reached No. 3 pop. Cyndi was one of the few artists to have their first and last hit be basically the same song, as "Girls Just Wanna Have Fun" reached No. 2 as her debut single in 1983 while "Hey Now (Girls Just Wanna have Fun)," her fourteenth and last charter, reached No. 87 in 1995.

January 17

Kate Bush's album *The Whole Story* topped the British charts for the first of two weeks.

January 21

Aretha Franklin was inducted into the Rock and Roll Hall of Fame by Rolling Stones member Keith Richards during the second annual awards presentation in New York City.

January 24

Carly Simon's "Coming Around Again" came around to No. 18 on the pop chart.

Exposé charted with "Come Go with Me" (No. 5). It was the first of their twelve hits through 1989.

January 26

Diana Ross hosted the fourteenth annual American Music Awards at the Shrine Auditorium in Los Angeles. Meanwhile, Janet Jackson, who was nominated in nine categories, walked away with two awards, Best Female R&B Video Artist and Best R&B Single for "Nasty."

February 7

Madonna's "Open Up Your Heart" became her fifth No. 1 and her third from the album *True Blue*.

February 14

Cyndi Lauper's "Change of Heart," though only reaching No. 67 in Britain, peaked at No. 3 in the States. The Esra Mohawk composition included backing vocals by the Bangles.

February 21

Aretha Franklin charted in a duet with George Michael on "I Knew You Were Waiting." It was her first No. 1 in twenty years (since "Respect," in 1967).

February 24

Reba McEntire's "Whoever's in New England" earned the country queen her first Grammy for Best Country Vocal Performance, Female, at the twenty-ninth annual Grammy Awards. Her career got a boast when she sang the national anthem at the National Rodeo finals in Oklahoma City, impressing singer Red Steagall, who encouraged her to go to Nashville.

March 4

Tina Turner began her Break Every Rule Tour, starting in Munich, West Germany, which did predictably break every box office record in thirteen countries.

March 7

Carole King and her songwriting partner/ex-husband Gerry Goffin were inducted into the Songwriters Hall of Fame at the eighteenth annual awards held at New York's Plaza Hotel.

March 9

Given a distinction few would be happy about, Madonna was voted Favorite Artist of Record Pirates by a special *Billboard* panel—an exasperating acknowledgment of her worldwide popularity.

March 14

Linda Ronstadt's duet with James Ingram, "Somewhere out There," peaked at No. 2. It was from the animated film *An American Tail*.

March 21

Emmy Lou Harris, Dolly Parton, and Linda Ronstadt's collaborative album, *Trio*, made it to No. 60 in the British isles.

March 23

Dionne Warwick and Luther Vandross co-hosted the initial Soul Train Music Awards in Hollywood, California. It was especially sweet for Vandross, who at age thirteen saw Warwick perform and decided there and then on a music career. Vandross, who at one time worked as a clerk for S & H Green Stamps, spent several years doing backup vocals for artists like Barbra Streisand, Chaka Khan, Carly Simon, and Donna Summer before earning his solo success.

March 28

The trio of Linda Ronstadt, Dolly Parton, and Emmylou Harris reached No. 6 with the fittingly titled *Trio* album, garnering a platinum disc for a million-plus sales.

April 25

Madonna became the only female artist to have four No. 1s in England, when "La Isla Bonita" topped the hit list.

May 9

More than two decades after the formation of Jefferson Airplane, its latest incarnation, Grace Slick and Starship, had their first British chart-topper, "Nothing's Gonna Stop Us Now," which stayed on top for four weeks and became the second biggest seller of the year in Britain.

June 4

The Eurythmics, featuring Annie Lennox, performed in Berlin as more than 1,000 East Berlin fans gathered at the great divide, chanting, "The wall must go."

June 6

Kim Wilde's "You Keep Me Hangin' On" topped the American charts, after reaching No. 2 in England eight months earlier. She consequently became only the fifth British female artist to reach No. 1 Stateside.

June 23

Tiffany (born Tiffany Darwish) began the unique Tiffany Shopping Mall Tour '87 in Paramus, New Jersey. She performed three free shows each weekend in shopping malls for passing customers, in a clever promotion that created tremendous media attention for the sixteen-year-old newcomer. When the summer shows ended, the teen returned to high school. She appeared on *The Tonight Show* with Johnny Carson.

June 27

Whitney Houston's "I Wanna Dance with Somebody" hit No. 1 while her album *Whitney* became the first album by a female singer to debut on *Billboard*'s chart at No. 1.

July 4

Bonnie Raitt sang at the July 4th Disarmament Festival in the Soviet Union, along with Santana, the Doobie Brothers, and James Taylor.

July 11

Heart's "Alone" topped the pop chart for the first of three weeks. It became the group's biggest hit single and was a cover of the little-known I-ten 1983 album cut. It was the third No. 1 in a row by a female, following Whitney Houston's "I Wanna Dance with Somebody" and Lisa Lisa's "Head to Toe." It was also their third and last No. 1.

July 25

Madonna made her debut tour of Britain, starting with a show in Leeds, West York, with the Who's That Girl Tour. The single "Who's That Girl" reached No. 1 there at the same time.

August 1

The rap trio Salt-N-Pepa's debut album, *Hot, Cool and Vicious,* charted, reaching No. 26 and lingering on the Top 200 for over a year, finally going platinum in 1988.

August 8

Siedah Garrett's duet with Michael Jackson, "I Just Can't Stop Loving You," charted, reaching No. 1 pop and R&B in Britain. The ballad was originally turned down by Whitney Houston and Barbra Streisand.

August 27

Donna Summer performed in Concord, California, starting her first American and European tour in four years.

September 5

Debbie Gibson's self-penned chart debut, "Only in My Dreams," reached No. 4 and went on to become the No. 1 12-inch dance single of the year. The prodigy had by seventeen become experienced as a writer, arranger, musician, and producer. At age twelve, she had already won $1,000 in a songwriting contest with her composition "I Come from America."

September 11

Paula Abdul won the Best Choreography Award at MTV's fourth annual Video Music Awards for "Nasty" by Janet Jackson, and would go on to choreograph videos for such broad-based talents as Dolly Parton, ZZ Top, Duran Duran, and Debbie Gibson.

September 23

Dionne Warwick was praised for her philanthropic work when the city of New York honored her for raising over a million dollars for AIDS research.

September 27

Dolly Parton's Wellness and Rehabilitation Center of Sevier County Medical Center opened as ABC-TV premiered *Dolly,* a short lived Sunday-night prime-time variety show.

September 28

Gladys Knight and Smokey Robinson guested for a week on the TV show *$10,000 Pyramid.*

September 30

Bonnie Raitt, Jennifer Warnes, and K. T. Oslin were a splendid and vibrant backing vocal group for Roy Orbison on his TV special *A Black and White Night*. It was a nightclub concert that took place at Los Angeles' famed Coconut Grove in the Ambassador Hotel. Backup musicians to Orbison that historic night included Bruce Springsteen and Elvis Costello.

October 23

Madonna's film *Who's That Girl?* opened in London.

October 28

Sheena Easton made her acting debut on NBC-TV's *Miami Vice* as Caitlin Davies, Sonny Crockett's girlfriend.

November 7

Sixteen-year-old Tiffany topped the charts with "I Think We're Alone Now," a chart hit for Tommy James and the Shondells four years before Tiffany was born.

Written by Christine McVie and her husband, Eddy Quintela, Fleetwood Mac's "Little Lies" hit No. 4 Stateside and No. 5 in Britain.

November 13

Sonny and Cher sang "I Got You Babe" together for the first time in ten years on *Late Night with David Letterman*.

November 21

Produced and written by Michael Bolton, "I Found Someone" by Cher charted today, on its way to becoming her first Top 10 hit (No. 10) in eight years.

November 28

Jennifer Warnes' duet with Bill Medley, "(I've Had) The Time of My Life," from the film *Dirty Dancing*, had the time of its life, making it to No. 1 and No. 6 in Great Britain.

December 5

Ex-Go-Go's member Belinda Carlisle stormed to No. 1 with "Heaven Is a Place on Earth." Helping to promote the single was a video directed by actress Diane Keaton.

k. d. lang and Roy Orbison's powerful duet on "Crying," from the film soundtrack of *Hiding Out* debuted on the country chart, eventually reaching only No. 42, but it would become a live performance highlight on her future tours. For some reason, the spiky-haired country artist with the penchant for a wardrobe of men's clothes always preferred to see her name in lowercase.. The k. d. stood for Katherine Dawn.

December 7

Judy Collins and Pat Benatar, along with Bruce Springsteen, Harry Belafonte, Graham Nash, Richie Havens, and the Hooters, took part in a Harry Chapin memorial concert, The Gold Medal Celebration, on what would have been the singer's forty-fifth birthday, at Carnegie Hall in New York.

December 26

Kim Wilde duetted with British comedian Mel Smith (as Mel and Kim) on a new version of Brenda Lee's "Rockin' Around the Christmas Tree," which reached No. 3 in Britain today. The proceeds from the record were given to the Comic Relief charity.

More Moments in 1987

Billie Holiday was posthumously awarded the Grammy Lifetime Achievement Award this year.

Mississippi "Hill Country" blues guitarist Jesse Mae Hemphill, known for her unorthodox playing technique (she often wore a tambourine on her foot to keep time), was awarded the prestigious W. C. Handy Award for Best Traditional Female Blues Artist in both 1987 and 1988, even though she had yet to release an album in the States!

In 1991, she released her second album (her first in the U.S.), titled *Feelin' Good,* winning the W. C. Handy Award again for Best Acoustic Album that year.

1988

January 9

Whitney Houston's "So Emotional" hit No. 1 pop, giving her six consecutive chart toppers.

January 16

Tina Turner performed before 180,000 fans at Rio de Janeiro's American Stadium. A box office record for a single artist.

January 19

A memorial in Janis Joplin's honor at the Southeast Texas Musical Heritage Exhibit in Port Arthur, Texas, was unveiled. More than 5,000 people attended the ceremony.

January 20

The Supremes were inducted into the Rock and Roll Hall of Fame during its third annual ceremony.

January 23

Sixteen-year-old Tiffany's self-titled album reached No. 1.

January 30

Tiffany's "I Think We're Alone Now" rushed to No. 1 in Great Britain for the first of three weeks. At the same time, the cute teen arrived in Britain to a media frenzy.

February 6

The Bangles' cover of Simon and Garfunkel's 1966 No. 13 "Hazy Shade of Winter" single hit No. 2, behind Tiffany's "Could've Been."

February 8

Bananarama performed "Love in the First Degree" at the seventh annual BRIT Awards at London's Royal Albert Hall. It would be group member Siobhan Fahey's last performance with the trio. She semi-retired to enjoy married life, before forming the duo Shakespeare's Sister with Marcella Detroit. A long-time Bananarama friend, Jacqui Sullivan, onetime vocalist with Siren and the Shillelagh Sisters, took over for Fahey.

February 20

After being turned down by every British major label, Kylie Minogue hit No. 1 with "I Should Be So Lucky" on the independent PWL imprint. Kylie was also a TV star from Australia, performing in *Neighbors,* a soap opera. She would go on to have thirty-one Top 30 hits in Britain.

February 28

k. d. lang performed at the Winter Olympics closing ceremony at McMahon Stadium in Calgary, Canada.

March 2

Linda Ronstadt won her third Grammy, for Best Country Vocal, Duo or Group, as part of a trio with Dolly Parton and Emmylou Harris on the *Trio* album at the thirtieth annual awards. It was Emmylou's fifth Grammy. Jennifer Warnes' duet with Bill Medley (formerly of the Righteous Brothers), "(I've Had) The Time of My Life," won the Best Pop Performance by a Duo or Group with Vocal category.

March 12

Gloria Estefan charted with "Anything for You," which became her first of three No. 1s.

March 26

While Tiffany's single "Could've Been" peaked at No. 5 in England, the traumatized teen ran away to live with her grandmother in La Mirada, California, after problems surfaced with her mother.

March 28

Tina Turner's Break Every Rule Tour ended today in Osaka, Japan, after she had performed 230 dates in twenty-five countries, playing to over 3 million people. The tour broke box office records in thirteen countries.

March 30

Gladys Knight and the Pips were honored with the Heritage Award at the second annual Soul Train Music Awards, coinciding with their thirtieth recording anniversary.

April 2

Due to disputes with her mother, a court gave temporary custody of Tiffany to her aunt in order for her to become the teen's guardian.

April 5

The RIAA certified 4 million copies sold of Tiffany's self-titled album.

April 11

Jennifer Warnes and Bill Medley (of the Righteous Brothers) sang "(I've Had) The Time of My Life" at the Academy Awards. It became the third Warnes-sung song to win an Oscar (see April 14).

April 23

Tiffany's "I Saw Him Standing There," a cover of the Beatles' 1964 hit, reached No. 7 pop.

Whitney Houston topped the pop charts with "Where Do Broken Hearts Go" while setting a record for most consecutive No. 1 singles. It was her seventh, beating out both the Bee Gees and the Beatles, who each had six in a row.

April 30

Talk about an international mélange, French Canadian Celine Dion performed for Switzerland, in the thirty-third annual Eurovision Song Contest held at the Royal Dublin Society in Dublin, Ireland with "Ne Partez Pas San Moi". . . and won!

May 3

Madonna began her run on Broadway at the Royal Theater in *Speed the Plow,* with Ron Silver and Joe Mantagna.

May 14

Gloria Estefan and the Miami Sound Machine's "Anything for You" became their biggest hit to date, topping the singles chart for a week.

May 28

k. d. lang debuted on the pop charts with *Shadowland.* The album featured Loretta Lynn, Brenda Lee, and the Jordonaires. While in her teens, lang placed eighth in a national javelin competition.

June 4

Armed with an anthropology degree from Tufts University (just in case), folk/R&B artist Tracy Chapman didn't need it when she cruised onto the charts with "Fast Car" (No. 6), her first of five hits through 1996.

June 11

Natalie Cole (in a rare live performance), Annie Lennox, Ashford and Simpson, Tracy Chapman, and the artist she emulated, Joan Armatrading, performed at Nelson Mandela's seventieth birthday concert at Wembley Stadium in England.

June 18

Belinda Carlisle visited Japan on a promo tour while "Circle in the Sand" reached No. 7 in the U.S. and No. 4 in the U.K., from the album *Heaven on Earth*, which also peaked at No. 4 in Britain.

Choreographer Paula Abdul punched her way onto the charts with "Knocked Out" (No. 41), her first of fourteen hits through 1995.

Melissa Etheridge's debut self-titled album, showcasing her raspy vocal style, entered the chart, on its way to No. 22 during a sixty-five week run. Melissa's career direction came into focus when her father gave her a guitar at the age of eight.

June 25

Debbie Gibson's "Foolish Beat" topped the pop chart, making the seventeen-year-old Gibson the youngest artist to write, produce, and perform a No. 1 single. It was her fourth straight chart record to reach No. 4 or better.

June 26

Debbie Gibson graduated with honors from Calhoun High School in Merrick, Long Island. The seventeen-year-old had already amassed four Top 5 hits before leaving school.

June 27

Cyndi Lauper, who had run off to Canada at age seventeen and never finished high school, received an honorary high school diploma at Richmond Hill High School in Queens, New York.

July 1

Debbie Gibson began her first headlining concert tour in Boston.

Melissa Etheridge performed at the Montreux Jazz Festival in Montreux, Switzerland. During the year, she would appear at concerts in America, Holland, Canada, Germany, England, and Italy as the opening act for both Huey Lewis and the News and Bruce Hornsby. Melissa attended Berklee College of Music in Boston at age eighteen, and then left for Los Angeles on her twenty-first birthday to seek a career in music.

July 11

Gloria Estefan and Linda Ronstadt performed at the first International Festival of Arts in New York's Central Park.

July 16

Seventeen-year-old Tiffany signed a deal to appear on Coco Puffs cereal boxes while "Feelings of Forever" peaked at No. 50 Stateside and No. 52 in Britain.

July 23

Former Polish-born vocalist for the British group Matt Bianco, Basia charted with "Time and Tide" (No. 26).

August 4

Brenda Lee sued MCA Records for failing to account for sales and licensing her records without her authorization. Within a year, all concerned would settle rather than go to court.

August 19

Folksinger Nanci Griffith's two performances at the Anderson Fair Club in Houston were recorded for subsequent release in November as the *One Fair Summer Evening* album. Nanci was inspired to begin a singing career by the likes of Bob Dylan and Carolyn Hester.

August 20

Karyn White, a former studio singer, assailed the R&B Top 100 with "The Way You Love Me," making it the first of three No. 1s in a row. The hits to follow were "Superwoman" and "Love Saw It."

August 22

Aretha Franklin: The Queen of Soul, a one-hour public television documentary, was aired. Appearing on the extravaganza with Aretha were Whitney Houston, Ray Charles, Smokey Robinson, and Eric Clapton.

August 28

Kylie Minogue sold over 2 million copies of her debut album, *Kylie,* in England. It became the biggest-selling album in England by a female artist to date.

September 2

A world-wide charity tour to raise money for Amnesty International began with a concert at London's Wembley Stadium, featuring Tracy Chapman, along with Bruce Springsteen and Sting.

September 28

Anita Baker and Luther Vandross performed in Washington, D.C., at the start of their The Heat Tour.

October 29

The first single by Enya (born Eithne Ni Bhraonain, Gaelic for Brennan), the ethereal "Orinoco Flow" (named after Venezuela's Orinoco River), surged to No. 1 in England, showcasing Enya's unique vocal style and innovative oceanic synthesizer sound. Her equally airy album, *Watermark,* soared to No. 5 in Britain the following week, staying on the Brit hit list for a remarkable sixty-three weeks.

October 31

Cher's "Believe" reached No. 1 in Britain, making her the first female artist over the age of fifty to reach the top spot.

Debbie Gibson reportedly held a séance at a Halloween party, in an attempt to contact Sid Vicious and Liberace, not necessarily in that order.

November 5

Taylor Dane ascended the Hot 100 with "Don't Rush Me" (No. 2), her fourth Top 10 single in a row.

November 22

Janet (Ertel) Bleyer was a member of a barbershop group turned pop, the Chordettes. They had fourteen hits in the '50s and early '60s, including "Lollipop" and "Mr. Sandman" on Cadence Records, owned by her husband and bandleader, Archie Bleyer. She died in her hometown of Sheboygan, Wisconsin, at age seventy-five.

December 3

Choreographer turned singer Paula Abdul charted with "Straight Up," a dance tune that zoomed to the top spot, becoming the first of her six No. 1s in less then three years.

December 10

Natalie Cole won NAACP's twenty-first Image Award for Best Female Artist.

December 12

Madonna signed a two-year deal with Columbia Pictures to do five films.

December 17

Anita Baker hit No. 3 on the pop charts with "Giving You the Best That I Got."
A week later (obviously in celebration of the hit), she married her longtime
boyfriend, Walter Bridgeforth.

1989

January 7

Kylie Minogue's "Especially for You" (a duet with Jason Donovan) began a
three-week stay at No. 1 in England, though it never charted in America.

January 11

The Karen Carpenter Story, a CBS-TV movie with Cynthia Gibb in the title
role, aired and topped the ratings.

January 14

Annie Lennox's first project outside of the Eurythmics, the duet with soulster
Al Green, "Put A Little Love in Your Heart," topped out at No. 9.

January 18

Tina Turner inducted legendary record producer Phil Spector into the Rock
and Roll Hall of Fame at its fourth ceremony. Spector produced and co-wrote
Tina's epic single "River Deep, Mountain High."

January 25

Tiffany received a platinum disc for the album *Hold an Old Friend's Hand* in
(not surprisingly) a shopping mall in Los Angeles. The seventeen-year-old
started her career performing free shows at shopping malls.

January 30

Gloria Estefan and the Miami Sound Machine won the Favorite Band, Duo or
Group, Pop/Rock, category at the sixteenth annual American Music Awards,
held at the Shrine Auditorium in Los Angeles.

Annie Lennox.

February 4

Enya's *Watermark* album debuted on the U.S. Top 200, eventually reaching No. 25 while selling over 8 million copies globally!

February 11

Paula Abdul's debut album, *Straight Up,* topped the national charts today. Not bad for a girl who began as a choreographer for the Los Angeles Lakers (for $50 per game) while still a freshman at Cal-State, Northridge, College.

February 12

Aretha Franklin was sued by a Broadway producer for $1 million because she failed to show up for rehearsals. The "Queen of Soul" blamed her fear of flying for not appearing in the show *Sing Mahalia Sing* (the story of legendary gospel artist Mahalia Jackson), but the judge ruled against her today.

February 13

Annie Lennox was named Best British Female Artist for the third time at the eighth annual BRIT Awards at the Royal Albert Hall, London.

February 18

Debbie Gibson hit the top of the album charts for the first of five weeks with *Electric Youth.*

February 22

Amy Grant's "Lead Me On" won the Best Gospel Performance, Female, category (even though it had an overt pop quality) at the thirty-first annual Grammy Awards.

March 2

Madonna became a $5 million winner as a sponsor for Pepsi-Cola. For the first time, a major star used a song for a TV commercial ahead of its retail release, when "Like a Prayer" aired during NBC-TV's *The Cosby Show.*

March 3

Madonna's "Like a Prayer" was not well received, as Italian TV refused to air her video clip believing it to be blasphemous.

March 11

Ann Wilson's duet with Cheap Trick's Robin Zander on "Surrender to Me," from the Kurt Russell film *Tequila Sunrise,* reached No. 6.

Debbie Gibson's album *Electric Youth,* recorded at Z Studio in Brooklyn, New York, began a five-week stay at No. 1.

March 25

Madonna's "Like a Prayer" reached No. 1 in Great Britain for the first of three weeks. Its promotional video caused a worldwide media and religious storm, and was banned by the Vatican because of its strong religious imagery. Pepsi-Cola, who paid Madonna $5 million as a spokesperson, dropped its commercial and withdrew Madonna's sponsorship, claiming consumer confusion between the commercial and the video.

March 30

After singing together as Gladys Knight and the Pips for thirty-one years, Gladys made her solo debut at Bally's Casino in Las Vegas.

April 1

Ethnically exotic Neneh Cherry (of Swedish and West African parentage) charted with "Buffalo Stance," from the film *Slaves of New York*. It peaked at No. 3.

Madonna's "Like a Prayer" hit No. 1 in the U.K. and would soon be No. 1 in the U.S. The promo video caused such a religious uproar that her tour was canceled, her sponsor Pepsi-Cola dropped her, and she was banned by the Vatican!!

April 4

Tiffany sang the national anthem on the opening day of the baseball season at the California Angels game at Anaheim Stadium.

April 15

Carly Simon's powerful "Let the River Run," the theme song to the Melanie Griffith film *Working Girl,* reached No. 49. Though a disappointment sales-wise, it would go on to win a Grammy and an Oscar.

Enya's "Orinoco Flow," now known as "Sail Away" in America, peaked at No. 24. Almost six months earlier, it had stormed its way to No. 1 in England and most of Europe. Enya was educated as a young teen at a convent in Millford, Ireland, and performed as a vocalist and keyboardist in the Irish band Clannad in 1980. She was the classically trained pianist daughter of show-band leader Lee O. Bhraonain.

April 22

Madonna had the No. 1 album and single in America with "Like a Prayer" and its album of the same name.

May 5

Natalie Cole appeared at the John Lennon Tribute Concert, singing "Lucy in the Sky with Diamonds" and "Ticket to Ride." The event was held at the Pier Head Arena in Merseyside, England.

May 11

Anita Baker co-hosted the twentieth annual Songwriters Hall of Fame Awards ceremony at Radio City Music Hall in New York with Dick Clark.

May 16

Janet Jackson was harassed by fans when she took a VIP tour of Universal

Studios. Adding insult to injury, the fans believed they were hounding her brother Michael. Her brother, on the other hand, went unnoticed on the tour while wearing a disguise.

June 3

The Shangri-La's reunite for the first time since the early seventies for Cousin Brucie's "First Palisades Amusement Park Reunion" at the Meadowlands in East Rutherford, New Jersey. Also appearing were Lesley Gore, the Tokens, Bobby Rydell, and Freddy Cannon.

June 8

Chrissie Hynde, a well-publicized vegetarian, stated at a Greenpeace Rainbow Warriors press conference in London that she once firebombed a McDonald's. The next day, a McDonald's in Milton Keynes, England, was firebombed. The McDonald's Corporation threatened legal action against Hynde and demanded she sign a letter not to repeat her statements.

June 10

Bette Midler reached No. 1 with her version of "Wind Beneath My Wings," which was prominent in her film *Beaches*. The soundtrack album hit No. 2 while making it to the same chart spot on the British charts. It was her first Top 10 single in nine years.

June 17

k. d. lang and the Reclines (her backup band named in honor of Patsy Cline) released an album, *Absolute Torch and Twang,* which began a year-long stay on the pop chart, peaking at No. 69 in March 1990.

June 21

Commenting in an interview on the upcoming Jefferson Airplane reunion album, Grace Slick said, "We're your parents' worst nightmare because now we are your parents."

June 24

Aretha Franklin and Whitney Houston's duet "It Isn't, It Wasn't, It Ain't Never Gonna Be" was released. It became Aretha's seventy-second chart rider (No. 41) and Whitney's twelfth, though it was the only single of her first fourteen that did not reach the Top 5.

June 25

Debbie Gibson sat in for Shadoe Stevens on his syndicated radio show, *American Top 40*.

July 10

The Shirelles appeared in Nashville, but not to sing in the usual sense. They were in federal court to sue local Gusto Records over improper payments of royalties on reissued hits. Ten months later, they won.

July 12

A Disney press release announced that Deborah Harry would play the Old Woman Who Lived in a Shoe in the Disney Channel's Shelly Duvall–produced *Mother Goose Rock 'n' Rhyme*.

July 15

Madonna's "Express Yourself" expressed itself to No. 2 as Madonna tied the Beatles all-time total of sixteen consecutive Top 5 hits. Her sixteen was still far removed from Elvis Presley's record of twenty-four.

July 18

The Jefferson Airplane reformed with original members (Grace Slick, Marty Balin, Paul Kantner, Jorma Kaukonen, and Jack Cassidy). The group then became Starship.

July 19

Joan Baez added her considerable talents to the seventh annual Prince's Trust Rock Gala with Van Morrison, Level 42, and others at the National Exhibition Center in Birmingham, West Midlands, England.

July 30

Emmylou Harris performed at the thirtieth annual Newport Folk Festival in Newport, Rhode Island, on a bill featuring Pete Seeger, John Lee Hooker, and John Prine, among others.

August 24

Patti LaBelle appeared in the Who's *Tommy* with an all-star cast, including Phil Collins and Elton John, at the Universal Amphitheater. She played the part of the Acid Queen.

Notable Moments of Women in Music

September 2

Carly Simon signed copies of her children's book, *Amy and the Dancing Bear,* at the Bunch O'Grapes bookstore in Vineyard Haven, Massachusetts.

Marianne Faithfull began teaching a three-day course, "Love, Fear, and the Ridiculous: Songwriting and Performing," at the Omega Institute in Rhinebeck, New York.

September 12

A written statement, titled "God Wants Us to Be Together," among other missives sent to recording artist Tiffany got a Santa Cruz, California, man, Jeffery Turner, in deep water and forced a Los Angeles court judge to issue a restraining order for his obsessive behavior toward her.

September 14

Shirley Alston Reeves of the Shirelles joined with members of the 5 Satins, the Belmonts, the Silhouettes, the Jive Five, and the Falcons in a doo-wop performance outside the Berklee Performance Center in Boston to promote the formation of the Doo-Wop Hall of Fame of America.

September 15

Natalie Cole hosted a forerunner of *American Idol* with her weekly show *Big Break.*

September 21

Formed in 1981, and after twelve Top 100 hits, the Bangles announced they were disbanding.

September 23

Nanci Griffith's *Storms* album reached No. 38 in Britain and would become her American chart debut, at No. 99, after eleven years of recording.

September 25

Four years after a Bette Midler impersonator (former Midler backup singer Ula Hedwig) sang "Do You Want to Dance" in a 1985 Mercury Sable commercial, a trial began in Midler's $10 million lawsuit against the Ford Motor Company and the Young and Rubicam Advertising Agency for using a sound-alike to impersonate Bette.

Gloria Estefan began three nights of performances at the Wembley Arena in Wembley, London.

October 3

Deborah Harry made her performance comeback in Great Britain after a seven-year absence at the small Borderline Club in London.

October 9

British thrushes Kylie Minogue, Sonia, and Hazel Dean began a tour called The Hitman Roadshow, named after their producer, Peter "Hitman" Waterman.

November 4

Belinda Carlisle's *Runaway Horses* album, featuring fellow Go-Go's Charlotte Coffey, Kathy Valentine, and Gina Schock guesting on "Shades of Michaelangelo" (with additional contributions from George Harrison and Bryan Adams), reached No. 4 in Britain during a year-and-a-half chart run.

November 5

Chaka Khan began a European tour in Hamburg, West Germany.

November 11

Lisa Stansfield's "All Around the World" soared to No. 1 in Britain for the first of two weeks. It would eventually be No. 1 in ten countries.

November 18

Two sixties vocal groups, the Shangri Las and the 3 Degrees, went to court in dispute over who owned their respective names. The Shangri Las won, but the 3 Degrees court ruling granted their name to former manager Richard Barrett.

December 2

Lisa Stansfield's debut album, *Affection,* hit No. 2 in Britain in its first week on the chart. It would soon sell over 4 million copies worldwide, making her a dominant new soul star.

December 9

Exposé's "Tell Me Why" reached the Hot 100, on its way to No. 9. It was the Miami trio's seventh straight Top 10 hit between 1987 and 1989.

Marianne Faithfull performed Kurt Weill and Bertholdt Brecht's "Seven Deadly Sins" at St. Ann's Cathedral in Brooklyn, New York.

December 13

Melissa Etheridge ended a seventeen-date European tour at the National Exhibition Center in Birmingham, West Midlands, England.

December 16

Joan Baez finished her current tour at the Universal Amphitheater in Los Angeles.

December 21

Martha and the Vandellas reunited for the first time in eighteen years, starting a British tour with a performance at the Talk of the Town in Manchester. When not working with Martha, Rosalind Ashford worked for the phone company and Annette Sterling was working in a hospital.

December 23

Madonna won the Top Adult Contemporary Artist Award in *Billboard*'s Year in Music annual survey

December 27

Bonnie Raitt played four sellout concerts at the Oakland—Alameda County Coliseum (starting today), supporting the Grateful Dead. The folk/blues artist was influenced by the recordings of Joan Baez, Bob Dylan, John Hammond, and Muddy Waters.

More Moments in 1989

At the age of eighteen, Buffalo-based singer/songwriter Ani DiFranco is courted by major labels, but shuns them in favor of creating Righteous Babe, her own label. DiFranco is criticized in the press for "making too much money" off each CD.

The eponymous debut from the Indigo Girls scores a single ("Closer to Fine") and a Grammy (Best Folk Recording). Shortly thereafter, Amy Ray—one-half of the duo—used that momentum to start her own co-op label, Daemon Records, championing indie artists.

Pioneer and "Empress of the Blues" Bessie Smith was inducted into the Rock and Roll Hall of Fame.

"Mariah has an amazing gift from God that has no color, no boundaries, and no limitations. You hear the passion and the honesty within her music." —Patti LaBelle

THE NASTY NINETIES

The fall of the Soviet Union was not the only collapse that captured the nation's attention. The onset of rap severely excluded melody and singing from the nation's music scene. For every rap record on the Top 100, there was one less opportunity for a singer to make their mark. With the near demise of new artists in rock, pop music leaned heavily

> **"We all come from dysfunctional families and these days I guess that's pretty normal."**
> —*Carnie Wilson*
> *(Wilson Phillips)*

on a re-energized R&B format and country music to act as the vehicles for women in music. Not to say that women (mostly young girls, actually) weren't making their voices heard in rap, but it was not through singing. It was talking rhythmically and in rhyme to a track of pared-down electronic instrumentation that blared at the masses. Lil' Kim, Missy Elliott, Foxy Brown, Lauryn Hill, Da Brat, MC Lyte, Eve, Lady Sovereign, and Rah Digga, among others, plied their wares, which luckily for them didn't require a two-to-three-and-a-half-octave range or the ability to stay on key, since there were essentially no keys!

Female rock artists who broke through into the mainstream, such as Sinead O' Connor and Alannah Myles, were rare. Artists from the sixties through the eighties kept their classic-rock audiences through concert performances, TV appearances, and occasional new releases. Cher, Blondie, Bonnie Raitt, Annie Lennox, Stevie Nicks, Pat Benatar, and Belinda Carlisle, among others, kept the past alive in the nineties and beyond.

Pop, however, was a different story, with the emergence of some of the most powerful singers in decades allowing the media to use the term "diva" not only for those who deserved it but for many who didn't. Among the superstar set of the 1990s and early 2000s were Celine Dion, Mariah Carey, LeAnn Rimes, Christina Aguilera, Ace of Base (featuring sisters Jenny and Linn Berggren), Sheryl Crow, Melissa Etheridge, Natalie Imbruglia, Lisa Loeb, Sarah McLachlan, Alanis Morissette, Jewel, Wilson Phillips, Taylor Dayne, and two of the biggest (if not the best), the Spice Girls and Britney Spears. Even Amy Grant drifted from contemporary Christian to secular music, scoring pop hits. And lest we forget the "Rolls-Royce" of female superstars, Madonna was still going strong as the former New York nude model hit age fifty.

> *"After we sold 3 or 4 million albums, we thought we wouldn't be treated like an all-girl band anymore but as a rock 'n' roll band. It never really worked."*
> —*Belinda Carlisle*

Country was still fertile ground for female artists, as the Dixie Chicks, Lorrie Morgan, Allison Krauss, Patti Loveless, Mary Chapin-Carpenter, Shania Twain, Wynonna, Trisha Yearwood, and LeAnn Rimes were joined by a carryover crop of greats from the 1980s, including Reba McEntire, Emmylou Harris, Dolly Parton, Tanya Tucker, and K. T. Oslin, who thrilled fans right into the new millennium.

> *"I'm ambitious. But if I weren't as talented as I am ambitious, I would be a gross monstrosity."*
> —*Madonna*

Though rap came almost exclusively out of the black community, it did not diminish the popularity or the number of R&B newcomers to the ranks of stars in both the urban and pop genres. Just some of the exciting acts to sing soulfully were Ashanti, Mary J. Blige, Toni Braxton, Faith Evans, Monica, Queen Latifah, Brandy, Destiny's Child, Beyoncé, and the white second coming of Teena Marie, Lisa Stansfield. World music, a hard to define but easy to listen to style, emerged, with one of its leading exponents being the Irish lass Enya.

The nineties carried on the growth, development, and discovery of new talent, while creating two distinctive, competing styles for women for the first time in music history: singer vs. rapper.

1990

January 8

Brenda Lee performed at the Elvis Presley Birthday Banquet at Graceland in Memphis to mark the fifteenth anniversary of his passing.

January 15

Patti LaBelle received a Lifetime Achievement Award at the annual CORE (Congress of Racial Equality) awards dinner in New York.

January 17

Carole King (and songwriting partner Gerry Goffin) were inducted into the Rock and Roll Hall of Fame at its fifth annual awards presentation, as was Legendary blues artist Ma Rainey. The awards show was held at the Waldorf Astoria Hotel in New York City.

January 22

Gloria Estefan co-hosted and performed at the seventeenth annual American Music Awards, held at the Shrine Auditorium in Los Angeles.

February 3

Sinead O'Connor's "Nothing Compares 2 U" reached No. 1 in Great Britain, where it would reside for five weeks. No. 2 was by Kyle Minogue and No. 3 by Technotronic. It was the first time in British history that the top three songs were all by non-British and non-American artists and two of the three were female.

February 9

Diana Ross performed at Detroit's Fox Theater, grossing over $700,000 for three shows over three days.

February 18

k. d. lang was pictured on the premiere cover of *Entertainment Weekly* while being depicted as a hot new artist.

February 21

Carly Simon's "Let the River Run" won the Best Song Written Specifically for a Motion Picture category at the thirty-second annual Grammy Awards. It would go on to win an Oscar for Best Song. She would later be hired to write the film score for *Postcards from the Edge*," thanks to her Oscar success. Also, Rickie Lee Jones' "Makin' Whoopee" won the Best Jazz Vocal Performance, Duo or Group, Award. Bette Midler's "Wind Beneath My Wings" won Record of the Year and song of the Year honors. Her performance of the song ended the show.

February 23

Bonnie Raitt had a field day at the thirty-second annual Grammy Awards, at the Shrine Auditorium in Los Angeles, winning Best Rock Vocal Performance Female ("Nick of Time"), Album of the Year (*Nick of Time*). Best Pop Vocal Performance, Female ("Nick of Time"), and Best Traditional Blues Recording ("I'm in the Mood," from John Lee Hooker's album *The Healer*).

February 24

Bonnie Raitt and k. d. lang took part in the Roy Orbison Concert Tribute to Benefit the Homeless, with host Whoopi Goldberg and performances by Bob Dylan, Roger McGuinn, Dwight Yoakam, David Crosby, Bruce Hornsby, Gary Busey, and B. B. King, among others, at the Universal Amphitheater in Universal City, California.

March 1

Janet Jackson began her first tour, the now-famous Rhythm Nation World Tour 1990, at the Miami Arena in Miami, Florida.

March 6

Gloria Estefan and the Miami Sound Machine received the Crystal Globe Award in recognition of the sale of more than 5 million albums outside their home country. The awards were held at the 21 Club in New York.

March 8

Bonnie Raitt won the Best Female Singer trophy in *Rolling Stone* magazine's Critic's Awards. Madonna came out at the opposite end when she was named Worst Female Singer and also was awarded the Worst Video citation ("Like A Prayer") in *Rolling Stone*'s poll.

Cher won two awards she could do with out: Worst Video for "If I Could Turn Back Time" and the Worst Dressed Award, according to *Rolling Stone* magazine.

March 10

Janet Jackson's "Escapade" spent it's second of three weeks at No. 1 R&B. It was Janet's sixth No. 1 in a row, going back to November 1986 and "Control."

March 17

Dionne Warwick performed at the fifteenth-anniversary celebration of her record label, Arista Records, at Radio City Music Hall in New York. She and other label performers would raise $2 million from the concert fund-raiser for AIDS organizations.

Wilson Phillips' debut single, "Hold On," charged onto the Top 100, quickly reaching No. 1. With seven hits in two and a half years, they were truly a short-lived success story.

March 20

Gloria Estefan was badly injured when her group's tour bus was rammed by a tractor-trailer near Scranton, Pennsylvania. Though suffering a fractured and dislocated vertebrae in her spine, she was back onstage performing at the American Music Awards less than eleven months later.

March 24

Sinead O'Connor's second album, *I Do Not Want What I Haven't Got,* debuted at No. 1 in Britain. It would remain charted for the rest of the year while eventually topping the charts in thirteen countries.

March 28

The Go-Go's regrouped for a one-shot benefit concert for the California Environmental Protection Initiative at the Universal Amphitheater in Los Angeles.

April 4

Phoebe Snow and Patti Austin performed at the first New York Rock and Soul Review at the Beacon Theater, along with Michael McDonald and Donald Fagen of Steely Dan.

"What pisses me off is when I've got seven or eight record company fat-pig men sitting there telling me what to wear." —Sinead O'Connor

April 7

After exactly one year, Bonnie Raitt's album *Nick of Time* finally climbed to No. 1 while its single "Have a Heart," featured in the Denzil Washington movie *Heart Condition,* reached No. 49.

Lisa Stansfield's "All Around the World," already No. 1 in England and various other countries, topped out at No. 3 Stateside. It would soon top the R&B chart, making Lisa only the second white artist to accomplish that feat.

Still a soft rock/pop force to be reckoned with in England, a new Carpenters TV-advertised compilation, *Only Yesterday,* topped the British chart during a three-month run in the Top 10, seven years after Karen Carpenter died.

April 14

Sinead O'Connor began a worldwide tour in Cornwall, England, calling it the Year of the Horse Tour.

April 15

The Carly Simon concert, *Carly in Concert: My Romance,* aired on HBO-TV, with Harry Connick Jr. as her guest.

April 16

Bonnie Raitt, Natalie Cole, Anita Baker, and Mica Paris performed at the "Nelson Mandela—An International Tribute to a Free South Africa" concert at Wembley Stadium in Wembley, England, singing Dylan's "Blowin' in the Wind." Raitt, who had taken up guitar at age eight, when she received a $25 instrument as a Christmas gift, went to Radcliffe College in 1967 to take courses in African studies.

April 23

Patti Austin and Phoebe Snow, along with Stevie Wonder and James Taylor, performed at New York's legendary Carnegie Hall at a fund-raiser for Special Olympics Africa.

April 24

Wilson Phillips (deciding on their group name after rejecting forty others, including Gypsy and Leda) made their network-TV debut on *Late Night with David Letterman*.

April 27

Tina Turner performed in Antwerp, Belgium, on the first night of her new Foreign Affair Tour, which would run for 121 shows.

April 28

Sinead O'Connor's *I Do Not Want What I Haven't Got* started a six-week run at the top spot on the album chart, eventually reaching triple-platinum status.

May 2

Belinda Carlisle announced she had dropped out of a $35,000 appearance scheduled for July 23 at the Frontier Days Rodeo in Cheyenne, Wyoming, citing her distaste for the maltreatment of livestock at such events.

May 4

Madonna's American leg of her Blonde Ambition Tour began at the Summit in Houston, Texas, before a sellout crowd.

May 5

En Vogue charted with "Hold On" (No. 2), their first of twelve hits through 1996.

May 12

The ever-contentious Sinead O'Connor refused to appear on NBC-TV's *Saturday Night Live* in protest over the inclusion of guest host, the equally controversial comedian Andrew "Dice" Clay. Talk about the pot calling the kettle black!

May 20

Gloria Estefan received the Crossover Artist of the Year Award at the second annual Latin Music Awards.

May 26

Confirming her position as the queen of contemporary Christian music, *Billboard*'s "Music of the '80s" poll named Amy Grant Gospel Artist of the Decade and her *Age to Age Gospel* collection Gospel Album of the Decade.

Heart's "All I Wanna Do Is Make Love to You" peaked at No. 2 Stateside after reaching No. 8 in the British Isles. The song was reportedly originally offered to Don Henley and was turned down.

Madonna's "Vogue" reached No. 1, and the Top 5 for the first time since June 1979 encompassed all female artists. No. 2 was by Heart ("All I Wanna Do Is Make Love to You"), No. 3 Sinead O'Connor ("Nothing Compares 2 U"), No. 4 Wilson Phillips ("Hold On"), and No. 5 Janet Jackson ("Alright").

May 27

Wilson Phillips performed at the nineteenth Tokyo Song Festival and then won the coveted grand prize with "Hold On," their first of three No. 1s over the next year. Members Carnie and Wendy Wilson are daughters of Beach Boys legend Brian Wilson and member Chynna Phillips is the daughter of the Mamas and the Papas' Michelle and John Phillips.

May 29

Madonna performed at the Sky Dome in Toronto, Canada, while local police scrutinized her concert very carefully due to a complaint about "lewdness."

June 2

Mariah Carey assaulted the Hot 100 with "Vision of Love," her first of five straight No. 1s. Idiosyncrasy alert! When Mariah performed, she demanded that her dressing room be filled with a variety of puppy dogs . . . real ones!

June 3

Folksinger Nanci Griffith performed in The Big Day, an open-air festival from various locations in Glasgow, Scotland, which aired live on C4-TV today.

June 7

Melissa Etheridge performed, starting tonight, for three nights at New York's Beacon Theater.

June 9

Wilson Phillips reached No. 1 with their debut single, "Hold On." Twenty-five years earlier to the day, the Wilson sisters' (Carnie and Wendy's) dad, Brian, and his Beach Boys hit No. 1 with "Help Me Rhonda."

June 28

Tina Turner became the first woman and only the second rock 'n' roll act (Pink Floyd being the other) to perform at the Palace of Versailles in France.

June 30

Mariah Carey's self-titled debut album charted. It would take the ten-song collection thirty-six weeks to make it to No. 1.

July 6

Wilson Phillips started a thirty-five-city tour with Richard Marx at the Concord Pavilion in Concord, California.

July 16

Wilson Phillips appeared on the first installment of *Into the Night Starring Rick Dees* on ABC-TV. Before the group formed, Chynna Phillips had been acting in films since the mid-'80s, including parts in *Some Kind of Wonderful, Caddyshack II,* and *Say Anything.*

July 19

Dionne Warwick appeared at the Greek Theater in Los Angeles alongside Johnny Mathis.

July 20

LaBelle joined forces with Dionne Warwick and Gladys Knight for "Superwoman," a cut on Gladys' new *Good Woman* album, which charted today, eventually reaching No. 45.

Madonna performed at Wembley Stadium at the start of the British leg of her world tour.

July 21

En Vogue reached No. 2 pop with "Hold On," their debut disc. The female quartet was put together by former Commodores member Thomas McElroy and partner Denzil Foster, who wanted to invent a funky, female, contemporary Supremes group.

Joni Mitchell, Marianne Faithfull, Cyndi Lauper, and Sinead O'Connor performed in Roger Waters' performance of *The Wall* at the site of the Berlin Wall in Berlin, Germany. The event, also released as an album and video, was broadcast live throughout the world, raising money for the Memorial Fund for Disaster Relief.

July 25

Bonnie Raitt, along with R&B legend Charles Brown, started a tour in Poughkeepsie, New York, where she had attended summer camp as a child.

August 1

Sinead O'Connor's tour took her to St. Paul, Minnesota (at which time, she reportedly checked into a Minneapolis Hospital to have an abortion).

August 4

Janet Jackson, while performing at a concert in St. Louis, collapsed from an ear infection and was hospitalized. She had only gotten through three songs at the time.

Wilson Phillips' debut album climbed to No. 2, on its way to sales of 7 million worldwide.

August 5

The *Madonna—Live! Blonde Ambition World Tour '90* concert aired on HBO and became the most watched show in the station's eighteen-year history.

August 9

Aretha Franklin performed at New York City's Radio City Music Hall.

August 11

Joan Baez performed at the Newport Folk Festival at Fort Adams State Park, Rhode Island. The sponsors were ice-cream entrepreneurs Ben and Jerry.

August 24

Sinead O'Connor refused to perform at New Jersey's Garden State Arts Center because they played the national anthem. She was protesting the idea of American patriotism. The incident became a major international news event. She could on principal despise patriotism, but it was seemingly all right at the time for her to be having a reported affair with her support act, British soul singer Hugh Harris, while she was still married.

August 26

Aretha Franklin, who failed to appear in the show *Sing Mahalia, Sing* was ordered by a New York judge to pay restitution in the amount of $209,364.07! (I wonder what the 7¢ was for?).

August 29

Wearing a wig and makeup to conceal her identity, Sinead O'Connor joined an anti-O'Connor demonstration outside her own concert prior to her performance in Saratoga Springs, New York. They were protesting because the "bald-headed banshee" refused to perform in New Jersey due to the venue playing the national anthem. Many radio stations began banning her records.

September 12

Stevie Nicks and Christine McVie announced their intention to leave Fleetwood Mac at the end of their current tour.

September 15

Dolly Parton was fined $20,000 by the Department of Labor for making her teenage staff work longer than 9 to 5 at her amusement park, Dollywood.

September 16

Janet Jackson performed at New York's Madison Square Garden. After the show, she presented a check to the United Negro College Fund in the amount of $450,000!

September 17

Natalie Cole married the former drummer for Rufus turned record producer, Andre Fischer.

September 27

Marianne Faithfull played a rare British date at the Borderline in London.

September 29

The Braxtons, a trio of teen sisters from Maryland, charted with their soul debut, "Good Life," reaching No. 79 R&B. One of the siblings would soon go on to solo success when Toni Braxton signed with Arista Records in 1991.

October 2

While visiting Mrs. Gouch's Natural Food store in Beverly Hills, a startled Sinead O'Connor witnessed a young meat-section worker sing the national anthem to her due to her anti-U.S. fervor. Proving there is no justice and certainly questioning freedom of speech, the patriotic American was summarily fired!!

October 3

Whitney Houston celebrated National Children's Day by performing at the White House in Washington.

October 4

Rickie Lee Jones, Bonnie Raitt, Melissa Etheridge, and Diane Reeves performed at a "vote-choice" concert to benefit the Hollywood Women's Political Committee at the Wadsworth Theater in Los Angeles.

October 21

Janet Jackson performed at Wembley Arena in London during her European tour.

November 2

During a promotional trip to Britain, Wilson Phillips appeared on the BBC-TV talk show *Wogan*.

November 4

Tina Turner's Foreign Affair Tour ended in Rotterdam, Holland. By the time it was over, more than 3 million people had seen Tina strut her stuff.

November 9

The regrouped Go-Go's guested on NBC-TV's *Late Night With David Letterman* on the eve of a comeback tour.

November 10

Carly Simon's *Have You Seen Me Lately?*, which included guest performances by her sister and former singing partners (the Simon Sisters), Lucy and Judy Collins, reached No. No. 60. It was her second album of the year, featuring eleven new songs written by Carly.

November 16

Bonnie Raitt joined Bruce Springsteen in two all-acoustic benefit concerts at the Shrine Auditorium in Los Angeles. The proceeds were to finance a lawsuit claiming that the government sanctioned drug trafficking and illegal arms sales to finance operations in the Iran-Contra affair. Somehow Joan Baez missed this one!

November 17

Wilson Phillips' single, "Impulsive," reached No. 2 in England.

November 21

En Vogue performed at the Summit in Houston during a tour as a supporting act for MC Hammer.

November 23

Madonna's "Justify My Love" video was banned by MTV.

November 25

Gladys Knight and the Pips reunited, but only for the *Motown 30: What's Goin' On!* CBS-TV special. Also performing were Patti LaBelle and Stevie Wonder.

November 26

Wilson Phillips won the Hot 100 Single category at the 1990 *Billboard* Music Awards with "Hold On."

December 1

Heart's "Stranded" reached No. 13, their last of fifteen singles to make the Top 15 nationally.

Rod Stewart's unlikely pairing in duet with Tina Turner resulted in a remake of Marvin Gaye and Tammi Terrell's "It Takes Two," which topped off at No. 5 in Britain today. It was never released in America as a single.

Whitney Houston's "I'm Your Baby Tonight" reached No. 1 on the pop charts and was written and produced by L. A. Reid and Babyface.

"[Celine Dion] One of the most technically astonishing instruments in pop music."
—Edna Gunderson, USA Today

December 5

Aretha Franklin was honored by the National Academy of Recording Arts and Science (NARAS) with a Living Legend Award.

December 7

Stevie Nicks and Christine McVie made their final appearance with Fleetwood Mac at the Great Western Forum in Inglewood, California, before a sellout crowd of over 16,000. A little over two years later, they would all reunite, well, for one night, anyway.

December 8

Celine Dion swept onto the charts with "Where Does My Heart Beat Now" (No. 4), her first hit.

December 9

Paula Abdul was hospitalized at North Hollywood Medical Center after a car crash in Los Angeles.

December 11

Chaka Khan performed on the *1990 Grammy Legends Show* on CBS-TV.

December 14

Dolly Parton appeared on NBC-TV's *The Tonight Show with Johnny Carson.*

December 21

Dolly Parton's *Christmas at Home* special aired on ABC-TV.

December 22

Wilson Phillips' "Impulsive" reached No. 4 on *Billboard*'s pop chart while the magazine honored the trio as the Top Singles Act and Top Pop Singles Artist, Duo or Group. They finished the year with twenty-seven consecutive weeks in the U.S. Top 10 album chart, an accomplishment not seen since the Supremes did it in 1967 with their *Greatest Hits* album.

December 23

Tiffany performed at Fort Campbell, Kentucky, home of the 101st Airborne Division's Screaming Eagles, before a crowd of 4,000 kids whose parents were serving in Saudi Arabia.

December 29

Patti LaBelle performed at the *Lou Rawls Parade of Stars Telethon* to raise money for the United Negro College Fund.

December 31

Wilson Phillips appeared on MTV's *New Year's Eve World Party* from the Ritz Hotel in New York City.

1991

January 9

Wilson Phillips video was certified gold by the RIAA. Carnie Wilson (daughter of Brian Wilson) made her vocal debut at the age of two in 1970 on the Beach Boys' "The Whole World," from their *Sunflower* album while the duo of sisters, Wendy Chynna Phillips (daughter of John and Michelle Phillips of the Mamas and the Papas fame) recorded their first (unreleased) song, "Take Me Out to the Ball Game," together, in 1974, as the Satellites. They were five and six years old, respectively, at the time.

Sinead O'Connor topped Mr. Blackwell's annual list of worst-dressed women. He called her "the bald-headed banshee of MTV."

January 12

When you're hot, you're *hot*! Whitney Houston received an award from the American Cinema Foundation for distinguished achievement, even though she had not yet starred in a film.

January 16

Tina Turner and ex-hubby, Ike Turner, were inducted into the Rock and Roll Hall of Fame at its sixth annual induction ceremonies. Producer Phil Spector accepted the award in their absence. Ike was in prison at the time for driving under the influence of cocaine. Also LaVern Baker was inducted, and Tracy Chapman inducted the Impressions.

January 19

Janet Jackson's "Love Will Never Do (Without You)" reached No. 1 pop, giving her the historic distinction of becoming the first artist to have seven Top 5 pop hits from the same album!

January 20

Anita Baker, who had won at least one Grammy in each of the last five seasons, was given the Best R&B Vocal Performance, Female, Award at the thirty-third awards ceremony at Radio City Music Hall in New York.

January 21

Tracy Chapman performed at the Martin Luther King Jr. celebration at the Guthrie Theater in Minneapolis, Minnesota. Tracy began writing songs when she just eight years old.

January 26

Cher, Bonnie Raitt, and Janet Jackson appeared in a special video, *Canteen*, made for U.S. troops serving in Desert Storm during the Gulf War.

Madonna's *The Immaculate Collection* album peaked at No. 2. Its American sales eventually topped 6 million.

January 27

Whitney Houston performed "The Star-Spangled Banner" at Super Bowl XXV in Miami. Response was so great that a single and video was rush-released. The record actually reached No. No. 20 on the Top 100.

January 29

Wilson Phillips sang an acoustic medley of their hits at the eighteenth American Music Awards, at the Shrine Auditorium in Los Angeles

Less than a year after receiving a severe injury in her tour bus (see March 20, 1990), Gloria Estefan made her live comeback, performing her new release, "Coming Out of the Dark," at the eighteenth annual American Music Awards.

January 31

A rabbi at the Simon Wiesenthal Center in Los Angeles, objecting to the apparent anti-Semitic lyrics in the Madonna song "Justify My Love" on her *The Immaculate Collection,* asked that copies be removed from record stores. Within a few years Madonna would become a Kabbalist (Jewish Mysticism) and marry a Jew, Guy Oseary.

Carly Simon made a rare television appearance on NBC-TV's *Late Night with David Letterman."*

February 1

Sinead O'Connor stated that she didn't like the music industry's values and that she would not be attending the Grammy Awards in a letter sent to the National Academy of Recording Arts and Sciences (NARAS). Off course, Sinead had no such complaint while attending both the MTV and the American Music Awards. Her camp has not yet reported if she intends to give back all the money she made from being in the music industry.

February 2

Debbie Gibson joined almost one hundred celebrities and artists in Burbank, California, to record *Voices That Care,* a charity record to benefit the American Red Cross Gulf Crisis Fund.

February 5

Wilson Phillips performed on TV's *The Tonight Show.*

February 9

Wilson Phillips' "You're in Love" hit the Top 100, rising to No. 1. It was their fourth Top 5 single and third chart topper in less than a year.

February 20

Chaka Khan and Ray Charles won Best R&B Performance by a Duo or Group with Vocal at the thirty-third Grammy Awards. The song was "I'll Be Good to You."

February 23

Whitney Houston reached No. 1 with "All the Man That I Need." Amazingly, it was her ninth chart topper in five years. Her formula of recording old hits continued to pay off as the original version was by Sister Sledge in 1982.

February 26

Joan Baez performed at a benefit dinner for the Shelter Partnership at the Biltmore Hotel, Los Angeles.

February 28

Gloria Estefan was profiled on *First Person with Maria Shriver* on NBC TV.

TLC signed with the Atlanta label LaFace Records, owned by Babyface and L. A. Reid. It didn't hurt that the group's manager was singer Pebbles, who just happened to be married to Reid.

March 1

Gloria Estefan started an eight-month world tour at the Miami Arena with a quintet-size backing-vocal group, including Jon Secada and soul pro Betty Wright.

March 2

Madonna's "Rescue Me" entered the national Hot 100 at No. 15, the highest-debuting single by a female artist in rock history up to that time. The single would, however, only reach No. No. 9.

Mariah Carey made the debut of debuts when she reached No. 1 for the first of eleven weeks with her self-titled album.

March 7

In a clear indication of "you love her or you hate her," Sinead O'Connor was named Best *and* Worst Female Singer in the annual *Rolling Stone* readers picks.

March 11

Janet Jackson, the youngest member of the Jackson clan, signed a $50 million contract with Virgin Records. The deal was for only two albums and was at the time the most lavish recording contract in history, though her brother Michael would soon eclipse her.

March 21

Celine Dion's English-language debut, "Where Does My Heart Beat," peaked at No. 4 in America. Before this recording, she had not learned to speak English. The youngest of fourteen children, she gave her first public performance at the age of five.

Cyndi Lauper performed at the first American Music Award's Concert Series in Yokohama Arena, Tokyo.

March 25

Madonna sang "Sooner or Later (I Always Get My Man)" at the sixty-third annual Academy Awards ceremony at the Shrine Auditorium in Los Angeles. The song from the film *Dick Tracy* won the Oscar for Best Song. Apparently running out of boyfriends, her escort for this evening was Michael Jackson.

March 30

Annie Lennox and Dave Stewart's (the Eurythmics') *Greatest Hits* debuted at No. 1 in Britain and remained on the charts into 1993.

Gloria Estefan's "Coming Out of the Dark" came into the light of No. 1 on the charts.

April 3

Queen Latifah, Big Daddy Cane, and Afrika Bambaataa appeared at the New York concert Rap Portraits and Lyrics of a Generation of Black Rockers.

April 6

Patti LaBelle performed on Bob Hope's Yellow Ribbon Party, in honor of returning troops from the first Gulf War.

April 14

The Pointer Sisters performed on *Welcome Home America,* an ABC-TV tribute to American armed forces returning from the Gulf War.

April 19

Whitney Houston was accused of "terrorist threatening" and allegedly punching a man in the eye when the man tried to break up a fight between her brother Michael and a third man at a Radisson Hotel in Lexington, Kentucky. The charges were later dismissed.

Queen Latifah.

April 20

Amy Grant's *Heart in Motion* album topped the Top Contemporary Christian Album chart, even though it was a pop album.

The fourth single from Wilson Phillips debut album, "You're in Love," soared to the pop-chart pinnacle. The vocal trio was now in second place behind the iconic Supremes among girl groups with No. 1 hits, as "You're in Love" was their third.

May 4

Cher reached No. 1 in Britain with "The Shoop Shoop Song (It's in His Kiss)." It was her first chart topper in England after a twenty-five-year career. The single was a cover of a song made popular by Betty Everett in '64 (and also covered by Linda Ronstadt, Aretha Franklin, the Supremes, and Lulu), which was featured a year earlier in the film *Mermaids,* also starring Cher.

Crystal Waters, niece of legendary vocalist Ethel Waters, vaulted onto the Top 100 with "Gypsy Woman" (No. 8).

May 6

Truth or Dare, the Madonna-commissioned bio-documentary premiered in Los Angeles.

May 12

Gloria Estefan performed live by satellite from Holland in The Simple Truth concert for Kurdish refugees.

May 14

Olivia Newton-John and Cliff Richard co-hosted the third annual World Music Awards in Monte Carlo.

May 31

Diana Ross performed at the Mid Hudson Civic Center in Poughkeepsie, New York, on the first night of her world tour. It was an encouraging start as she broke the house attendance record previously held by John Denver.

June 4

The Shirelles performed at Los Angeles' Pantages Theater in the Celebrate the Soul of American Music concert to raise money for the Thurgood Marshall Scholarship Fund, named after the former Supreme Court justice.

June 8

Diana Ross showed another side of her talents when she filled in for a week for a British disc jockey on BBC Radio 1 in London, starting today.

The Chordettes, who reformed in 1988 after twenty-seven years, were featured as special guests at Radio City Music Hall for *The Royal New York Doo-Wop Show.*

June 10

Aretha Franklin and Stevie Wonder sang at the burial of the Temptations lead singer, David Ruffin, and Michael Jackson paid for the funeral.

June 18

Gloria Estefan performed at a White House state dinner for Brazilian President Fernando Collor de Mello in Washington, D.C.

June 29

Dionne Warwick, Chaka Khan, En Vogue, and Dianne Reeves, among others, performed on the *Celebrate the Soul of American Music* TV show.

July 21

Joan Baez, ever the humanitarian, sang "You'll Never Walk Alone" as 13,000 people walked over 6 miles through Golden Gate Park, San Francisco, to raise money for AIDS research.

July 27

When Natalie Cole brought the idea of singing a duet album with her father Nat "King" Cole's old recordings to her label, EMI refused, so she signed with Electra Records, recorded the album *Unforgettable . . . With Love,* and today it topped the album charts.

July 30

Arsenio Hall's entire TV program was devoted to Patti LaBelle.

Maria Carey and Debbie Gibson, among others, performed at New York radio station WHTZ's eighth-birthday party.

August 3

Jasmine Guy, Salt-N-Pepa, Tara Kemp, Heavy D, and Monie Love performed at the Shoreline Amphitheater in Mountain View, California, in the KMEL Summer Jam '91.

August 9

The Shirelles performed at The Apollo R&B Reunion to help raise funds for the financially strapped theater in New York.

August 10

The 5th Dimension received a star on Hollywood's Walk of Fame, and then the original quintet began a reunion tour after being two separate entities (the 5th Dimension, Marilyn McCoo and Billy Davis) for sixteen years.

August 15

Debbie Gibson sang her second No. 1 record, "Lost in Your Eyes," on ABC-TV's *The International Special Olympics All-Star Gala*.

August 19

Joan Baez sang "We Shall Overcome," along with a Russian protest song, over a phone to Radio Free Europe, which broadcast it to the Soviet Union.

August 25

Celine Dion was the opening act for Michael Bolton on a Canadian tour that stopped this night at the CNE venue in Toronto. Celine's first break in the business came when at the age of twelve, she recorded a demo tape that her brother Michael sent to an address on the back of an album by her idol, French singer Ginette Reno. The address belonged to Reno's manager, Rene Angelil, a Quebec-based music entrepreneur. Angelil, so taken by the young thrush's sound remortgaged his house to finance the recording of her maiden album in 1981, titled *La Voix Du Bon Dieu*.

August 28

PBS-TV aired *Going Home to Gospel with Patti LaBelle* from Quinn Chapel in Chicago.

September 4

Country artist Dottie West (born Dorothy Marie Marsh) spent over twenty years on the charts, from 1963 to 1985. The Tennessee native had two solo No. 1s ("A Lesson in Leavin'" and "Are You Happy Baby?"), but was even more popular in duet with Kenny Rogers, with whom she won Vocal Duo of the Year awards with in 1978 and 1979. All told, she had sixty-three country hits before her untimely demise in a car accident in the parking lot of the Grand Ole Opry at age fifty-eight.

September 5

Mariah Carey sang her hit "Emotions" (No. 1) at the eighth annual MTV Awards ceremony at the Universal Amphitheater in Universal City, California.

September 15

Whitney Houston spoke at London's Hyde Park at the Reach Out and Touch People with HIV and AIDS rally.

Notable Moments of Women in Music

September 21

Diana Ross performed the last of three sellout shows at New York's Radio City Music Hall, grossing over $650,000 (not a bad weekend's work).

September 30

Diana Ross, spokeswoman for the National Children's Day Foundation, spoke before a House Select Committee on Children, Youth, and Families in Washington D.C.

October 1

Anita Baker paid $100,000 for author Alex Haley's personal copy of *The Autobiography of Malcolm X* at an auction of Haley's works on his Knoxville, Tennessee, farm.

October 12

Hole, featuring Courtney Love (born Courtney Michelle Harrison), had their first album, *Pretty on the Inside,* issued, and it charted today in Britain at No. 59. With a repertoire of songs like "Retard Girl" and "Teenage Whore," the three-girl and one-guy grunge band was not destined to be the next Dixie Chicks. Courtney's rebellious life began with stealing a Kiss T-shirt from a Seattle Woolworths and winding up in a number of reform schools. She decided on a music career after hearing the Sex Pistols' *Never Mind the Bollocks* album in the late '70s, a dubious role model if there ever was one.

October 15

Cher was named the Worst Dressed Woman of the Last Three Decades" by fashion critic Mr. Blackwell, who said in summation: "From toes to nose, she's the tacky tattoo'd terror of the 20th century. A Bono-fied fashion fiasco of the legendary kind."

October 17

British thrush Sandi Shaw was arrested outside her London apartment for refusing to give a breathalyzer test to a bobby.

October 21

Tori Amos signed to the London-based Atlantic affiliate, East West Records. The label then released a four-track EP, *Me and a Gun,* the title cut referring traumatically to an incident in Los Angeles in 1985, when Amos was raped at gunpoint by a man who had given her a ride home after her performance in a bar.

Courtney Love.

October 27

Britain's Smash Hits Pool Awards gave Kylie Minogue the Worst Female Singer trophy. What do you want to bet she didn't show up to receive the award?

November 3

Joan Baez and Tracy Chapman participated in the Laughter, Love, and Music memorial concert for rock promoter Bill Graham at the Polo Fields in San Francisco's Golden Gate Park before a crowd estimated to be around 350,000.

November 5

Bette Midler appeared on Barbara Walters' ABC-TV special.

November 7

Sheena Easton, suffering from an intestinal disorder, was helped offstage by costar Raul Julia on her debut evening in a stage production of *Man of La Mancha*. She spent the night in a hospital.

November 10

Roberta Flack performed at a benefit to help families of ill children at Symphony Hall in Boston, Massachusetts, for the Cohen Hillel Academy in Marblehead, Massachusetts.

November 11

In an hysterical episode of CBS-TV's *Murphy Brown*, Aretha Franklin played herself next to worshipping but totally out of tune Candice Bergen (as Murphy). Their show closing "You Make Me Feel Like a Natural Woman" was the highlight of the season.

Natalie Cole, Dionne Warwick, Stevie Wonder, and Isaac Hayes, among others, performed at the Celebrity Theater in Los Angeles to raise money for cancer patient and former Motown star Mary Wells. Sadly, Mary would die within nine months at age forty-nine.

November 15

Deborah Harry took on the acting role of a phone-sex operator in an episode of cable TV network Showtime's *Intimate Stranger*.

November 16

Enya's *Shepherd Moons* album debuted at No. 1 in Britain. It was recorded at her home in Eire. Enya's first break came when lyricist Roma Ryan sent Enya's tapes to a number of film producers, including David Puttnam, who brought her in to do the score to his 1985 feature *The Frog Prince*.

November 23

Patti LaBelle sang "Over the Rainbow" on CBS-TV's *Party for Richard Pryor*. She loved the song so much, she recorded it twice and it was a single release for her both times.

November 24

Cyndi Lauper married David Thornton in Manhattan, New York. Patti LaBelle sang "A Whiter Shade of Pale," and none other than Little Richard presided over the event.

November 25

After British TV station TVS aired a show with a comedian portraying Dusty Springfield as a drunk, Dusty sued and won £75,000 (about $140,000) in a libel suit against the station.

November 26

ABC-TV aired *Gladys Knight Holiday Family Reunion,* which originally taped in September on the UCLA campus in Los Angeles.

November 30

Bette Midler's album *For the Boys* charted (No. 22), becoming her thirteenth of fifteen hit albums between 1972 and 1993.

Tori Amos' emotional ballad "Silent All These Years" became her debut single charter, reaching No. 51 in the U.K. Though her early success was in England, Tori was actually from Newton, North Carolina, and has both Cherokee Indian and Scottish family roots and is the daughter of a Methodist minister.

December 9

The Boring Institute of Maple, New Jersey, named Madonna Most Boring Personality of 1991, claiming that "she's parlayed a bad attitude into superstardom." (Note: See June 16,1992, for the other side of the coin).

December 13

Mavis Staples of the Staple Singers performed at UCLA's Royce Hall at the annual Stellar Awards for Gospel Music.

December 21

Queen Latifah (born Dana Owens) hit the R&B charts with "Latifah's Had It Up to Here," reaching No. 13. Considering her name means "sensitive and delicate," the brash and bellicose Queen must enjoy the irony. Nevertheless, the bawdy broad sure can sing!

December 23

British TV's BBC-2 aired *Christmas in Vienna,* with Diana Ross and Placido Domingo from the Vienna City Hall.

More Moments in 1991

Cordell Jackson may be best known as the rockin' grandma who plays rings around rockabilly guitarist Brian Setzer in a 1991 Budweiser ad, but she was an early Rockabilly pioneer and one of the first women to write, sing, accompany, record, engineer, and produce a record. Perhaps because of this "rediscovery," Jackson made appearances in and around this year on national talk shows like the *Late Night with David Letterman*. She died in 2004.

The Shirelles won a legal case to regain unpaid royalties.

1992

January 3

Queen Latifah, Naughty by Nature, MC Lyte, Public Enemy, and the Geto Boys performed at Madison Square Garden in New York for what was billed as "The World's Greatest Rap Show Ever."

January 4

Chrissie Hynde, a noted vegetarian, ate a "groenteburger" (vegetable burger) at a McDonalds in Amsterdam, Holland, as a publicity stunt.

January 7

Debbie Gibson (managed by her mother) opened on Broadway in *Les Miserables,* playing Eponine.

January 11

Patti LaBelle was named Entertainer of the Year at the NAACP twenty-fourth annual Image Awards at the Wiltern Theater in Los Angeles.

January 15

On TV's *Entertainment Tonight,* Brenda Lee, the diminutive, dynamite damsel, suggested that that year's all-male lineup of inductees for the Rock and Roll Hall of Fame should've included the likes of the Shirelles, Mary Wells, Dionne Warwick, Connie Francis, and herself: "The women who pioneered rock 'n' roll . . . were just as important as the males," she stated.

January 21

Melissa Etheridge performed at a Voters for Choice concert in Washington, D.C.

Tori Amos performed at the annual MIDEM Festival in Cannes, France, in the side bar of the famed Martinez Hotel. She attended the ultra-strict Peabody Conservatory in Baltimore, starting at age five, where she had a piano scholarship (and was kicked out by age eleven for playing by ear).

Wilson Phillips performed at the annual music industry festival MIDEM at the Palais des Festivals in Cannes, France. In the group's early days, the trio was actually a quartet, with Owen Elliot, daughter of the Mamas and the Papas' Cass Elliot, on board.

January 22

Mariah Carey's stepfather sued her. Having paid for her dental work, car, and an apartment in her early days, she was supposedly to repay him when she became a success.

January 25

Tori Amos' single "Little Earthquakes," showcasing her literate songwriting skills, reached No. 14 in the U.K. Tori was influenced by the music of Fats Waller, John Lennon, and George Gershwin, among others, and began playing in bars in Washington, D.C., and Baltimore in her late teens.

January 26

Gloria Estefan performed during halftime at Super Bowl XXVI, between the Washington Redskins and the Buffalo Bills, in Minneapolis.

February 1

Vanessa Williams soared onto the Top 100 with "Save The Best for Last." It was her biggest hit, reaching No. 1 both pop and R&B. Nine years earlier, Vanessa became the first black woman to win the Miss America pageant.

February 7

Gloria Estefan sang at the Palacio de los Deportes in Mexico City, Mexico, grossing over $2 million in two nights. It was the start of a sellout journey, taking her to Aruba, Puerto Rico, Columbia, and Venezuela.

February 8

Rickie Lee Jones performed at the Wiltern Theater in Los Angeles.

February 15

Sarah Mclachlan's "Into the Fire" debuted on the modern-rock chart, eventually rising to No. 4.

February 21

Natalie Cole performed at the famed Apollo Theater in New York. She then donated her receipts to help save the financially strapped landmark.

February 22

Bonnie Raitt was named Musicares' 1992 Person of the Year at their annual NARAS-sponsored Musicares Foundation Dinner at the Waldorf Astoria in New York. Also performing were Natalie Cole, Jackson Brown, and David Crosby.

Shakespeare's Sister (former Bananarama member Siobhan Fahey and Marcella Detroit) hit No. 1 in Britain with "Stay." The single retained the top spot for eight weeks.

TLC charted with their debut recording, "Ain't 2 Proud 2 Beg," reaching No. 2 R&B and No. 6 pop. The record consisted of samples from five acts, including Bob James, James Brown, Kool and the Gang, Silver Convention, and Average White Band. One wonders if there was any room left for anything original!

February 24

Courtney Love married Nirvana leader Kurt Cobain in Hawaii. Several months earlier, Love's then-new boyfriend Cobain informed viewers of C4-TV's *The Word* that "Courtney Love's the best fuck in the world." Ahhh, a match made in heaven.

February 25

Natalie Cole was the big winner with Grammys for Record of the Year, Song of the Year, Traditional Pop Performance Album of the Year, and Best Engineered Album (non-classical) while Mary Chapin-Carpenter received the Best Country Vocal Performance, Female (for "Down at the Twist and Shout"), at the thirty-fourth annual Grammy Awards, held at Radio City Music Hall in New York.

Tina Turner's British-TV special biopic, *The Girl from Nutbush,* aired on BBC1 in England.

February 26

Aretha Franklin received the Lifetime Achievement Award at the Rhythm and Blues Foundation's third annual Pioneer Awards in New York.

March 18

Donna Summer received a star on the Hollywood Walk of Fame.

March 20

Rickie Lee Jones performed at London's Dominion Theater during a brief British tour, her first since 1983.

March 24

Sarah McLachlan appeared on NBC-TV's *Late Night with David Letterman*.

March 28

Enya's *Shepherd Moons* album peaked at No. 17 in America and would eventually spend 235 weeks on the pop chart.

March 30

Celine Dion's duet with Peabo Bryson, "Beauty and the Beast," from the Disney movie of the same name, won the Best Song Written for a Motion Picture or Television category at the sixty-fifth annual Academy Awards, held in Los Angeles. The same night, Celine was once again named Female Vocalist of the Year at the twenty-first annual Canadian Juno Awards. Not a bad couple of birthday presents for the twenty-fourth-year-old.

March 31

Amy Grant ended a British tour at the Apollo Theater in Manchester, England.

April 1

Emmylou Harris performed at the silver anniversary of the Country Music Hall of Fame from the Grand Ole Opry in Nashville (the show would air on May 2 on CBS).

April 3

k. d. lang appeared on NBC's-TV's *The Tonight Show with Johnny Carson*.

April 5

The Supremes, the Marvelettes, Martha Reeves and the Vandellas, the Temptations, and the Four Tops performed on the Giants of the Motown Show at Wembley Arena in Wembley, London, England.

April 11

Tina Turner, the Four Tops, and the Temptations were grand-opening performers for Euro-Disney Amusement Park outside Paris, France.

April 18

Annie Lennox appeared on NBC-TV's *Saturday Night Live* while her album *Diva* debuted at No. 1 in England. Her first solo album, it would become one of the year's biggest sellers in Europe.

April 20

Time Warner announced a new seven-year, multimedia contract with Madonna under her newly formed Maverick group of companies, with a record label, publishing company, book, TV, merchandising, and motion-picture subsidiaries, to be run from Los Angeles, New York, and London.

April 23

Tori Amos made her American TV debut on NBC-TV's *Late Night with David Letterman*. Five years earlier, she was promoted as a scantily clad rocker, leading the rock outfit Y Kant Tori Read, which bombed with an album of the same name.

April 25

Amy Grant appeared at an all-star concert at the Irvine Meadows Amphitheater in Laguna Hills, California, to benefit the Pediatric AIDS Foundation. Earlier that month, she had been named Artist of the Year at the twenty-third annual (Christian) Dove Awards.

April 29

Paula Abdul married actor (and son of Martin Sheen) Emilio Estevez. That lasted about two years.

May 1

Released twenty-six years after her last British chart hit, Connie Francis' album *The Singles Collection* reached No. 12 in England.

May 6

Whitney Houston performed on her first network-TV special, *Whitney Houston—This Is My Life,* on ABC-TV. The show was produced by her own Nippy Inc. production company. Nippy was her nickname as a child.

May 8

The Dixie Cups, of "Chapel of Love" fame, reunited and performed at Radio City Music Hall in New York for WCBS-FM's twentieth anniversary concert.

May 16

Bonnie Raitt performed with her father, Broadway actor/singer John Raitt, and the Boston Pops Orchestra at Symphony Hall in Boston. They sang "Blowin' Away."

Emmylou Harris performed at the Gene Autry Western Museum outside Los Angeles, as part of a tribute to singing cowboys and cowgirls, hosted by TV star Dennis Weaver.

May 21

Singing her way into Johnny Carson's heart, Bette Midler vamped her way through "One for My Baby (And One More for the Road")" on Carson's last-ever *Tonight Show* telecast.

May 22

Wilson Phillips performed on Britain's BBC1-TV's *Wogan* show.

May 29

With obviously little else to do since crime in 1992 was nonexistent, the FBI raided an establishment and recovered forty-four nude photographs of Madonna stolen from a collection by photographer Steven Meisel. Ironically the following month, the June issue of *Playboy* featured naked shots of her royal nudeness from the same beach-location session.

June 4

Dionne Warwick sang at the Hammersmith Odeon in London at the end of a ten-performance trip through England.

June 12

Cyndi Lauper starred in the comedy/thriller *Off and Running,* which made its British debut today.

Even though she had suffered chronic back pain that saw her collapse at the L.A. international airport, Dionne Warwick still had the temerity to attend and perform at her record company president's (Clive Davis') Man of the Year honors at the New York Waldorf Astoria, singing "That's What Friends Are For" with Whitney Houston.

June 13

Cyndi Lauper was featured on England's BBC1-TV's *Top of the Pops.*

Wilson Phillips' second album, *Shadows and Light,* debuted at its No. 6 peak in Britain.

June 16

The first "Madonna Appreciation Convention" (the Madonnathon) was held at the Holiday Inn in Southfield, Michigan, on the singer's thirty-fourth birthday.

June 17

Gloria Estefan received the Humanitarian Award at the twenty-eighth annual Music and Performing Arts Unit of B'inai B'rith at the Imperial Ballroom in the Sheraton Hotel, New York.

June 30

Polly Jean (P. J.) Harvey released her first full-length recording, *Dry,* to worldwide critical acclaim. *Rolling Stone* magazine names her Best Songwriter and Best New Female Singer.

July 1

Judy Collins, Barbra Streisand, Chynna Phillips, Mary Chapin-Carpenter, Patti Austin, and Vanessa Williams (Dinah Washington's goddaughter) participated in a fundraiser for the Hollywood Women's Political Committee, raising over $350,000.

July 2

Celine Dion began her first U.S. tour, opening for Michael Bolton, at the Coca-Cola Starplex Amphitheater in Dallas, Texas.

July 11

Jazz prodigy Patti Austin, along with Vanessa Williams, performed at the Hollywood Women's Political Committee fund-raiser.

Patti LaBelle's 1989 No. 79 original, "If You Asked Me To," reached No. 4 today via Celine Dion's remake.

July 12

Rickie Lee Jones appeared at London's Royal Festival Hall for the Capital Radio Jazz Festival.

July 14

Aretha Franklin sang "The Star-Spangled Banner" on the second night of the Democratic National Convention.

Olivia Newton-John revealed she was battling breast cancer, declaring, "I am making this information public myself, to save inquiring minds ninety-five cents." She then promptly postponed her upcoming tour.

The Pointer Sisters performed at the Valley Forge Music Fair in Devon, Pennsylvania.

Wilson Phillips performed the national anthem at Baseball's sixty-third All-Star Game at Jack Murphy Stadium in San Diego.

July 26

Mary Wells was Motown's first million-selling singer when she hit with "My Guy." She came to Motown as an aspiring songwriter with a tune intended for Jackie Wilson, but Berry Gordy heard her and recorded the seventeen-year-old on her song "Bye Bye Baby." She went on to have twenty-three hits through 1968. She died of cancer at forty-nine today.

August 1

Stevie Nicks, along with Roseanne and Tom Arnold, joined Ringo Star on stage to sing "With a Little Help from My Friends" at his Greek Theater, Los Angeles, show. Not bad for a girl who worked as a Bob's Big Boy hamburger hostess, a waitress, and a sometimes house cleaner in Hollywood in her pre–Fleetwood Mac days.

August 3

Dolly Parton donated $500,000 to improve public education in her childhood home county, the Sevier Country School system.

August 10

k. d. lang performed on *The Arsenio Hall Show*.

August 15

Mary J. Blige's first single, "You Remind Me," peaked at No. 29 on the pop charts while going on to No. 1 R&B. Mary, who sang in a Pentecostal church choir while living in Savannah, Georgia, started her career pursuit with a demo she did of Anita Baker's "Caught Up in the Rapture" on a Yonkers, New York, shopping-mall karaoke machine.

August 18

Chaka Khan performed at New York's Beacon Theater. Two months earlier, Chaka became a grandmother at age thirty-nine!

August 29

k. d. lang's "Crying" reached No. 13 in Great Britain, almost five years after charting in America. During the year, lang stated she was a lesbian and also mentioned that regarding her celebrity, "in some instances it got a little crazy, sort of like Beatlemania."

September 2

Gloria and Emilio Estefan began a relief effort following the devastation caused by Hurricane Andrew in Florida. They quickly converted their Miami offices into a distribution center for donated food and water.

September 13

Patti Austin and James Ingram performed on PBS-TV's *Evening at the Pops* with John Williams and the Boston Pops Orchestra.

September 14

British songstress Joan Armatrading appeared on NBC-TV's *The Tonight Show* with Jay Leno.

September 16

Dionne Warwick appeared at a fund-raiser for presidential hopeful Bill Clinton at millionaire Ted Field's Beverly Hills mansion and sang "Amazing Grace."

September 17

As if there wasn't enough worldwide Madonna madness, the bed used as a prop in the *In Bed with Madonna* film was bought by a fifteen-year-old Dutch girl at a UNICEF fund-raising auction for $7,700.

September 19

Patti LaBelle's NBC-TV *Out All Night* sitcom debuted with the diva playing a singer in her own Los Angeles nightclub.

September 20

Tracy Chapman performed at the Greek Theater in Los Angeles. A far cry from her singing career, she originally majored in anthropology and African studies. While in college and during her sophomore year at Wooster, her school chaplain took up a collection to buy Tracy a new guitar.

September 24

Madonna performed in the AMFAR AIDS fashion benefit at the Shrine Auditorium in Los Angeles. As if the crowd of 6,000 hadn't seen enough,

Madonna found the need to expose her breasts! Well, what do you expect from a girl who started out doing nude modeling.

September 25
Roberta Flack and Dionne Warwick, known for their numerous benefit performances, once again helped out at the Caring in Concert AIDS benefit TV special, broadcast from the Mann Music Center in Philadelphia.

September 26
Gloria Estefan headlined an all-star benefit she organized for Hurricane Andrew victims at Joe Robbie Stadium, Miami, which raised over $1 million toward the relief effort. The performers included Bonnie Raitt , Whoppi Goldberg, Paul Simon, Crosby, Stills Nash, and Jon Secada.

The Best of Belinda Carlisle, Volume 1 topped the British album chart.

October 3
Sinead O'Connor sang a noxious interpretation of the song "War" to stunned audience silence on NBC-TV's *Saturday Night Live.* She then tore apart a photo of the Pope and stated: "Fight the real enemy." The show's producer Lorne Michaels said: "We were sort of shocked, the way you would be at a house guest pissing on the flower arrangement in the dining room." She was banned for life from the show.

October 6
Annie Lennox was interviewed on Whoopi Goldberg's syndicated TV talk show.

October 15
Madonna's infamous "sex" party to promote her impending album and book (also called *Sex,* a metal-covered collection of provocative photographs featuring Madonna) was held in Manhattan for 800 invited guests. Her royal nudeness showed up carrying a toy lamb while dressed as Little Bo Peep. Her book would go on to reportedly sell 500,000 copies in its first week of release.

October 16
Tracy Chapman sang "The Times They Are A-Changin'" and Chrissie Hynde sang "I Shall Be Released" at the Bob Dylan thirtieth-anniversary celebration, held at New York's Madison Square Garden. In her early days, Chrissie had a job at London's *New Musical Express* magazine, where she became a contributing writer. Her first review was of a Neil Diamond album.

October 17

Chaka Khan, Ike Turner, Lou Rawls, Bobby Womack Al Green, and Bill Withers performed at two concerts in Redondo Beach, California, as benefits for deceased former Temptations member Eddie Kendrick's family.

October 19

Donna Summer performed at the Palais Omnisports in Paris, France.

October 21

The anti-Sinead brigade, known as the National Ethnic Coalition of Organizations, destroyed more than 200 albums, CDs, and cassettes provided by people incensed with Sinead O'Connor's infamous "ripping of the Pope" episode on *Saturday Night Live.* Adding a New York touch, a steam roller crushed the recordings on a Manhattan street.

October 25

The "Sinead Brigade," mostly wearing Sinead O'Connor face masks, gathered outside St. Patrick's Cathedral in New York City, tearing up pictures of the pope. It must have pleased the former part-time kiss-o-gram girl, who liked to dress up as a French maid.

October 26

Emmylou Harris and Dolly Parton performed on cable network TNN's *Hats Off to Minnie—America Honors Minnie Pearl* special.

Judy Collins, Carly Simon, Lucy Simon (Carly's sister), Lesley Gore, Odetta, Maureen McGovern, Cissy Houston, and the Roaches recorded "America the Beautiful" and " Michael Row the Boat Ashore" as the Clintones for torch-light parades across America to promote the Women Light the Way for Change cause on October 28.

November 1

Nancy Wilson hosted a benefit at UCLA for the National Council of Negro Women. Among the guests were Dionne Warwick.

November 9

Sinead O'Connor continued attacking the Catholic Church in a *Time* magazine interview. Born in Dublin, Ireland, she was placed in a Dominican center run by nuns for girls with behavioral problems. Seems she had been caught shoplifting.

December 6

Emmylou Harris appeared as grand marshal of the fortieth annual Nashville Christmas Parade.

December 10

Tori Amos was voted Best New Female Artist in *Rolling Stone*'s annual readers poll.

December 11

Emmylou Harris headlined the third annual Gift of the Heart concert at the First Unity Church. The proceeds went to the Nashville Family Center for the homeless.

"All That She Wants" became Ace of Base's first chart release, hitting No. 3 in Sweden and No. 1 in Norway, Finland, and Denmark. Its popularity led Metronome Musik in Hamburg, Germany, to sign the female-led group for releases in the rest of Europe and the Far East.

December 19

Janet Jackson's *Rhythm Nation 1814* album was certified six-times platinum (6 million copies) by the RIAA.

The Carpenters' classic first-hits compilation, *The Singles 1969–1973*, was certified by the RIAA with 4 million sales.

Regina Belle, featured female vocalist with the Manhattans in the mid-'80s, made a case for her solo success when "A Whole New World" hit the Hot 100, on the way to No. 1.

Whitney Houston's "I Will Always Love You" sold a record 399,000 copies in one week. The former record was held by Bryan Adams' single "(Everything I Do) I Do for You" a year earlier.

December 21

Sade performed on *Saturday Night Live.*

December 25

Whitney Houston's film debut, *The Bodyguard,* opened nationally. The film co-starring Kevin Costner was written twenty years earlier and was originally intended for Diana Ross and Ryan O'Neal.

Carnie and Wendy Wilson of Wilson Phillips had their holiday compilation, *Hey Santa!* debut at No. 116.

December 26

Amy Grant's second seasonal collection, *Home for the Holidays,* reached No. 2. She was kept from No. 1 by Whitney Houston's *The Bodyguard* soundtrack album.

Dionne Warwick participated in the annual Lou Rawls Parade of Stars telethon in Los Angeles to raise money for the United Negro College Fund, which raised over $11 million.

December 28

Whitney Houston's "I Will Always Love You" reached No. 1 R&B for eleven weeks and No. 1 pop for fourteen weeks. The original version of the song was by Dolly Parton, in 1982. Kevin Costner, Houston's co-star in *The Bodyguard,* suggested she record it. It would become her biggest hit.

More Moments in 1992

Britney Spears landed a spot on the pop TV show *Star Search,* but was cut after the first round of competitions. At age eleven, she returned to the Disney Channel for a spot on the *New Mickey Mouse Club* show from 1993 to 1994. (Spears had been turned down years earlier, when she was thought to be too young for the show. She was only eight years old!). Other future celebrities on that show included Christina Aguilera, 'N Sync members Justin Timberlake and J. C. Chasez, *Felicity* actress Keri Russell, and *The Notebook* star Ryan Gosling.

1993

January 1

Melissa Etheridge performed at the Triangle Ball, a gay and lesbian fete, as part of President Clinton's inaugural celebrations in Washington, D.C. Melissa used the opportunity to publicly announce that she was a lesbian.

January 9

Chrissie Hynde performed at PETA's 1993 Animal Ball during inauguration festivities for President Bill Clinton in Washington, D.C.

January 17

Dionne Warwick and Luther Vandross performed at the Lincoln Memorial in Washington, D.C., at An American Reunion: The People's Inaugural Celebration.

Roseanne Cash, Shawn Colvin, and Mary Chapin-Carpenter performed at The Bob Dylan Thirtieth Anniversary Celebration held at New York's Madison Square Garden.

January 19

Emmylou Harris performed at the Salute to Children concert as part of the presidential inauguration celebrations from the Kennedy Center for the Performing Arts. The show aired later that day on the Disney Channel.

Fleetwood Mac's most popular lineup of Christy McVie, Stevie Nicks, Mick Fleetwood, and Lindsey Buckingham reunited for one performance of "Don't Stop" (which incoming President Bill Clinton had used as his theme song during his campaign)at the presidential inaugural concert from the Capital Center in Landover, Maryland.

k. d. lang performed at PETA's "Animals Ball" during the Presidential inauguration festivities for Bill Clinton in Washington, D.C.

January 20

Carole King performed in the "Arkansas Ball" on the day of President Clinton's inauguration in Washington, D.C. (Barbra Streisand had also performed at another presidential inauguration gala previously, at Lyndon B. Johnson's in 1965.)

En Vogue performed at MTV's Rock and Roll Inaugural Ball in Washington, D.C., singing the Star-Spangled Banner.

January 24

Chaka Khan sang "Ain't That Peculiar" and "How Sweet It Is" at a tribute to Marvin Gaye in France during the twenty-seventh annual MIDEM convention.

January 25

Mariah Carey received the Favorite Female Artist, Pop/Rock, and Favorite Album, Adult Contemporary, trophies at the twentieth annual American Music Awards.

January 28

Hit British artist Lulu, who began her career in 1963 as lead singer of Lulu and the Lovers, performed on BBC1-TV's *Top of the Pops,* the only female vocalist to appear on that long-running show in each of the last four decades.

February 11

Patti LaBelle guested on Arsenio Hall's TV show.

February 13

Dolly Parton's "Romeo" romanced its way onto the country singles chart to the tune of No. 27. Her all-star backup vocal group included Tanya Tucker, Mary-Chapin Carpenter, Kathy Mattea, and Pam Tillis.

February 17

As if there weren't enough awards shows, Emmylou Harris won the Female Vocalist Award at the first German American Country Music Federation Awards . . . in Nashville!

February 18

Tapestry, an off-Broadway revue of Carole King's songs, debuted in New York.

February 24

Enya's *Shepherd Moons* received the Best New Age Album Grammy, and k. d. lang received the Best Pop Female Vocal Award (her third win) at the thirty-fifth annual Grammy Awards, held at the Shrine Auditorium in Los Angeles.

February 25

Bonnie Raitt co-hosted the fourth annual Rhythm and Blues Foundation Awards in Hollywood. Receiving Pioneer Awards that night were Carla Thomas and Martha and the Vandellas.

The Carly Simon–written, hour-long children's opera, *Romulus Hunt,* a touching story of the unsuccessful efforts of a son to reunite his divorced parents, premiered at the John Jay Theater in New York.

February 27

After 14 weeks at No. 1, Whitney Houston's "I Will Always Love You" became the longest-running chart topper, eclipsing Boys to Men's 1992 smash, "End of the Road." Additionally, the 4 million–selling single was No. 1 in over a dozen countries. It became the second-largest-selling single in U.S. history behind only "We Are the World" by USA for Africa.

March 1

Annie Lennox's solo album, *Diva,* reached No. 1 in England, eventually selling over 5.5 million copies worldwide.

March 4

"I feel like a queen," Patti LaBelle exclaimed as she was honored with a star on Hollywood's Walk of Fame.

k. d. lang was named Best Female Singer in *Rolling Stone*'s Music Awards Critics' Picks.

March 5

Patti LaBelle, Natalie Cole, and Luther Vandross co-hosted the seventh annual Soul Train Music Awards.

March 19

Mary J. Blige was awarded the Best New R&B Artist and Best R&B Album, Female, for *What's the 411?* at the seventh annual Soul Train Music Awards in Los Angeles. Among Mary J's quirky concert performance demands was that the first $100,000 be paid in $100 Bills.

March 20

Nanci Griffith's *Other Voices, Other Rooms* album (named after a 1948 Truman Copote book) peaked at its No. 54 American and No. 18 British debut. The collection of Griffith's covers of her favorite songs included guest vocals by Emmylou Harris, Carolyn Hester, Indigo Girls, Chet Atkins, Bob Dylan, Leo Kottke, John Prine, and Arlo Guthrie.

Vanessa Williams and Brian McKnight reached the R&B hit list with "Love Is," rising to No. 55, though it scored big at No. 3 pop. It was the Miss America pageant winner's ninth of thirteen pop hits through 1996.

March 21

Canadian k. d. lang's album *Ingénue* won Album of the Year, as well as Songwriter of the Year and Co-Producer of the Year, for "Constant Craving" and "The Mind of Love" at the twenty-second annual Juno Awards in Toronto, Canada. Despite her great popularity, "Constant Craving" was her only American chart single (No. 38) through 2002.

Connie Francis returned to the Westbury Music Fair in Westbury, Long Island, New York, the town where she was raped nineteen years earlier, to perform for a sellout crowd. She had been performing for almost forty years.

March 22

Sade performed at New York's Paramount Theater and must have felt quite comfortable as she did the whole show bare foot.

March 23

To benefit the Country Music Foundation and the Rhythm and Blues Foundation, a concert called The Rhythm, Country and Blues concert was held at the Universal Amphitheater in Los Angeles starring the Pointer Sisters.

March 25

Lulu performed a duet with Bobby Womack on the British TV show *Top of the Pops*.

March 27

Shania Twain's debut single, "What Made You Say That," entered the country singles chart, on its way to No. 55. Her musical influences included the Carpenters, the Mamas and the Papas, and a variety of Motown recordings. Among her idiosyncrasies: Shania demanded a bomb-sniffing dog check her rooms backstage.

April 6

Ann and Nancy Wilson sang the national anthem at the Seattle Mariners' season opener against the Toronto Blue Jays at the Kingdome in Seattle.

April 10

As a legendary protest figure for over three decades, Joan Baez continued another year of fund-raising, protesting, cause-rallying, and performing. This time using a truck as a stage, Baez participated in the first date of a benefit tour in shell-shocked Bosnia, singing to refugees in Zagreb, Croatia, prior to a television show the following night in war-torn Sarajevo.

April 14

Enya was named the Top Irish Female Artist at the annual IRMA (Irish Recorded Music Industry) Awards, held at the National Concert Hall in Dublin.

April 15

Sade began a tour in Copenhagen, Denmark, that would include thirty-five shows, ending in London.

April 16

k. d. lang appeared at the Earth Day benefit concert, headlined by Paul McCartney, at the Hollywood Bowl in Hollywood, California, with proceeds going to animal activist organizations, PETA, and Greenpeace.

April 18

Millie Jackson, B. B. King, and Bobby "Blue" Bland performed at the Westbury Music Fair in Westbury, New York.

April 27

Aretha Franklin's first TV special was taped at New York's Neaderlander Theater and featured duets with Bonnie Raitt, singing "Since You've Been Gone," and "Natural Woman" with Raitt and Gloria Estefan. The show to benefit the Gay Men's Health Crisis aired on May 9 on Fox TV.

May 1

Shirley Owens Reeves of the Shirelles received the Lifetime Achievement Award at the opening of the Doo-Wop Hall of Fame in Providence, Rhode Island.

May 3

Jewel performed on San Diego's local 99X FM's new artists' *Loudspeaker* show. The folk-flavored singer-songwriter, originally from Anchorage, Alaska, was at the time living in a Volkswagen van, which was parked in a parking lot near the beach, while she survived mainly on a diet of peanut butter and carrots.

May 4

Janis Ian's first album in over a decade, *Breaking Silence,* was issued. Its title was about a reference to her lesbianism, which she had become open about in interviews.

May 12

Tina Turner was given an Outstanding Contribution to the Music Industry Award at the World Music Awards' fifth annual ceremony in the Sporting Club, Monte Carlo, Monaco.

May 14

Dolly Parton performed at New York's Carnegie Hall during the Country Takes Manhattan showcase of sold-out performances. By the time she had her last of seventy-eight solo country chart singles, in 1993, Dolly had racked up a total of twenty-three No. 1s.

May 19

Jewel made her first performance appearance at the Interchange Coffeehouse in Pacific Beach, San Diego, where she developed a strong local following.

May 20

Pat Benatar performed at a sellout date at the Whisky a Go Go in Los Angeles.

May 21

Joan Baez performed at London's Dominion Theater during a British concert trip to promote her Virgin Records album *Play Me Backwards*.

May 22

Ace of Base's No. 1 in Germany "All That She Wants," an infectious pop-reggae tune, reached No. 1 in Britain. The group, led by Jenny Berggren and Linn Berggren, originally performed under the name Tech Noir (named after the discotheque featured in *The Terminator* film).

Carnie and Wendy Wilson (Wilson Phillips) spent the day working behind the counter of a record store in Los Angeles to benefit LIFEbeat's CounterAID, a fund-raiser for those with HIV/AIDS.

Salt-N-Pepa performed at a benefit to raise money for AIDS patients called LIFEbeat's CounterAID. They had intended to become nurses, but wound up as telephone sales operators before striking gold as a rap act.

May 24

Dionne Warwick performed at ASCAP's tenth annual Pop Awards at the Beverly Hilton Hotel in Beverly Hills, performing Bacharach and David songs.

May 29

Janet Jackson's album, *Janet*, reached No. 1 in England. The recordings included a diverse guest artist list, including opera singer Kathleen Battle and Public Enemy's Chuck D.

June 5

Mariah Carey married Sony Music President Tommy Mottola at St. Thomas Episcopal Church in New York. Among the guests were Barbra Streisand, Bruce Springsteen, and Billy Joel.

June 6

Joni Mitchell performed at the Troubadours of Folk Festival at UCLA's Drake Stadium, Los Angeles

The biopic *What's Love Got to Do With It,* based on Tina Turner's life and her 1986 autobiography, premiered.

June 9

Debbie Gibson, who was a huge attraction in Japan, began a tour, opening at Nakano Sun Plaza Hall in Tokyo.

June 10

Janis Ian appeared on NBC-TV's *The Tonight Show.*

June 15

Diana Ross performed "God Bless the Child" at the first Apollo Theater Hall of Fame concert from the historic venue.

June 19

Ace of Base's *Happy Nation,* their European-only debut album, peaked at No. 21 in the U.K. It had stopped at No. 4 in their homeland of Sweden the month before.

July 3

Shania Twain's sophomore single, "Dance with the One That Brought You," hit the country singles chart, reaching the same position as her first, No. 55. The video was directed by actor Sean Penn. Born Eileen Regina Edwards, she took the name of her Objibway Indian stepfather and adopted the Indian name Shania (meaning "I'm on the way") in 1990.

July 8

Patti Smith performed in Central Park, New York, as part of the city's Summerstage series.

July 10

While on a European tour, Chaka Khan performed at the Montreux Jazz Festival in Montreux, Switzerland, and continued on to the JVC Jazz Festival in Nice, France, and the North Sea Jazz Festival in the Hague, the Netherlands.

July 15

Debbie Gibson opened in the twentieth-anniversary production of *Grease* at London's Dominion Theater, playing the featured role of Sandy.

July 17

Kim Wilde's remake of Yvonne Elliman's 1978 hit, "If I Can't Have You," made it to No. 12 in Britain. While Elliman's version reached No. 1 in America, Wilde's never charted here.

July 31

Updating the John Travolta/Olivia Newton-John original "You're the One That I Want," Debbie Gibson's duet with fellow *Grease* star Craig McLachlan reached No. 13 in Britain.

August 3

Sheryl Crow's first single, "Run Baby Run," was issued, but elicited little interest. It would be almost a year before she would have her first big hit, "All I Wanna Do."

August 7

Joan Baez performed in New York's Central Park as Vanguard prepared to release a three-CD 60-track anthology, *Rare, Live and Classic,* covering her iconic career from 1958 to 1989 and including a previously unreleased duet with Bob Dylan, "Blowin' in the Wind," and cuts from the her 1981 sessions with the Grateful Dead.

August 26

Shawn Colvin, Melissa Etheridge, and Heart performed at the Voices for Choices benefit concert in Santa Monica, California.

September 7

Sinead O'Connor reportedly attempted suicide by taking an overdose of pills and vodka.

September 11

Janet Jackson made her film debut when the motion picture *Poetic Justice* hit theaters today.

September 13

Gloria Estefan was honored with the Hispanic Heritage Award by Housing Secretary Henry Cisneros at a Washington, D.C., reception.

September 14

Bette Midler's Nobody Beats the Wiz concert series opened at Radio City Music Hall, set to run for five weeks. (It was her first concert performance in ten years, and she was given a $25,000 Tiffany diamond band to mark the occasion.)

September 30

Kate Pierson (B-52's) was charged with trespassing and criminal mischief during an anti-fur protest at the New York office of *Vogue* magazine.

Whitney Houston and husband, Bobby Brown, had their limousine pulled over at Kennedy International Airport, New York, by nine police officers with guns drawn, looking for drugs.

October 16

Aretha Franklin sang the national anthem at the Skydome in Toronto before the first game of the World Series between the Philadelphia Phillies and the Toronto Blue Jays.

October 23

Toni Braxton had her first of two R&B No. 1 singles when "Seven Whole Days" reached the top. She previously had three singles peak at No. 2 before reaching the milestone. They were "Give U My Heart," "Love Shoulda Brought You Home," and "Another Sad Love Song."

October 29

Melissa Etheridge's *Yes I Am* album debuted on the chart at No. 16. It would stay on the Top 200 hit list for over two years.

November 6

"All That She Wants" by Ace of Base hit No. 2 in America after first conquering the European continent. After their demo was rejected by ABBA's Polar label in Stockholm, the group sent their cassette to Mega Records in Copenhagen, Denmark, which signed Ace of Base for £2,900 in March of 1992.

November 7

Janis Ian, in a rare visit to England, performed at the Cambridge Theater in London.

November 20

Anita Baker's "Witchcraft" duet with Frank Sinatra on his *Duets* album reached its peak at No. 2 pop in its first week on the charts. The *Duets* album also included two Carly Simon performances on "In the Wee Small Hours of the Morning" and "Guess I'll Hang My Tears Out to Dry" and peaked at No. 129 in its first week on the pop Top 200.

November 27

Celine Dionne powered her way onto the charts with "The Power of Love," the first No. 1 in America for the French Canadian.

December 4

k. d. lang sang a duet with Elton John on "Teardrops" for his *Duets* album, and today it hit No. 4 in its week of entry on the British chart. It would hit No. 25 Stateside the following week.

December 12

Patti LaBelle performed at the twelfth annual Christmas in Washington benefit.

December 15

Bette Midler became the highest-grossing artist in the twenty-one year history of the Universal Theater with her nine-date shows, adding up to $2,200,000.

December 31

Donna Summer performed at the Resorts Casino Hotel in Atlantic City for Merv Griffin's *New Year's Eve Third Annual Special,* which was shown on Fox TV. It was also Donna's forty-fifth birthday.

Janis Ian participated in shock jock Howard Stern's *The Miss Howard Stern New Year's Eve Pageant* TV special. She was quoted speaking of the event: "It was absolutely the most disgusting thing I've ever been a part of, and I hope they ask me back next year."

More Moments in 1993

Although the band 4 Non-Blondes had a short shelf life, they were included on VH1's "100 Greatest One-Hit Wonders" list for their '93 single, "What's Up?" (garnering tons of airplay worldwide and reaching No. 14 on the U.S. *Billboard* Hot 100). Singer Linda Perry got a second wind as a producer and songwriter in the next decade. She went on to pen hits for artists like Pink, Gwen Stefani, Courtney Love, and Christina Aguilera.

On the morning of July 7, singer Mia Zapata of the Seattle band the Gits is found murdered. The music community fears the killer is someone known to Mia. Despite numerous benefit efforts, a segment on *America's Most Wanted*, and Joan Jett's appearances with the other band members performing as Evil Stig ("Gits Live" backwards), the killer, Jesus Mezquia, is not found until more than a decade later, thanks to DNA. It turns out to have been a random attack by a total stranger.

1994

January 20

The Pointer Sisters received a star on the Hollywood Walk of Fame and became only the second female group to receive one. The first was the Supremes.

January 27

Janet Jackson was touted as Best Female Sex Symbol and Best Female Singer in *Rolling Stone*'s Music Awards and readers poll.

Still performing occasional live dates in Great Britain, Suzi Quatro appeared on BBC-TV's popular comedy series *Absolutely Fabulous*. On this same date in 1974, Suzi's "Stumblin' In" charted, on its way to No. 1 in America, her biggest Stateside success.

January 29

Mary Wilson of the Supremes was seriously injured (though she recovered) in a car accident on a California highway. (Not a good day for women on the road!)

January 30

Natalie Cole sang the national anthem at Super Bowl XXVIII in the Georgia Dome in Atlanta, Georgia.

February 2

"To think I've been doing this for thirty fucking years," Diana Ross reflected while performing at MIDEM '94 in Cannes, France, where she received the Commander in the Order of Arts and Letters Award from the French Minister of Culture.

February 6

Celine Dion was featured in a one-hour special on the *Disney Channel*.

February 12

Celine Dion's cover of "The Power of Love," formerly a No. 1 in England for Jennifer Rush, topped the American charts while reaching No. 4 in Britain.

Tori Amos' album *Under the Pink* hit No. 1 in Britain in its first week on the charts.

February 19

Tori Amos' *Under the Pink* album debuted and peaked at No. 12 in America.

February 23

Dionne Warwick attended a federal hearing by a Judiciary Juvenile Justice Sub-Committee in Washington, D.C., that referenced gangsta rap as "pornography."

February 26

Toni Braxton's self-titled album reached No. 1 pop, almost eight months after its first release. She was influenced by Chaka Khan, Stevie Wonder, Whitney Houston, and Quincy Jones.

March 1

Reba McEntire's ballad "Does He Love You?," a duet with Linda Davis, won the Best Country Vocal Collaboration Award at the thirty-sixth annual Grammys at New York's Radio City Music Hall. Gloria Estefan won her first Grammy for the Best Tropical Album (Mi Tierra) category. Toni Braxton received the Best New Artist and Best R&B Vocal Performance, Female, trophy for the song "Another Sad Love Song." Whitney Houston was also a big winner with Record of the Year, Best Pop Vocal Performance, Female, for "I Will Always Love You" and Album of the Year for *The Bodyguard*. Mary Chapin-Carpenter earned the Best Country Vocal Performance, Female, trophy (for "Passionate Kisses"). Apparently she would not need her degree from Brown University in American civilization. Nanci Griffith won the Best Contemporary Folk Album category for *Other Voices, Other Rooms*.

March 2

The Shirelles, Mabel John, and Irma Thomas were honored with Pioneer Awards at the Rhythm and Blues Foundation's fifth annual awards at the Roseland Ballroom in New York City.

March 16

The other side of stardom is living with the risks that come with that stardom. Roberta Flack, who had been stalked on several occasions by a deranged New York cab driver, was under siege while he attempted to get in her apartment as he screamed: "I'll kill her if I see her." He was promptly arrested.

March 23

The Staple Singers and Patti LaBelle performed at a joint benefit for the Rhythm and Blues Foundation and the Country Music Foundation at the Universal Amphitheater in Los Angeles.

April 2

Ace of Base's *The Sign* (a repackaged version of the European album *Happy Nation*), including four new tracks for the American scene, reached No. 1 in the U.S. The significance was historic as they became the first Swedish act to top the American albums chart, an accomplishment not even achieved by the iconic ABBA.

April 4

Sheryl Crow performed at the Orpheum Theater in Boston, opening for Crowded House. She began playing piano by ear at the age of six. Having attended her first concert at age thirteen (to see Peter Frampton), she started writing songs immediately after.

April 8

Courtney Love's husband, Nirvana's Kurt Cobain, was found dead at the couple's Seattle home. The drugged-out grunge rocker committed suicide by sitting in his chair, looking out the window, while pulling the trigger on a shotgun. Courtney Love thus became an instant celebrity in the upside-down media-hungry world. It didn't hurt the absurdity of her life that she reportedly carried Coban's ashes with her wherever she went. Oh, and to top it off, her group Hole's DGC label debut was scheduled for release the following week.

April 9

Whitney Houston performed at Carnegie Hall in New York, along with James Taylor, Elton John, Aaron Neville, Branford Marsalis, and Sting, among others, at the fifth annual Rain Forest Benefit Concert.

Notable Moments of Women in Music

April 21

Ace of Base member Jenny Berggren was attached while sleeping in a bedroom of her parents home in Gothenburg, Sweden. The knife-wielding German lunatic was arrested, jailed for only a year, but banned from Sweden for the following ten years.

April 22

Chaka Khan and Brian McKnight sang "Bridge over Troubled Waters" at New York's Paramount Theater for the seventh annual Essence Awards.

April 26

Grace Slick of Starship pled guilty to pointing a shotgun at a cop in her home. She claimed great stress as the reason. Can only imagine how stressful the 200 hours of community service was.

Salt-N-Pepa performed at the James L. Knight Center in Miami, Florida.

April 30

Aaliyah's "Back and Forth" debuted on the pop charts and eventually reached No. 5. It was her first of sixteen hits in her brief career as she died in a plane crash in 2001 at the age of twenty-two. Six months after she charted, she married R. Kelly, but it was annulled because she was underage.

The Staple Singers performed at the twenty-fifth annual New Orleans Jazz and Heritage Festival.

May 2

The Shirelles were inducted into the Rhythm and Blues Foundation with a Pioneer Award and performed "Dedicated to the One I Love" for the first time in seventeen years.

May 4

Toni Braxton was named the World's Bestselling R&B Newcomer of the Year at the sixth World Music Awards in Monte Carlo, Monaco, while Whitney Houston received the World's Bestselling Pop Artist of the Year, Female Recording Artist of the Year, American Recording Artist, R&B Artist of the Year, and Overall Recording Artist awards.

May 7

Chrissie Hynde and the Pretenders appeared on TV's *Saturday Night Live.*

May 14

Janet Jackson performed on NBC-TV's *Saturday Night Live.*

May 26

The world is still scratching its collective head over this one. The King of Pop and the daughter of the King of Rock and Roll were married today. Lisa Marie Presley and Michael Jackson tied the knot in La Vega, Dominican Republic. Obviously proud of their union, the two denied it ever happened for two months.

June 4

Carole King took over for Petula Clark in the Broadway play *Blood Brother* and stayed with the show through January 1995.

Tori Amos' "Past the Mission" single, with Trent Reznor of Nine Inch Nails guesting, reached No. 31 in England. For whatever ghoulish reason, it was recorded at the house in which actress Sharon Tate was murdered in 1969.

June 5

Donna Summer performed with the Nashville Symphony at the town's Summer Lights Arts Festival.

June 7

Grace Slick was sentenced to 200 hours of community service and four A.A. meetings a week for three months after pointing a loaded gun at a police officer, called to her Tiburon, California, home to investigate a domestic dispute in March.

The all-female British group Touch started a two-week stint at the charity-funded Trinity Studios in Woking, England. Within months, the group would change its name to Spice and then to the Spice Girls, based on a song written for them called "Sugar and Spice."

June 9

TLC member Lisa "Left Eye" Lopes set fire to her boyfriend's (professional football player Andre Rison's) home. (And you thought TLC stood for Tender Loving Care).

June 11

Emmylou Harris sang at the Roots of Country concert, celebrating the reopening of the famed Ryman Auditorium, the original Grand Ole Opry venue.

June 16

Two months after Courtney Love's husband killed himself, Courtney's bassist in Hole, twenty-seven-year-old Kirsten Pfaff, was found dead in her bathtub from a heroin overdose.

June 20

Aretha Franklin performed at the White House in Washington for President and Mrs. Clinton.

June 24

Melissa Etheridge, k. d. lang, and Sarah McLachlan appeared at a LifeBeat benefit concert, at the Beacon Theater in New York.

July 7

Sheryl Crow started a U.S. tour as the opening act for the reunited Eagles at the Cleveland Municipal Stadium in Ohio. Ten years earlier, she graduated with a classical music degree at the University of Missouri and relocated to St. Louis to teach music at an elementary school, before moving to Los Angeles in 1986.

July 8

Emmylou Harris sang with the San Diego Symphony Orchestra at the Summer Pops Bowl Amphitheater in San Diego.

July 17

Whitney Houston performed at the World Cup soccer finals between Italy and Brazil at the Rose Bowl in Pasadena, California.

July 28

Patti LaBelle, Ruth Pointer, and Bette Midler performed "Over the Rainbow" at the Harbor light Pavilion in Boston during Patti's tour.

August 6

Former public school teacher Sheryl Crow charted, on the road to immense success and frustration when "All I Wanna Do" peaked at No. 2—for six straight weeks!

Melissa Etheridge hit the singles survey with "I'm the Only One" (No. 8).

August 12

Around 30,000 people showed up at Yasgur's Farm in upstate New York to relive Woodstock on its twenty-fifth anniversary. Performing as they did a quarter of a century earlier were a radiant Melanie and Richie Havens, along with Arlo Guthrie, among others. Though it was on the original site, they had to call it Bethal' 94 (after the town near Woodstock) because a rival festival named Woodstock 94 in Saugerties, New York, with a cast of contemporary wannabe Woodstockers was competing nearby, including acts like Sheryl Crow, Melissa Etheridge, and Salt-N-Pepa.

Dionne Warwick guested on the *Geraldo* (Rivera) TV show, but drew criticism when she supported and sympathized with O. J. Simpson regarding the murder of his wife.

Heart began performing for five nights at Seattle's semi-intimate Backstage Club and took the opportunity to record for an all-acoustic album called *The Road Home.*

August 29

Marianne Faithfull's autobiography, *Faithfull,* was published to tie in with the September release of her compilation album *Faithfull: A Collection of Her Best Recordings.*

August 31

R. Kelly married new chart sensation Aaliyah in Rosemont, Illinois. The marriage was later annulled as Aaliyah was only fifteen years old at the time, and the state law required new brides to be at least sixteen years old.

September 3

Bette Midler made her first appearance in Las Vegas in eighteen years at the MGM Grand Garden.

September 7

During a tour opening for Nine Inch Nails, Courtney Love and Hole performed at the Riverside Theatre in Milwaukee, Wisconsin. Courtney, who'd supported her self as a stripper prior to her Hole days, came to Los Angeles in 1989 and placed a free ad in the *Recycler* newspaper, reading: "I want to start a band. My influences are Big Black, Sonic Youth, and Fleetwood Mac."

September 16

Whitney Houston began the first of seven performances at Radio City Music Hall in New York. Each one was a sellout, grossing over $2,500,000.

September 17

Mariah Carey and Luther Vandross reached No. 3 in the chart debut in England of their remake of the Diana Ross–Lionel Richie hit "Endless Love." It would reach No. 2 Stateside and No. 7 R&B.

September 27

A Go Go's two-CD, thirty-six-track retrospective, *Return to the Valley of the Go-Go's*, was released, including three newly recorded tracks to coincide with a reunion tour, which included ex-Bangle Vicki Peterson replacing pregnant guitarist Charlotte Caffey.

October 1

Actress/singer Brandy charted with "I Wanna Be Down" (No. 6), her first of six hits through 1996.

October 3

Whitney Houston returned to the White House, this time to perform in the Rose Garden, to celebrate the visit of Nelson Mandela at a state dinner.

October 6

Patti LaBelle debuted at her own hometown nightclub, Chez LaBelle in Philadelphia.

October 8

Marianne Faithfull sang "Crayfish" at Elvis Aaron Presley: The Tribute, an all-star tribute to the late king of rock held at the Pyramid Arena in Memphis, Tennessee. Ann Wilson sang "I Want You, I Need You, I Love You," and Sheryl Crow performed "Don't Be Cruel" while "All I Wanna Do" stopped at No. 2 on the national charts, behind Boyz II Men's "I'll Make Love to You."

October 10

Folk artist Nanci Griffith performed at London's Royal Albert Hall accompanied by a full orchestra.

October 18

Sheryl Crow was the opening act for Bob Dylan at the Roseland Ballroom in New York. Seven years earlier, she got her first break by performing as a backing singer on Michael Jackson's eighteen-month Bad world tour, beginning in September 1987.

November 1

Reba McEntire's face got a lift on this day when Frito Lay launched the shipment of 3 million Frito snacks with her face on the front.

November 5

Brandy's debut single, I Wanna Be Down," went gold while still rising up the charts, on its way to No. 6 pop. The fifteen-year-old beauty was already an accomplished actress, having appeared in the TV shows *Thea* and *Moesha.*

Nanci Griffith played four shows at the Richard Rodgers Theater in New York.

November 12

Gloria Estefan's "Hold Me, Thrill Me, Kiss Me," a remake of the Mel Carter hit, reached No. 9.

Melissa Etheridge gave a benefit concert on Melissa Etheridge Day at her old high school in Leavenworth, Kansas. The show was to raise money for a ball field to be named after her father, John Etheridge, a teacher, counselor, and athletic director at the school.

November 15

Gladys Knight and Stevie Wonder sang "For Once in My Life" with Frank Sinatra on his *Duets II* album, which released today.

November 18

Deborah Harry and Blondie's *The Platinum Collection,* a forty-seven-song CD anthology, including their 1975 demo "Once I Had a Love," which was re-recorded as "Heart of Glass," was issued in America.

November 19

Mary Chapin-Carpenter's "Shut Up and Kiss Me" became her first country single No. 1.

November 21

Joni Mitchell played an acoustic showcase at Queens Gate Terrace in London— her first British performance in twelve years.

The Go Go's performed at Los Angeles' famed Troubadour on their current reunion tour.

November 24

Reba McEntire's autobiography *Reba: My Story,* published by Bantam, hit the *New York Times* bestseller list.

November 25

Sheryl Crow duetted with Mick Jagger on "Under My Thumb" at a Rolling Stones concert at Joe Robbie Stadium in Miami, Florida.

November 26

Chrissie Hynde's duet with the "Chairman of the Board," "Luck Be A Lady," on Frank Sinatra's *Duets II* album peaked at No. 29.

Sheena Easton, Roberta Flack, James Ingram, and Peabo Bryson began The Colors of Christmas tour in the Palace of Auburn Hills in Auburn Hills, Michigan.

November 30

En Vogue performed at Wembley Arena in England and then ostensibly quit the tour due to member Cindy Herron's pregnancy, though rumors indicated it was due to stress related to working with Luther Vandross.

Melissa Etheridge met with fourteen students to discuss her career as a musician and songwriter as part of the Grammy in the Schools "Soundcheck" program before a performance with Hootie and the Blowfish.

December 5

On a bill as diverse as you can get, Courtney Love and Hole performed in Z100's "Acoustic Christmas," held in New York's Madison Square Garden with Sheryl Crow, Melissa Etheridge, Indigo Girls, Weezer, Bon Jovi, and Toad the Wet Sprocket.

December 6

Kylie Minogue, Belinda Carlisle, Mary Chapin-Carpenter, and the Kinks, among others, appeared at B.T.'s Tenth Anniversary Concert at the London Arena.

December 7

Celine Dion performed at the "Gala for the President" before President Clinton at Ford's Theater in Washington, D.C. Though it aired tonight, it was originally recorded on October 30.

Reba McEntire was named Top Female Country Artist of the Year at the fifth *Billboard* Music Awards at the Universal Amphitheater in Universal City, California.

December 17

Twenty-six-year-old Celine Dion married her fifty-two-year-old manager Rene Angelil at the Notre Dame Basilica in Montreal.

December 28

Among the seventeenth annual Kennedy Center Honors, shown on CBS-TV this night, Aretha Franklin was given a tribute, along with Patti LaBelle, the Four Tops, and Detroit's New Bethel Baptist Church choir performing.

December 31

Sheryl Crow performed at a New Year's Eve show at the Hard Rock Café in Maui, Hawaii.

More Moments in 1994

The U.S. Postal Service introduced a Billie Holiday postage stamp.

Stax founder Estelle Axton passed away on February 25. Axton and brother, Jim Stewart, were the co-founders of the legendary Memphis soul-recording label, Stax Records (taking its name from Jim and Estelle's surnames). In 2006 (Grammy parent) The Recording Academy honored Estelle with a Trustees Award.

Sarah McLachlan is sued by an obsessed fan and stalker for copyright infringement after she writes the song "Possession," based on lines from one of his letters. The lawsuit never came to trial as the plaintiff committed suicide.

Liz Phair appears on the cover of the October 6, 1994, *Rolling Stone* magazine's "Women in Rock" issue, setting off a media firestorm heralding 1994 as the year of women in rock. Seems you couldn't turn on a TV news report or pick up a music magazine without the reference. Phair's debut, *Exile in Guyville*, was chosen as one of *Rolling Stone*'s 500 Greatest Albums of All Time.

Tori Amos co-founds RAINN (The Rape Abuse and Incest National Network) to provide support and resources for rape victims.

Sonic Youth super couple, Thurston Moore and Kim Gordon, give birth to daughter, Coco.

1995

January 10

Chaka Khan, Dionne Warwick, and Patti LaBelle, among others, performed at the Universal Amphitheater in Universal City, California, at a tribute concert honoring Ella Fitzgerald.

January 12

The B-52's inducted Martha and the Vandellas into the Rock and Roll Hall of Fame at its tenth annual induction ceremonies at New York's Waldorf Astoria. Also, Melissa Etheridge performed Janis Joplin's "Piece of My Heart." Prior to that, she had the honor of inducting the late Ms. Joplin into the Hall.

January 13

Folk artist Nanci Griffith began a tour at the Andrew Jackson Hall in Nashville, Tennessee, which was set to end at New York's Beacon Theater on April 18.

January 21

Courtney Love was arrested for offensive behavior on board a Quantas Airways plane, flying between Brisbane and Melbourne, Australia. By this time, she was being hailed as the queen of the riot grrrl movement, a media invention. What an honor!

Melissa Etheridge's "I'm the Only One" peaked at No. 8. It entered the chart six months earlier and stayed in the Top 100 for forty weeks, making it her biggest hit single.

January 22

Janet Jackson was honored at the International Dance Awards in London with an award for her achievements in dance music.

January 28

It took ten months after originally charting, but Celine Dion's "The Colour of My Love" finally topped the British charts today.

January 30

The Go Go's performed "Tutti Frutti" with the legendary Little Richard to open the twenty-second American Music Awards, held at Los Angeles' Shrine Auditorium.

February 3

Joni Mitchell appeared on TV, by her own recollection, for the first time in twenty-five years (*The Johnny Cash Show,* in 1970) on NBC-TV's *The Tonight Show.*

February 9

Madonna's *True Blue* (7 million) and *Like a Virgin* (9 million) were certified multi-platinum by the RIAA.

February 11

Cyndi Lauper's "I'm Gonna Be Strong," originally recorded in 1981 with her first group, Blue Angel, peaked at No. 37 in Britain. At the same time, Cyndi played the first of two nights at London's Royal Albert Hall.

February 12

The RIAA certified three million sales of Celine Dion's "The Colour of My Love." By the end of the year, the album would sell over 2 million copies in the U.K., over one million in Japan, and 1.4 million in Canada.

February 25

Madonna's "Take a Bow" reached No. 1. She became the first female artist to have eleven U.S. chart-toppers, now at No. 5 on the all-time list behind the Beatles, Elvis Presley, the Supremes, and Michael Jackson.

February 27

k. d. lang was named Best International Female Artist at the thirteenth Annual BRIT Awards, held at London's Alexandra Palace.

February 28

Annie Lennox, Sarah MacLachlan, and Melissa Etheridge sang backup for Carly Simon on "You're So Vain" at Clive Davis' annual pre-Grammy party at the House of Blues in Los Angeles. Clive was not offended at the title as he knew the song was written by Carly about Kris Kristofferson.

March 1

Sheryl Crow was voted Best New Artist and performed "All I Wanna Do" at the thirty-seventh annual Grammy Awards, held at Los Angeles' Shrine Auditorium. She also received Record of the Year and Best Pop Vocal Performance, Female, awards that night. Meanwhile, Carly Simon and Tori

Amos presented the annual Best Male awards. For some inexplicable reason, Simon found the post-Grammy press conference an appropriate time to state that she had lived in O. J. Simpson's "murder house" in Brentwood, California, in 1976, for five months.

March 2

The Rhythm and Blues Foundation in Los Angeles held its sixth annual Pioneer Awards presentation, with Cissy Houston (whose daughter, Whitney, made the presentation) on the receiving end.

March 3

Carly Simon began her first tour in fifteen years (a seven-date tryst) in front of a sellout crowd at the Galaxy Theater in Santa Ana, California. She noted to the audience that she had only done sixty concerts in her entire career.

March 4

Celine Dion's "Think Twice" reached U.K. No. 1 at the same time as her *The Colour of My Love*" album topped the British charts, both for five weeks, making her the first artist since the Beatles ("I Feel Fine") to hold the top spot on both hit lists for five consecutive weeks.

March 10

Sheryl Crow performed at the opening-night gala of the Hard Rock Hotel and Casino in Las Vegas, Nevada.

March 16

Anita Baker and Babyface were at it again, co-hosting the ninth annual Soul Train Music Awards, this time with additional host, legendary diva Patti LaBelle. Anita also received the Best R&B/Soul Female Single and Best R&B Soul Female Album awards that night.

March 18

Annie Lennox appeared on NBC TV's *Saturday Night Live*. The same day her *Medusa* album of cover recordings, featuring "A Whiter Shade of Pale" (the first record she bought at age fourteen), reached No. 1 in Britain.

March 23

Mary Chapin-Carpenter was named Best International Female Vocalist at the Inaugural Great Country Music Awards, held in (of all places) Birmingham,

England. She couldn't attend as she was performing at the Sioux City Convention Center Auditorium in Iowa.

March 31

Known as the "Mexican Madonna," Selena (born Selena Quintanilla-Perez) was a singer on the verge of greatness. She recorded five albums in Spanish, including the Latin pop chart No. 1 *Amor Prohibido* and won a Grammy for her *Live* album in 1993. She was working on her first English-language album when she was shot to death by her fan club president (who was embezzling from Selena) in a Corpus Christi, Texas, motel room. Her posthumous English album, *Dreaming Of You,* sold over a million copies.

April 4

Melissa Etheridge posed nude in a PETA ad in the *Advocate* magazine, protesting fur sales with her gal-pal, Julie Cypher.

April 5

Whitney Houston's first album, *Whitney Houston,* was certified a 12-million seller by the RIAA.

April 10

Joan Baez did the first of four dates at the Bottom Line in New York, which would be recorded for a future release, with guests Janis Ian, Mary-Chapin Carpenter, and Kate and Anna McGarrigle.

April 11

Carole King broke her arm when Bob Dylan hugged her and she fell into the photographer's pit at his Dublin gig, during an encore of "Real Real Gone" with Elvis Costello and Van Morrison.

In a testament to her fan base, Amy Grant's *Home for Christmas* album was certified by the RIAA for 2 million in sales.

April 16

Trisha Yearwood and Emmylou Harris performed at London's Royal Albert Hall as part of the New American Music Tour '95.

April 23

Dolly Parton's Dollywood amusement park opened in Pigeon Falls, Tennessee.

April 25

Thirty minutes into an Amsterdam, Holland, show, Courtney Love walked off the stage after an audience member threw a cup containing a liquid at her.

April 26

Courtney Love reportedly turned down an offer of $1 million to pose nude in *Playboy* magazine, but she would bare her breasts on David Letterman's TV show some nine years later.

May 3

Celine Dion earned the World's Bestselling French-Canadian and Canadian Female Artist of the Year awards at the seventh annual World Music Awards, held at the Sporting Club in Monte Carlo, Monoco.

May 5

In a campaign for Major League Baseball, Aretha Franklin appeared with the Detroit Tigers, singing "Take Me Out to the Ball Game," in their promotional video.

May 6

Joni Mitchell played the twenty-sixth annual New Orleans Jazz & Heritage Festival.

May 10

Reba McEntire was named Entertainer of the Year at the thirtieth annual Academy of Country Music Awards. She was the first woman in fifteen year to win since Barbara Mandrell did it in 1980.

May 15

Jewel made her television debut on NBC-TV's *Conan O'Brien Show*. The appearance was reportedly seen by actor Sean Penn, who called her and invited her to the Venice Film Festival in Italy.

May 18

Bette Midler appeared on NBC-TV's *Seinfeld* episode "The Understudy."

May 23

Donna Summer performed in Sao Paolo, Brazil.

May 28

Mary Chapin-Carpenter headlined the Songs for the Heartland benefit concert at the Oklahoma Civic Center to raise money for families of victims in the recent Oklahoma City terrorist bombing.

June 3

Sheryl Crow was named Top New Artist at the first Blockbuster Entertainment Awards, held at Hollywood's Pantages Theater. Her pre-hit artistic career included recordings by Eric Clapton, Celine Dion, and Wynona Judd of songs she wrote, backup singing on Don Henley's 1989 album, *The End of the Innocence,* and tours with George Harrison, Rod Stewart, and Joe Cocker.

June 10

TLC sang their hit "Waterfalls" at the MTV Movie Awards.

June 11

Courtney Love was hospitalized at Harborview Medical Center in Seattle after apparently taking too much prescription medicine.

June 13

Alanis Morissette's debut album, *Jagged Little Pill,* was issued on Madonna's Maverick label, exemplifying a rebellious and impetuous writing and performing style that was immediately accepted by Gen Xers.

June 15

Sinead O'Connor hit two Israeli photographers and damaged their equipment during a visit to Jerusalem's Holy Sepulcher Church.

June 16

Diana Ross performed in Moscow at the Kremlin Palace of Congresses.

June 17

Janet and Michael Jackson's duet on "Scream" reached No. 5 in its debut week on the pop charts, the highest debut of any single up to that time. A week earlier, the single had reached No. 3 in England in its first week on the charts.

June 30

Brandy, Blackstreet, Notorious B.I.G., Naughty by Nature, and Method Man,

Alanis Morisette.

among others, performed at the Byrne Meadowlands Arena in East Rutherford, New Jersey, at the Hot 97 Summer Jam.

Mary J. Blige, Boyz II Men, and Montell Jordan performed at the Starwood Amphitheater in Antioch, Tennessee.

July 4

The Lollopalooza '95 touring festival, including Courtney Love and Hole and Sinead O'Connor (another conservative wench), among others, began at the Gorge, in George, Washington. Love celebrated the occasion by having a backstage brawl with singer Kathleen Hanna of Bikini Kill, who would file assault charges. During one of the Lollopalooza shows in Kansas, Love notified the crowd that "I'm going to abuse you, because you fucking deserve it, you shits!"

July 8

A remix of Deborah Harry and Blondie's "Heart of Glass" reached No. 15 in Britain, sixteen years after the original version reached No. 1.

TLC's "Waterfalls" reached No. 1 pop for seven weeks and No. 4 R&B. It was the trio's second of four No. 1s, including "Creep," "No Scrubs," and "Unpretty."

July 11

Donna Summer sang at the Nautica Stage in Cleveland, Ohio, at the start of a U.S. tour.

July 17

The RIAA certified Carole King's *Tapestry* album at 10 million copies sold, becoming the second-highest-selling album by a female artist (first was Whitney Houston's debut).

July 20

TLC's album *Waterfalls* headed toward 9 million in sales while the group (who obviously didn't know how to manage their money) filed for chapter 11 bankruptcy.

July 26

Mary Chapin-Carpenter's PBS-TV special, *In The Spotlight,* aired in America and included duets with Joan Baez and Shawn Colvin.

July 28

Patti Smith appeared unannounced at the Lollapalooza gig in New York, performing a forty-five-minute set.

July 29

Shania Twain's *The Woman in Me* album rose to No. 6 on the Top 200. As a teenager, the bountiful beauty worked with her stepfather in the Canadian forests as part of a restoration crew, learning to use chain saws and axes while planting trees.

July 31

Courtney Love walked off a Lollapalooza tour performance in Burgetstown, Pennsylvania, after a so called fan threw a shotgun shell on the stage.

August 4

"Luck Love," the first single from Ace of Base's second album, premiered at the World Games opening ceremony in Gothenburg, Sweden, an event that was broadcast live throughout Europe.

August 9

Celebrating the closure of the Lollapalooza trek, Courtney Love was carried off the stage by a security guard during the final concert, after swearing at fans and twice jumping into the crowd to attack them.

August 11

Reba McEntire performed at the Bradley Center in Milwaukee during her summer tour. Meanwhile, the RIAA certified platinum sales for *The Last One to Know* and multi-platinum sales for *For My Broken Heart* (3 million), *Read My Mind* (3 million), *Greatest Hits* (3 million), and *Greatest Hits, Volume II* (4 million). Not a bad day for Reba.

August 30

For the first time since 1979, Carly Simon reunited with former husband, James Taylor, at a benefit concert unofficially known as "Livestock 95" for the Martha's Vineyard Agricultural Society at the society's Fairgrounds in West Tisbury, Massachusetts. The audience of over 10,000 saw them do separate sets before joining together for two numbers.

August 31

Gloria Estefan performed before a crowd of 16,000 Cuban refugees at the Guantanamo Navel base in Cuba. Interesting in that she was the daughter of a Cuban soldier and bodyguard to former President Fulgencio Batista, who was ousted from power by Fidel Castro when she was three years old.

September 2

The Rock and Roll Hall of Fame Museum opened its doors in Cleveland, Ohio. A concert to honor the event featured Annie Lennox, Martha and the Vandellas, Aretha Franklin, Chrissie Hynde and the Pretenders, Chuck Berry, Little Richard, and Bruce Springsteen. In an obvious tribute to the '60s girl group the Shangri-Las, Melissa Etheridge performed "Leader of the Pack."

September 4

Carnie Wilson's (of Wilson Phillips) new daytime talk show premiered on independent TV stations and would last a year in the competitive talk-show marketplace.

September 8

Annie Lennox performed at a free concert in Central Park, New York City, her first New York performance in seven years.

September 17

Alanis Morissette performed at the John Anson Ford Theater in Hollywood. Unlike fellow Canadian Joni Mitchell, who began writing at age twenty, Alanis wrote her first songs at the age of nine, having begun playing piano at age six.

September 21

Michelle Wright, Shania Twayne, Sarah McLachlan, and the Nylons performed on the "Horizon," an inaugural celebration bill at the General Motors Place in Vancouver, Canada.

September 25

Courtney Love (who's last name was obviously a contradiction to her behavior) was found guilty of assaulting Kathleen Hanna of Bikini Kill and sentenced to one year in prison and an anger-management course.

September 28

Courtney Love pleaded guilty to a charge of fourth-degree assault regarding her attack on a woman during the July 4 Lollapalooza gig and was given a one-year suspended sentence, conditional to her refraining from violence for two years and enroll in anger-management classes. (Yeah, that'll work!)

September 29

Gladys Knight, Aretha Franklin, Kool and the Gang, and the Isley Brothers performed at New York's Madison Square Garden at the KISS-FM Classic Soul concert.

October 3

The RIAA announced that Reba McEntire was now the third-bestselling female artist of all time, with twenty-eight million albums sold. No. 1 and No. 2 were Barbra Streisand and Linda Ronstadt, respectively. The same day, Reba celebrated twenty years in the business with the release of her sixteenth MCA album, *Starting Over.*

October 5

Mary J. Blige, Brandy, Salt-N-Pepa, Wu-Tang Clan, Jodeci, Run D.M.C., and Notorious B.I.G., among others, performed in an all-star hip hop/rap show at Madison Square Garden in New York.

October 7

A one-time-only reuniting of LaBelle on record resulted in the No. 1 hit (on the dance charts) "Turn It Out," from the film *To Wong Foo, Thanks for Everything, Julie Newmar.*

Alanis Morissette topped the album chart with *Jagged Little Pill* and became the first Canadian female artist to reach No. 1 in the U.S. (that's right! Joni Mitchell only reached No. 2 . . . twice!) In 1988, at the age of fourteen, Alanis was an opening act for rapper Vanilla Ice.

Celine Dion's *D'Eux* debuted and peaked at No. 7 in Britain. It would go on to sell over 3 million copies in France.

October 15

Jonathan Hogan filed a complaint in the Santa Clara County, California, court, claiming that Courtney Love punched and kicked him in the groin when he climbed on the stage at the Edge nightclub in Palo Alto in an attempt to dance with her.

October 16

k. d. lang "cybertalked" with fans on America Online.

October 21

Rickie Lee Jones pulled out of an Irish TV show in Dublin, Ireland, when the producers refused to allow her to sing "The Altar Boy," because they felt it might offend some religious groups.

October 24

Chrissie Hynde sang the national anthem before the third game of the World Series between the Atlanta Braves and the Cleveland Indians at Jacobs Field in Cleveland, Ohio.

October 28

Alanis Morissette appeared on NBC-TV's *Saturday Night Live.* In 1984, she began her career with an acting part in the Nickelodeon TV show *You Can't*

Do That on Television, which led to her appearing in a movie playing a singer called Alanis (opposite future *Friends* TV star Matt LeBlanc as her boyfriend).

November 2

Chrissie Hynde acted and played on an episode of NBC-TV's *Friends.*

With no business acumen or musical training, Florence Greenberg, a housewife from New Jersey, started one of the premier indie-record companies of the '60s, Scepter Records. She discovered the Shirelles ("Will You Love Me Tomorrow") and Dionne Warwick and had hits with B. J. Thomas, the Kingsmen, Chuck Jackson, and numerous others. She died of a stroke at age eighty-two today.

November 5

Jewel played the part of Dorothy in an all-star production of *The Wizard Of Oz,* with Natalie Cole, Roger Daltry, Jackson Browne, and Nathan Lane at New York's Avery Fisher Hall, with proceeds benefiting the Children's Defense Fund.

November 7

Chynna Phillips' (of Wilson Phillips) debut solo album, *Naked and Sacred,* was issued while Carnie and Wendy Wilson backed their father, Brian, on a remake of his Beach Boys hit "Do It Again" for his *I Just Wasn't Made for These Times* album.

November 18

The James Bond film *Goldeneye* premiered with the Tina Turner title theme song. The single reached its peak in England at No. 10 in its first week of release. However, it would only make it to No. 89 R&B and No. 102 pop in America.

November 25

The album *Tapestry Revisited: A Tribute to Carole King* peaked at No. 88. It featured various artists' doing their own interpretations of the songs from *Tapestry,* including those by Celine Dion, Faith Hill, Aretha Franklin, Amy Grant, the Bee Gees, Rod Stewart, and Richard Marx, among others.

December 2

Mariah Carey, singing lead for Boyz II Men, reached the bestseller list with "One Sweet Day," a recording that spent an incredible sixteen weeks at No. 1, making it the No. 1 hit of the rock era.

The *Guinness Book of Records* stated that Ace of Base's *Happy Nation* album was the bestselling debut album of all time. The worldwide sales of that album had just exceeded 19 million on this day. Meanwhile, their follow-up set, *The Bridge,* reached its peak at No. 6 in Britain.

December 3

k. d. lang, who preferred to dress in masculine attire, was ironically the entertainment at the inaugural VH1 Fashion and Music Awards in Manhattan.

December 4

Celine Dion's "To Love You More," recorded by Celine with Kryzler and Company, a Japanese instrumental trio, became the first non-Japanese-language song to hit No. 1 on the Japanese chart since the 1983 Irene Cara smash "Flashdance."

December 6

Joni Mitchell received the prestigious Century Award, a form of lifetime achievement award, at the 1995 *Billboard* Music Awards, broadcast live from New York's Coliseum on Fox TV. Mary J. Blige's *My Life* was honored as the Top R&B Album.

December 7

Patti Smith started an eight-date northeastern tour, opening for Bob Dylan, in Danbury, Connecticut.

Super Jam 95 at Boston's Fleet Center featured Salt-N-Pepa, Shai, Brian McKnight, Montell Jordan, Coolio, After Seven, and Silk, among others. The day before, Salt-N-Pepa had received a citation from the governor of Massachusetts for portraying positive images for woman.

December 8

Courtney Love appeared on the TV show *10 Most Fascinating People,* saying that she wished she had done "eight thousand million things differently" to help stop the suicide of her husband, Nirvana's Kurt Cobain. This from the woman who in 1989 got married for the first time to cross-dresser lead singer James Moreland of the L.A. punk band Leaving Trains in Las Vegas. Needless to say it, was a short romance.

December 9

Enya's newest album, *The Memory of Trees,* grew to No. 5 in Britain. Her international recorded sales to date were reported to be over 18 million.

December 22

Bette Midler's beachfront home on the island of Kauai, Hawaii, was burned down by an arsonist.

December 31

Chaka Khan performed at a New Years Eve show at the Beacon Theater in New York.

More Moments in 1995

Bassist Kelley Deal of the Pixies was arrested for possession of heroin.

1996

January 2

Nanci Griffith contributed the song "Well All Right" to the *Notfadeaway, Remembering Buddy Holly* album, accompanied by the Crickets, which was released today. She revealed at the time that she had wanted to be a member of the Crickets as a young girl.

January 4

Dolly Parton and Emmylou Harris were guest artists on *The Grand Ole Opry Seventieth Anniversary*" show, which aired on CBS. Dolly first joined the Opry twenty-seven years earlier to the day, though she had been singing there for thirty-eight years!

January 6

In a bizarre incident of unneeded publicity for a record, O. J. Simpson called a Los Angeles radio station and requested Mariah Carey and Boyz II Men's mega hit "One Sweet Day" be played in dedication to his murdered wife, Nicole.

January 9

Courtney Love finally wound up on an entertainment list that justified her talent. She was included on fashion guru Mr. Blackwell's worst-dressed list. Also having the dubious honor that year was Melissa Etheridge.

January 12

Janet Jackson signed a recording extension worth over $80 million dollars with Virgin Records on a four album deal, which included a $35 million advance and a reported 24 percent royalty, more than twice what most artists were getting.

January 17

Gladys Knight and the Pips were inducted into the Rock and Roll Hall of Fame by Mariah Carey at the eleventh annual awards. Marianne Faithful inducted the legendary Shirelles. Also inducted were Jefferson Airplane.

January 22

Celine Dion performed at the Palais des Festivals in Cannes, marking her return to MIDEM following her 1983 debut at the age of fourteen.

January 23

Carly Simon and Hall and Oates played four shows, in support of the American Indian College Fund, at the Fox Arena, Foxwoods Resort Casino, in Ledyard, Connecticut.

January 27

Mary J. Blige charted both pop and R&B today with what would become her biggest hit, "Not Gonna Cry," from the movie *Waiting to Exhale.* It attained the No. 1 spot for two weeks and No. 1 R&B for five weeks.

January 29

Shania Twain was named Favorite New Country Artist at the twenty-third annual American Music Awards in Los Angeles' Shrine Auditorium.

January 30

Reba McEntire was named Favorite Female Country Artist for an unprecedented tenth consecutive year at the twenty-third annual American Music Awards.

January 31

Carole King's 1961 Shirelles standard, "Will You Love Me Tomorrow," finished a three-month run as the first legally licensed commercial music jingle in Russia. It was used for McVine's Hob Nobs cookies. The song reached No. 1 thirty-five years ago yesterday.

February 6

Ace of Base's *The Sign* (a revised version of *Happy Nation*) was certified for 9 million in sales in America by the RIAA.

Madonna held a press conference in Buenos Aires, Argentina, as location work on the movie *Evita* began.

February 7

Jewel performed at Farmington High School in Detroit after she was mistakenly booked because the agent thought she was the rap artist Jewell.

February 9

Joan Baez performed at Los Angeles' Wiltern Theater.

February 10

Enya's *The Memory of Trees* album peaked at No. 9. It replaced her *Shepherd Moons* CD at No. 1 on the New Age survey as well.

Tori Amos charted with the album *Boys for Pele*, which would go on to reach No. 2 and become her biggest U.S. hit.

February 19

Annie Lennox was once again named Best Female Artist at the fifteenth annual BRIT Awards, held at London's Exhibition Center. It was her sixth award, a British record.

Bjork, the diminutive Icelandic artist, was seen on British TV attacking a news reporter after arriving in Thailand. Apparently she didn't like the questions being asked as she slammed the female reporter to the ground while emphasizing her displeasure with accented banging of the girl's head on the floor. She later apologized.

February 23

Wynonna Judd's CBS-TV special, *Wynonna Revelations* aired with guest star Bette Midler.

February 28

Joni Mitchell beat out Mariah Carey and Madonna to earn the Best Pop Album category for *Turbulent Indigo* at the thirty-eighth annual Grammy Awards, held at Los Angeles' Shrine Auditorium. Her artwork for the album was named Best Recording Package. Not surprising since, before she became enamored with music, she had her sights on a career as a commercial artist at Alberta College in Calgary, Canada. Emmylou Harris' *Wrecking Ball* was named Best Contemporary Folk Album and Alanis Morissette won for the Album of the Year, Best Rock Album (*Jagged Little Pill*), Best Rock Song, and Best Female Rock Vocal (both for "You Oughta Know").

Bjork.

February 29

The Chantels were inducted into the Rhythm and Blues Foundation at its seventh annual awards dinner. One of the highlights of the evening was the pairing of awards presenter Patti Austin with Darlene Love and Staples Singers' Mavis Staples, belting out "Just One Look."

March 6

Donna Summer did her thing at Radio City Music Hall in New York.

March 8

Tina Turner, known for legs that go on forever, was named the Hanes Hosiery spokeswoman/model.

March 10

Madonna lip-synched "Don't Cry for Me Argentina" in her role as Eva Peron on the balcony of the presidential palace, where the First Lady of Argentina told a crowd she was dying in 1951. The president of Argentina earlier refused to allow the shooting (probably the only shooting they didn't allow), saying, "A total and utter disgrace, pornographic and blasphemous—an insult to Argentine women." One can only speculate as to what changed hi$$$$$$ mind.

March 23

Celine Dion's "Because You Loved Me," taken from the *Up Close and Personal* film soundtrack, topped the American chart while the companion album, *Falling into You,* debuted on the British charts at No. 1.

March 25

Sheryl Crow performed in Baumholder, Germany, for families of American troops stationed in Bosnia-Herzegovina. It was at the invitation of First Lady Hillary Rodham Clinton, who was there on a support mission for the troops.

March 29

Patti LaBelle was honored with the Heritage Award and sang "Over the Rainbow" at the tenth annual Soul Train Music Awards, held at Los Angeles' Shrine Auditorium. The award was presented by Bill Cosby. Hosting the show were Anita Baker, Brandy, and LL Cool J.

April 6

Mariah Carey's "Always Be My Baby" charted, on its way to No. 1. It was her seventeenth hit in six years, eleven of which were No. 1s.

April 13

Jewel began a week-long tour, opening for Bob Dylan, at the Simon Forum in Madison, New Jersey.

April 18

Sheryl Crow visited Capital Hill to promote the new Rock the Vote online vote-registration drive.

April 22

Jewel performed on CBS-TV's *Late Night with David Letterman.*

May 5

Dolores O'Riordan of the Cranberries received an apology and $12,500 (which she donated to the Warchild Charity) from *The Sport* newspaper after they ran a story that she wore no underwear at a Hamburg performance.

May 8

Mary J. Blige was sued by her ex-managers for $1 million in royalties attributed to the success of her album *What's The 411?*

Shania Twain was honored as Top Female Country Artist at the annual World Music Awards at the Sporting Club in Monte Carlo, Monaco.

May 13

Patti LaBelle taped a TV special with the Boston Pops Orchestra.

Tori Amos performed at an in-store live broadcast from the Virgin Megastore in Manhattan at the beginning of her three sold-out dates in Madison Square Garden.

May 16

Dolly Parton performed at the Ryman Auditorium in Nashville for the *Grand Ole Opry Tribute: Minnie Pearl*, which aired on CBS-TV.

May 20

Melissa Etheridge was named Songwriter of the Year at the thirteenth annual ASCAP Pop Music Awards, held at the Beverly Hilton Hotel in Beverly Hills, California.

May 30

One of England's most revered female vocalists, Joan Armatrading was honored at the forty-first Ivor Novello Awards with the Outstanding Contemporary Song Collection Award in London.

June 8

The Fugees, with Lauryn Hill leading, reached No. 1 in England with "Killing Me Softly," a remake of Roberta Flack's hit from 1973. A week later, it became the first single to reach No. 1 in Germany in its first week on the charts. In contrast, it never made the U.S. pop or R&B Top 100 lists, though it did reach No. 2 in pop airplay.

June 10

Amy Grant received the Minnie Pearl Award for humanitarian and community work at the TNN channel's Music City News Country Awards, held at the Grand Ole Opry in Nashville.

Diana Ross performed at Boston Symphony Hall at a benefit for the Anti-Defamation League. The diva raised $450,000!

June 18

Patti Smith performed on NBC-TV's *Saturday Night Live*. It was her first American TV appearance since 1978.

Though raised in New York, Fiona Apple's debut, *Tidal*, a gloomy, angst-ridden album, was issued in Europe today. Fiona was the daughter of actor Brandon Maggertt and singer Diane McAfie. To say she was brought up in a dysfunctional environment is an understatement. Fiona saw her first therapist at the age of ten and was raped in the hallway outside her divorced mother's Upper West Side apartment the day prior to Thanksgiving at age twelve.

July 9

Sarah McLachlan performed the national anthem at the Major League Baseball All-Star Game in Philadelphia.

July 19

Celine Dion sang "The Power of the Dream" at the opening ceremonies of the centennial Olympic Games in Atlanta, Georgia.

The Spice Girls, an as yet relatively unknown British all-girl quintet, appeared on BBC-TV's *Top of the Pops* live via satellite from Japan. The girls carefully planned publicity campaign was kicked into gear with the nicknaming of each girl: Geri Haliwell "Ginger Spice," Melanie Brown "Scary Spice," Victoria Adams "Posh Spice," Melanie Chisholm "Sporty Spice," and Emma Bunton "Baby Spice."

July 27

The Spice Girls' catchy pop single "Wannabe" soared to No. 1 in England and would go on to sell over 1.25 million copies, officially starting Spice Girls mania. The group signed with Virgin Records in 1995 for a reported $3.5 million.

July 28

Margie Ganser was a member of the "Queens of Musical Melodrama," the Shangri-Las. She and her twin sister, Mary Ann, joined sisters Mary and Betty Weiss to form the group in high school. Discovered by "Svengali" George "Shadow" Morton, they turned out teen angst classics like "Remember," "Leader of the Pack" and "Give Us Your Blessings." Blending sensuality with innocence, they traversed the charts eleven times, from 1964 through 1966. Margie died of breast cancer at age forty-nine today.

August 3

Jewel's "Who Will Save Your Soul" reached No. 1.

August 17

The Spice Girls worked behind the counter at Ainleys record store in Leicester, England, raising money for the local Emily Fortey School for special children with special needs.

August 20

The Emotions, Billy Preston, the Brothers Johnson, and Isaac Hayes performed at the Universal Amphitheater in Universal City, California.

August 24

Brandy, with help from Gladys Knight, Chaka Khan, and Tamia, charted with "Missing You" (No. 25).

August 29

Emmylou Harris sang Dion's classic "Abraham, Martin and John" at the Democratic National Convention in Chicago.

September 10

Outraged by the fact that the supposedly consumer friendly Wal-Mart chain was selling guns in the same stores they sell food and toys, Sheryl Crow wrote on a cut of her new album, "Watch our children as they kill each other, with a gun they bought at Wal-Mart discount stores." Wal-Mart promptly banned the sale of that album.

September 15

Bonnie Raitt, the born pacifist, was arrested for trespassing as a member of a demonstration against logging in the world's last privately owned grove of redwood trees at Pacific Lumber Co.'s Carlotta Mill, north of San Francisco.

September 17

A bomb was found at a London post office addressed to Bjork by a deranged man, who police found dead after he videotaped himself building it and then committing suicide.

September 21

A remixed hip-hop version of Roberta Flack's 1973 hit "Killing Me Softly with His Song" hit No. 1 on the Hot Dance Music chart. The remix release was motivated by the success of the Fugees' cover of "Killing Me" from earlier in the year.

Gloria Estefan Live in Concert from Miami Arena aired live on HBO-TV.

Vanessa Williams, the Harlem Boys Choir, Babyface, Seal, and Elton John, among others, entertained at the MGM Grand in Las Vegas at a benefit concert held by tennis star Andre Agassi called Agassi Slam for Children.

September 28
Gladys Knight, Chaka Khan, Brandy, and Tamia sang together on the hit "Missing You," from the film *Set It Off.* The record reached No. 25 pop today as well as No. 10 R&B

October 4
Gladys Knight and the O'Jays performed at the Universal Amphitheater in Universal City, California.

October 12
Sheryl Crow's second album, the self-produced and mostly self-penned *Sheryl Crow,* peaked at No. 6 in America and No. 5 in Britain, even with the Wal-Mart chain banning the album from its stores.

October 19
Joan Baez performed at Alcatraz prison in San Francisco Bay for the Bread and Roses concert, held annually to benefit inmates across the country. The folk legend would continue to perform into the twenty-first century.

October 20
Carly Simon had an attack of stage fright and refused to leave her stateroom. She was scheduled to sing before 1,200 guests at a party for *Travel and Leisure* magazine aboard the *Queen Elizabeth 2,* which was docked in New York.

October 21
Olivia Newton-John hosted the Lifetime TV channel's *Lifetime Applauds the Fight Against Breast Cancer,* a television concert special held at the Pantages Theater in Los Angeles.

October 25
Madonna was listed at No. 82 in *Entertainment Weekly*'s Power 101 survey of the most influential people in the entertainment business. Not too shabby for a girl who started out working in a doughnut shop in New York's Times Square.

October 26

Former member of the all-sisters group the Braxtons, Toni Braxton hurdled the Hot 100 with "Un-Break My Heart" (No. 1), her eleventh hit since 1992.

The Spice Girls' "Say You'll Be There" flew to No. 1 in England. Geri Haliwell of the quintet started out as a hostess on a Turkish TV game show called *Sechakalim.*

October 30

The RIAA certified 4 million in sales of Celine Dion's *Colour of Love.* During the month, she received an award to commemorate the sale of 10 million copies of her four English-language American releases. As if that wasn't enough, Celine was confirmed to be the first Canadian female vocalist to have three multi-platinum albums.

November 7

The Spice Girls turned on the Christmas lights on Oxford Street from HMV record store. Emma Bunton of the group started out as a child model.

November 8

Alanis Morissette was named Best New Act at the annual Q Awards, held at London's Park Lane Hotel.

November 9

En Vogue charted, en route to No. 1 R&B (No. 2 pop) with "Don't Let Go (Love)" from the film *Set It Off,* starring Queen Latifah. It was their last of six No. 1s among seventeen charters through 2000 and eighteen pop hits through 2001.

November 10

Tina Turner was interviewed on *60 Minutes,* the acclaimed TV newsmagazine show on CBS.

November 14

Alanis Morissette earned the Best Female Artist Award at the third annual MTV Europe Music Awards, held at London's Alexandra Palace. She began her music career at the age of fourteen, when, incredibly, MCA publishing in Toronto signed her to a songwriting contract. That led to a recording deal with MCA Records (Canada).

November 16

The Spice Girls' debut album, *Spice,* entered the British chart at No. 1. A pop teen panacea, *Spice* would go on to be the most popular album worldwide by a female group.

November 17

Patti LaBelle, Stevie Wonder, and Luther Vandross performed at Celebrate the Dream: Fifty years of Ebony Magazine at Los Angeles' Shrine Auditorium.

November 30

Sheryl Crow's "Every Day Is a Winding Road" navigated its way to No. 12 in Britain.

December 3

Gladys Knight performed at the Christmas tree-lighting ceremony in New York's Rockefeller Center.

December 4

Madonna received the Artist Achievement Award at the seventh annual *Billboard* Music Awards, held at the Aladdin Hotel Theater in Las Vegas. Alanis Morissette was named Artist of the Year as *Jagged Little Pill* was named Album of the Year and Shania Twain's *The Woman in Me* was named Country Album of the Year.

December 5

Shawn Colvin, Sheryl Crow, Susannah Hoffs, Patty Rothberg, Jewel, Sarah McLachlan, Leah Andreone, and Tracy Chapman appeared at the Z-100 Jingle Ball held at Madison Square Garden in New York.

December 7

Toni Braxton's "Un-Break My Heart" hit No. 1 on the pop charts and stayed their for eleven weeks. It would become her fourth No. 2 hit on the R&B charts. The song featured backing vocals by Shanice Wilson.

December 8

Emmylou Harris sang "Ring of Fire" as part of the tribute to Johnny Cash at the nineteenth annual The Kennedy Center Honors: A Celebration of the Performing Arts.

December 11

Gloria Estefan, Donna Summer, and Chaka Khan performed as the *Three Divas on Broadway* at the Lunt Fontanne Theater in New York.

December 12

Proving that anyone playing themselves in a film can get recognition, Courtney Love won the award for Best Supporting Actress for her portrayal as a off-the-wall wife in *The People Vs. Larry Flint* at the sixty-second New York Film Critics Awards.

December 14

Natalie Merchant, Sarah Mclachlan, Tori Amos, Sheryl Crow, and others performed at the KROQ Almost Acoustic Christmas concert at the Universal Amphitheater in Universal City, California.

December 18

Dionne Warwick appeared at the Vatican in Rome, but not to perform. She had a special audience with Pope John Paul II. (One can but wonder if her friends at the Psychic Friends Network had foretold of the meeting.)

December 19

Amy Grant's Tennessee Christmas broke the house record, becoming the highest grosser ever at the Nashville Arena, before two sellout crowds of over 25,000 fans.

December 25

Madonna's film *Evita* opened in theaters across America to a positive response.

The Spice Girls hosted the annual Christmas edition of British TV's *Top of the Pops* in London, England.

December 28

Promoted to death with national media and fan frenzy formerly reserved for acts like the Beatles, the Spice Girls' single "2 Become 1" debuted at No. 1 in Britain, making the "girls" the first female act to have its first three singles top the British singles chart.

More Moments in 1996

Diane Warren, one of the most prolific contemporary American songwriters, won a Grammy for "Because You Loved Me,"" written for the film *Up Close and Personal* (and made famous by Céline Dion). The song also received Academy Awards and Golden Globes nominations.

1997

January 19

Madonna was named Best Actress in a motion picture, musical or comedy (for *Evita*) at the Golden Globe Awards, held in Los Angeles.

The Shirelles were honored in their hometown of Passaic, New Jersey, when Passaic High School renamed their assembly Shirelle Auditorium.

January 24

Marianne Faithfull's American tour, titled 20th Century Blues: An Evening in the Weimar Republic, started at the Brooklyn Academy of Music in Brooklyn, New York.

January 25

The Spice Girls tied the record held by Alanis Morisette for the highest charting American single by a debut act as "Wannabe" reached No. 11.

January 27

Shania Twain was named Top Country Female Artist at the twenty-fourth annual American Music Awards at the Shrine Auditorium in Los Angeles, the first time an artist other than Reba McIntire had won in eleven years.

January 28

When a pop group has a mercurial a rise as the Spice Girls, there are bound to be naysayers, and readers of Britain's *New Musical Express* voted their single "Wannabe" as the Worst Single at the 1997 NME BRAT Awards at the Camden Center in London.

February 8

Erykah Badu topped the R&B charts today with her single "On and On." She would go on to have six more charters through 2002. The Dallas vocalist was influenced by such artists as Rick James, Teena Marie, Marvin Gaye, and Chaka Khan.

February 10

Ginger Spice and Sporty Spice of the Spice Girls tried to join British band Blur onstage at the Astoria in London, but bouncers who did not recognize them unceremoniously threw them offstage.

February 14

Alanis Morissette's *Jagged Little Pill* album was certified by the RIAA to have sold 15 million copies, the biggest selling debut by any female artist in music history. By July 29, 1998, it had sold 16 million copies.

February 21

The Spice Girls received the Best International Pop Album Award at the twelfth annual Irish Record Music Association (IRMA) Awards at Dublin's Burlington Hotel.

February 22

Jennifer Lopez married Ojani Noa, a waiter, but she didn't wait long (one year) to leave him.

The Spice Girls phenomena continued, with their single "Wannabe" reaching No. 1 in America.

February 25

Sade was arrested in Montego Bay, Jamaica, for disorderly conduct, disobeying a policeman, and dangerous driving. In that particular incident, she was obviously not a "Smooth Operator."

Tracy Chapman was named Best Acoustic Guitarist, Female, at the 1997 Orville H. Gibson Guitar Awards, held at New York's Hard Rock Café. She was discovered by fellow student Brian Koppelman after recording demos at her university's campus radio station, WMFO, which led to his recommending her to his father, Charles Koppelman, president of SBK Publishing. (Nice to have a publisher in the family.) Also, Mary Chapin-Carpenter was named Best Country Guitarist, Female.

February 26

Bonnie Raitt, Chaka Khan, and Shawn Colvin backed Ellen DeGeneres on the opening number at the Grammy Awards while soul divas Whitney Houston, Brandy, Mary, J. Blige, Toni Braxton, Aretha Franklin, Chaka Khan, and CeCe Winans sang a medley from *Waiting to Exhale* at the thirty-ninth annual event at New York's Madison Square Garden.

March 1

More than two years after its original release, Jewel's album *Pieces of You* finally peaked at No. 4. It took a year-long chart trek and would eventually sell over 10 million albums worldwide.

March 6

The Spice Girls, a huge international success story, were named Best International New Act at the sixth annual Echo Awards, held at the Congress Center in Hamburg, Germany.

March 7

A legendary vocalist from the "Wall of Sound" era, Darlene Love was awarded $263,500 in past-due royalties from her former producer and owner of Philles Records, Phil Spector. It only took about thirty years for her to get the judgment.

March 9

Celine Dion, Alanis Morissette, and Shania Twain shared the Best Country Female Vocalist honors for the International Achievement Awards at the twenty-sixth annual Juno Awards at Copps Coliseum in Hamilton, Ontario, Canada. By now Shania's fame was such that a Twain look-alike, Donna Huber, was touring Canada impersonating Twain.

March 10

Anita Baker, Jewel, and Mary Chapin-Carpenter were part of a musical contingent lobbying Capitol Hill for greater support of the arts at the beginning of the week-long Arts Advocacy Celebration in Washington, D.C.

March 13

Reba McEntire took questions on "Reba's Worldwide Cybercast" live on America Online and the CMT cable network.

March 25

Jewel made her British debut, opening for Johnny Cash at the legendary Royal Albert Hall in London.

April 2

Joni Mitchell was reunited with her daughter, Klauren Gibb, who she had given up for adoption in 1965. Joni was a struggling twenty-year-old art student at the time.

April 5

Sheryl Crow's "Every Day Is a Winding Road" rose to No. 11 in America, more than four months after it had hit No. 12 in Britain.

April 8

Mother of writer/singer Hoyt Axton, Mae Boren Axton, had a varied career, especially during a period in America when a woman's place was in the home. Mae was a country music DJ, and became a publicist for country star Hank Snow in the early '50s. She also was a songwriter and brought a tune to manager Tom Parker at his hotel in Nashville. Parker liked it enough to give it to his budding star, Elvis Presley, who turned it into his first No. 1 (for eight weeks). The song was "Heartbreak Hotel." Mae died accidentally when she drowned in her hot tub at her Henderson, Tennessee, home. She was eighty-two.

April 11

The Spice Girls signed 500 copies of their book *Girl Power!* in two hours at B. Dalton bookstore in Manhattan.

April 17

The Spice Girls were named Best Female Newcomers in the ninth annual World Music Awards, held at the Sporting Club in Monte Carlo, Monaco. The group was created by two managers who placed an advertisement in the British theater newspaper, the *Stage,* looking for a female version of the hit act Take That, saying, "Are you 18–23 with the ability to sing/dance. Are you streetwise, outgoing, ambitious and dedicated?" Four hundred girls showed up at a London studio and were given thirty seconds each to perform.

April 24

Marianne Faithfull did the first of two shows at London's Bloomsbury Theater.

April 30

Ellen DeGeneres presented k. d. lang with the Creative Integrity Award at a benefit that raised over $200,000 for the Los Angeles Gay and Lesbian Center's women's programs. Meanwhile, ABC TV aired the *Ellen* "coming out" episode, in which lang appeared.

May 1

The Pointer Sisters performed in Washington, D.C., at the Democratic National Committee gala.

May 2

Cyndi Lauper began a tour with Tina Turner at the Cynthia Woods Mitchell Pavilion in the Woodlands, Texas.

May 4

Courtney Love put the house she shared with Nirvana's Curt Cobain up for sale at $3 million.

May 9

The Spice Girls performed at the Prince's Trust Royal Gala Charity Concert at the Opera House in Manchester, England, in the presence of Britain's Prince Charles.

May 11

k. d. lang appeared in an acting role in the miniseries *Mario Puzo's the Last Don* on CBS-TV.

May 15

Jewel was featured on the front cover of *Rolling Stone.*

The Spice Girls' "Mama" entered the British chart at No. 1. The group became the first act since Tiffany, in 1988, to top the English and American charts at the same time.

May 16

Carly Simon filmed a set for the VH1-TV special *Bill Clinton, Rock and Roll President* set to air June 23.

May 24

The Spice Girls album, *Spice,* reached No. 1 in America, making the vocal quintet only the third all-girl group to reach the album's peak spot, following the Supremes and the Go-Go's, and the first British all-female aggregation to do it.

May 31

The Spice Girls' "Say You'll Be There" peaked at No. 3, having entered the American Hot 100 at No. 5. It was the highest position a British act's recording had debuted at on the *Billboard* chart, having surpassed the Beatles' "Let It Be" at No. 6, in 1970, a record the Fab Four held for twenty-seven years.

June 11

Joni Mitchell was inducted into the Songwriters Hall of Fame at the twenty-fifth annual dinner, held at the Sheraton Hotel in New York. As she could not attend, her award was accepted by Judy Collins, who had recorded Mitchell's first recorded song, "Both Sides Now," in 1967.

June 16

Responding to threats after her attack on photographers the day before, Sinead O'Connor canceled a "Sharing Jerusalem: Two Capitals for Two States" concert in the holy city. She was supposed to be supporting peaceful coexistence but obviously was not the appropriate spokesperson. There's no truth to the rumor that a considered substitute was Courtney Love!

June 21

Jewel took part in Blockbuster Rockfest '97 at the Texas Motor Speedway in Fort Worth, Texas, with Paula Cole, among others. She had recently been voted No. 1 in a CD Now Web survey as the female singer with whom men would most like to be stranded on a desert island with.

June 23

Brandy appeared in the lead role of the ABC/Disney TV production of *Cinderella*. She also had a part in the hit teen-horror flick *I Know What You Did Last Summer*.

June 28

Sheryl Crow began a British tour at London's Royal Albert Hall.

June 30

Erykah Badu, George Clinton, and Cypress Hill began the House of Blues Smokin' Grooves Tour at the Great Woods Center for the Performing Arts in Mansfield, Massachusetts. Badu originally performed under the name M. C. Apples in a rap trio before becoming part of the duo Erykah Free.

July 4

Roberta Flack performed in Boston at the Hatch Shell with the Boston Pops Orchestra.

July 5

Brooklyn rapper Lil' Kim charted with "Not Tonight," reaching No. 33 R&B and No. 6 pop, with the recording help of Missy "Misdemeanor" Elliott, Lisa

"Left Eye" Lopes, Da Brat, and Angie Martinez. Kim would go on to have twenty-two hits through 2004 and a conviction for lying to a grand jury, perjury, and conspiracy in an investigation into a shooting. She would eventually go to jail for a year.

Sarah McLachlan's all-female singer-songwriter touring troupe, the thirty-five-date Lilith Fair tour got underway at the Gorge in George, Washington. The rotating lineup included Jewel, Mary Chapin-Carpenter, Tracy Chapman, Paula Cole, Indigo Girls, Shawn Colvin, Suzanne Vega, Lisa Loeb, the Cardigans, and Joan Osbourne. Despite catty press, the tour became one of the most popular, and the highest grossing, traveling festivals in the U.S. that summer. It continued for another couple of years until 1999.

July 10

Jewel, Sarah Mc Lachlan, Suzanne Vega, Mary Chapin-Carpenter, and Paula Cole performed at the all-female Lilith Fair '97 caravan at the Blockbuster Desert Sky Pavillion in Phoenix, Arizona.

July 12

The O Zone: Spice Girls special aired on BBC1. That same week, *Top of the Pops* magazine published an issue that included a blow-up doll of each of the five Spice Girls.

July 13

The Spice Girls recorded three songs at London's Royal Albert Hall for inclusion in their upcoming movie.

July 14

Walkers, a British potato chip company, debuted its Spice Girls Crisps, which went on sale in Great Britain today. Within six months, the company would announce sales of more than 16 million bags.

July 15

Fiona Apple made her first performance appearance as part of the all-female Lilith Fair '97 at the Riverport Amphitheater in Maryland Heights, Missouri.

July 30

Sarah McLachlan, Emmylou Harris, the Indigo Girls, and Jewel continued the Lilith Fair '97 tour at Hardee's Walnut Creek Amphitheater in Raleigh, North Carolina.

August 5

Connie Francis, along with other *American Bandstand* mainstays Chubby Checker, Fabian, and Bobby Rydell, attended "Bandstand Day" in Philadelphia, rededicating the former WFIL-TV building as the West Philadelphia Enterprise Center.

August 9

Janis Ian performed at Ben and Jerry's Newport Folk Festival in Newport, Rhode island.

With Bananarama and the Spice Girls having opened the door for British all-girl singing groups, All Saints had their first major exposure, performing on BBC-TV's *National Lottery*. The girls, Melanie Blatt (named after popular folk artist Melanie), Shazney Lewis, and Natalie and Nicole Appleton, met and named themselves after All Saints Road in London's Notting Hill district.

August 16

Mary J. Blige, Chaka Khan, k. d. lang, Toni Braxton, Rod Stewart, Jon Bon Jovi, and Seal, among others, performed at London's Wembley Stadium for the Songs and Visions—The Carlsberg Concert '97 show.

Patti LaBelle's "When You Talk About Love" reached No. 56 pop, becoming her last of twelve solo Top 100 hits through 1997.

September 4

Jewel won the Best Female Video trophy ("You Were Meant for Me") and performed "Foolish Games" at the fourteenth annual MTV Video Music Awards, held at New York's Radio City Music Hall. The Spice Girls received the Best Dance Video trophy for "Wannabe" and dedicated their performance of "Say You'll Be There" to the late Princess Diana.

September 5

Erykah Badu received four awards at the third annual Soul Train Lady of Soul Awards, winning Best Album, Best New Artist, Best Single, and Best Song. The visibly pregnant performer co-hosted the show with one of her idols, Chaka Khan. Also honored was Janet Jackson, who received the Lena Horne Award for Outstanding Career Achievement.

September 6

All Saints, the all-girl British singing group, hit No. 4 in England with "I Know

Where It's At." Member Melanie Blatt was named after her mother's favorite singer, folk artist Melanie. Blatt, who attended the Sylvia Young Theatre School when she was eleven (at the same time as Emma Bunton, who would go on to be Baby Spice of the Spice Girls), would act in a Mentadent toothpaste television commercial with Emma.

September 12

Nanci Griffith performed for a sellout crowd at New York's Hammerstein Ballroom at the Manhattan Center.

September 24

Debbie Gibson, realizing her recording audience was diminishing ("Losing Myself," her last of eleven chart singles, from 1987 through 1993, only reached No. 86), took on the role of Belle in the Broadway production of *Beauty and the Beast.*" It followed a national tour of *Funny Girl* in 1996.

October 4

Fiona Apple's only chart single, "Criminal," debuted, eventually reaching No. 21. Apple's musical break came when a friend babysat for noted music publicist Kathy Schenker and passed on Fiona's demo. Schenker in turn gave it to Clean Slate Record's honcho, Andy Slater, who signed Apple to his label. Even so, Slater nurtured her talent for two years before releasing any material.

October 18

Gloria Estefan sang the national anthem before game 1 of the World Series between the Cleveland Indians and the Florida Marlins at Pro Player Park in Miami, Florida.

October 20

Sheryl Crow played the first of six gigs, opening for the Rolling Stones at Foxboro Stadium in Foxborough, Massachusetts.

October 28

Annie Lennox was noted as being Britain's thirty-fourth-wealthiest rock star, with a reputed personal wealth of $43 million, according to *Business Age* magazine. The magazine also reported that the individual Spice Girls were the country's forty-second-wealthiest rock stars, with presumed personal wealth of $24 million each.

Fiona Apple.

November 1

England's Prince Charles and Prince Harry meet the Spice Girls before they performed at the Two Nations in Concert benefit in Johannesburg, South Africa.

Whitney Houston starred in *Cinderella* as fairy godmother to Brandy. The ABC-TV movie cost over $10 million to make, a record for the time.

November 4

Bonnie Raitt backed Beth Nelsen Chapman on syndicated TV's *Rosie O'Donnell Show.*

Patti Smith appeared at England's eighth annual *Q* Awards, where she received the *Q* Inspiration Award at London's Park Lane Hotel. Also, legendary record producer Phil Spector, while making a rare public appearance to collect his trophy at the annual *Q Awards* in London, couldn't resist taking a swipe (as many now were) in his acceptance speech, when he stated, "Am I the only one who believes that the Spice Girls are the Antichrist?"

November 6

Janet Jackson was honored as the Best Female Artist at MTV's European Awards in Rotterdam, the Netherlands.

Sarah McLachlan was honored by the city of Milwaukee for a $25,000 donation from Lilith Fair to a local women's shelter. Milwaukee Mayor John Nordquist declared it "Sarah Mclachlan Day" during the presentation. She was touring through Milwaukee at the time.

November 8

Shania Twain's "Love Gets Me All the Time" topped the country singles chart.

November 11

Cyndi Lauper appeared on NBC-TV's *Conan O'Brien Show.*

November 15

The Spice Girls' second album, *Spiceworld,* entered the British chart at No. 1. Their debut album had already sold over 18 million copies around the globe, and singles from that set had sold a total of 10 million copies.

November 16

Amy Grant talked with fans online in a live cyber-cast from Nashville's Bluebird Café.

The Spice Girls performed an impromptu free concert from their hotel balcony in Rome, singing (what else) "Spice Up Your Life."

November 22

Shania Twain's pop/country album *Come on Over,* peaked at No. 2 pop in its first week and reached No. 1 country (also in its first week on the chart).

November 29

When Whitney Houston was belatedly informed that the Washington, D.C., concert she was to appear at was actually a mass wedding for 25,000 couples of "Moonies," she apparently came down with flu-styled symptoms that prevented her from performing. The show would have earned her a cool million dollars!

November 30

As could only happen in England, the Spice Girls received both the Best Group and Worst Group trophies at the Smash Hits Awards in London. Ginger Spice was also honored (if you could call it that) as the Worst Dressed Female.

December 2

Patti Smith started her first headlining tour in almost two decades at Lupo's in Providence, Rhode Island.

December 4

Salt-N-Pepa, LL Cool J, Ginuwine, and Shaggy, among others, performed at Super Jam '97 at the Fleet Center in Boston.

December 6

Erykah Badu's album *Live* peaked at No. 4 on the Top 200 chart in its debut week. It would soon reach No. 1 for three weeks on the R&B chart. Badu began as a teen rapper when she appeared at age fourteen on Dallas radio station KNON-FM.

The Spice Girls and Celine Dion performed at the sixty-ninth Royal Variety Performance, held at the Victoria Palace, London, in the presence of Queen Elizabeth.

December 7

All Saints took part in the Concert of Hope benefit in memory of Diana, Princess of Wales, at Battersea Power Station in London.

December 8

The Spice Girls performed at the eighth annual *Billboard* Music Awards in Las Vegas' MGM Grand Garden Arena, which was broadcast live by FOX-TV. The quintet also received awards for Album of the Year and New Artist of the Year.

December 9

The RIAA certifies 10 million sales of Celine Dion's *Falling into You.*

December 10

Shawn Colvin, Celine Dion, and Mary Chapin-Carpenter performed at the seventeenth annual Gift of Song concert, honoring the fiftieth anniversary of UNICEF, at New York's Beacon Theater. Also on the bill were Garth Brooks, the Fugees, George Michael, and Steve Windwood.

December 19

Celine Dion was featured on CBS-TV's *Ladies' Home Journal's Most Fascinating Women of '97.*

Chaka Khan and B. B. King performed at Vatican City in Italy for the annual Vatican Christmas Concert.

December 20

Jewel broke the record for the longest unbroken Hot 100 singles chart run as "Foolish Games/You Were Meant for Me," in its fifty-sixth consecutive week on the survey, broke the fifty-five-week record previously held by both Everything But the Girl's "Missing" and Duncan Sheik's "Barely Breathing."

December 24

The *Spice Girls Top of the Pops Special* aired on BBC-TV in England.

More Moments in 1997

Joni Mitchell and gospel singer Mahalia Jackson are inducted into the Rock and Roll Hall of Fame.

After success on the Lilith Fair tour, Paula Cole's single "Where Have All the Cowboys Gone" (from the '96 release, *This Fire*) became the inescapable hit of the summer and garners Cole a Grammy for Best New Artist.

Diane Warren's "How Do I Live," recorded by both Trisha Yearwood and LeAnn Rhimes, garners Yearwood a Grammy for Best Female Country Vocal Performance. In a somewhat ironic twist, the song was originally written for Rhimes to sing for the *Con Air* movie soundtrack, but when producers felt the version was too "pop" and asked her to re-record it, she declined. Yearwood stepped in, and her more country-flavored version fit the bill. When the song was released, Rimes heard the news and quickly released her own version. Although Yearwood got the Grammy, Rimes' version outsold Yearwood's by a longshot.

Meredith Brooks had a hit with the song "Bitch," but the title is bleeped on radio station airwaves.

The Spice Girls movie debut, *Spiceworld: The Movie,* opened to lukewarm reception from the critics. But what do they know!? The comedy, featuring a cavalcade of stars (Roger Moore, Elton John, and Meat Loaf), raked in millions at the box office and was nominated for seven awards at the 1999 Golden Raspberry Awards, where they won the award for Worst Actress.

1998

January 7

Sarah McLachlan appeared on ABC-TV's *Ellen*. Sarah's biggest hit, "Adia," would come four months later (No. 3 pop). Her follow-up, from the film *City of Angels,* was called "Adia/Angel," but two weeks later, the label changed it to "Angel/Adia," and a week after that to just "Angel." To add to the confusion, her label then cut the single altogether. Despite all this, it reached No. 4 pop.

January 9

Janet Jackson received her eighteenth gold RIAA certification, this time for "Together Again." It put her in first place among female artists with the most gold singles.

January 10

Reba McEntire co-hosted with Ray Romano at the twenty-fourth annual People's Choice Awards, held at the Santa Monica Airport.

January 12

Dusty Springfield was given a tribute at the Rock and Roll Hall of Fame's thirteenth annual induction diner at New York's Waldorf-Astoria Hotel. Nona Hendryx (of LaBelle) sang Dusty's song "Son of a Preacher Man" to Springfield, who was fighting cancer at the time. Though her doctors were optimistic, the powerhouse Brit would lose the fight in less than a year. Also, Sheryl Crow inducted Stevie Nicks, Christine McVie, and the rest of Fleetwood Mac, while Shania Twain, a huge fan who was heavily influenced by the Mamas and the Papas, had the honor of inducting the group.

Madonna was included on fashion expert Mr. Blackwell's thirtieth annual Ten Worst Dressed Women list.

January 14

Celine Dion's "My Heart Will Go On" set a new record for reaching the largest American radio audience, garnering 116 million plays in a single week.

Mr. Blackwell (you knew he was going to love this group) put the Spice Girls at No. 1 in his thirty-eighth annual Worst Dressed Women list, saying, "The Spice Girls are five candy-colored beauties trapped in fashion waste."

January 17

Fiona Apple opened for the Rolling Stones at New York's Madison Square Garden.

The all-girl group All Saints' single "Never Ever" reached No. 1 on the British chart while their debut album, *All Saints,* reached No. 2 in the U.K. Prior to their first hit, their brash and confident new manager John Benson promised to garner the girls a record deal within a month. He came through in ten days, landing the group at London Records.

January 22

The Spice Girls were named the year's Biggest Hype in the annual *Rolling Stone* readers poll.

January 25

Posh Spice (Victoria Adams) and English soccer star David Beckham announced their engagement. They met after a local soccer match.

Queen Latifah and Martha and the Vandellas sang during halftime at Super Bowl XXXII at Qualcomm Stadium in San Diego while Jewel sang the national anthem.

January 26

The Spice Girls received Favorite New Artist and Favorite Band, Duo or Group, awards and their album *Spice* was named Favorite Album in the pop/rock field at the twenty-fifth Annual American Music Awards at the Shrine Auditorium in Los Angeles.

January 27

The Spice Girls' "Spice Up Your Life" and "Mama" were nominated in the Worst Single of the Year category by readers of Britain's *New Musical Express.*

February 4

Dionne Warwick performed at New York's Apollo Theater.

February 8

All Saints won Best Single and Best Video honors and performed "Never Ever" at the seventeenth annual BRIT Awards. They were now officially the number-two all-girl group in Britain behind the Spice Girls.

February 14

Celine Dion's incessantly played single "My Heart Will Go On" set an all-time record for most times played on the radio in one week, 116 million!

Madonna gave her first club performance in ten years at the "Ice Ball" at New York's Roxy Dance Club.

February 15

Sheryl Crow sang "Honky Tonk Women" with Mick Jagger at the Rolling Stones' "Joint in Las Vegas" show.

February 20

Bonnie Raitt, Rosemary Butler, and Carole King performed together at a tribute concert for Nicolette Larson at the Santa Monica Civic Auditorium, raising money for UCLA Children's Hospital Foundation's "Lotta Love" benefit. They sang "Up on the Roof," "Lotta Love," and "I Feel the Earth Move."

February 21

Celine Dion's "My Heat Will Go On," featured in the movie blockbuster *Titanic* reached No. 1 in England and the same day topped the U.S. Hot Latin Tracks chart, the first English-language record ever to do so.

February 25

Erykah Badu won Best Female R&B Vocal Performance and Best R&B Album at the fortieth Grammy Awards ceremonies. Fiona Apple received the Best Female Rock Performance Award for her single "Criminal."

February 26

Gladys Knight and the Pips received a Lifetime Achievement Award (presented by Stevie Wonder) at the Rhythm and Blues Foundation Awards in New York City.

February 27

Janet Jackson was a guest on Rosie O'Donnell's TV show to discuss the question on the world's collective mind, the position of her tattoos on her body!

March 5

Toni Braxton was given the annual Echo Awards at the Congress Center in Hamburg, Germany, for Best International Female Artist.

March 9

The female quartet All Saints came to America on a promotional tour. The tour had an auspicious start as their passports went missing upon their landing in New York.

March 11

The Spice Girls album *Spice World* was certified with 3 million sales by the RIAA as the group was named Favorite Pop Group at the fourth annual Blockbuster Entertainment Awards at Hollywood's Pantages Theater.

March 16

Celine Dion contributed her version of "Here, There and Everywhere" to Beatles producer, George Martin's tribute album, *In My Life*. Her recording was produced by Martin himself.

Donna Summer sang at a benefit for the City Men's Health Crisis at New York's Carnegie Hall. Her performance lasted over two hours.

March 26

Patti LaBelle appeared at the Boston department store Filene's, while promoting her newest endeavor, Patti LaBelle's Signature Fragrance Collection.

April 5

The Spice Girls performed their first U.K. live concert in Glasgow, Scotland.

April 6

"The First Lady of Country Music" Alabama-native Tammy Wynette was a super star with seventy hits between 1966 and 1980. Originally a beautician in Birmingham, she moved to Nashville in 1966 and began a string of twenty No. 1s, including the anti-feminist standard "Stand by Your Man." She died while taking a nap on her couch from a blood clot in her lung. She was fifty-five years old.

Wendy O. Williams of the Plasmatics died of a self-inflicted gunshot wound.

April 7

Mary J. Blige performed on NBC-TV's *The Tonight Show with Jay Leno*.

April 8

Chrissie Hynde sang "Baby It's You" and "Message to Michael" at the "One Amazing Night" tribute to Burt Bacharach at the Hammerstein Ballroom in

New York while the British quartet All Saints sang "Always Something There to Remind Me."

April 9

Dolly Parton performed at Tammy Wynette's memorial service at the Ryman Auditorium in Nashville. Earlier in the day, at a private service, Dolly, who was inconsolable, broke down while singing "Shine On" and was unable to finish.

April 11

Patti Austin, Nancy Wilson, Stevie Wonder, Smokey Robinson, Ray Charles, and James Ingram appeared on *Quincy Jones . . . The First 50 years,* a tribute to the legendary record producer, which was televised on ABC-TV.

April 14

Carole King, Celine Dion, Mariah Carey, Shania Twain, Aretha Franklin, and Gloria Estefan performed in the "Divas Live: An Honors Concert for VH1 Save the Music" at New York's Beacon Theater.

April 16

Joni Mitchell, Stevie Nicks, Natalie Cole, Gwen Stefani, Paula Cole, Sheryl Crow, Shawn Colvin, Bjork, and Trisha Yearwood took part in the all-female "Stormy Weather '98 benefit concert for Walden Woods at the Wiltern Theater in Los Angeles.

April 27

Roberta Flack, Wynonna Judd, and Madonna performed with the East Harlem Violin Project at the finale of the ninth annual Rain Forest Foundation Benefit Concert in New York's Carnegie Hall.

April 30

Stevie Nicks appeared on NBC-TV's *The Tonight Show with Jay Leno.*

May 2

Carly Simon received an honorary doctorate from Berklee College in Boston and sang an a cappella verse (obviously tongue-in-cheek) from her hit single "Anticipation."

May 6

The Spice Girls were named World's Best Selling Pop Artists of the Year and the World's Best Selling British Artists of the Year at the tenth annual World Music Awards in Monte Carlo.

May 11

Tori Amos appeared on NBC-TV's *The Tonight Show With Jay Leno*.

May 14

Joni Mitchell began a North American tour with Bob Dylan at the General Motors Place in Vancouver, British Columbia.

May 16

Tori Amos' self-produced and written *From the Choirgirl Hotel* peaked at No. 6 in Britain. The album was recorded in Cornwall, England, in a two-hundred-year-old barn.

May 29

Ginger Spice missed the second concert in a row (of a two-show stay) at the Spektrum in Oslo, Norway, fueling speculation that she was quitting the Spice Girls.

May 31

Ginger Spice (Geri Haliwell) announced through her lawyer that she was leaving the Spice Girls, saying, "This is because of differences between us." Somehow the world managed to continue rotating.

Olivia Newton-John duetted with Mariah Carey on "Hopelessly Devoted to You" at Radio City Music Hall for WHTZ New York's "Z-Day" concert.

June 2

Mariah Carey joined Patti LaBelle on her *Patti LaBelle in Concert on Broadway* show at the Hammerstein Ballroom in New York. The show would later be aired on PBS-TV.

June 9

Celine Dion, the Spice Girls, Stevie Wonder, Jon Bon Jovi, and others performed at the third annual Pavarotti and Friends benefit concert in Modena, Italy. The Spice Girls (now down to a quartet) sang their new single, "Stop," with host Luciano Pavarotti. That must have been akin to Caruso singing with backup by Bananarama!

June 10

Diana Ross received the Hitmaker Award at the Songwriters Hall of Fame's twenty-ninth annual awards in New York. The presentation was made by Whitney Houston, and it's interesting to note that Diana never wrote any of her hits and her presenter never wrote any either. Maybe they ran out of writers to honor!

June 12

Olivia Newton-John performed in a downpour at NBC-TV's *Today* summer concert series. At about this time, her forty-first, and last, chart single was rising, eventually reaching No. 67. It was a remake of her 1974 hit "I Honestly Love You," with Babyface.

June 14

The Indigo Girls, Roseanne Cash, and Tracy Chapman, among others, performed in "Fleadh" at Downing Stadium in Randalls Island, New York.

June 16

ASCAP's first Rhythm and Soul Heritage Award was given to Chaka Khan at their eleventh annual Rhythm and Soul Awards in New York.

July 4

Aretha Franklin charted for the ninety-seventh time when "Here We Go Again" hit, eventually reaching No. 24 R&B. Among her R&B chart totals were twenty No. 1s over a thirty-eight-year period.

July 5

Sarah McLachlan came down with food poisoning, which sidelined the singer at the Lilith Fair in Columbus, Ohio. It was her first performance cancellation in over twelve years.

July 9

During Heart's tour with the Tubes, a Philadelphia concert was cut short after Ann Wilson experienced shortness of breath when a front-row imbecile sprayed pepper spray into the air.

July 20

Stevie Nicks was granted a restraining order from a Los Angeles Superior Court commissioner against a greatly disturbed Ronald Anacelteo from all concerts and recording studios where she performed, as well as her home and workplace. He believed she was a witch and could cure him of homosexuality.

July 22

Petula Clark received her Commander of the British Empire (CBE) medal at an investiture ceremony at Buckingham Palace in London.

August 8

Melissa Etheridge sang "Ave Maria" at the Los Angeles wedding of actress Kathy Najimy and Dan Finnerty. None other than feminist Gloria Steinem officiated at the ceremonies.

August 14

Stevie Nicks took part in "A Day in the Garden" in Bethel, New York, to celebrate the anniversary of Woodstock.

August 15

Joni Mitchell participated in "A Day in the Garden" in Bethel, New York, to celebrate the anniversary of the Woodstock festival exactly twenty-nine years earlier.

Obviously a good day for Mary J. Blige, her fifth album, *The Tour*, topped off at No. 7 R&B. Three of Mary's five albums (*What's the 411?*, *My Life*, and *Share My World*) had reached the top spot between 1992 and 1997.

August 20

Joan Baez, Nanci Griffith, Lucinda Williams, and Bela Fleck, among others, played at the Pine Knob Music Theater in Clarkson, Missouri, while on the road with the Newport Folk Festival tour.

August 21

Patti Smith began a tour with Bob Dylan at Melbourne Park in Melbourne, Australia.

August 22

All Saints' "Never Ever" reached No. 4 in the States, their first American chart triumph.

August 28

Talk about irony, fans mobbed a stage in Venice Beach, California, when All

Saints was forced to cancel a benefit performance for an anti-violence charity because they didn't have a performance permit.

August 29

A two-CD, thirty-two-track compilation on Janis Joplin called *The Ultimate Collection,* featuring photography by Linda McCartney, peaked at No. 26 in Great Britain.

Janet Jackson was honored with the International Female Artist of the Year Award in Oslo, Norway, at their Oslo's first annual Hitawards.

Mary J. Blige, Mariah Carey, Missy Elliot, Maze, and others performed in the KMEL-FM All Star Jam at the Shoreline Amphitheater in Mountain View, California.

September 9

Toni Braxton took over the role of Belle in the Broadway musical *Beauty and the Beast* at the Palace Theater in New York.

September 12

All Saints received the award for Breakthrough Act at the MTV Europe Music Awards in Milan, Italy. The group sang the LaBelle hit "Lady Marmalade" that night.

September 16

A Union Jack dress owned by Spice Girl Ginger Spice was sold at auction by Sotheby's of London for $70,244.

September 23

Chaka Khan, Prince, and Larry Graham played at the MCI Center in Washington, D.C.

September 24

Aretha Franklin, Natalie Cole, and Boys II Men performed at the Mentoring Big Night at the Garden benefit at New York's Madison Square Garden,.

October 9

Emmylou Harris, Sheryl Crow, Lucinda Williams, and Willie Nelson performed at the Campaign for a Landmine-Free World concert at the DAR Constitution Hall in Washington, D.C.

October 26

Deborah Harry and a reunited Blondie performed at the Circus in Stockholm, Sweden, at the beginning of their comeback Euro '98 twenty-two-date concert tour.

October 30

The Vocal Group Hall of Fame and Museum in Sharon, Pennsylvania, held its inaugural inductions. It was hosted by legendary DJs Jack "The Rapper" Gibson, Martha Jean "The Queen" Steinberg (the first black female DJ), and publisher/author Jay Warner. Among the fourteen groups enshrined were the Supremes, the Platters, the Drifters (with Clyde McPhatter), the Five Blind Boys of Mississippi, the Ravens, the Mills Brothers, the Golden Gate Quartet, and Sonny Til, and the Orioles.

November 12

Ex-Fugee member Lauryn Hill gave birth to a daughter, Seluh Marley, in New York. The father was her fiancé, Rohan Marley, son of reggae star Bob Marley.

November 17

Janet Jackson, while on a South African tour, met President Nelson Mandela at his home, along with all twenty-nine of his grandchildren.

November 19

Natalie Cole sang "They Can't Take That Away from Me" at Frank Sinatra's eightieth birthday party at the Shrine Auditorium in Los Angeles. If that didn't do it for Ole Blue Eyes, Little Richard's rendition of "Old Black Magic" surely did.

November 20

Alanis Morissette performed at the newly opened Tower Records store in Buenos Aires, Argentina.

November 21

Alanis Morissette's *Supposed Former Infatuation Junkie* album debuted at No. 1.

December 2

Jewel performed at the sixty-sixth annual lighting of the Christmas tree at the Rockefeller Center in New York City.

December 3

Shania Twain's *The Woman in Me* became the third-bestselling album of all time by a female artist and the biggest-selling album by a female country artist ever, according to the RIAA, which certified 11 million copies sold.

December 5

Brandy charted with "Have You Ever," which would soon become her second No. 1 pop in less than seven months. Not bad for a teen heartthrob who decided she wanted to be an entertainer after watching Whitney Houston's video "How Will I Know" and then being totally influenced at the age of eleven when she attended a Little Richard concert.

Lauryn Hill performed on NBC-TV's *Saturday Night Live,* with guest host Jay Leno.

December 7

Shania Twain was honored as Female Artist of the Year and Female Artist of the Year, and "Your Still the One" was named Best Selling Country Single of the Year at the annual *Billboard* Music Awards at the MGM Grand Garden in Las Vegas.

December 11

Alanis Morissette performed at the fifth Nobel Peace Prize Concert at the Spektrum Stadium in Oslo, Norway.

Cher, Bette Midler, Deborah Cox, and Ace of Base performed at WKTU's "Miracle on 34th Street Concert" radio station show at New York's Hammerstein Ballroom.

December 17

Tracy Chapman, Sheryl Crow, Jon Bon Jovi, and Eric Clapton performed holiday favorites at the "A Very Special Christmas" benefit at the White House in the presence of President Bill Clinton and First Lady Hillary Clinton.

December 23

Cissy Houston, Roberta Flack, and Phoebe Snow backed Darlene Love as she did her yearly rendition of the immortal Phil Spector–produced record "Christmas Baby Please Come Home" on David Letterman's *Late Night* TV show on CBS.

December 30

Patti Smith appeared on CBS-TV's *Late Show with David Letterman.*

December 31

Deborah Harry and Blondie ended their reunion year by headlining The Fall Festival '98 at Otway Ranges near Lorne, Australia.

More Moments in 1998

Diane Warren has a hit on an unlikely pairing with Aerosmith on the power ballad "I Don't Want to Miss a Thing," featured in the film *Armageddon.* The song debuted No. 1 on the *Billboard* Hot 100 (the band's first-ever such song after twenty-eight years together) and was nominated for an Academy Award for Best Song. It simultaneously hit No. 1 on the country charts in a version by Mark Chestnutt.

Lauryn Hill's debut, *The Miseducation of Lauryn Hill,* was released, sweeping the Grammy Awards after being nominated for eleven and winning five.

1999

January 2

Faith Evans, with a little help from Puff Daddy, entered the R&B hit list with "All Night Long," peaking at No. 3 R&B and No. 9 pop.

Shania Twain's seven-month tour finished up at the MGM Grand Garden in Las Vegas. The eighty-four shows grossed $36 million, making it the top tour of the year.

January 9

Courtney Love and members of her band, Hole, played an acoustic set at Los Angeles' Viper Room to benefit the Center for Living, a local nonprofit organization that teaches yoga and meditation.

January 11

Deborah Harry and Blondie made their first U.S. network-television appearance in sixteen years, performing at the twenty-sixth annual American Music Awards, held at Los Angeles' Shrine Auditorium.

January 16

Brandy's "Have You Ever" hit No. 1 pop for the first of two weeks. It was her ninth of an eventual fifteen charters, from 1994 through 2002, for the *Moesha* TV star.

January 21

Lauryn Hill opened her world tour at the Budokan in Tokyo, Japan.

January 25

Judy Collins, Phoebe Snow, Janis Ian, Jewel, Paula Cole, and Odetta performed at the Women in Music 1960–1999 concert, at Madison Square Garden in New York.

January 28

Belinda Carlisle started a ten-date British tour at the Eden Court Theater in Inverness, Scotland. Surprisingly and to her chagrin, she was always more popular in Britain than in her native America.

January 30

Britain's *New Musical Express* conducted a poll to find "The pop personality that you would like as your doctor." Australian singer Natalie Imbruglia won.

February 2

Ontario, Canada, beauty Shania Twain was honored by *Cosmopolitan* magazine as its Fun Fearless Female of the Year. She began performing under the name Eileen Twain in the late '80s before becoming Shania in 1990.

February 7

Deborah Harry and Blondie reached No. 1 in Britain with "Maria," their sixth No. 1 there over a twenty-year span.

February 8

The Spice Girls' motion picture, *Spice World,* was nominated for the annual Golden Raspberry Award as the Worst Film of the Year.

February 13

Deborah Harry and Blondie became the only group to score a No. 1 hit on the British charts in the '70s, '80s, and '90s when "Maria" reached the top spot in its first week of release.

February 16

Stevie Wonder presented the reunited Eurythmics (Annie Lennox and Dave Stewart) with the Outstanding Contribution to British Music honor at the eighteenth annual BRIT Awards in London. They wore matching Union Jack suits while performing a number of their greatest successes and solemnly dedicating their performance to Stephen Lawrence and Michael Menson, both victims of racist murders.

February 23

Melissa Etheridge received the Best Blues Guitarist, Female, Award at the Orville H. Gibson Guitar Awards, held at the Hard Rock Cafe Los Angeles.

February 24

Celine Dion won two Grammys for Best Female Pop Vocal Performance and Best Song Written Specifically for a Motion Picture or for Television for "My Heart Will Go On" at the forty-first annual Grammy Awards. The song was also named Song of the Year and Record of the Year. Sheryl Crow won Best Rock Album for *The Globe Sessions*. She was nominated in six categories. Meanwhile, Lauryn Hill received five Grammys, including Best R&B Song and Best Female R&B Vocal Performance (for "Doo Wop (That Thing)"), and Best New Artist, Album of the Year, and Best R&B Album (for *The Miseducation of Lauryn Hill*).

February 27

Britney Spears hit No. 1 in England with "Baby One More Time." Aside from going to the top in the States, it became Britain's biggest seller of the year.

March 2

Newly elected Rock and Roll Hall of Fame member Dusty Springfield died of breast cancer at her Henley-on-Thames home, just west of London. She was due to accept an honor from the queen of England (an OBE, officer of the Order of the British Empire) on the day she passed away. Dusty was fifty-nine.

March 3

Shania Twain's Winter Break, her first TV special, aired on CBS-TV, with Elton John duetting on "You're Still the One."

March 7

Celine Dion won Best Female Vocalist, Best Album, and Best Selling Album, International or Domestic, (for *Let's Talk About Love*), Best Selling Francophone Album (for *S'il Suffisait D'Aimer*), and the prestigious International Achievement Award at Canada's twentieth annual Juno Awards in Hamilton, Ontario. It gave her an astounding total of twenty Juno Awards.

March 12

One of Britain's most beloved artists, Dusty Springfield, who had died ten days earlier, was transported in a horse-drawn carriage for her funeral at St. Mary's Church in Henley-on-Thames, England. Thousands lined the streets in a driving downpour to see Dusty's final appearance. The funeral was attended by such stars as Lulu, Elvis Costello, Kiki Dee, and the Pet Shop Boys, among others.

March 15

Elton John inducted Dusty Springfield into the Rock and Roll Hall of Fame, and the Staple Singers were inducted at the fourteenth annual festivities in New York. Meanwhile, Bonnie Raitt inducted Charles Brown and sang "Runaway" as a tribute to Del Shannon at their posthumous induction.

March 23

Lauryn Hill began the first of three sold-out concerts at Madison Square Garden in New York. The highlight was a duet with Mary J. Blige on "I Used to Love Him." She later donated $50,000 to a refugee fund-raising project.

March 28

Bonnie Raitt performed at the Karl Marx Theater in Havana, Cuba (that's right! Havana!) during the "Music Bridges Around the World" cultural exchange between American and Cuban musicians.

April 10

Chrissie Hynde organized a tribute to Linda McCartney. The "Here, There and Everywhere—A Tribute to Linda" benefit concert took place at London's Royal Albert Hall, with Sinead O'Connor, Marianne Faithfull, George Michael, Tom Jones, and others.

April 13

Tina Turner, Cher, Whitney Houston, Mary J. Blige, and TLC performed at New York's Beacon Theater for VH-1's *Diva's Live '99* show.

April 22

A Dublin, Ireland, bookmaker with a great sense of humor opened a book on Sinead O'Connor becoming the next Pope. The odds were quoted at 10,000 to 1. This after the "Pope ripper" was ordained as a priest (not kidding) in the renegade Roman Catholic Latin Tridentine Church in Lourdes, France.

April 29

Now calling herself Mother Bernadette Mary of the Order of Mater Dei (but she'll always be "the baldheaded banshee" to the rest of us), Sinead O'Connor withdrew a contribution she made seven days earlier to the Tridentine Church in the amount of $200,000.

May 15

Janis Ian performed at a Rock and Roll Hall of Fame tribute to folksinger Phil Ochs.

July 3

Nineteen-year-old Christina Aguilera's debut, "Genie in a Bottle," charted, en route to No. 1 for five weeks. Born in Staten Island, New York, the former latter-day Mickey Mouse Club regular went on to have eleven hits through 2002, including six Top 5 hits, such as "What a Girl Wants" and "Come On Over Baby," both No. 1s.

July 4

Victoria Adams (Posh Spice of the Spice Girls) married soccer star David Beckham at a castle in Ireland. British rag *OK* magazine paid $1.7 million for the exclusive rights to the wedding photos.

July 31

Christina Aguilera managed her first No. 1 when "Genie in a Bottle" reached the top of the pop charts.

August 18

Tori Amos and Alanis Morissette began their 5 1/2 Weeks Tour at the National Car Rental Center in Fort Lauderdale, Florida. No, they were not performing at a car rental office, it was an indoor stadium.

September 22

Diana Ross is not one to be hassled. She was arrested on the Concorde after a row at London's Heathrow Airport, where she rubbed her hands down the front of a female security guard after the guard reportedly touched Diana's breasts. Obviously not what Diana had in mind when she sang "Touch Me in the Morning."

October 16

Ella Mae Morse, who had Capitol Records first million-selling hit, "Cow, Cow Boogie," in 1942, died in Bullhead City, Arizona. The Texas-born singer combined boogie-woogie, jazz, blues, swing, and country influences during the '40s and '50s, helping to create a pioneering pop sound that would later become rock 'n' roll. Elvis Presley once praised her for teaching him how to sing. She was seventy-five.

November 8

Gwen Gordy Fuqua, who convinced her family to stake brother Berry Gordy the $800 he needed to start Motown Records, died in San Diego. Fuqua, former wife of Moonglows leader Harvey Fuqua, started Motown's artist development department, guiding the careers of acts like the Supremes and Temptations. She was seventy-one.

November 11

The RIAA (Recording Industry Association of America) named Barbra Streisand the most successful female artist of the century. Streisand had sold over 62 million records over the last thirty-eight years.

November 17

Mariah Carey had to cancel her performance on Tome's famous Spanish steps when she was physically overwhelmed by fans. She took refuge in a nearby shop and left only after a squad of police came to escort her to safety.

December 18

The Spice Girls wax statues were unveiled at London's Madame Tussaud's Gallery. The five figures cost a total of six figures ($595,000).

December

Britney Spears won four *Billboard* Music Awards, including Female Artist of the Year. A month later, she took home the Favorite Pop/Rock New Artist Award at the American Music Awards.

More Moments in 1999

Sheryl Crow appears uber-sexy at forty on the cover of *Maxim* magazine's July issue.

Soul and gospel legends the Staples Singers are inducted into the Rock and Roll Hall of Fame. Mavis Staples, who was included in VH1's *100 Greatest Women of Rock and Roll* also graced *People* magazine's "Top Ten Albums of 1993" list for *The Voice,* the second of two solo albums for Prince's Paisley Park label.

VH1 compiled its *100 Greatest Women of Rock and Roll.* The coveted Top 10 places were held respectively by Aretha Franklin, Tina Turner, Janis Joplin, Bonnie Raitt, Joni Mitchell, Billie Holiday, Chrissie Hynde, Madonna, Annie Lennox, and Carole King

Ronnie Spector made a comeback record produced by Joey Ramone and released by Olympia, Washington, indie label Kill Rock Stars. Kind of ironic, as her famous ex, Phil Spector, produced the much-publicized Ramones album *End of the Century* back in 1980!

Britney Spears began her reign of outrageousness, appearing on the cover of *Rolling Stone* magazine in April at age sixteen holding Teletubbies. Inside shots portray the teen as a sexy, Catholic school Lolita, upsetting parents worldwide.

Lauryn Hill sparks Grammy controversy after receiving the Best New Artist Award despite prior huge hits with the Fugees.

The *New York Times* heralded the age of the independent singer-songwriter with a long piece about Aimee Mann's turbulent years fighting the major label system. Jonathan Van Meter's exhaustive piece, "What's a Record Exec to Do with Aimee Mann?," hit newsstands on July 11.

Sarah Dash, Nona Hendryx, Cindy Birdsong, and Patricia Holt, better known as Patti LaBelle and the Blue-Belles, appeared together for the first time in thirty-one years, singing a stirring "You'll Never Walk Alone" at the Rhythm and Blues Foundation's Pioneer Awards in Los Angeles. The group was presented its award by five-time Grammy winner Lauryn Hill.

"*My justification is that most people my age spend a lot of time thinking about what they're going to do for the next five or ten years. The time they spend thinking about their life, I just spend drinking. I'm either a really good drunk or I'm an out-and-out sh*t, horrible, violent, abusive, emotional drunk.*"—Amy Winehouse

THE NAUGHTIES

The First Decade of the Twenty-first Century

In a decade punctuated by 9/11, the Iraq War, and an alarmingly unpopular Bush presidency, music was not at the forefront of civil protest as it had been in the "protest era" of the '60s during the Vietnam War. The "me" mentality of President Reagan's '80s generation had lots of carryover and combined with the Internet to enable the "instant gratification age," creating a generation of teens and twenty-somethings who felt that everything should be free, and one of the biggest losers in that moral breakdown was the recording business. This decade has seen sales of bestselling CDs down from an average of 3 to 5 million copies to around a million, and though the mediums for exposure were more numerous (YouTube, MySpace, ring tones, downloads, etc.), the creators were frequently either giving music away as a marketing ploy or just having the music stolen on the Internet.

Still the resilience of music managed to bring new voices to the landscape. For women artists, it was no less vexing a problem than for men, though paradoxically it was a

> *"Anybody who tries to say I haven't paid my dues, I guarantee you, hasn't been on American Idol."*
> —*Carrie Underwood*

decade when more and more females were getting musical recognition. The biggest difference maker for musical exposure was probably the emergence of Fox-TV's cash cow *American Idol*. Women did particularly well in this "*Star Search* on steroids" talent contest, and some of the more outstanding acts to emerge included Kelly Clarkson, Carrie Underwood, Fantasia Barrio, Jordin Sparks, and Jennifer Hudson, who would help reestablish the theatrical movie musical with her Oscar-winning performance in *Dreamgirls*. It's

> *"People are all the time asking me if I hated Simon for mentioning my weight, and I really do not. I am proud of who I am, that is why I auditioned for the show, because I thought that I had something to bring to the table. Now, as for my favorite . . . that would be Randy, of course. He took a chance on me."*
>
> *—Jennifer Hudson*

hard to believe that if it wasn't for Simon Cowell (whose true calling should have been that of a CIA interrogator) and fellow judges Randy Jackson and '80s pop artist Paul Abdul, this collection of powerful vocalists might never have been discovered, let alone reach the pinnacle of success they've attained. One can only hope that as "cream rises to the top," these ladies would have found their way to success through one of the more conventional routes. *American Idol* just made it happen faster and with more fury, just as the Internet did for instantaneous delivery of music, news, and information.

The pop field was particularly well represented by newcomers Avril Lavigne, Gwen Stefani, Natasha Bedingfield, Jessica Simpson, the aforementioned Clarkson and Sparks, Kelly Sweet, Rhianna, Pink, Sarah Bereilles, and the troubled soul named Amy Winehouse, who barely got out of drug and alcohol rehab in time to appear by satellite on the 2008 Grammy Awards, singing her hit, ironically called "Rehab." Talk about using your experiences for profit! Mainstays from past decades,

> *"I've been known to run around naked when I'm drunk. One time I was drinking whiskey, and I was so loud, someone called the police. I have a side to me that's a bit delinquent and I get myself in trouble."*
>
> *—Avril Lavigne*

like Sheryl Crow, Celine Dion, Alanis Morrisette, and a reunited Spice Girls, also continued pop's predominance.

Britney Spears continued to captivate her large and loyal following, despite her illogical and disturbing behavior during the mid-naughties, which included head shaving, not wearing panties in public, a dysfunctional, trance-like performance at the MTV Video Music Awards in 2007, two forced trips to a psych ward, and losing custody of her children, however titillating the media and public may have found her antics. Britney's trials and tribulations were of greater interest because of what she represented, being the poster child for the twenty-first-century version of paparazzi madness. Britney became the vehicle for the newest strain of media disease, the combination of extreme paparazzism and instant

> *"The best part [of being a star] is the fans, like, loving you—and the free clothes . . . . Sundance is weird. The movies are weird—you actually have to think about them when you watch them. . . . I always like performing overseas. Like Canada."*
> —*Britney Spears*

information, where what an artist (usually a female) does now is, through the magic of digital media, around the world and in your face in ten minutes. Of course, the flipside to this hypermedia is that a no-talent celebrity like Paris Hilton can turn her non-newsworthy attention into a recording career.

The 2008 Grammys epitomized the melding of the past with the present when Beyoncé duetted with Tina Turner on a smoking version of "Proud Mary." On the pop teen-idol front, fifteen-year-old Miley Cyrus (daughter of country artist Billy Ray Cyrus) mined recording and performing gold by portraying Hannah Montana. The Disney TV series was reminiscent of the '90s *Mickey Mouse Club* and served as a launching pad for musical talents, just as the *Mouse* had been for the likes of Britney and Christina Aguilera a decade before.

Meanwhile, R&B, hip-hop, and soul were thriving, with such fresh and fabulous voices as Alicia Keys, the aforementioned *Idol* stars Jennifer Hudson and Fantasia Barrino, Fergie of the Black-Eyed Peas, Keyshia Cole, and Joss Stone. Stars from the '80s and '90s, like Beyoncé, Mariah Carey, Mary J. Blige, Teena Marie, and Janet Jackson, added to those successful styles. Speaking of Teena Marie, the Rick James protégé made a monster comeback after a

> *"I like somebody who is ambitious, who is very strong-minded but still sensitive, and I like somebody who knows how to talk and how to listen. . . . And I love kick boxing. It's a lot of fun. It gives you a lot of confidence when you can kick somebody in the head."*
> —*Alicia Keys*

ten-year retirement (to raise her daughter) to go Top 5 with the hit album *La Dona,* in 2004. Jazz was surprisingly and refreshingly well represented by artists like Norah Jones, Diana Krall, Queen Latifah (who can

> *"I've had lesbian experiences in the past. I won't say how many men I've had sex with—but I'm a very sexual person."*
> —Fergie

sing just about anything), Jane Monheit, stalwart Patti Austin, and the strikingly beautiful blond saxophonist/singer Mindi Abair. Punk rock's banner was proudly and energetically waved by American-born, British hit sensation Roxy Saint. Known as the Queen of Punk, whose outrageously sexy videos and equally outrageous performances with everyone from Korn, Linkin Park, Metallica, Green Day, and 50 Cent to Morrissey, the Offspring, and the White Stripes made for a reemergence of the form.

Country, too, had its share of solid singers, including *American Idol*'s Carrie Underwood, Lee Ann Womack (whose "I Hope You Dance" is one of the most compelling singles of the decade), Faith Hill, Taylor Swift, and perennials LeAnn Rimes and Reba McEntire. Many other country stalwarts, like Dolly Parton, Tricia Yearwood, Allison Krause, Martina McBride, and the Dixie Chicks, continued to tour and record for

> *"Without a piano I don't know how to stand, don't know what to do with my hands."*
> —Norah Jones

an ever-loyal fan base, but due to country radio's age discrimination of not playing most artists over thirty years old, they've deprived a whole generation of listeners the opportunity to broaden the scope of their female favorites.

All in all, as the naughties rush to a close, the first decade of the new millennium has featured an imposing, alluring, zany, often controversial, brazen, brave, vehement, captivating, inspired, fascinating, vulnerable, tempestuous, frantic, energetic, heavenly, impressionable, and never boring collection of women, who have not only competed with the men in music but have often dominated the scene, and likely will for decades to come, with the feminist sound and mystique on full display.

Where the music's going is anyone's guess, but where it's been is unmistakably historic, and women's vast contribution to it is undeniable.

2000

January 7

Bernice Petkere, known as the "Queen of Tin Pan Alley" in the 1930s, died at the age of ninety-eight. Her first song, "Starlight," was recorded by Bing Crosby. Others who recorded her songs included Kate Smith, Tony Bennett, and Nancy Wilson. She also wrote music for radio shows and the score for the MGM musical *Ice Follies of 1939,* starring Joan Crawford and James Stewart.

January 8

Christina Aguilera hit No. 1 for the first of two weeks with "What a Girl Wants." The recording became her second of four No. 1s in a year and a half. Christina, of Ecuadorian and Irish descent, was a regular on *The Mickey Mouse Club* in 1992 and '93.

January 11

Whitney Houston was detained when she tried to sneak over fifteen grams of marijuana out of Hawaii.

January 12

Charlotte Church, the teen darling of Britain, fired her manager, Jonathan Shalit. A bit ungrateful when you consider he negotiated a five-album deal with Sony Records for her and helped her earn over $10 million.

February 4

ABBA turned down almost $100 million to reunite for a world tour of a hundred concerts. The group, who split up seventeen years earlier, were the most commercially successful pop act of the '70s.

February 11

Aprilla motorcycles sued the Spice Girls over lost advertising as sponsors of the 1998 Spiceworld Tour. Geri Halliwell of the fem quintet appeared in court today to testify. It didn't do much good as the group lost.

Does anyone remember anything about this night besides the green scarf "dress" worn by J. Lo at the forty-ninth annual Grammy Awards show? Surprisingly, she didn't make Mr. Blackwell's worst-dressed list for the year.

February 12

Mariah Carey began a two-week stay at No. 1 with her single "Thank G-d I Found You."

March 7

The first black woman to conduct the symphony orchestras of Chicago, Los Angeles, Detroit, and thirteen other American cities, Margaret Rosezarian Harris died of a heart attack today at age fifty-six. Originally a pianist, Harris gained her greatest acclaim as a conductor. She also worked on Broadway, most notably as music director of the musical *Hair*.

March 10

Chrissie Hynde of the Pretenders was arrested when she led an animal rights protest in Manhattan. She was protesting against Gap stores, who were reportedly using leather from cows slaughtered cruelly and illegally.

March 14

Though it was billed as the Supremes Reunion Tour, Diana Ross was really the only original member after the promoters insulted Mary Wilson with an offer of $2 million while Diana was to get $20 million, according to TV's *Access Hollywood*. Undeterred, Diana went out with Scherrie Payne and Lynda Laurence, who weren't even in the group until years after Diana left. Cindy Birdsong, the original replacement for deceased Florence Ballard, wasn't even mentioned.

March 26

Whitney Houston, Queen Latifah, Ray Charles, and Isaac Hayes sang a special medley of previously nominated Oscar songs at the Academy Awards presentation in Los Angeles.

April 7

A tribute concert was held in New York to honor Joni Mitchell. Performers included Cyndi Lauper, k. d. lang, Shawn Colvin, Mary Chapin Carpenter, and Elton John.

April 13

Revlon sponsored its tenth-anniversary Carnegie Hall benefit concert to protect the rain forest with performances by Gladys Knight, Martha Reeves, Elton John, Billy Joel, James Taylor, Sting, the Impressions, and Percy Sledge.

Britney Spears.

April 27

Daughter of folksinger Jolly Robinson, Vicki Sue Robinson was an actress/singer and Philadelphia native, who had one of the quintessential disco hits of the '70s with "Turn the Beat Around." She performed at the Philadelphia Folk Festival when she was six years old and was in the original cast of the Broadway musicals *Hair* and *Jesus Christ Superstar.* She died today of cancer at age forty-five.

May 15

Britney Spears informed a German magazine that she intended to refrain from sex until her wedding night. Yeah! And no one in the '60s took drugs!

May 16

Britney Spears' second LP, *Oops! . . . I Did It Again,* debuted at No. 1, selling 1.3 million copies, making it the highest debut by a female artist in U.S. history. Across the pond, she debuted her live act in England, performing to three sellout crowds at London's Wembley Arena.

Courtney Love gave a speech at the Digital Hollywood Online Entertainment Internet Conference in New York on piracy in the music business that draws praise.

June 9

The mother of two, Sinead O'Connor announced to the world in *Curve* magazine that she was a lesbian.

June 20

After a fifteen-year legal battle, a New York judge awarded the Ronettes $2.6 million from producer Phil Spector, saying Spector had cheated them out of royalties. The ruling eased the way for veteran artists of the fifties and sixties to collect past-due royalties on their old recordings.

June

Simple Machines founders Jenny Toomey and Kristin Thomson created the Future of Music Coalition, devoted to artist rights. Their annual conference features politicians and musicians working together to enact fair copyright and royalty legislation. Toomey fronted the indie-rock band Tsunami for much of the 1990s.

August 22

Now in her fifties, singer/guitarist Barbara Lynn returned with *Hot Night Tonight* after a lengthy hiatus. Although she recorded sporadically throughout the '60s, '70s, and '90s, she's most known for her 1962 self-penned ballad "You'll Lose a Good Thing," which became a national hit, hitting No. 1 on the R&B charts and was in the Top 10 on the pop charts.

September 13

A British newspaper (the *Mirror*) stated that Toni Braxton refused to appear at the American Mobo Awards after one of her breast enlargements exploded. Toni referred to it as "a mystery illness," but the dry-witted Brits of the *Mirror* said she bowed out "after her boob implant burst."

September 18

You know it's the twenty-first century when you're sued by an Internet company. That was Britney Spears' fate when DNA Visual Business Solutions filed suit because she allegedly didn't pay for her Web site's redesign.

September 24

Canadian songstress Nelly Furtado's debut, *Whoa, Nelly!*, features her break-through Grammy Award–winning single, "I'm like a Bird," for Best Female Pop Vocal Performance.

November 2

A British TV poll to find the sexiest female act voted All Saints No. 1, beating out the Spice Girls, who finished second. Interestingly the '50s vocal trio the Beverly Sisters reached eleventh place, beating out TLC. (Must have been an older viewing audience.).

November 2–4

The ROCKRGRL Music Conference, the largest assembly of female musicians ever held, convened in Seattle, Washington, with Ronnie Spector, Amy Ray, and Courtney Love as keynote speakers. The band Heart was presented with the first Women of Valor Award, and more than 250 female artists performed.

November 6

Madonna performed onstage for the first time in eight years at the Roseland Ballroom in New York. Her set lasted twenty minutes, and she wore a black vest with the name Britney Spears emblazoned in sequins on her chest.

November 12

Destiny's Child's single "Independent Woman Pt. 1" reached No. 1 and stayed there for eleven weeks.

More Moments in 2000

The World Music Awards named Mariah Carey the bestselling female artist of all time, with the most U.S. No. 1 singles for a female artist. According to *Billboard* magazine, she was the most successful artist of the 1990s in the United States.

2001

January 4

Courtney Love filed a lawsuit against an alleged stalker, claiming the woman drove over Courtney's foot, costing her both a role in a film and the subsequent fee of $340,000.

January 8

Laura Webb Childress, tenor vocalist for the Bobbettes, died. She and her four schoolmates were barely in their teens when they formed the Harlem Queens, but soon became the rage with their classic "Mr. Lee," a song they wrote about their fifth-grade teacher, which went to No. 1 R&B and No. 6 pop in 1957. It made them the first all-girl rock 'n' roll group to have a Top 10 hit.

January 9

Lynn Dixon Denicker, lead singer of the Aquatones, passed away. The group, formed in Valley Stream, Long Island, New York, in 1957, had a hit with their first single, "You' (No. 21 pop, No. 11 R&B), but couldn't chart again despite seven excellent follow-up singles and disbanded in 1960. They were the first male group with a female lead to have a hit, both pop and R&B, in the rock 'n' roll era. Lynn was trained as an operatic soprano.

January 28

Jennifer Lopez, aka J.Lo, a nickname that would bring abbreviated names into vogue, hit No. 1 with her album, entitled *J.Lo.* Among her special needs at concerts: white flowers, furniture, and carpeting backstage.

February 7

Dale Evans, known as the "Queen of the West," was the wife of country and western singer and Western movie star Roy Rogers. She wrote their biggest hit, "Happy Trails," and sang it with Roy for almost fifty years. She originally sang with the Jay Mills Orchestra and is in the National Cowgirl Hall of Fame. Dale passed away today at age eighty-eight.

February 22

Macy Gray won the Grammy for Best Female Pop Vocal with "I Try" at the forty-third Grammy Awards.

March 12

A U.S. poll of critics, musicians, and fans named Judy Garland's recording of "Over the Rainbow" the song of the twentieth century.

March 14

Spice Girl Geri Haliwell lost her driving privileges for six weeks for speeding in the London area and was fined $680. Poor dear was doing 60 mph in a 30 mph zone in her Aston Martin DB7.

March 25

Unconventional as ever, Bjork shows up at the seventy-third Academy Awards show to perform "I've Seen It All" from the film *Dancer in the Dark* wearing a swan outfit, making the quirky Icelandic singer a household name. Not surprisingly, she appeared on Mr. Blackwell's "Ten Worst Dressed Women" list that year.

April 3

Mariah Carey signed the biggest recording contract in music history when she inked a deal with Virgin Records for three albums worth a guaranteed $102 million.

April 22

Destiny's Child reached No. 1 in England with "Survivor."

May 27

Mya, Pink, Christina Aguilera, and Lil' Kim began five weeks at No. 1 with Labelle's hit "Lady Marmalade."

June 5

The much-anticipated debut from Alicia Keys, *Songs in A Minor,* sold a ton of units (over 235,000 copies in its first week), making her one of the bestselling new artists of 2001. The first single, "Fallin'," spent six weeks at No. 1 on the U.S. *Billboard* Hot 100. Keys won five Grammy Awards in 2002, including Best New Artist and Song of the Year for "Fallin'."

Lucinda Williams' *Essence* is released, debuting on the *Billboard* 200 at No. 28. She won the 2002 Grammy Award for Best Female Rock Performance for the single "Get Right with God."

July 8

Alicia Keyes reached No. 1 with her album *Songs In A Minor.*

August 4

It was reported that Mariah Carey had hired a private investigator to spy on her former husband, Sony Records President Tommy Mottola. Mariah believed Tommy was orchestrating a smear campaign against her.

August 6

Whitney Houston signed a deal with Arista Records for $100 million.

August 14

Singer-songwriter Michelle Branch released her first major-label CD, *The Spirit Room,* on Maverick Records, peaking at No. 28 on the U.S. *Billboard* 200 chart and producing three top *Billboard* hits ("Everywhere," "All You Wanted," and "Goodbye to You"). Her follow-up, *Hotel Paper,* released in '03, scored a Top 20 hit for its single "Are You Happy Now?"

August 25

Aaliyah (born Aaliyah Haughton) died when the plane she was in crashed in the Caribbean. She had been filming a video on the island. The young singer/actress had already had sixteen pop-chart singles, including her No. 1, "Try Again," in 2000. She was only twenty-two years old.

September 1

Bjork charted on the Hot 100 singles sales list with "Hidden Place." She became the only artist from Iceland to ever hit an American chart.

September 23

Macy Gray reached No. 1 in Britain with her *The Id* album.

October 9

A man "borrowed" Missy Elliot's Lamborghini Diablo (valued at $300,000) for a joyride and promptly crashed it into a traffic sign. His escapade cost him three years in jail.

November 5

The *London Times* reported that the highest-earning woman in England that year was Madonna, with income of $51 million.

November 20

Former 4 Non Blondes singer Linda Perry got a second wind as producer and chief songwriter for Pink's breakout album *M!ssundaztood,* featuring the hit, "Get the Party Started." Perry, who also contributed heavily to albums by Gwen Stefani, Kelly Osbourne, and Courtney Love, scored another hit with Christina Aguilera's version of "Beautiful" (from *Stripped*).

December 9

It's rare that a TV network apologizes for anything, but NBC-TV did after

Madonna was able to utter the word "motherfucker" during a live broadcast from the Tate Art Gallery before the censors could use their bleeper.

December 15

Lead singer Bianca Halstead (aka Bianca Butthole) of the all-female band Betty Blowtorch, was killed post-gig in New Orleans when she was an unfortunate passenger riding with a drunk driver who was taking her back to her hotel. In a sobering twist, Bianca had been sober for ten years.

December 16

Nicole Kidman and Robbie Williams reached No. 1 in England with "Something Stupid," a remake of the Nancy and Frank Sinatra hit.

More Moments in 2001

Madonna's "What It Feels Like for a Girl" video was banned from MTV.

Founded by former roadie Misty McElroy, the Portland Rock and Roll Camp for Girls was launched and became a phenomenon, copied worldwide.

After receiving *Billboard*'s Artist of the Decade Award in the '90s, Mariah Carey parted ways with Columbia Records after a long relationship. She signed with Virgin Records for a reported $80 million. During this year, her erratic behavior became public, including an unscheduled visit to MTV's *Total Request Live,* where she handed out Popsicles to the audience. And in an example of art imitating life, Mariah Carey starred in *Glitter,* a film about a young singer desperately seeking stardom who dates a DJ, who helps her break into the music business. The film was released and flopped, heralding a nervous breakdown for Carey.

2002

February 27

The unlikely winner for Album of the Year" at the forty-fourth annual Grammy Awards was the soundtrack *O Brother, Where Art Thou?* from the Coen brothers movie starring George Clooney. Produced by T-Bone Burnett, the soundtrack prominently featured old-time roots music performed by mainly contemporary Americana artists, including Gillian Welch, Alison Krauss, and Emmylou Harris.

March 14

Alicia Keyes performed in a suite at Britain's House of Commons, courtesy of member of parliament David Lammy, whose reasoning was he wanted parliament to be more open to young people. No word on whether the rest of parliament were invited to attend the performance.

March 30

Mary J. Blige charted with "Rainy Dayz," an eventual No. 12 pop hit and her twenty-fifth charter since "You Remind Me," in 1992.

April 20

Calling her "irrational, mercurial, self-centered, unmanageable, inconsistent, and unpredictable" and claiming a contract was invalid because she was "stoned" at the time, two former members of Nirvana argued that Courtney Love should not have the rights to her husband Curt Cobain's and Nirvana's recordings. The judge gave them to her anyway.

April 25

Lisa "Left Eye" Lopes of TLC was killed in a car accident. The singer/arsonist was thirty years old (ironically her age is a newspaper term meaning "the End").

May 29

Natalie Imbruglia signed a $170,000 deal to be the face of French cosmetics company L'Oreal.

June 29

Rosemary Clooney was one of the best-loved pop singers of the fifties and by the seventies was popular as a jazz artist. She charted twenty-five times between 1951 and 1960 with songs like "Hey There," "This Ole House" and "Come On-a My House." Her nephew is movie star George Clooney. She died today at age seventy-four.

June

Breathy "Straight Up" singer and former Laker Girl Paula Abdul was hired to be a judge on *American Idol*, a phenomenon in the making. Three years later, she was accused of having an affair with one of the contestants, which was reported on by every entertainment news show. Abdul showed her sense of humor by appearing in a *Saturday Night Live* skit spoof.

July 27

Mariah Carey checked into a hospital suffering from extreme exhaustion.

August 6

In a macabre report, 560 British undertakers polled said that grieving families preferred pop songs to hymns at funerals. Among the desired for the departed were "I Will Always Love You" by Whitney Houston and the favorite on the grim reaper hit parade was Bette Midler's "Wind Beneath My Wings."

August 10

Lisa Marie Presley, daughter of Elvis Presley, married actor Nicholas Cage. It lasted four months until Cage filed for divorce.

August 27

After redefining country music with their two previous releases, *Wide Open Spaces and Fly,* the Dixie Chicks released *Home,* and score their first Top 10 single with "Long Time Gone." Home sold over 6 million copies and garnered the chicks four Grammy Awards in 2003, including Best Country Album.

September 2

Bjork's London apartment was broken into and robbed of recording equipment while the Icelandic vocalist was asleep in her bedroom.

September 17

Season one *American Idol* winner Kelly Clarkson released first single, "A Moment Like This" (later appearing on her debut outing, *Thankful*), setting a *Billboard* record when it rose from No. 52 to No. 1—largely in part to its first-week sales of over 200,000 copies!

September 28

Madonna was voted the greatest female singer of all time in a VH-1 poll of over 750,000 obviously uninformed and delusional ballot casters.

September

No Doubt's platinum front woman Gwen Stefani married Bush guitarist Gavin Rossdale in two separate ceremonies on both sides of the Atlantic, the first at St. Paul's Church in London's Covent Garden and in Los Angeles two weeks later. The two have a son, Kingston, born in 2006.

October 6

Underdog pop singer Jessica Simpson came into her own when she married 98 Degrees singer Nick Lachey and became a newlywed with her own MTV reality sitcom, *Newlyweds: Nick and Jessica*. The show tortured audiences for two seasons, starting in 2003, offering up lots of vacuous banter from Simpson and fodder for *Saturday Night Live* skits.

October 13

Celine Dion was sued by the British rock band Muse after she announced her show would be called "Muse." The group's vocalist indignantly stated: "We don't want anyone to think were Celine Dion's backing band." (Yeah . . . that's going to happen.)

October 22

Singer-songwriter Michelle Branch's collaboration with Santana "The Game of Love," won a Grammy Award for "Best Pop Collaboration with Vocals". Tina Turner originally recorded the track with Santana, but it was not released until October 16, 2007.

November 2

Heavily armed British police arrested a terrorist group who were planning the kidnapping of the Spice Girls' Victoria Beckham. They planned to ransom Posh Spice and her two kids for $8.5 million dollars.

November 9

Madonna's movie *Swept Away* was cancelled for British release because the film did so badly in America.

December 4

Whitney Houston stated in a TV interview that she was addicted to sex and that drugs and drinking almost killed her.

December 29

Readers of *Sugar* magazine (who obviously had the collective IQ of sperm) voted for their No. 1 role model. Are you Ready? No. 1 Pink, No. 2 Britney Spears, No. 3 Ms. Dynamite, No. 4 (I love this one!) Kelly Osbourne, No. 5 Kylie Minogue.

December 30

Diana Ross was arrested by an Arizona highway patrol officer for drunk driving. The diva couldn't stand on one foot, walk a straight line without falling down, and couldn't count to thirty. She was cited for three misdemeanors, and it wasn't even New Years Eve yet!

More Moments in 2002

Ousted Destiny's Child singers LeToya Luckett and Latavia Roberson sued the band, claiming they were slighted in the lyrics of the 2001 hit song "Survivor."

2003

January 11

Cheryl Tweedy of the British group Girls Aloud was arrested for allegedly hitting a lavatory attendant in Guildford, England.

January 13

Diana Ross appeared in court for drunk driving in Tucson, Arizona. The police report stated she could not (among other things) touch her nose, walk a straight line, or count up to thirty. She was stopped while swerving across a road.

January 19

Norah Jones reached No. 1 with her *Come Away with Me* album. The album was also No. 1 in England.

February 2

Girl duo Tatu began four weeks on top of the British charts with "All the Things She Said." The girls were the first artists from Russia to have a hit in England.

February 4

Courtney Love was arrested at Heathrow Airport for "endangering an aircraft." She was on a flight from Los Angeles to London when she began verbally abusing the cabin crew for not letting her nurse, who was in the economy section, come up and see her in the first-class section.

Norah Jones.

February 9

Norah Jones' second outing, *Feels like Home,* was released. Within a week, it had sold over a million copies, making it the highest-selling album in the history of Blue Note Records. *Time* magazine included Jones on the "Time 100," list of the most influential people of that year.

February 23

Jazz pop artist Norah Jones swept the competition at the forty-fifth Grammys for her debut, *Come Away with Me,* winning Album of the Year, Best New Artist, Best Female Pop Vocal, Song of the Year, and Record of the Year ("Don't Know Why") while Sheryl Crow won the Best Female Rock Vocal Award.

March

Hard-rocking Canadian all-female band Kittie sued their label, Artemis, for unpaid royalties. The band settled and put out one final album on the label before starting their own.

April 7

Avril Lavigne pretty much swept the Canadian Juno Awards, including Best New Artist, Best Single, and Best Album.

April 24

Christina Aguilera's "Beautiful" became the first No. 1 on the new British Download chart.

April 25

Britain's *Sunday Times* noted that the only female in their "Rich List" Top 5 survey was Madonna at No. 4, with a fortune of over $386 million.

May 14

Britney Spears and the footwear company Skechers settled a lawsuit out of court over an agreement for the artist to promote a line of roller skates.

May 15

June Carter Cash, famed country singer and wife of Johnny Cash, died today at age seventy-three.

May 22

Madame Tussaud's Wax Museum in London unveiled its newest feature, a wax work of Jennifer Lopez that cost $88,400 to make.

June 24

Beyoncé Knowles released her solo debut, *Dangerously in Love,* becoming one of the year's biggest commercial hits, spawning two number-one singles and earning the former Destiny's Child front woman five Grammy Awards in 2004.

June 29

Former Destiny's Child lead Beyoncé was No. 1 in both the U.S. and Great Britain with her solo album *Dangerously in Love.*

August 17

Eva Cassidy hit No. 1 in Britain with her album *American Tune.* It was the American artist's third chart topper in England.

August 29

Madonna startled the MTV Video Music Awards audience by passionately kissing Christina Aguilera and Britney Spears on the lips during a sexy performance of "Like a Virgin."

September 11

Jennifer Lopez and actor Ben Affleck had to postpone their nuptials because their supposedly well-kept secret as to where they were to wed (a private estate in Santa Barbara, California) was leaked to the paparazzi.

September 16

The Vocal Group Hall of Fame held its sixth annual induction ceremonies in Sharon, Pennsylvania. Co-hosts Mary Wilson of the Supremes and publisher/author Jay Warner anchored the proceedings that saw Martha and the Vandellas, the Whispers, the Five Satins, the Charioteers, the Isley Brothers, the Impressions, Earth, Wind and Fire, and the Commodores inducted.

October 9

A Sheryl Crow "admirer" was charged with stalking and harassment when he tried to get into her limo after a performance in New York.

November 6

Honoring pop artists during the MTV Europe Music Awards, the city of Hamburg, Germany, where the awards were held, renamed several avenues after acts, such as Janet Jackson and Madonna, at least until the show was over.

November 17

Britney Spears became the youngest singer to ever get a star on Hollywood's Walk of Fame. She was twenty-one.

December 2

Alicia Keys released the follow-up to her debut, *The Diary of Alicia Keys.* "If I Ain't Got You" became the first single by a female artist to stay on *Billboard*'s Hot R&B/Hip-Hop chart for more than one year, surpassing Mary J. Blige's "Your Child" (forty-nine weeks). Keys went on to become the bestselling female R&B artist of 2004 and took home Best R&B Video at the 2004 MTV Video Music Awards, and four Grammy Awards, for Best R&B Album, Best Female R&B Vocal Performance ("If I Ain't Got You"), Best R&B Song ("You Don't Know My Name"), and Best R&B Performance by a Duo or Group ("My Boo" with Usher). She was also nominated for several other awards, including Album of the Year and Song of the Year.

December 5

Courtney Love received an eighteen-month sentence in drug rehab after she admitted she was addicted to cocaine.

December 6

Diana Krall married singer Elvis Costello at Elton John's British mansion.

December 13

Lauryn Hill (formerly of the Fugees) performed at a Christmas show in Vatican City and used the occasion to verbally assault the Catholic church for its "head in the sand" attitude toward sexual abuse by priests when she berated them to repent. She certainly had a captive audience as the spectators were bishops, cardinals, and the elite of Italian society. Needless to say, she has not been asked to make a return engagement.

December

The third studio album from Kelis, *Nasty,* contained her biggest hit to date: a little double-entendre ditty called "Milkshake" (allegedly about her boobs). A cleaned-up version of the song was ironically featured in commercials from fast-food chains Hardee's and Carl's Jr.!

More Moments in 2003

Sex author Madonna releases her first children's book, *The English Roses,* debuting at No. 1 on the *New York Times* bestseller list. Quite a divergent path from her previous foray in publishing in 1992 and 1994 (*Sex* and *The Girlie Show*).

2004

January 4

Britney Spears had her two-day-old marriage to childhood friend Jason Alexander (no, not the Seinfeld star) annulled. Her lawyers stated: "She lacked understanding of her actions to the extent she was incapable of agreeing to the marriage." Wonder what her lawyers would have thought about her shaving her head in February 2007!

January

Jennifer "Jenny from the Block" Lopez's on-again, off-again engagement to actor Ben Affleck was the talk of the town (and every tabloid rag and TV show) for months! The pair finally called off their engagement, sparing everyone the detailed daily media scrutiny. (Lopez did return the Harry Winston 6.1-carat pink diamond!) Was it the disastrous reviews for their collaborative film, *Gigli*? The rumors of Ben's predilection for strippers? Who knows?

Notable Moments of Women in Music

February 1

Janet Jackson's unfortunate Super Bowl incident with Justin Timberlake introduced the phrase "wardrobe malfunction" into the vernacular. Broadcast live on CBS from Houston, Texas, "Nipplegate" led to a crackdown and widespread debate on perceived indecency in broadcasting, outrageous fines, and an overall perception of decreasing cultural morality.

February 6

Faith Evans enrolled in a rehab program to avoid charges of cocaine possession. Prosecutors agreed the charges would be dropped if she completed the thirteen-week program.

February 10

Diana Ross was sentenced to two days in jail for her December drunk-driving arrest in Tucson. Showing that stars were of course treated no differently than the general public, she was allowed to plead guilty over the phone from New York and serve her time near her Los Angeles home.

December 16

Doris Troy, who had the 1963 hit "Just One Look," died today. Doris had been a background singer for Dionne Warwick and sang on Pink Floyd's *Dark Side of the Moon* album.

March 18

It was a busy night for Courtney Love as she flashed her bust at TV host David Letterman while singing "Danny Boy" on his show and then found time to throw a microphone stand at a man in the crowd at an after hours nightclub party. No penalties for the former, but she was charged with assault for the latter.

April 4

Alanis Morissette hosted the Juno Awards (Canada's version of the Grammys) in a bathrobe, which she took off to reveal a nude-colored leotard. The antic was her response to the censorship backlash caused by Janet Jackson's breast-revealing Super Bowl incident earlier this year.

June 5

Jennifer Lopez and Marc Anthony were secretly married at her home in Beverly Hills, California—just four days after his divorce was final.

Roxy Saint, queen of the underground punk movement, performed at the Download Festival in Donington, England, with Korn, Iggy Pop, Lincoln Park, Metallica, Slayer, and Slipknot for over 70,000 people.

June 29

Courtney Love pleaded guilty to disorderly conduct in a Los Angeles court and was ordered to join a drug program and pay the victims' medical expenses. The court's penalties apparently had little concern for Courtney as she showed up five hours late.

August 28

The queen of British punk Roxy Saint performed at the Reading Festival with Morrissey, 50 cent, the White Stripes, Green Day, and the Offspring for a raucous crowd of over 60,000 people.

September 6

Brit pop tart Natasha Bedingfield released her debut, *Unwritten,* a hit around the globe. Its lengthy shelf life spawned three hit singles—"Single," "These Words," and "Unwritten"—the third of which received a Grammy Award nomination for Best Female Pop Vocal Performance in 2007. The song was picked up as the theme for the MTV reality series *The Hills* and was featured on a Pantene shampoo commercial.

September 12

Natasha Bedingfield reached No. 1 in England with her debut album, *Unwritten.*

October 14

A British publication, the *Newspaper,* issued its "Pop Stars' Pet Hates" survey, which among other lunacies mentioned that Posh Spice Victoria Adams hated the name Vicky, Britney Spears despised her feet, and Geri Halliwell of the Spice Girls disliked guys who smell. (Someone had a lot of time on their hands.)

October 24

Ashlee Simpson took the heat by doing a "hoe down" jig to get offstage when she started singing to the wrong track on *Saturday Night Live,* igniting a firestorm about lip-synching. (Her manager/father claims it was due to her "acid reflux disease").

October 28

Courtney Love was ordered to stand trial for assault with a deadly weapon after she threw a lit candle and a bottle at Kristin King. Apparently Courtney was angered to find Ms. King at the home of a former boyfriend when Love showed up in the wee hours.

November 10

Liza Minelli's former bodyguard sued the songstress for $100 million, claiming she forced him to have sex with her and after repeated attempts, he succumbed.

November 23

Gwen Stefani steps out on her own with her first solo album, *Love. Angel. Music. Baby.*, and the lead single "Hollaback Girl," allegedly one of the first digital downloads to sell 1 million copies. Her L.A.M.B. clothing line was launched the previous year, further confirming her stature as a fashion icon!

December 17

Lisa Marie Presley agreed to sell 85 percent of her father, Elvis Presley's estate to Robert Sillerman. The deal was worth $100 million. Elvis must be turning in his grave.

December 18

A school book report done by Britney Spears sold at auction in New York for $1,860. No word on what grade Britney got on the report.

2005

February 10

Rolling Stone named Madonna its second-biggest money earner of the year. Her take was almost $55 million. Prince was No. 1 with $90 million.

February 13

Recently recovered cancer survivor Melissa Etheridge outshines Joss Stone on a Janis Joplin duet sung at the forty-seventh annual Grammy Awards show.

April 30

Fifty-nine-year-old Cher absolutely, positively (supposedly) made her last concert tour performance when she appeared at the Hollywood Bowl, at the end of a three-year "farewell" world tour that included 325 performances. She was only nineteen years old when she and Sonny Bono, her performing partner and husband, played the Hollywood Bowl forty years earlier at the start of her career.

April

After a tumultuous few years, Mariah Carey made a stunning comeback with *The Emancipation of Mimi*. It debuted at No. 1, and the Def Jam label reported that the album had shipped 10 million copies by June '06. The record, the biggest of her career to date, won a Grammy for Best Contemporary R&B Album, and the No. 1 single, "We Belong Together," scored her two Grammys (Best Female R&B Vocal Performance and Best R&B Song).

June

Destiny's Child officially broke up, paving the way for the one-woman media blitz known as Beyoncé.

July 2 and 8

Ten simultaneous Live 8 benefit concerts were held around the globe, in London, Paris, Berlin, Philadelphia, Rome, Tokyo, Canada, South Africa, Moscow, and Scotland. More than 1,000 musicians performed and the various venues, including Madonna, Alicia Keys, Destiny's Child, Mariah Carey, Dido, Annie Lennox, Joss Stone, Lauryn Hill, Sarah McLachlan, Shakira, Bjork, Faith Hill, and Garbage. The concerts were broadcast on 182 TV networks and 2,000 radio networks and watched by an estimated 3 billion people! Live 8 was timed to coincide with the G8 conference and summit in Scotlandin order to help raise awareness of poverty around the world. The event also coincided with the twentieth anniversary of Live Aid.

July

Michelle Branch forms the Wreckers with country singer Jessica Harp. The first single from their 2006 release, *Stand Still, Look Pretty,* was "Leave the Pieces." It was nominated for a Grammy Award (Best Country Performance by a Duo or Group with Vocal) in December 2006.

August 2

Faith Hill's country comeback, *Fireflies,* landed at No. 1 on both the *Billboard* 200 and top country albums chart. The single, "Mississippi Girl," became Hill's highest-debuting single. In her long and varied career, Hill has been honored by the Country Music Association, the Academy of Country Music, the Grammy Awards, the American Music Awards, and the People's Choice Awards.

August 7

American-born British punk/rock star Roxy Saint performed at the ESPN X-Games at the Staples Center Los Angeles with the Dead Kennedys, Pennywise, and Death by Stereo.

September 27

Seventies soul singer Bettye LaVette made a comeback with *I've Got My Own Hell to Raise.* Featuring cover songs in duet with Sinéad O'Connor, Lucinda Williams, Aimee Mann, Roseanne Cash, Dolly Parton, and Fiona Apple, the recording was chosen as one of Amazon.com's Top 100 Editor's Picks of 2005.

Her follow-up CD, *The Scene of the Crime,* also on Anti, was released in September 2007 and was recorded at the famed FAME Studios in Muscle Shoals, Alabama.

October

Fiona Apple released her long-awaited *Extraordinary Machine*—six years after her last studio album. A demo version of the record was leaked in 2003, causing a stir in the music industry. It was named in many year-end "best of" lists, including *Entertainment Weekly, Rolling Stone, Blender,* and *Spin.*

November 10–12

The second ROCKRGRL Music Conference was held in Seattle. Keynote speakers were Patti Smith and Johnette Napolitano of Concrete Blonde. Patti Smith is awarded the Woman of Valor Award, an 8-track tape of her album *Horses* mounted on a plaque. The award has a place of honor on the piano in her home.

November 15

Pop country singer Carrie Underwood launched her post–*American Idol* career with *Some Hearts,* the biggest-selling debut album by a female country music artist in history. Underwood is the first *American Idol* winner to sweep up honors at all three major music awards in the same awards-show season ('06—'07: four American Music Awards, thirteen *Billboard* Music Awards, and two Grammy Awards (including Best New Artist). *Some Hearts* has produced five No. 1 hits to date ("Inside Your Heaven," "Jesus, Take the Wheel," "Don't Forget to Remember Me," "Wasted," and "Before He Cheats").

Madonna's *Confessions on a Dance Floor* hit No. 1 in forty countries, a new record. (The Beatles previously held this record, when *The Beatles 1* went to No. 1 in thirty-six countries, in 2000.) *Confessions on a Dance Floor* won the Grammy for Best Electronic/Dance Album. Tickets for her 2006 tour sold out within minutes in the U.S., Europe, and Asia and was the highest-grossing tour in history by a female artist.

December 20

"Queen of Hip-Hop Soul" Mary J. Blige released her seventh studio album, *The Breakthrough,* pulling out all the big producer guns, from the Black Eyed

"Ms. [Mary J.] Blige brings together hip-hop realism and soul's higher aspirations, hip-hop's digitized crispness and soul's slow-building testimonies." —Jon Pareles, The New York Times

Peas' will.i.am to Dr. Dre. The album debuted at No. 1 on both the *Billboard* 200 Albums and Top R&B/Hip-Hop Albums charts, and has sold over 7 million copies worldwide, racking up an incredible number of awards in the process: *Billboard* Music Awards (9), American Music Awards (2), BET Awards (2), NAACP Image Awards (2), and a Soul Train Award. She also received the most Grammy Award nominations (eight total) at the 2007 Grammy Awards, taking home three for Best R&B Album, Best Female R&B Vocal Performance, and Best R&B Song (the latter two for the single "Be Without You").

December

R&B vocalist Alicia Keys and U2 front man Bono recorded a cover of the Peter Gabriel/Kate Bush single "Don" Give Up" for World AIDS Day. Released exclusively on iTunes, all proceeds went to the Keep a Child Alive charity.

More Moments in 2005

Norah Jones received three Grammy Awards in 2005, including Record of the Year and Best Pop Collaboration with Vocals (both for her pairing with the late Ray Charles on "Here We Go Again"). The single "Sunrise" (from the 2004 multi-platinum album *Feels Like Home*) garnered a Grammy for Best Female Pop Vocal Performance—her eighth Grammy (and eleventh overall)!

Melissa Etheridge releases *Greatest Hits: The Road Less Traveled*, which includes the song "I Run for Life." Etheridge, a breast cancer survivor, wrote the song in support of the Susan B. Komen Race for the Cure.

2006

January 24

Jenny Lewis of indie band Rilo Kiley released her first solo CD, *Rabbit Fur Coat,* to rave reviews. Appearances on *The Late Show with David Letterman, The Late Late Show with Craig Ferguson, Late Night with Conan O'Brien,* and *Later with Jools Holland* follow. Lewis was awarded *Esquire* magazine's Esky Award for Best Temperature Raiser in its April issue.

American singer-songwriter Chan Marshall, aka Cat Power, released *The Greatest* and canceled her upcoming U.S. tour, citing "health-related issues." She was admitted to the psychiatric ward at Miami's Mount Sinai Medical Center and spoke of the episode in the November issue of *Spin.*

February 15

Former Prince side-gals Wendy and Lisa accompany him onstage at the Brit Awards in London, where they performed hits songs, including "Purple Rain." It was the first time in twenty years that the three had played together live (Sheila E. also joined the band).

February

Colombian singer Shakira shimmies her way to becoming a global pop-culture sensation with "Hips Don't Lie" (with Wyclef Jean)—the second single from her *Oral Fixation Vol. 2*. The No. 1 single was one of the hottest summer songs of this year and scored a Grammy for Best Pop Collaboration with Vocals. The pair steamed up TV sets on shows like *American Idol, The Ellen DeGeneres Show, Live with Regis and Kelly, The Today Show,* and *Total Request Live.*

April 21

Country superstar couple Faith Hill and Tim McGraw kicked off their successful Soul2Soul II Tour. The tour became the highest-grossing country music tour ever and was named Major Tour of the Year by the prestigious *Pollstar* magazine, beating out road veterans Madonna and the Rolling Stones.

April 24

Emmylou Harris' collaboration with Dire Straits' Mark Knopfler, *All the Roadrunning,* was released to critical acclaim. The album rose to No. 8 and No. 17 on the U.K. Album and *Billboard* 200 charts, respectively.

June 9

A revamped, sexier Nelly Furtado released her third album, *Loose,* spawning several hit singles, including "Maneater," "Say It Right," "All Good Things (Come to an End)," "Do It," and "Promiscuous" (featuring Timbaland). "Promiscuous" would become Furtado's first No. 1 single, winning a 2006 *Billboard* Music Award for Pop Single of the Year, and was nominated for a Grammy in 2007 (Best Pop Collaboration with Vocals). The song was also included in three "best of" lists for 2006, in *Blender* magazine, the *Village Voice,* and *Rolling Stone.*

June 27

She may have lost the *American Idol* crown in season five to Taylor "Soul Patrol" Hicks, but Katharine McPhee proved she's no loser. Her debut, double A-side single, "Over the Rainbow/My Destiny," was released on RCA Records, peaking at No. 12 on the *Billboard* Hot 100. It was second highest bestselling single of 2006 (ironically just behind Taylor Hicks' "Do I Make You Proud?"). The gorgeous multi-faceted performer was named one of the "100 Most Beautiful People of 2007" by *People* magazine. And the dudes liked her, too. She landed at No. 2 on *FHM* magazine's "100 Sexiest Women in the World of 2007" and at No. 47 on *Maxim*'s "Hot 100 Women of 2007."

June

After seven albums and eleven years together, the all-girl indie-rock band Sleater-Kinney announced they're on "indefinite hiatus." It's a dignified end for a group cited as "America's Best" rock band by rock critic Greil Marcus in *Time* magazine (2001).

June

Mariah Carey received a 2007 recording star on the Hollywood Walk of Fame, along with other female artists Crystal Gayle, LeAnn Rimes, and Shania Twain.

June

Joan Jett crossed generational lines as a headliner with her Blackhearts band on the Warped Tour, kicking off in June .

July 21

Ani DiFranco received the Woman of Courage Award at the National Organization for Women (NOW) conference. Past winners include Barbra Streisand and Senator Barbara Boxer.

August 22

She's a model. She's an actress. She's an author. She's an ex-con. But wait! She's also a recording artist! Paris Hilton released her (surprise) self-titled debut on her Heiress Records label, an imprint of Warner Bros. Although the album reached No. 6 on the *Billboard* 200 for a week, its total sales were pretty dismal. On the positive note, she provided plenty of fodder for all the late-night talk show hosts! Hilton joined the ranks of celebutante/actresses-turned-"singers," including Lindsay Lohan, Hilary Duff, Jennifer Love Hewitt, Juliette Lewis, and Minnie Driver.

Girl group Danity Kane, formed on the ABC/MTV reality show *Making the Band 3* (featuring Sean "Diddy" Combs at the helm), released their self-titled debut. Produced by a host of top producers (Timbaland, Scott Storch, Rodney Jerkins), the album surprisingly sold over 90,000 copies in the first day of release and landed at No. 1 on the *Billboard* 200, knocking Christina Aguilera's *Back to Basics* from the top spot and outselling hip-hop duo OutKast. Who knew!

September 19

The Black Eyed Peas' funky front woman, Fergie, kicked off a solo career with her debut, *The Dutchess,* spawning five hit singles, including "London Bridge," "Glamorous," "Big Girls Don't Cry," "Fergalicious," and "Clumsy." She won a slew of awards in 2007, including the Teen Choice Awards' Choice Female Artist, MTV Video Music Awards' Best Female Artist, American Music Awards' Best Pop/Rock Female Artist, and was nominated for a Grammy in 2008 for Best Female Pop Vocal Performance for "Big Girls Don't Cry."

October 15

After thirty-three years, the legendary New York City punk landmark CBGB closed after a lengthy rent dispute. Patti Smith performed the final show at the club, accompanied by her longtime band members, Lenny Kaye, Jay Dee Daugherty, and Tony Shanahan, in a three-and-a-half-hour show. The venue is slated to relocate to Las Vegas. Oy vey.

October 31

British rapper Lady Sovereign (born Louise Amanda Harman) released her debut outing, *Public Warning,* on Def Jam. She was signed to the label after a meeting with CEO Jay-Z (where the hip-hop mogul asked her to do an impromptu freestyle). One of the singles, "Love Me or Hate Me," was featured in an ad for Verizon Wireless. She opened for Gwen Stefani's The Sweet Escape Tour in 2007.

October

Amy Winehouse, the beehive-wearing, heavy eyeliner sporting, U.K. retro-soul singer, hit a home run with her second outing, *Back to Black.* The critically acclaimed recording, highlighted by the single "Rehab," climbed to No. 1 on the U.K. Albums chart and No. 7 on the U.S. *Billboard* 200—the highest debut entry for an album by a British female solo artist. (She was unseated, however, several weeks later by Joss Stone). The CD was considered one of the bestselling albums of 2007, and she collected a bunch of accolades as a result, including six Grammy Award nominations and a BRIT Award for Best British Female Artist. But her rampant professional success has been mired by equally out-of-control personal dramas (drugs, relationships, jail, show cancellations), which unfolded in the tabloids.

"Maverick defiance has always been the best part of the Dixie Chicks' appeal, along with the determination to hold on to something down-home as they reach for a mass audience." —Jon Pareles, The New York Times

November 10

The Dixie Chicks' documentary, *Shut Up and Sing,* was released, capturing the backlash surrounding the March 2003 incident where chief Chick Natalie Mains dissed the president. Mains (a native Texan) announced to a U.K. audience that she was embarrassed to be from the same state as George W. Bush. The band became country music pariah, and fallout from the incident included boycotts from angry fans and the media, and the band even received a few death threats.

November

Faith Hill's stunned reaction at the CMA Awards after losing the Female Vocalist of the Year Award to Carrie Underwood made big waves in the tabloids. When the results were revealed, she was seen throwing both hands in the air as if she had won and then mouthing the word "What!?" into the camera. Hill claimed her reaction was a joke.

December 25

American Idol "loser" Jennifer Hudson outshined onscreen rival Beyoncé in her portrayal of Effie White in the film *Dreamgirls.* Hudson's stunning performance earned her numerous awards, including an Oscar and a Golden Globe.

More Moments in 2006

Love, Janis, the musical stage show about the life and music of rock 'n' roll singer Janis Joplin, debuted.

2007

January 26

R&B singer-turned-actress Alicia Keys co-stared as an assassin in the film *Smokin' Aces,* along with fellow performer Common and actors Ben Affleck, Ray Liotta, Andy Garcia, Jeremy Piven, and Ryan Reynolds. Keys' second film appearance was in *The Nanny Diaries,* released on August 24, 2007.

January

Not Too Late, Norah Jones' third outing for Blue Note, was released worldwide this month, debuting at No. 1 on both the U.S. *Billboard* 200 and U.K. Albums chart lists and reaching No. 1 in seventeen countries, including Germany and France. It was certified gold or platinum in twenty-one countries, as of February 2007.

"Before I met her [Alicia Keys], I felt that what I was hearing in her voice was in her heart. That's important. You can sing well. You can play well, but the key is that you can feel her heart in it." —Stevie Wonder

February 11

At the forty-ninth Grammy Awards show in 2007, the Dixie Chicks swept all five categories for which they were nominated, including the coveted Song of the Year, Record of the Year, and Album of the Year categories.

February 13

West, the eighth studio album from Lucinda Williams, debuted at No. 14 on the *Billboard* 200 (the highest chart position of her career) and was nominated for a 2008 Grammy for Best Rock Song ("Come On").

February 25

Melissa Etheridge takes home the Oscar for Best Original Song for "I Need to Wake Up," a socially conscious tune she penned for the 2006 film on global warming, *An Inconvenient Truth.*

March 17

The fabulous Ronettes were inducted into the Rock and Roll Hall of Fame by Keith Richards of the Rolling Stones, who reminisced how he first heard them in a North England show and thought he'd overdosed and was being sung to by angels. The awards were held on March 12, 2007, but aired tonight on VH-1. The trio of Ronnie, Estelle, and Nedra sang their signature rock classic "Be My Baby," the song Brian Wilson of the Beach Boys called the most perfect rock record ever made. Ronnie, in her acceptance speech, thanked everyone but her abusive ex-husband, the man who created their sound, Phil Spector. Spector, however, apparently wanting to be a continual part of history, despite being under the pressure of his murder trial starting the next day, sent a congratulatory telegram to the group, which was read on the show by Paul Shaeffer.

March 27

Jennifer Lopez had a hit with *Como Ama una Mujer,* recorded entirely in Spanish and co-produced by hubbie Marc Anthony. The album peaked at No. 10 on the U.S. *Billboard* 200 and No. 1 on both U.S. Latin Album and Pop Album charts, and was a success around the globe, attaining the highest sales of a Spanish-language album debut

April 1

A cheeky cover-version video of the Black Eyed Peas' "My Humps" hit YouTube by none other than Alanis Morisette. The parody received more than 8 mil-

"She's [Christina Aguilera] one of the greatest. She was born to sing."
—*Ron Fair, executive producer*

lion views and was given the thumbs-up from Peas singer Fergie, who sent her a butt-shaped cake!

April 20

The first all-female rock band to put out a full-length album, Fanny received the ROCKRGRL Women of Valor Award at Berklee College of Music in Boston, and three of the four members perform together for the first time in twenty years. The award was presented by singer-songwriter Toshi Reagon.

June

Christina Aguilera received a recording star on Hollywood's Walk of Fame.

July 1

In honor of the tenth anniversary of the death of Princess Diana, the Concert for Diana was held at London's Wembley Stadium and broadcast around the world. Some of the invited performers were Lily Allen, Fergie, Joss Stone, Natasha Bedingfield, Anastacia, and Nelly Furtado (who sang her event-inappropriate "Maneater").

July 24

Jennifer Lopez and Marc Anthony announced a "co-headline" world tour called Juntos en Concierto, starting in the fall—along with the news that she's pregnant with her first child.

July

One of the most visible MySpace success stories is Lily Allen, who created a MySpace page and gained international buzz back in November 2005. Her debut, *Alright, Still,* was released this month, the first single of which, "Smile," reached No. 1 on the U.K. singles chart. The CD was nominated for Best British Album at the BRIT Awards and for Best New Artist at the 2007 MTV Video Music Awards, as well as a 2008 Grammy Award nomination for Best Alternative Music Album.

September 9

Beleaguered star Britney Spears appeared on the MTV Music Awards with a half-hearted dance to promote her single, "Gimme More." The "performance" unleashes a media frenzy to monitor her erratic escapades.

October 18

"Hannah Mania" ensued with the kickoff of the sold-out Best of Both Worlds Tour, featuring 'tween singer Miley Cyrus and her Disney Channel alter-ego character, Hannah Montana. Following on the heels of the double-album release, *Hannah Montana 2/Meet Miley Cyrus* (which has sold over 1 million copies since its release in June), tour ticket sales in most locations allegedly sold out within minutes of going on sale and sparked controversy related to ticket prices (high) and the resulting ticket scalping (higher). Let's hope she's making dad, Billy Ray, proud!

November 13

Alicia Keys' third studio album, *As I Am,* was released. The single "No One" was nominated for two Grammy Awards, including Best Female R&B Vocal Performance and Best R&B Song.

November 15

The year 2007 was one for comeback as bands from Asia to Zeppelin reformed—and why the heck not the Spice Girls!? Nine years in the making, the pre-tour kickoff show was at the Victoria's Secret fashion show in Los Angeles.

When tickets went on sale for the first London date of the world tour, it allegedly sold out in thirty-eight seconds!

December

The U.K.'s *Mojo* magazine awards its Solo Artist of the Year title to P. J. Harvey. Her *White Chalk* release appeared at No. 8 in its Top 10 Albums of 2007.

2008

April 15

Sony Pictures released the eventual horror cult-classic film *Zombie Strippers,* starring the outrageous British punk rocker Roxy Saint alongside sex star Jenna Jameson. The highlight of the film came as Roxy killed off legendary horror fiend Freddy Kruger.

"I'm a legend, not a superstar or it would have been much easier to spread my legs and fuck everybody in the music biz."—Roxy Saint

HAL LEONARD BOOKS BY JAY WARNER

Music, music history, music industry, entertainment, and educational books for all ages

How to Have Your Hit Song Published

In its fourth edition, this bible for songwriters has been in print for thirty consecutive years and has been endorsed by everyone from Barry Manilow, Dick Clark, and Rick James to Whitney Houston's writer Michael Masser, Elvis's writer Ben Weisman, and Beatles publisher Irwin Pincus. *How to Have Your Hit Song Published* was the first, and continues to be the most beneficial, of all works to help songwriters succeed in the multi-billion dollar songwriting business of today. Everything from how to make contacts and network, promoting your songs and your writing career, and how publishing companies *really* work, to setting up your own publishing company, learning how the laws can be used in your favor, using twenty-first-century technologies to your advantage, and much more is all included in the only volume written for everyone, from the veteran professional to the newcomer, in simplified layman's terms. *How to Have Your Hit Song Published* also includes actual contracts and licenses used by publishers, record companies, film companies, and TV companies every day. Only this edition includes paragraph breakdowns and explanations of what they mean and how they actually effect you. The work also has twelve massive lists of nearly 1,000 contacts, including record companies, publishers and songwriter associations, film and TV music supervisors, record producers, record distributors, entertainment attorneys, film and TV studios, and for the first time in any publication available to the general public, a vast contact list of foreign publishers in more than twenty countries, with phone, fax, e-mail, and snail-mail addresses. *How to Have Your Hit Song Published* takes you from the creative process to the process of gaining exposure and marketing your songs and your writing career.

On This Day in Music History

Brimming with more than 2,000 fascinating pieces of history and trivia about music from rock 'n' roll, R & B, and country, *On This Day in Music History* seems like a straightforward, entertaining reference work, but connecting the stories and facts over the days and months, it reveals the rich mosaic that makes up the history of modern music over the past fifty years. By combining a calendar format with more than 180 photos, the "on this day" concept sets a new trend in books, allowing for instant gratification in a to-the-point history. With a foreword by Beatles producer George Martin and endorsements by the likes of Neil Diamond, Rick James, John Kay of Steppenwolf, and Maurice White of Earth, Wind and Fire, this tour through music history touches on everyone from Elvis, Streisand, and the Beatles to Elton John, the Rolling Stones, Celine Dion, and Madonna.

On This Day in Black Music History

The second in the "On This Day" series, *Black Music* is a first-of-its-kind, entertaining reference source, covering a hundred-year spectrum of all genres of black music. R & B, doo-wop, soul, gospel, hip-hop, rap, rock 'n' roll, jazz, and everything outside and in between is chronicled here for music and entertainment lovers of all ages. With a foreword by the legendary Quincy Jones, it is music-history appreciation adapted for the twenty-first century. It is perfect for our instant-gratification age—offering more than 2,000 facts about hundreds of artists, including Aretha Franklin, Ella Fitzgerald, Whitney Houston, Stevie Wonder, Count Basie, Queen Latifah, Ray Charles, Dizzy Gillespie, Miles Davis, James Brown, Snoop Dogg, Alicia Keyes, TLC, Michael Jackson, Mary J. Blige, B. B. King, R. Kelly, and Babyface. Each page also includes the No. 1 hit on that day by the best of black music's legendary performers.

American Singing Groups: A History from 1940 to Today

American Singing Groups is the definitive history of vocal groups, encompassing the doo-wop of Dion and the Belmonts, the Motown sound of the Supremes, the surf sound of the Beach Boys, the country rock of

Crosby, Stills, Nash and Young, the solid soul of the timeless Temptations, the magical pop rock of the Mamas and the Papas, and the contemporary pop of groups like 'N Sync and the Backstreet Boys. With over 400 groups' histories, each entry details the act's career, key members, and influences. With extensive discographies and rare photos, this one-of-a-kind, almost-600-page, entertaining reference is filled with musical facts that will fascinate fans and collectors. Updating its original 1992 bestselling edition, published as *The Billboard Book of American Singing Groups*, this work also chronicles the revival of vocal groups in the nineties and the new millennium. This is an essential and comprehensive guide to an evolving and ever-popular musical art form.

ABOUT THE AUTHOR

Jay Warner is a six-time Grammy-winning music publisher, recipient of the Heroes and Legends Foundation's Pioneer Award, and the first publisher to be entered into the Congressional Record for his contributions to the music industry. He has turned his meticulous passion for information into a distinct and separate career as an author and music historian, with a series of bestselling books and his definitive series of Music-Cals™, the mini-book in a day-by-day format.

As a music publisher, Warner has represented writers, artists, and celebrities as diverse as Bruce Springsteen, Barry Manilow, Wesley Snipes, the Emotions, Jimmy Webb, B. B. King, Neil Diamond, the Rascals, Tony Orlando and Dawn, the Whispers, Evander Holyfield, Teena Marie, the Four Seasons, and Rick James, and has published over 100 Top 40 hits, including "Blinded by the Light" (Manfred Mann), "Born to Run" (Bruce Springsteen), "Up, Up and Away" (the 5th Dimension), "People Gotta Be Free" (Rascals), "Dawn" (the Four Seasons), "Sun Ain't Gonna Shine Anymore" (Walker Brothers), "Who Do You Think You Are" (Bo Donaldson and the Heywoods), "It's a Miracle" (Barry Manilow), "Someone for Me" (Whitney Houston), "By the Time I Get to Phoenix" (Glen Campbell), "How Can I Be Sure" (the Rascals), "Knock Three Times" (Tony Orlando), Midnight Train to Georgia" (Gladys Knight and the Pips), "Prisoner" (Barbra Streisand), "Worst That Could Happen" (Brooklyn Bridge), "Groovin'" (the Rascals), "Who Loves You" (the Four Seasons), "You Send the Rain Away" (Rebbie Jackson and Robin Zander), "Cold Blooded" (Rick James), "Party All the Time" (Eddie Murphy), "In My House" (Mary Jane

Girls), "Baby I'm Hooked" (Confunkshun), "Love Is All We Need" (Mary J. Blige), and many more.

In 1978, Warner wrote the first in-depth text on publishing, songwriting, and copyright law in layman's terms, *How to Have Your Hit Song Published* (Hal Leonard). Thirty years later, it is in its fourth printing, is still the definitive text on the subject, and has never been out of print.

In 1993, Warner's encyclopedic work, *The Billboard Book of American Singing Groups: A History, 1940–1990,* was published to rave reviews as the ultimate resource on the subject. The book was updated in 2005 (Hal Leonard) to coincide with the seventh annual Vocal Group Hall of Fame Awards show, which aired on PBS and was co-hosted by the author and Mary Wilson of the Supremes.

In 1997, Warner's *Billboard's American Rock 'n' Roll in Review* continued his streak of entertaining reference works, and in 2001, his *Just Walkin' in the Rain* (the true story of a convict quintet, a liberal governor, and how they changed Southern history through rhythm and blues) shook up the establishment, becoming a bestseller. In 2004, Warner started a new series of books with *On This Day in Music History* (with a foreword by Beatles producer Sir George Martin), followed by *On This Day in Black Music History* (with a forward by Grammy winner Quincy Jones) in 2006, both published by Hal Leonard.

Jay Warner lives in Los Angeles with his wife, Jackie, and favorite four-legged friends, Napoleon and Sunny.